SMALL CORPUS STUDIES AND ELT

SCL

Studies in Corpus Linguistics

Studies in Corpus Linguistics aims to provide insights into the way a corpus can be used, the type of findings that can be obtained, the possible applications of these findings as well as the theoretical changes that corpus work can bring into linguistics and language engineering. The main concern of SCL is to present findings based on, or related to, the cumulative effect of naturally occuring language and on the interpretation of frequency and distributional data.

General Editor
Elena Tognini-Bonelli

Consulting Editor
Wolfgang Teubert

Volume 5

Mohsen Ghadessy, Alex Henry and Robert L. Roseberry

Small Corpus Studies and ELT
Theory and practice

June 2002, TWC
To Yoko
with very best wishes!
Elena

Small Corpus Studies and ELT

Theory and practice

MOHSEN GHADESSY

Zhongshan University, Guangzhou, P.R.C.

ALEX HENRY

ROBERT L. ROSEBERRY

University of Brunei Darussalam

JOHN BENJAMINS PUBLISHING COMPANY

AMSTERDAM / PHILADELPHIA

™ The paper used in this publication meets the minimum requirements of American National Standard for Information Sciences — Permanence of Paper for Printed Library Materials, ANSI Z39.48–1984.

Cover design: Françoise Berserik
Cover illustration from original painting *Random Order*
by Lorenzo Pezzatini, Florence, 1996.

Library of Congress Cataloging-in-Publication Data

Small corpus studies and ELT : theory and practice / [edited by] Mohsen Ghadessy, Alex Henry, Robert L. Roseberry.
    p.   cm. -- (Studies in corpus linguistics, ISSN 1388-0373 ; v. 5)
Includes bibliographical references and index.
    1. Language and languages--Computer-assisted instruction. 2. English language--Computer-assisted instruction. I. Ghadessy, Mohsen, 1935- II. Henry, Alex. III. Roseberry, Robert L., 1945- IV. Series.

P53.28 .S6   2001
418'.0285--dc21   00-067436

ISBN 90 272 2275 4 (Eur.) / 1 58811 035 4 (US) (Hb; alk. paper)

John Benjamins Publishing Co. · P.O.Box 75577 · 1070 AN AMSTERDAM · The Netherlands
John Benjamins North America · P.O.Box 27519 · Philadelphia PA 19118-0519 · USA

Table of contents

Preface

J.M.Sinclair

There are several reasons why it is a pleasure to write a preface to this collection of papers showing what can be done with small corpora. For one thing, many of the authors are personal friends, former colleagues and students who have chosen to work with corpora, and I hope that the encouragement of this work in Birmingham and the provision of the resources they found there may have helped them to focus on corpus linguistics. Another reason for wanting to identify with small corpora is that since my own main work over many years has been with the largest available corpora of the period, some commentators have concluded that I have a low opinion of small corpus work. I hope that not only this preface, but my co-authorship of one of the papers herein, will put paid to such nonsense. The type of work will certainly be constrained by the corpus size, but that has nothing to do with the quality.

Let me first of all review the way in which the dimensions of corpora have developed since they first became available for study; then deal briefly with large corpora, and why they are necessary at all, for I am unrepentant of my constant pressure to make more language data available. From this discussion it can be seen what jobs are well suited to small corpora, and what jobs are better left to large corpora. Then I will point to the differences between language data seen as a set of texts and seen as a corpus; and finally celebrate the genuine strengths of small corpora.

The incredible shrinking corpora

In the early sixties work began on both sides of the Atlantic on corpora to be held in electronic form and to be processed by computer. The two projects were unaware of each other until 1965. At Brown University in Rhode Island, USA, Nelson Francis and Henry Kuçera set out to compile a million-word sample of published American English of the year 1961, which was the last year for which publication records were available when they began their work (Francis and Kuçera 1979). Meanwhile at the University of Edinburgh in Scotland, a corpus was taking shape, consisting of transcriptions of informal spoken interaction among speakers of British English. Because of the greater amount of labour involved in spoken language collection, this corpus only reached some 300,000 words, of which 166,000 were regularly used in research. Edinburgh University did not possess a computer at the time, so arrangements were made with Manchester University to carry out preliminary processing; the project moved to Birmingham in 1965 (Sinclair et al 1970, Jones and Sinclair 1973).

These corpora were simultaneously the largest and smallest of their type, being the only ones, and they remained so for a number of years. In fact the Brown size and structure proved to be well-judged, and was followed by an equivalent corpus of British printed English for the same year (LOB — the Lancaster-Oslo-Bergen Corpus, Johansson et al. 1978). In 1982 Yang Hui-Zhong compiled JDEST (English for Science and Technology, Shanghai Jiao Tong University, Yang 1985) following the Brown size and structure, and several were compiled in Birmingham in the seventies, beginning with Peter Roe's (Roe 1977); these kept to the size of a million words but contained full texts, rather than the 2000-word samples of the Brown style.

The million-word tradition continues, and there are now modern equivalents of Brown and LOB compiled at the University of Freiburg in Germany, and called "Flob" and "Frown". They are identical in size and structure with Brown. All of these corpora, and several more, can be found on a compact disk published by ICAME, the International Computer Archive of Modern English, which has pioneered the archiving of language data for over twenty years (Hofland et al. 1999).

But million-word corpora must now be regarded as small by today's standards. As the power and storage capacity of computers has risen sharply, and very large amounts of text have become available in electronic form, they are dwarfed by the current norms; what were large corpora have become small ones — yet the first seemed to contain unheard-of riches when it was first released to the world.

Now the largest available corpus is The Bank of English[1], some 410 times the size of the Brown family. Spoken corpora have also grown very fast despite the problems they pose; the first one to be widely used, the London-Lund corpus, was about 500,000 words in length (Svartvik and Quirk 1980); now the Bank of English contains 50 million words of transcribed speech, about 300 times the size of the original Edinburgh corpus. Nevertheless, one spoken corpus is living proof that small can be beautiful — the Longman/Lancaster Spoken English Corpus contains only 53,000 words (Taylor and Knowles 1988).

So there is a kind of relativity in corpus sizing — the dimensions of a "small" corpus vary with the date it is compiled; the apparently massive corpora of a few years ago are now perceived as tiny, and in another decade or two, anything less than a few billion words will count as a small corpus, because there is every reason to make bigger and bigger corpora, and the job becomes easier as the size goes up.

No data like more data

This slogan comes from the Linguistic Data Consortium (LDC), established in the USA a decade ago, and devoted to distributing language data, whether organised as corpora or not. The United States, after the brilliant start given by the Brown Corpus, then lagged behind Europe for twenty years (indeed the American National Corpus, cloned from the British one of ten years ago, is at the planning stage as I write), and the impetus to start LDC came because of pressure from statisticians, whose primary need was a large amount of language in order to advance research such as Speech Recognition.

LDC is not a corpus and does not claim to be one; it is an archive and a distribution service, and it contains whatever material, in any language, is made available to it. Its attitude and slogan were important a few years ago because many students of language were so accustomed to working with very small amounts of data, and were unfamiliar with the methods of handling large amounts, that there was a good deal of resistance to the arrival of the cornucopias of language that LDC proposed to gather. One has to remember, too, that the dominant attitude to language in USA over forty years has been concerned with language in the mind, and not language on paper or in the air; hence large quantities of it were simply not required.

Phrasemaking

What do you get from a large corpus that you do not get from a small one? Essentially you get repetitions of multi-word choices in combination. The large number of words in a language, and their characteristically uneven distribution (Zipf 1935) mean that despite the clear tendency of languages to practice coselection, that coselection is subject to so much variation that if one wants to study collocation or phraseology by automatic methods then even the 9-figure corpora are pitifully small.

Try the following test: first fix on a figure of the number of occurrences of a word that you need for a job — maybe fifty for personal study, 250 if the computer will be asked to detect significant patterns in the concordance. Then select a word that is frequent in the corpus but not one of the "grammatical" words which are frequent in any corpus. Note the frequency of your selected word, and also of its most frequent collocate — again leave the grammatical words on one side. It is very likely that the frequency of the pair in collocation with each other is an order of magnitude below the frequency of the single word, unless you have chosen a word like kith, which will not normally occur except with kin. If the frequency of the collocation is still substantial, then add a third word, namely the word which most frequently occurs with the pair. You should drop an order of magnitude again.

In this way you can make an assessment of which features of which words can be studied in any given corpus. For example, if you are studying the contextual patterns of words, then you will almost certainly be looking for repetitions. So it is bad news that around half of the vocabulary of any corpus (ie the number of different word-forms) consists of single occurrences. On the other hand, if you are studying an author's use of single occurrences as an indication of style, then even a very small collection can be useful because the phenomenon is so common (Marcinkevičinė 1998).

Methodology

It is clear from the above discussion that factors other than being "small" or "large" must be used to distinguish two different kinds of corpus. Until recently they were not perceived as different in anything but size, but there has been a development in thinking, of which this book is the first monument; now "small" and "large" corpora are seen as in contrast with each other. So the difference must be methodological, because it cannot be just size, whether relative or absolute size.

The Editors hint at this towards the end of their Introduction, "the methodologies are ... intuitive". A small corpus is seen as a body of relevant and reliable evidence, and is either small enough to be analysed manually, or is processed by the computer in a preliminary fashion, using the kinds of tools presented in Section II; thereafter the evidence is interpreted by the scholar directly. There is no need to collect the quantities of data needed in order to delay the direct participation of the human being.

There is thus a fairly sharp contrast in method; the so-called Small Corpora are those designed for early human intervention (EHI) while the Large Corpora are designed for late or delayed human intervention (DHI). (Of course in DHI the human being is indirectly controlling the process, and the process has probably been built up over many EHI sessions, and the human being must eventually participate in order to interpret the results.[2])

So this book is essentially a celebration of the EHI method. The researchers have a clear goal in mind, and they build a corpus for an investigation, or if they are lucky enough, use one that is already available. The processing is usually with standard tools, so packages like WordSmith are invaluable for EHI, but occasionally these are adapted, or special ones devised for the job.

Text and Corpus

There is another methodological point to be made, to clarify what is meant by calling a collection of texts a corpus. It is still, after all, a collection of texts, so what is different about it when it is seen as a corpus?

By calling a group of texts or text samples a corpus we are investing it with linguistic status. The corpus is gathered on the basis of *external* criteria (Clear 1992), to do with the sociocultural roles of the texts it contains, and the claim is implicitly made that an investigation into the *internal* patterns of the language used will be fruitful and linguistically illuminating. So if it is a general corpus, researchers expect to find in it information about the language as a whole, and if it is a more specialised corpus, then the characteristics of the genre will be discoverable.[3]

A text is a single, unified, meaningful event, an artefact; it is read and stud-

ied as such; a corpus is a multiple set of events, and is studied for the similarities and differences among its events, and the component parts of its events. So
in principle the same piece of language can be treated as a text or a corpus, and
different points will emerge (Tognini Bonelli forthcoming 2000, Introduction).

Working with small corpora, then, is not the same as working with texts,
and the papers in this book make that clear, in their innovative research strategies and novel results.

Comparison

The main investigative technique that is used here, and in most EHI studies, is
comparison; comparison uncovers differences almost regardless of size.
Samples from different genres are typical of EHI work, where the computer
detects proportional differences or the presence or absence of particular phenomena, and the researcher interprets this information. The Brown corpus was
designed with this kind of study in mind, and although it was also used to
establish very basic facts about American published English as a whole, the
aspect of comparison has dominated research — the cluster of similar corpora
that are mentioned above form various axes of comparison, US/UK English
with Lob, 1960s/1990s English with Frown and Flob, etc. One of the most
recent flowerings of comparative EHI research is the large Longman Grammar
of Spoken and Written English (Biber et al. 1999). The core corpus that
informs this work consists of just under 20 million words, in four components
of 4–5 million words each, covering conversation, fiction, news and academic
prose.

Across languages, the comparative method is a very good starting point,
and in recent years *parallel* corpora, sets of translated texts, have become very
popular. The texts are aligned with respect to each other, using a variety of
simple aligners, or by hand if the corpora are very small, and translation equiv-
alences can then be studied.

Language Teaching

The focus of this collection is the application of small corpus – EHI – research
to the business of teaching and learning languages. As the papers show, corpus

evidence can illuminate language teaching from many different angles; as well as the comparisons mentioned above there is the accurate description of structure, reliable models of usage, how words and phrases are actually translated, what are the essentials in a syllabus, what are the characteristic errors of learners, etc. Small corpora can be put together quickly for a classroom job or an individual need, and can be honed to very specific genres and sub-genres. Corpus resources can be placed under the control of the students, and "self-access" can take on a new and rich meaning.

The origin of this lively movement is not in corpus linguistics as such, but in the tiny computers of twenty years ago, which in UK were associated with the name of Clive Sinclair (no relation). The early models were quite unable to handle corpora, having memories as small as 1 kilobyte, but with the ingenuity of Tim Johns and others (eg Higgins and Johns 1984) could be given a highly motivating role in language learning. As the small computers gained power, and the microprocessor developed into the PC, then the notions of "classroom concordancing" and "data-driven learning" became popular. These were adaptations of mainframe computer routines to the smaller machines, and the miniaturisation gave rise to Microconcord (Johns 1986), the precursor of WordSmith. At around this time, in the middle eighties, the mainframe was going out of fashion for large-scale data processing, and distributed computing over a network of minicomputers was preferred; in this way, and within the broad heading of language pedagogy, the two communities of linguistic computing converged. There was, and is, still a demarcation line in the operating systems on which software is mounted; the "micro" tradition is dependent on DOS/Windows, whereas the "mini" group use Unix/Linux

The re-emergence, then, of the small corpus has a broader base in applications than just language teaching, and although this book is focused on the teaching side there is mention of other applications, in translation studies, literary studies etc. Indeed the application to literary stylistics is a rather separate line of development, with origins even earlier than the first "general" corpora.

There is no special virtue in being small, except that many scholars like to keep the dimensions of their studies modest in order to be manageable without requiring special expensive equipment or a high level of technical skill. As linguistic computing gets ever easier and more flexible and more powerful, the meaning of "small" will be frequently reinterpreted, and the only distinction that is here to stay is the methodological one, the type of human intervention and the timing of it.

Notes

1. For up-to-date information on The Bank of English, see the Cobuild Web-page, www.cobuild.collins.co.uk.

2. Some resource packages use fully automatic analysis and leave the interpretation to the user — eg Cobuild Collocations CD-ROM. The corpus was mildly pre-processed for reasons like the protection of anonymity, but the results are not edited in any way.

3. Some discussion of these and other relevant points can be found in the EAGLES Project Reports of 1996–see http://www.ilc.pi.cnr.it/EAGLES96/browse.html#wg1, the Corpus Working Group and the files corpustyp.ps and texttyp.ps.

References

Biber, D., Johansson, S., Leech, G.N., Conrad, S. and Finegan, E. 1999. *Longman Grammar of Spoken and Written English*. Harlow: Pearson Education Ltd.

Clear, J.H. 1992. "Corpus sampling". In *New Directions in English Language Corpus Methodology*. G.Leitner (ed), 21–31, Berlin: Mouton de Gruyter.

Francis, W.N. and Kuçera, H. 1979. *Manual of Information to accompany a Standard Sample of Present-day Edited American English, for use with digital computers*. Providence, R.I.: Department of Linguistics, Brown University.

Higgins, J. and Johns, T.F. 1984. *Computers in Language Learning*. London and Glasgow: Collins ELT.

Hofland, K., Lindeberg, A. and Thunestvedt, J. 1999. *ICAME Collection of English Language Corpora*, Second Edition. The HIT Centre, University of Bergen, Norway. (CD-ROM).

Johansson, S., Leech, G.N. and Goodluck, H. 1978. *Manual of Information to accompany The Lancaster-Oslo/Bergen Corpus of British English, for use with digital computers*. University of Oslo, Department of English.

Johns, T.F. 1986. "Micro-concord: a language-learner's research tool". *System* 14(2): 151–162.

Jones, S. and Sinclair, J.M. 1973. "English lexical collocations: A study in computational linguistics". *Cahiers de Lexicologie* XXIII-II.

Marcinkevičinė, R. 1998. "Hapax legomena as a platform for text alignment". In *Translation Equivalence: Proceedings of the Third European Seminar*. W. Teubert, E. Tognini Bonelli and N. Volz (eds), 125–136, Mannheim: The TELRI Association e.V. and Pescia, The Tuscan Word Centre.

Roe, P. 1977. *Scientific Text*, ELR Monographs no 4. University of Birmingham, Department of English.

Sinclair, J.M., Jones, S. and Daley, R. 1970. *English Lexical Studies*. Final Report to OSTI on Project C/LP/08. University of Birmingham, Department of English.

Svartvik, J. and Quirk, R. (eds), 1980. *A Corpus of English Conversation*. Lund: Lund University Press.

Taylor, L. and Knowles, G. 1988. *Manual of Information to Accompany the SEC Corpus*. UCREL, University of Lancaster.

Tognini Bonelli, E. 2001. *Corpus Linguistics at Work*. Amsterdam and Philadelphia: John benjamins.

Yang Huizhong 1985. "The use of computers in English teaching and research in China". In *English in the World*, R. Quirk and H.G.Widdowson (eds), 86–100. Cambridge: CUP.

Zipf, G.K. 1935. *The Psychobiology of Language*. Houghton Mifflin, reprinted 1965, Cambridge, MA: MIT Press.

Introduction

The emergence of a new approach to language studies based on collections, or corpora, of texts, has revolutionised the teaching and learning of languages. Made possible in the last few years by the development of powerful yet relatively inexpensive computer systems, corpus analysis, as this field is called, has changed our view of what language is and how it is used. For the first time, researchers, teachers, and students have been able to explore huge collections of texts consisting of hundreds of millions of words to discover such facts about a language as which words are commonly used together with others (collocations), what grammatical patterns are associated with a given word (colligations and lexical phrase frames), which words are used more frequently than others, which meanings of a word are most frequently invoked, and so on. Information such as this has not only changed the way dictionaries are made and used, but has also made remarkable contributions to language teaching and to understanding the way language is used in literature, business, and the professions.

Parallel to the rapid development of large corpus studies, an interest in the analysis of small textual corpora has arisen. Small corpus language studies have undoubtedly been with us in some sense since the first time a human attempted to learn another language by referring to native-speaker usage as a model. At first glance then, small corpus analysis may seem to be almost trivial: something that every language-learner subconsciously does when trying to learn an additional language. However, systematic development of this field over the last ten years or so has yielded discoveries about language that are no less remarkable or important than those derived from the study of huge corpora. Furthermore, most of this additional knowledge about language could not have been discovered through the analysis of large corpora or through any other known method of language analysis.

This book presents the field of small corpus analysis through individual contributions by a number of the leading researchers working in this area. The contributions have been selected to show both the breadth and depth of the field, and they have been carefully written to make them accessible, not only to fellow researchers, but also to teachers and students of language teaching. A wide range of topics has been included, providing the reader with a variety of concepts and practical outcomes. As in all new, important, and rapidly developing disciplines, the contributions presented here represent a variety of diverse views and approaches, but they share the common goal of revealing small corpus analysis as a powerful tool for the teaching and learning of *authentic* language.

The book is divided into six sections. Section I deals with the emergence and development of corpus linguistics in its traditional sense and suggests how a similar analysis of small corpora can provide important but different kinds of information for language learning. Section II presents and explains some tools of the trade — some computer programmes for personal computers — that are commonly employed in small corpus research. In Section III, the concept of genre, or type of text, becomes uppermost, and the four chapters of this section deal with several kinds of important language information that can be derived from small corpora that focus narrowly on a single genre. Section IV looks at a topic normally thought of as a matter for large corpus analysis only: the structure of English. The two papers in this section explore this topic in quite different ways, drawing interestingly divergent conclusions about the nature of grammar. Section V contains three papers exploring the use of "parallel" corpora. These corpora examine a text and its parallel translation into another language or another dialect, such as a learner's dialect. Clearly, by examining the way in which learners structure the language they are learning, the analysis of small parallel corpora has much to offer the language classroom. A focus on learners' language alone comprises the final section, Section VI. The two papers in this section contribute further important methods and approaches to the teaching of English as an additional language.

Overview of the chapters

I Background: Large and small corpora

In Section I, Robert de Beaugrande examines the changing view of language in the twentieth century and shows how corpus analysis has altered our understanding of language and discourse and has begun to bring these two concepts together by showing how language works for real purposes in real situations. By focusing on a tranche, or slice, of language taken from a large corpus, he demonstrates how large corpus analysis reveals important facts about fluency, naturalness, and idiomaticity of language. Having provided a background to the workings and outcomes of large corpus linguistics, de Beaugrande then moves toward a science of small corpus analysis, suggesting that similar techniques could be employed there as well. He defines two types of small corpora that are of particular interest in second-language teaching: the learnable corpus, matched to the relative fluency of the target group; and the specialised corpus, determined by "register, discourse domain, or subject matter".

II Tools for small corpus analysis

Moving from de Beaugrande's overview of the field, Section II looks at some popular and useful PC computer tools for small corpus analysis. The first paper in this section, by Paul Nation, demonstrates the use of two computerised vocabulary research tools to analyze reading texts and to provide lists of required vocabulary for study in the second-language classroom. Extensive and detailed lists and tables are provided to show the step-by-step operation of the programmes and the value of the information that they reveal. Nation also investigates the concept of readability in connection with lists of the most frequently used words in English and presents some research questions in this field, intended to aid teachers in their own research.

In the other paper in this section, Mike Scott describes his WordSmith Tools suite of text analysis software, a popular set of computer programmes for the PC, used and referred to by a number of contributors to this collection. Although by its very nature, much of the analysis of small corpora needs to be done by the human analyst without computer assistance, there are various kinds of important information that can be gleaned most easily with the help of text analysis programmes. WordSmith Tools provides almost instantaneous displays of word frequency lists; concordances, which show all the uses of a given word in its cotexts; and lists of keywords, words that appear more often in a corpus than chance alone would dictate. This suite of tools provides several additional functions of use to the analyses of both single and parallel corpora. One of the most fascinating parts of Scott's chapter shows the use of WordSmith Tools to enhance appreciation and comprehension of a literary text.

III Establishing genres

With Section III, our attention is drawn to the investigation of genres, or types of texts. This is an area that is not well suited to the use of large corpora, in which a number of very different genres are typically mixed together. Small corpus analysis of genres, however, provides bountiful and crucial information for language teaching and other purposes related to business and the professions.

The first paper in this section is John Flowerdew's "Concordancing as a tool in course design", an early and important contribution to this field, reprinted here by permission. Flowerdew was one of the first to show how computerised concordancing of a small corpus of similar texts could provide important and easily learnable language patterns drawn from authentic texts. This paper presents a clear approach to the working methods of small corpus analysis and is recommended as a starting point, especially for those who are just getting started in this area.

Next, Alex Henry and Robert L. Roseberry expand on the work of Flowerdew and others by demonstrating two parallel analyses of what they call "move registers", or the language of similar parts of different texts of the same genre. They show that such analyses can be instrumental in providing crucial and, at the same time, easily learnable authentic language belonging to the genre. Henry and Roseberry further show how this methodology can pick up the essential language differences between two apparently similar genres. They conclude by demonstrating a set of computerised learning materials, drawn from the analysis and suitable for use either as classroom or as self-access materials.

In the third paper in this section, Marina Bondi looks at different genres within a given discourse area, in this case the discourse of economics, and investigates ways in which small corpus analysis can reveal information about language variation across genres. Her study ranges from an analysis of functional units to patterns of words and grammar in "self-projection" and "other-projection" as used in the argumentative features of the discourse. She concludes by identifying a number of implications of interest especially to language teachers.

Section III ends with a paper by Vincent Ooi, who uses the World Wide Web, or Internet, as a fruitful source of texts for the analysis of genres. Not only is the Internet an increasingly popular source of texts on a multitude of topics, but it is also a breeding ground for many new and mixed genres. Using many of the methodologies described above, Ooi shows how the Internet can be easily adapted for classroom use, providing both teachers and students with easily accessible and analysable sources of important data.

IV Use of Systemic Functional Linguistics

Peter Ragan opens Section IV with a paper that demonstrates how a systemic functional small learner corpus can be used in the language classroom. He focuses on features of discourse and wording in this study, which contrasts the way in which native and non-native speakers give instructions for a simple task.

While Ragan's students seem capable of operating successfully within a functional framework of language structure, Geoff Barnbrook and John Sinclair point to the shortcomings of functional grammars and opt for local grammars derived from a specialised corpus. Their paper analyses the patterns of definition used in the Collins Cobuild Student's Dictionary and is unique in this collection for being function-based, rather than genre-based.

V Use of parallel corpora

Three papers, comprising Section V, investigate the use of parallel corpora as a source of data for language learning. In the first of these, Ann Lawson explains the nature of parallel corpora and shows how they can be used, particularly in the area of translation. Her data are drawn from the Trans-European Language Resources Infrastructure Project, a parallel corpus that will eventually be made available over the Internet. She points out that, in general, the Internet, as Ooi demonstrated in Section III, is a fruitful source for corpus data in various areas of discourse.

Making use of techniques and methodologies such as those described by Lawson, Geoff Thompson investigates "small corpora of equivalent genres in different languages". As a result of his investigation, Thompson argues strongly in favour of including language forms even within primarily communicative lessons. However, he stresses that such language data should be presented coherently in its natural context, thus showing its value to the discourse from which it comes. According to Thompson, "Using parallel corpora of familiar genres as the basis for language awareness activities can help learners explore the ways in which language is deployed in the FL [foreign language] to achieve particular communicative goals."

Section V ends with a paper by Mohsen Ghadessy and Yanjie Gao, who use a small parallel corpus to compare thematic organisation in Chinese and English. The authors base their classification of theme on Halliday's (1994) categories and come to the conclusion that, in spite of some important differences, there is a large degree of correlation between thematic patterning in the two languages. From this finding, the authors are able to draw implications for teaching translation and for identifying text-types across languages.

VI Implications and applications

In the final section, Section VI, two papers discuss specific applications of small corpora of learner English to the development of materials for the language classroom. Lynne Flowerdew begins this section with a paper that investigates "collocational patterning, pragmatic appropriacy and discourse features" in learner English. She points to the usefulness of a small corpus of learners' English in deriving this information but also cautions against some of the obstacles inherent in this process.

The final paper in the collection, by Christopher Tribble, again draws on the Internet as a source of "web-published 'leaflets'" which Tribble uses as a source of materials for a pedagogy of writing. He stresses that four kinds of knowledge are needed in order to succeed at a writing task: knowledge of content, writing process, context, and language system. The corpus can provide learners with a valuable resource for such knowledge. Tribble differentiates between two kinds of corpora that are useful in his methodology, arguing for "a corpus-informed pedagogy of writing in which the comparative analysis of small exemplar corpora in relation to larger reference corpora becomes part of the repertoire of the teachers and students of writing."

The papers collected in this volume represent some of the most up-to-date and most valuable research being done in English Language Teaching today. They show that language, far from being the idealised and perfectly rational system envisaged by some of the leading linguists of the nineteenth and twentieth centuries, is instead a developing, vibrant, and even volatile manifestation of our thought processes and has no existence apart from the social purposes for which it is intended. Humans use language in patterned ways for a multitude of purposes; and small corpus analysis, by focusing on types of texts and the purposes they are intended to achieve, offers us a window of understanding into the workings of language. In part with the aid of computers, we can observe for ourselves the vocabulary, functions and discourse patterns of texts created for specific purposes. By involving our students in this process, we can help them to raise their awareness of the language patterns they are trying to learn. Through parallel corpora, we, together with our students, can explore the similarities and differences between first and target languages, as an aid to learning the latter. And, although no corpus, no matter how large or how narrowly focused, can show us all there is to know about a language in use, the papers in this collection present a convincing argument in favour of using authentic texts as the basis of language learning.

Happily, the necessary tools and materials for small corpus analysis are relatively inexpensive and easily available. The methodologies are simple and intuitive, yet powerful in their outcomes. And the results of learning with the aid of these methodologies are impressive. It is our hope that this book will provide an impetus for more and more teachers to involve their students in *hands-on* exploration of authentic spoken and written texts. Likewise we hope that researchers will continue to add to the remarkable knowledge of language that corpus analysis — on both a large and small scale — has thus far provided.

Mohsen Ghadessy
Alex Henry
Robert L. Roseberry

June 2000, Brunei Darussalam

SECTION 1

CHAPTER 1

Large Corpora, Small Corpora, and the Learning of "Language"

Robert de Beaugrande

United Arab Emirates University

Abstract

The evolution of multiple corpora may not merely give us a more complete and accurate picture of language and discourse, but may transform the meaning of *language* and *discourse* as terms and as concepts in both theoretical and applied linguistics. In the past, language has often been idealised to be a complete and well-defined system, whereas discourse has been considered fragmentary and poorly-defined. Corpus data now signal some "missing links" between those two sides through regularities that are more specific than language yet more general than discourse. These regularities could help to explain why native speakers of English sound "fluent" and why their usage sounds "natural" or "idiomatic". Useful resources might therefore be achieved for designing innovative programmes in the teaching and learning of English by non-native speakers. Here, I would propose to distinguish the resources by two types of *small corpus*: (1) the *learnable corpus* delimited by the respective fluency levels of learner groups; and (2) the *specialised corpus* delimited by a specific register, discourse domain, or subject matter.

What is "language"?

Large corpora have been around a number of years, but their full significance and value is only recently coming to be appreciated (compare Altenberg 1991; McEnery and Wilson 1996; Pearson 1998). These collections of authentic data in unprecedented quantities and degrees of delicacy may fundamentally transform our ways of addressing the question *what is language?* In particular, we may reconcile the meanings of the term *language* as it figures in *general discourse* and as it figures in *specialised discourse,* such as that of linguistics, the established science of language.

One strategy for promoting such a reconciliation might be to compare the data from a *large corpus of general discourse* with data from a *small corpus of specialised discourse.* On the general side, we might collect and examine examples of the word *language* in the *Bank of English,* the world's largest general corpus stored on computers at Birmingham University:[1]

(1)   you should be pleased that the French *language* has been spared

(2)   he has no qualifications in teaching of English as a Foreign *Language*

(3)   it's old-fashioned, and it's in a foreign *language*. People are frightened of it

(4)   I was told afterward that my *language* was most entertaining

(5)   fatally damaged? I don't want to use *language* of that sort

(6)   there is a lot of bad *language* and gratuitously oafish behaviour

(7)   General Kryuchkov used the *language* of the Cold War when he accused the US

(8)   He violently opposes the new *language* law, which makes major concessions

What meanings might apply here? Example (1) concerns the *French language* spoken by a whole nation of native speakers, whereas example (2) concerns the *English language* as a subject-matter to be taught to and learned by non-natives. Example (3) suggests that being *in a foreign language* may contribute to *frightening people.* Examples (4), (5), and (6) indicate how particular uses of *language* may be evaluated. In example (7), *language* stands for both the style and the content of what a Russian general said — hostile and belligerent, as suited the *Cold War.* And example (8) concerns an official *law* regulating which *languages* should be used and when — an explosive issue in many regions of the world today.

All these uses of the term *language* in general discourse deal with real-life concerns of people who put *language* into practice, or else are prevented from doing so because they have *no qualifications* (2), or because the *language* is *foreign* (3) or is restricted by a *language law* (8), and so on. Typically, these practices in turn have real-life consequences, as when someone's language gets judged *entertaining* (5) and someone else's gets judged *bad* or *oafish* (6); or when *the language* of the *Cold War* (8) pushes us closer to the brink of a hot war.

On the specialised side, I turn to the small corpus of some 15,00,000 words of distinguished British and American writers I compiled by downloading from the *Bibliomania* website on the Internet (http://www.bibliomania.com/Fiction):

(9)   Gabriel strove to restrain himself from breaking out into brutal *language* about the sottish Malins (*Dubliners*)

(10)   Elizabeth was at first sorry for the pain he was to receive; till, roused to resentment by his subsequent *language*, she lost all compassion in anger. She tried, however, to compose herself (*Pride and Prejudice*)

(11)   Lady Catherine was extremely indignant on the marriage of her nephew; and as she gave way to all the genuine frankness of her character, [...] she sent him *language* so very abusive that for some time all intercourse was at an end. (*Pride and Prejudice*)

(12)   I vociferated curses enough to annihilate any fiend in Christendom; [...] "A wicked boy", remarked the old lady, "and quite unfit for a decent house! Did you notice his *language*, Linton? I'm shocked that my children should have heard it." (*Wuthering Heights*)

(13)   There were not merely no grammatical errors, but as a composition it would not have disgraced a gentleman; the *language*, though plain, was strong and unaffected, and the sentiments it conveyed very much to the credit of the writer. [...] "No doubt he is a sensible man, and I suppose may have a natural talent for — thinks strongly and clearly — and when he takes a pen in hand, his thoughts naturally find proper words." (*Emma*)

(14)   There had been no real affection either in his *language* or manners. Sighs and fine words had been given in abundance; but she could hardly devise any set of expressions, or fancy any tone of voice, less allied with real love. (*Emma*)

(15)   And now nothing remains for me but to assure you in the most animated *language* of the violence of my affection. (*Pride and Prejudice*)

(16)   He wished she knew his impressions; but he would as soon have thought of carrying an odour in a net as of attempting to convey the intangibilities of his feeling in the coarse meshes of *language*. So he remained silent. (*Madding Crowd*)

(17)   These familiar flowers, these well-remembered bird-notes [...] such things as these are the mother tongue of our imagination, the *language* that is laden with all the subtle inextricable associations the fleeting hours of our childhood left behind (*Mill on the Floss*)

(18)   The artist can express everything. Thought and *language* are to the artist instruments of an art. (*Dorian Gray*)

We again see, now expressed in more articulate styles, the evaluations of language being improper, e.g., *brutal* (9), *abusive* (11), or *shocking* (12). In conformity with social codes, the speaker may *strive to restrain himself* (9) or *compose herself* (10), but may give way to *resentment, anger,* or *indignation* (10–11). More specialised and literary are usages which evaluate *language* by its discernment and powers in doing *credit to the writer* by being *strong* and *unaffected* and by finding *proper words* for one's *thoughts* and *sentiments* (13). Reciprocally, *language* may be judged devoid of *real affection* or *real love* despite *fine words* like Mr Elton's (14), or like Mr Collins' absurdly *animated assurance* of *violent affection* (15). Even more specialised and literary is the perception that language offers *coarse meshes* incapable of *conveying the intangibilities of feeling* (16); or that our *imagination* and *subtle inextricable associations* are best expressed in a *language* of images and sounds, not words (17). All these meanings deconstruct the magisterial optimism that *the artist can express everything* through the *instruments* of *thought* and *language* (18); the Modal Verb *can* leaves open the prospect of an endlessly unfilled potential.

Again on the specialised side, I shall turn to the small corpus of about 250,000 words I hand-compiled from influential discourses in modern linguistics.[2] Sometimes, we find *language* being hailed in terms that sound even more effusive than do literary data like (18) (quoted from Bloomfield 1933:3; Hjelmslev 1969 [original 1943]:3):

(19)   The effects of language are remarkable, and include much of what distinguishes man from the animals

(20)   Language — human speech — is an inexhaustible abundance of manifold treasures.

(21)   Language is the instrument with which man forms thought and feeling, mood, aspiration, will and act, the instrument by whose means he influences and is influenced, the ultimate and deepest foundation of human society

(22)   Language [...] is the ultimate, indispensable sustainer of the human individual, his refuge in hours of loneliness, when the mind wrestles with existence and the conflict is resolved in the monologue of the poet and the thinker.

Yet the spirit of such declarations is utterly remote from the sober, brittle conceptions of language usually proposed within the discipline of linguistics.

Admittedly, my data show those conceptions to be far from uniform. Sometimes, linguists have envisioned supplying general audiences with accessible information about *language*, e.g.:

(23)   of what use is linguistics? [...] That linguistics should continue to be the prerogative of a few specialists would be unthinkable — everyone is concerned with it in one way or another. (Saussure 1966 [1916]:7)

(24)   This little book aims to give a perspective [that] will be useful, I hope, both to linguistic students and to the outside public that is half inclined to dismiss linguistic notions as the private pedantries of essentially idle minds. Knowledge of the wider relations of their science is essential to professional students of language if they are to be saved from a sterile and purely technical attitude. (Sapir 1921:v)

(25)   The deep-rooted things about language, which mean the most to us, are usually ignored in all but very advanced studies; this book tries to tell about them in simple terms and show their bearing on human affairs. (Bloomfield 1933:xv)

(26)   It must now be quite clear to all linguists that there is a new awareness everywhere of the powers and problems of speech and language. [...] There are signs of [...] an eagerness to develop linguistic science so that it may get to grips with its subject-matter. [However,] there is a distinct danger that the more technical it becomes, [...] the less it can contain the humanism of speech and language. (Firth 1957 [original 1948]:141)

Yet sometimes linguists warned that prevailing notions about *language* might be wholly misguided:

(27)   Many people have difficulty at the beginning of language study, not in grasping the methods or results, which are simple enough, but in stripping off the preconceptions that are forced upon us [by] our traditional notions. (Bloomfield 1933:3f)

(28)   there is no other field in which so many absurd notions, prejudices, mirages, and fictions have sprung up. […] The task of the linguist is, above all else, to condemn and dispel them (Saussure 1966 [original 1916]:7)

Linguists would thus be called upon to supply *new* and *scientific* views of language:

(29)   We must call in a new type of facts to illuminate the special nature of language. (Saussure 1966 [1916]:16)

(30)   We must therefore welcome new systems of linguistic thought with their terminology as contributions to […] linguistic science (Firth 1957 [1948]:141)

One way might be to follow the standard scientific procedure of making careful observations of large quantities of data:

(31)   language has been studied in a scientific way by careful and comprehensive observation (Bloomfield 1933:3)

But my small corpus detected linguists suggesting that such procedures would not work:

(32)   To be rid of illusions we must first be convinced that the concrete entities of language are not directly accessible. (Saussure 1966 [1916]:110)

(33)   The true and unique object of linguistics is language studied in and for itself (Saussure 1966 [1916]:232)

(34)   Knowledge of the language, like most facts of interest and importance, is neither presented for direct observation nor extractable from data by inductive procedures of any known sort. (Chomsky 1965:18)

And the stage was strategically set for presenting specialised definitions of *language* which in effect replaced the medium of real-life communication with an abstract idealisation (Beaugrande 1998), e.g.:

(35) language [is] an organised totality with linguistic structure as the dominating principle. (Hjelmslev 1969 [1943]:8)

(36) a language [is] an infinite set of sentences, each finite in length and constructed out of a finite set of elements. (Chomsky 1957:15)

(37) Our discussion of natural languages will be restricted to the formal treatment of English. [We] will assume that the sentences of English are to be obtained from the sentences of a λ-categorial language by deletion of the logical symbols, [where] λ is a logical constant with a fixed interpretation. (Cresswell 1973:127, 84)

The *unthinkable* for Saussure, Sapir, and Firth seems to have happened: at least a major part of *linguistics* became *the prerogative of a few specialists* (23); it has adopted *a sterile and purely technical attitude* (24) and lost sight of *the humanism of speech and language* (26).

In return, a number of authorities in modern linguistics have arrived at the notion that authentic discourse is too disorderly to be a proper object of investigation. Apparently, even such *language* as Mr Martin's letter, though couched in *proper words* and freed of *grammatical errors* (13), would be unworthy to be *studied* or *placed in any category of human facts*:

(38) language is a well-defined object in the heterogeneous mass of speech facts; [...] speech cannot be studied; [...] we cannot put it in any category of human facts, for we cannot discover its unity. (Saussure 1966 [1916]: 14, 19, 9)

(39) observed use of language [...] surely cannot constitute the subject-matter of linguistics, if this is to be a serious discipline; [...] much of the actual speech observed consists of fragments and deviant expressions of a variety of sorts. (Chomsky 1965:4, 201)

Discourse is naturally evaluated so unfavourably because it fails to match the conception of *language* being an ideal system wherein everything is timelessly and perfectly *well-defined*.

These examples may suffice to make my point. Comparing data from large corpora of general discourse with data from small corpora of specialised discourse is a useful tactic for exploring vital differences among general and specialised meanings of important terms, such as *language*. Paradoxically, the shift of a term from general usage to specialised usage may not bring a direct gain in precision or clarity, but in fact a margin of gratuitous uncertainty and obscurity. Students of *language* should be aware — and wary.

Linguistics might have fared far better by not trying to foreclose and freeze the meaning of *language* with doctrinaire moves like examples (32) through (38). Instead, we might envision multiple meanings to reflect our broader motivations for approaching or studying language:

> (40)   [For] the question "what is language?", [...] the only satisfactory
>   response is "why do you want to know?" [Are you] interested in
>   language planning in multilingual communities? Or in aphasia and
>   language disorders? Or in dialects and those who speak them? Or
>   in how come one language differs from another? Or in the formal
>   properties of language as a system? Or in the functions of lan-
>   guage and the demands we make upon it? Or in language as an art
>   medium? (Halliday 1973:9)

Halliday's canny advice seems apt for the uses of language corpora today. If you ask *what is language?* in a *general* sense, then the place to look is a *very large corpus*–ideally much larger than any we have today. But if you ask *what is language?* in a *special* sense, say, because you are developing projects to assist non-native learners of English in appreciating the language of literature (as I am), then the place to look is a *small corpus* representing the language from a suitably specific point of view.

The uses of corpora are surely most urgent for non-native speakers who have not had extensive exposure to fluent English. Our major problem is so much not *bad English* or *incorrect English*, as is often lamented, but rather *insufficient English*. Such is patently true here in the Emirate of Abu Dhabi. My learners use Arabic for most purposes of daily life, especially within the family circles, which are relatively self-contained, at least for women. In those areas of our curriculum where English is the medium of instruction, we must not take it for granted that the learners will command the general fluency such instruction routinely presupposes, nor that they will develop the specialised fluency needed for the discourse of the subject-matter. Without strategic sup-port, they suffer from a substantial margin of communicative inefficiency and information loss. To detect and offset this tendency, I have adopted the strategy of having my students write a summary of the lecture at the end of the class: the feedback alerts me to problems I could not isolate any other way.

In such settings, access to corpora of authentic usage of English would be the most realistic resource for achieving significant improvements. A dual approach with two types of *small corpora* would seem most promising. The *learnable corpus* would be a small corpus delimited by the respective levels of our learners; its entries would be expressly selected to be manageable with a modest fluency in grammar and vocabulary. Such might be similar to the "learner corpus" proposed by Peter Ragan, and the "exemplar corpus" proposed by Chris Tribble (both in this volume). In contrast, the *specialised corpus* would be a small corpus delimited by a specific register, discourse domain, or subject matter, similar to the proposals by Alex Henry and Bob Roseberry, as well as by Vincent Ooi and by Lynne Flowerdew (again in this volume). Ideally, these two senses of *small corpus* would complement each other within an integrated and co-ordinated programme for non-native learners; the selection of general English would be consciously designed to support later work with specialised English in the same curriculum.

The question "what is language?" revisited

I have been arguing so far that the question *what is language?* has rarely been seriously addressed, and when it has, the answers have seldom managed to balance theoretical factors with practical ones. Linguistics has aspired to define *language* in resolutely specialised terms as an ideal system isolated from discourse, and has thus failed to sustain a firm foundation upon substantive observed evidence.

I would now argue that corpus data can supply some "missing links" by indicating regularities that are *more specific than language* yet *more general than discourse* (Beaugrande 2000). For that purpose, a shift in perspective seems fitting: the most essential trait of the units of language is not to be *well-defined* or *distinctive* (as linguistics has claimed) but rather to be *selectable* and *combinable*. Instead of constituting a *closed set of formal rules* which precisely determine the *well-formed strings*, a language constitutes an *open repertory of rich guidelines* for constructing *meaningful discourse events*.

Research on corpus data has recognised two modes of being selectable and combinable, complementing the well-established distinction between "grammar" and "lexicon" (or "vocabulary") (cf. Firth 1957 [original 1934–51]; 1968 [1952–59]; Greenbaum 1974; Francis 1993). Items that tend to be selected together in *grammatical* combinations are said to be *colligable*, and the result is called a *colligation*. Items that tend to be selected together in lexical combinations are said to be *collocable*, and the result is called a *collocation*. These terms are not ideal, since you have to pronounce them carefully to keep them distinct in speech. But they are distinct in writing, and their derivations are clear: you can think of *co-* for "together", as in "co-operate", plus *ligament* for "link up" and *locate* for "put in a particular place".

A language like English, and discourse in English too, can accordingly be said to be based upon extensive and delicate reserves of *colligability* and *collocability*. If they were not, people would encounter harrowing difficulties in deciding what to say. Any word could be combined equally well with any other word, and the language would be completely flat and uniform, like a featureless desert of sand particles. But in reality, the English language is far more similar to an astonishingly diverse and well-tended landscape; and the closer you look at real language, the more delicate details you will find, much like a landscape viewed from the window as the airliner descends from the higher altitudes down toward the ground.

So instead of being *well-defined in advance*, language is a system that is *always in the process of getting defined* wherever discourse takes place; and discourse normally performs this defining quite well. Language evolves on large scales in *historical time*, e.g., as the grammar of English has worn away the distinction between *thou* and *you*, and the vocabulary has picked up a wealth of new expressions like *desertification*. But the language also evolves on small scales in *discursive time*, e.g., as a textbook progresses from the general introduction to the presentation of more specialised sub-topics. At any given point, the colligability and collocability are also evolving and richly constraining the range of the choices a speaker or writer actively considers.

Moreover, colligability and collocability help to determine whether a discourse sounds more or less *fluent, natural,* or *idiomatic* (cf. Sinclair 1984). These three factors have long been intuitively applied when comparing the discourse of native speakers to non-native learners of English. Now we can finally gather explicit evidence about how they are determined in practice by systematically consulting and comparing corpus data.

We should emphasise that colligability and collocability do not dictate what native speakers must say, but rather constitute the background of expectations about what native speakers usually say. The precise order of actual discourse is generated whilst the grammatical colligations and lexical collocations partially *realise* colligability and collocability, and partly *vary* them or *innovate upon* them. Thus, many of the unpredictable, novel, or even unprecedented combinations in discourse are easily produced and understood by analogy to similar ones (Sinclair 1991). When a collocation or colligation is actually found in a corpus, we can say it has been *attested*; but no amount of attestations could ever include all the combinations that are possible or even probable when language becomes discourse.

Learning English as a native language could be described as a process of steadily refining and tuning your sensitivity toward colligability and collocability. You don't just learn what the words are and what they mean, but also which words tend to go together, often producing new meanings along the way. You also learn which types of words or meanings tend to go together, so that you can interchange words of a similar type or meaning without special effort. The learning process is nearly always successful because you hear or see such a huge set of example discourses, rather like a building a large personal corpus of English that gets stored in your memory and experience rather than in a computer.

We might attempt a parallel description for the process of learning English as a non-native language, but we would need to highlight some major differences. The process must contend with the projection of expectations derived from the colligability and collocability in the native language. As for colligability, my own learners here in Abu Dhabi keep inventing ways to build English after the pattern of Arabic. For example, the Verb *be* is omitted in the Present (41), whereas other Verbs appear as Present Participles (42). Since Arabic has no Infinitive, Verbs tend to agree when they shouldn't, whether in Present (43) or the Past (44). Since Arabic can distinguish Grammatical Subject from Clause Topic, the Noun in the Subject of a Clause may by followed by an extra Pronoun, most often the Relative *which* (45) that so often appears after a Noun; in exchange, the Relative gets omitted where English requires it but Arabic would not (46). Or again, the Topic gets postponed until after some rhetorical flourish (47–48).

(41)   The UAE desert rich with green plants.

(42)   Sheikh Zayed still *encouraging* people to revive these sports.

(43)   The teacher has to *manages* the problems and to *reacts* to them.

(44)   In addition, I can't go away and *left* this small girl from himself in the desert.

(45)   Diurnal animals *which* are active at daytime.

(46)   we arrived to the police centre, there I heard some *sound came*

from small room in the office. I went there, and I found *woman sat* on the chair.

(47)   *The most important thing to say that* there are no weak animals in the desert.

(48)   *In addition of that we must not forget that* teacher consider as prophet has an great message to all humanity.

As for collocability, my students produce solecisms which sound distinctly non-fluent, though readily understandable, e.g.:

(49)   A politician job is a dream cannot *cross to my reality.*

(50)   In winter Abu Dhabi have many *immigrated birds.*

(51)   Students will support their country and make its *flag flappers high in the sky.*

Designing the two types of small corpora I have cited in the previous section — the learnable corpus and the specialised corpus — could substantially benefit the teachers, the learners, and even the designers of the corpora. Working through a set of authentic examples in corpus data impels us to notice meanings and contexts that might go totally unnoticed if we encountered a single example or just invented one for casual illustration. This work does not require any high level of theoretical training or technical terminology. On the contrary, it should be expressly kept user-friendly enough for teachers and learners to browse on their own initiative and to share their insights or observations.

The learnable small corpus

To explore the benefits of corpusbrowsing, I now return to the Bank of English for some data I extracted on the common English verb *see*. Most people, if asked, would probably give a meaning corresponding to the definition we find in first place in a typical dictionary: "to perceive with the eye; to view" (*Random House Webster's*, p. 1213). The same dictionary lists a number of less obvious meanings, some with illustrative data and some without, such as: "to perceive mentally; understand; to construct a mental image; visualise; to be cognisant of; recognise: *to see one's mistake*; to accept or imagine as accept-able: *I can't see him as president*; to foresee: *he doesn't see us in a war.*" We can't tell from such examples how the compilers selected their definitions, decided which ones to illustrate, and constructed illustrative data like *to see one's mistake*. Yet if you are deriving your dictionary from a corpus, you are obliged not just to provide real data to illustrate your definitions, but also to use real data when formulating your definitions.

Two of the data illustrations for the meanings of *see* just quoted contain Negation. Yet the compilers and users of such a dictionary would be nonplussed by the prospect of making a special entry for *don't see*, regarding which my large-corpus data revealed some specific and interesting traits in its colligability and collocability.

The data in this my demonstration will be examined across just one sampling, culled from the 365 data lines returned for the key-word combination *don't see*, i.e., only for colligations in the Negative Simple Present Tense, apart from the Third Person Singular Tense and from Past or Future Tense, plus Modal Auxiliaries.[3]

For the colligability, one striking discovery was the proportions among the Pronouns as Subjects, which together accounted for 335 lines (about 92%) in contrast to only 16 Noun Subjects.[4] Among those, the Subject *I* was attested in no fewer than 223 lines (about 61% of the total), *you* in 64, *they* in 38, and *we* in only 10. Among the few Nouns, *people* was most frequent in 4 lines, *analysts* followed in 2, whilst all the others appeared just once, some with loose similarities in meaning: *experts, academics, doctors, shrinks, countries, Americans, Christians, kids, children*. Now, frequencies in large corpus data may not be easy or secure to interpret, but they can prompt us to pose further questions, such as: why should *don't see* take *I* as a Subject six times more often than *they*?

To probe such questions, let's shift our attention from the left-hand Subjects of *don't see* over to the right-hand Objects. By far the most common, occurring in 80 lines, was a framed *that*-Proposition Clause, [5] like those shown in (52–57).

(52)   taken over power, but I don't see that anything has changed.

(53)   But I still don't see that it makes any difference.

(54)   particularly pleased, but I don't see that it matters to anyone else

(55)   he said finally, "I don't see that you've got an option, son".

(56)   say you've guessed correctly. I don't see that you've incriminated Deidre.

(57)   we still don't see that the teachers are well-trained

This framing can serve the social function of mediating between a strong unframed denial (e.g. *the teachers are still not well-trained*) on the one side, and a weaker frame on the other side (e.g. *I don't think/believe that the teachers are well-trained*). Unlike those weaker frames, the frame *I don't see that ...* can imply having looked for evidence and not found it. Interestingly, some of these things could hardly be *seen* in any concrete sense, such as *it mattering to anyone* (54). And, as I shall be pointing out later, visibility was indeed often not decisive in the choices of Objects.

The stance of the speaker (or writer)[6] regarding the evidence also strongly influenced the preferences for Subjects being First Person Singular versus Third Person Plural. If *I don't see* it, then it usually because it just isn't the case, as in (52–56). If *they don't see* it, then usually because they are not being attentive, open-minded, thoughtful, and so on, as in (58–60). The choice of *you* Subjects could have same social function as *I*, e.g. (51), but most of them were more like *they — you don't see* what's really there, as in (62–63).

(58)   bureaucrats. They don't see the difference. They simply
(59)   conditions getting worse. They don't see the economic reforms
(60)   they can't react. Perhaps countries don't see the gravity of the situation, but
(61)   stopping in black towns, you don't see them kissing black babies
(62)   You don't see the beauty of the bay
(63)   so few casualties. If you don't see the hand of God in something like this

However, the implications shifted dramatically when the Enumerator *many* appeared just to the right of *don't see*, which I found in 30 lines. Here, the preferred Subject was not *I* in just 8 lines like (64), but *you* in 20 lines like (65–66); and now the denial means *you don't see many* because there aren't many.

(64)   I hope this one does, but I don't see many signs, frankly, of doing it.
(65)   you don't see many boarded-up storefronts
(66)   because boys programme them. You don't see many women practising their golf
(66a)   I don't see any women practising their golf
(66b)   women don't practise their golf, it's a man's sport ...

By using *you* and *many*, the speaker can doubly weaken responsibility for the denial. Such is quite useful if your denial might be controversial, as you can see by comparing (66) with (66a) and (66b).[7]

The huge proportion of *I* Subjects may indicate a preference for pronouncing one's own view on what is not the case, especially when other people might expect or believe that it is the case. One symptomatic signal for such a preference was *but* appearing immediately to the left of Subject + *don't see that* in 12 lines, as shown back in (52–54); plus *still* in two lines, e.g. (53). In one revealing instance, a *proud feminist* defensively declared: *I don't see that my running for homecoming queen in any way contradicts that.*

I also noted six lines with *really* being used in these two differing social functions. Placing the item to left of *don't see* implied not seeing something because it's not real (67); placing it to the right could have either that same implication, as in (68), or the implication of not seeing something even though it is real, as in (69).

(67)   I really don't see the government doing that
(68)   I don't see that there's anything really wrong
(69)   Alvarez says the Americans don't see the Japanese as they really are

As we can see by contrasting (68) against (69), the choice of Subject follows suit: First Person for what's not real, and Third Person for what is real but not *seen*.

The collocation *don't see that* was followed by the Existential[8] *there's* or *there is* in 17 lines, such as (70–71). How might this colligation differ from a version with just a Direct Object, as in (70a–71a)?

(70)   I don't see that there's anything funny about it
(70a)   I don't see anything funny about it
(71)   I don't see that there's any natural conflict
(71a)   I don't see any natural conflict

Perhaps a strengthening effect can be achieved by having the key item which is *not seen* placed as the Subject of its own Existential Clause — not only don't I see it, there's no such thing.

Attempting to sort out the other right-hand data, I tabulated all the choices of Direct Object Nouns which might conform to the presumably basic meaning of *see* noted above and listed in first place in a dictionary, namely *to per-*

ceive with the eye. My findings confirmed what John Sinclair has repeatedly pointed out: the presumed basic meaning in dictionaries or textbooks may not be the meaning in most common usage (e.g. Sinclair 1998). My tabulation found only 18 fully plausible attestations (about 5%), as in (72–76):

(72)   You don't see the blood until you take off a glove
(73)   you just don't see the flag much in Japan
(74)   with radio you don't see the candidate's face
(75)   we don't see the moon very much here
(76)   it's nice to be where I don't see the anti-Semitic graffiti

A small portion of these data involved Objects that would be visible but in unspecified ways:

(77)   they don't see the reality of war
(78)   you don't see the horrors of the bombing
(79)   Hurricane Hugo. You don't see the suffering that people are going through

In these data sets, especially the second type (77–79), the dominant implication is not seeing something that is actually there — and so the Subject is rarely *I*.

Two colligations with Noun Object each preferred just one Noun for a non-visible thing so frequently that they indisputably count as solid collocations. The more frequent, appearing in 38 lines, was *any reason* which nearly always had one of three colligations further to the right: *why* (19 lines), *to* (10 lines), and *for* (7 lines).[9] After *why* came a Clause consisting of Subject + a Modal Verb *should/shouldn't* or *can't* + Process Verb, as in (80–81); after *to* came a Verb in the Infinitive, as in (82); and after *for* came either Noun as Actor + *to* + Verb in the Infinitive, as in (83); or else Verb as Present Participle, as in (84). These three colligations could presumably be interchanged, e.g. in (80a, 82a, 83a). But each may be felt to place its own focus by moving the respective items close to the *reason*: *why* focuses on motivation, *to* focuses on the Action, and *for* focuses on the Actor.

(80)   If that's your true pattern, I don't see any reason why you should change it
(80a)   If that's your true pattern, I don't see any reason for you to change it

(81)   I don't see any reason why Canada can't compete
(82)   top managers don't see any reason to retreat from stocks
(82a)   top managers don't see any reason for retreating from stocks
(83)   we don't see any reason for the U.N. to investigate
(83a)   we don't see any reason why the U.N. should investigate
(84)   when I find a colour I like, I don't see any reason for changing it

Curiously, the data did not attest the combination *I don't see why* (without adding *any reason*), which I had intuitively expected; perhaps speakers prefer to suggest that they would need *reasons* before they would accept a scenario. Nor did I find *I don't see the reason* with Definite Article; perhaps Negation + *any* is thought to make a stronger denial.

The second most frequent Noun Object, appearing in 28 lines, was *the point*, which, like *reason*, is not a visible thing. The social function should be subtly different. If you say you *don't see any reason* for doing something, you imply that doing it anyway would be unreasonable, unmotivated, unjustified, and so on; so it probably won't be done. But if you say *don't see the point*, you imply that doing it anyway would be pointless, idle, unproductive and so on; yet it may be done, or is being done anyway, as in these data (85–88). *Worrying* is no less common for being *point*-less (85). Someone was apparently just *passing the time* (86). And many people certainly *have dual nationality* (I do) (87), and *ski downhill* (88) as contrasted, I suppose, to *skiing cross-country*, rather than *skiing uphill* (a scenario whose point is hardly worth contesting).

(85)   and panic. I don't see the point of worrying until I have
(86)   not particularly demanding but I don't see the point in him "passing the time"
(87)   I don't see the point in having dual nationality
(88)   And what's more, secretly, I don't see the point of downhill skiing

To the right of *point* I found *of* in 10 lines, and *in* in 8 lines. Either Preposition could be followed by Verb as Present Participle, as we see here in (85–88).

Eight attestations were simply about *not seeing the point* of what somebody is doing or saying. Using *see* for an audible modality like talk underscores how far the meaning of *understand* or *grasp* can displace the meaning *perceive by the eye*.

(89)   I really don't see the point of this, Chief Inspector.
(90)   about this story. I really don't see the point you're making, Colin

A similar displacement could be inferred for some other Noun-Object collocates, such as *relevance* (91), *logic* (92), *need* (93), *advantages* (94), *problem* (95), *danger* (96), or *threat* (97).

(91)   if it has a multicultural policy, I don't see the relevance of this question

(92)   it's stupid, I just don't see the logic in it

(93)   have been returned unopposed. I don't see the need for an election

(94)   not ready for Europe, they don't see the advantages it offers

(95)   whites don't see the problem nearly the same way

(96)   John Major Supporter: I don't see the slightest danger of that

(97)   But other analysts don't see the threat that Dr Kramer sees

All these are not visual, or only vaguely so.

In most of the corpus data, the right-hand colligations were more complicated than just *don't see* + Noun as Direct Object. Some illustrations we have seen already, such as *that*-Proposition Clause and *reason why* + Clause. These preferred colligations were Clause-like without actually having the Subject + Agreeing Verb that a genuine Clause requires. One collocation, attested in 28 lines, was constructed with *don't see* + Object as Actor + Participial Verb as Action, where the social function was to express an unforeseen scenario, as in (98–101). Even an Object or Actor that was not human or animate was expressed as if it could act under its own power, as we see in (100–101). Alternative Clause versions are not hard to imagine, as in (100a–101a), but the originals seem to have a smoother prosody.

(98)   to prove we are the best. You don't see many people smiling at a John Major speech

(99)   you don't see many ploughman plodding their weary way

(100)   Mr Scalfaro and others don't see the currency decisively sliding

(100a) Mr Scalfaro and others don't see that the currency will decisively slide

(101)   if we make any speed at all, I don't see the watertight bulkheads standing up

(101a) I don't see that the watertight bulkheads are going to stand up

Notice again the preferred implication, reinforced by signals like *many* (98–99) and *I*-Subject (101), that what you *don't see* just isn't there (or won't be).

An alternative Clause-like colligation, found in 23 lines, was constructed with *don't see* + Object + *as* + Object Complement as Modifier (102) or as Noun (103), where the social function was apparently to repudiate an assessment.

(102)   I don't see the deficit as insurmountable
(103)   because they're only pictured, I don't see women as any sort of threat

As before, what isn't *seen* just isn't there when *I* is the Subject.

Interestingly, both of these colligations clearly preferred Personal Pronouns for Objects. The most common was *myself* in no fewer than 27 lines, e.g. (104–110). The most numerous were repudiated assessments with *as* (in 16 lines), e.g. (104–105), then unforeseen scenarios with Present Participles (in 5 lines), e.g. (106–107). The 4 attestations with both *as* and Present Participle in the same data line, e.g. (108), might indicate that the two colligations are fairly close in their social functions. A few with Prepositional Phrases (in 4 lines), e.g. (109–110), might be either assessments or scenarios.

(104)   I don't see myself as an Asian, but as a Muslim
(105)   Banton says "I don't see myself as a homophobic artist"
(106)   plans to expand the business. I don't see myself having a huge store
(107)   I'm over 70 now, and I don't see myself starting again.
(108)   when I walk down the street, I don't see myself as attracting attention.
(109)   I don't see myself on a Versace runway.
(110)   I don't see myself in the role of a teacher,

The high frequency of *myself*-Objects might be due to widespread concern for self-images among the participants in media discourse. Notice how a speaker can invoke the possibility of a flattering image — e.g., owning *a huge store* (106), or qualifying to be a fashion model for *Versace* (109) — in the same speech act as repudiating it.

I have now surveyed the colligability and collocability of *don't see* and attempted to describe some of the relevant social functions. Especially when used with the Subject *I*, or with the Subject *you* + the Enumerator *many*, a major function is for the speaker to deny, with a fairly mild force, that something is true, likely, plausible, reasonable, and so on, contrary to the beliefs of other people. Considerably less often, the speaker asserts rather than denies, but again with contrariness.

If I were building a learnable corpus, I would need to decide which data deserved to be included. For *don't see*, plausible candidates might be examples (53), (68), (70), (80), and (90). But trying to build together a corpus of selected data lines would contradict the essential architecture of corpora, which are built of whole texts and discourses. The data lines are temporary artefacts; while displaying one regularity they may be concealing or truncating another. We can pull them out of corpus materials but we should not isolate them.

So the task of constructing a learnable corpus will require extensive explorations of socially functional colligations and collocations in order to select a set of learnable texts which exemplify them. I could not simply pick out a set of user-friendly data about *don't see* and insert it into a corpus. Instead, I would need to examine various data clustered around a social function such as expressing mild denials, and to identify the types of texts which exploit them.

The task will undoubtedly be immense and laborious, more like map-making back in the early ages of exploration than like language analysis by the conventional methods of today. To recall my analogy (proposed in the previous section) of viewing a landscape from the window of a descending airliner, the explorer sees steadily finer details. But a grand irony intrudes: the explorer's own vision is the agent for mapping out a vast wilderness area from several altitudes, and ultimately even for creating the landing field!

Yet once heavy labours of constructing learnable corpora have been performed, the labours of acquiring fluent English will be substantially lightened. Teachers and learners will become explorers in their turn but now in a tamed landscape, less like a wilderness than a nature park. Instead of working through prefabricated and arbitrary lists of grammatical rules or vocabulary items whose use is merely hypothetical, they will discover grammar and vocabulary in thickets of real usage as they interactively browse the corpus and seek to explain the patterns they find.

Along the way, the staid division between grammar and vocabulary will fade away, like an artificial boundary between two interacting ecosystems. If, as I have pointed out, colligations and collocations are less general than a language yet more so than a discourse, so too are they less general than grammar yet more so than vocabulary as these two areas are usually treated in the classroom. And if the polarisation of language and discourse (or langue and parole, or competence and performance) has stunted the progress of language science, so too has the polarisation of grammar and vocabulary stunted the progress of language learning.

The specialised small corpus

Constructing a specialised small corpus delimited by a register, discourse domain, or subject-matter involves heavy labours of a subtly different kind. Again, we want to support explorations of language resources in authentic usage, but with a conscious focus on the resources that are not typical of general discourse. Unfortunately, a large portion of specialised discourse, even in textbooks, is not user-friendly for prospective readers or learners, but gratuitously academic, verbose, or obscure (Beaugrande 1992, 1994, 1999). So we can anticipate some systematic tension or trade-off between learnability and specialisation.

I shall give just some brief illustrations from my work using WordPilot©, a corpus-based resource program developed by John Milton at the Hong Kong University of Science and Technology (available at www.compulang.com/ wordpilot.htm). It is designed to support word-processing activities and can be accessed directly from WORD to display examples of authentic usage for specific expressions. It also offers lists for working on words that are (a) frequently misused; (b) frequently used or confused on the Test of English as a Foreign Language (TOEFL); or (c) frequently tested on the Scholastic Aptitude Test (SAT). Moreover, the latest version (CompuLang Word Pilot 2000 Premium Edition) includes (a) a set of small corpora from such domains as business, accounting, academic reports, legal reports, biographies, and public speeches; (b) links to monolingual and multilingual dictionaries and to a thesaurus on the Web; (c) links to writing tutorials for applications like "job search" and "résumé writing"; and (d) a voice synthesiser to pronounce words selected either from the current text or from an amazingly erudite list including items like *monophthalmus* and *ligustrum obtusifolium*.

Here at the United Arab Emirates University, I have been using *WordPilot* to compile small corpora for various uses in my own teaching. My corpus of British novels I have mentioned before (in the section "What is "language"?). This one I have deployed to bridge the subject-matter of my courses in Syntax, Semantics, or Stylistics, with the literary side of our programme.

To escape the vacuity of the assigned textbook on *Semantics* with its mind-numbing examples like *John is as tall as himself* and *Cats are not vegetables*, I introduced data to explore how meanings arise and evolve in contexts. In Jane Austen's *Pride and Prejudice*, which my students were reading in another course, the reader is positioned to attribute the *pride* to Mr Darcy and thus to be caught in the *prejudice* against him harboured by Elizabeth Bennet. But if we search and collate all occurrences of *pride* and *proud* in the whole text, we can notice that the attributions typically appear framed as opinions of unidentified persons, such as *everybody* (111–112). Just because he failed to be sociable at one assembly — he was in fact acting aloof to hide his shyness toward strangers — his proudness was instantly and irrevocably *discovered* and *decided*, where the colligation with Passive Verbs and the collocation *most...in the world* subtly deconstruct the force of what is apparently asserted as absolute truth (113–114). Then we encounter the personal testimony of the ambivalent Mr Wickham, which Elizabeth innocently believes and condemns the *pride* as *abominable* (115). Later still, when Elizabeth repeats Mr Wickham's account, a truly elaborate framing is created: Mrs Gardiner rummages in her memory and finally dredges up a foggy *recollection* of another unidentified attribution about a *reputed disposition* (116).

(111)   everybody says that he is ate up with *pride*

(112)   He is not at all liked in Hertfordshire. Every body is disgusted with his *pride*.

(113)   he was discovered to be *proud* , to be above his company, and above being pleased;

(114)   His character was decided. He was the *proudest*, most disagreeable man in the world.

(115)   "It is wonderful," — replied Wickham, — for almost all his actions may be traced to pride." "Can such abominable pride as his, have ever done him good?"

(116)   she tried to remember something of that gentleman's reputed disposition, when quite a lad, [...] and was confident at last that she recollected having heard Mr. Fitzwilliam Darcy formerly spoken of as a very *proud*, ill-natured boy.

Treating a literary work as a special kind small corpus can thus support a deeper appreciation of how the reader joins in constructing an alternative world of human experience on the basis of multiple and possibly conflicting language data that merit special attention.

Another small corpus I compiled from the Web (a mere 50,000 words so far) was for use in a Methods of Research course module on the topic of "deserts" and "desertification". Despite my university being located at the very gateway of the immense Rub al-Khali, known to antiquity as Arabia Deserta, my students proved to have scant knowledge about deserts; perhaps their diet of British novels had kept them preoccupied with landscapes like Hertfordshire.

One term and concept they had not encountered before was *arid*. I searched my corpus and picked out attestations like (117–120). I used underlining to highlight contextual items that seemed helpful in determining or elaborating the meaning of the key word.

(117) half the countries on earth lie partly or entirely in *arid* and semi-*arid* zones, which cover one-third of the planet's land surface

(118) *arid* lands are defined on the basis of climate, ecology, and land-use characteristics.

(119) *Arid* land: Mean annual precipitation up to about 200 mm in winter rainfall areas and 300 mm in summer rainfall areas

(120) Semi-*arid* lands receive annual rainfall of between 500 and 800 mm

(121) *Desertification* occurs when land in *arid* or semi-*arid* regions is degraded by human activity or prolonged drought brought about by global warming.

First, example (117) alerts us to how important *aridity* is by its sheer extent. Then, (118) states multiple criteria for *defining* it, whilst (119) and (120) narrow these down to amounts of *precipitation* or *rainfall*, and contrast *arid* with *semi-arid lands*.

From there, a link is made to the equally unfamiliar term *desertification* (121). The challenge now is to understand the process of creating a desert as compared to describing a desert like the Rub Al-Khali ,which has existed for thousands of years much as we see it here today. So I ran another search and chose data like (122–128). Again, the data indicated the size of the issue getting *recognition* from *world leaders* (122). Numerous collocates highlighted the negative meanings associated with a serious threat: *disturbance, wastelands, breakdown, degradation* (123–124). The causes are linked not to abstract natural forces but to concrete human activities of *inappropriate land use,* such as *overcultivation, overgrazing,* or *deforestation* (126). Yet these in turn are linked to the *underlying socioeconomic* and *political reasons* which are still not being addressed even by anti-*desertification programs* (127). One major reason is forcing *poor countries* to produce *cash crops* regardless of environmental consequences (128), which point up the need for global action by *world leaders*.

(122)   in the last few years, <u>world leaders</u> have started to recognize the need to <u>combat</u> *desertification*

(123)   *Desertification* is the process of <u>land disturbance</u> that ultimately leads to the transformation of productive land into these <u>ecological wastelands</u>

(124)   a <u>breakdown</u> in the <u>sustainability</u> of these systems, primarily because of <u>environmental degradation</u> of *arid* lands is the process called *desertification*

(126)   Human activities include <u>overcultivation</u>, <u>overgrazing</u>, <u>deforestation</u>, <u>poor irrigation practices</u> and any other <u>inappropriate land use</u> and <u>human management of ecosystems</u>.

(127)   Anti-*desertification* programs have made little effort at <u>solving the underlying socioeconomic and political reasons for unsustainable land-use practices</u>

(128)   A more general cause for *desertification* is the <u>pressure put on poor countries</u> to include them into the <u>world market economy</u> through the <u>cultivation</u> of <u>cash crops</u>

To make the topic more animated and immediate, I presented videos such as *River of Sand* (featuring Bruce Cockburn) and *Seeds of Survival* produced by USC Canada in Mali and Ethiopia.[10]

Conclusion

The next stage would be to turn our teachers and learners loose on some small corpora and to interface their uses with activities such as reading and writing in English. *WordPilot* is well-designed for such interfacing, but the small corpora will need considerable further designing for reasons I have attempt to describe in this paper. No doubt other specifications for the design will emerge as the implementation passes through its developmental stages, and the wilderness grows more hospitable.

Notes

1.   I am most indebted to John Sinclair for helping me learn to access the system and allowing me to use his personal terminal.

2. A detailed analysis of these discourses has been presented in Beaugrande (1991).

3. I shall identify the grammatical terms here by Capitalising them. The full grammar is presented in Beaugrande (1997) as derived and modified from Halliday (1994).

4. These proportions could be different if I had included the Third Person Singular (*doesn't see*), but the tendencies I shall explore indicate that the differences might not have been significant. Minor discrepancies in total numbers, here and further on, arose from not counting lines where data were missing, unclear, or duplicated.

5. The term "framing" refers to the means for saying what is expressed as being *said, thought, believed,* and so on rather than asserted just then by the speaker; the term "Proposition" is often used for the content of what gets framed.

6. I shall use the term "speaker" in this section on the understanding that a writer is often implied, though the differences in usages between speaking versus writing certainly deserve to be explored, notably by contrasting spoken corpora with written corpora.

7. Examples whose number carries a letter as in (66a), are hypothetical, just for comparison.

8. The term "Existential" is used by Halliday and others for Clauses beginning with *there is…* or with *there are…* to assert that something exists.

9. In the remaining cases, *why* was optionally omitted, as in *I don't see any reason the Irish would want to*; or *any reason* was at the end of the text; or the Preposition was *of*, which I don't find idiomatic.

10. Available from Kensington Communications Inc., 20 Maud Street Suite 402, Toronto, Ontario, Canada M5V 2M5; Fax. 001/613/234–6842.

References

Altenberg, B. 1991. "A bibliography of publications relating to English computer corpora". In S. Johansson and A. B. Stenström (eds), *English Computer Corpora: Selected papers and research guide*. Berlin: Mouton.

Baker, M., Francis, G. and Tognini-Bonelli, E. (eds), 1993. *Text and Technology: In honour of John McHardy Sinclair*. Amsterdam: John Benjamins.

Beaugrande, R. de. 1991. *Linguistic Theory: The discourse of fundamental works*. London: Longman.

Beaugrande, R. de. 1992. "Knowledge and discourse in geometry: Intuition, experience, logic". *Journal of the International Institute for Terminology Research* 3(2):29–125.

Beaugrande, R. de. 1994. "Special purpose language in the discourse of epistemology: The 'genetic psychology' of Jean Piaget". In M. Brekkle, Ø. Andersen, T. Dahl, and J. Myking (eds), *Applications and Implications of Current LSP Research,*

16–32. Bergen: Fagbokforlaget.

Beaugrande, R. de. 1997. *New Foundations for a Science of Text and Discourse.* Stamford, CT: Ablex.

Beaugrande, R. de. 1998. "Performative speech acts in linguistic theory: The programme of Noam Chomsky". *Journal of Pragmatics* 29:765–803.

Beaugrande, R. de. 1999. "User-friendly communication skills in the teaching and learning of Business English". *English for Special Purposes* 18.

Beaugrande, R. de. 2000. "Text linguistics at the millennium: Corpus data and missing links". *Text* 20.

Bloomfield, L. 1933. *Language.* New York: Holt.

Chomsky, N. 1957. *Syntactic Structures.* The Hague:Mouton.

Chomsky, N. 1965. *Aspects of the Theory of Syntax.* Cambridge MA: MIT Press.

Cresswell, M. 1973. *Logics and Languages.* London: Methuen.

Firth, J. R. 1957. *Papers in Linguistics 1934–1951.* London: OUP.

Firth, J. R. 1968. *Selected Papers of J. R. Firth 1952–1959,* F. R. Palmer (ed). London: Longman.

Francis, G. 1993. "A corpus-driven approach to grammar". In M. Baker, G. Francis, and E. Tognini-Bonelli (eds), 137–156.

Greenbaum, S. 1974. "Some verb-intensifier collocations in American and British English". *American Speech* 49:79–89.

Halliday, M. A. K. 1973. *Explorations in the Function of Language.* London: Arnold.

Halliday, M. A. K. 1994. *An Introduction to Functional Grammar.* Second revised edition. London: Arnold.

Hjelmslev, L. 1969 [orig. 1943]. *Prolegomena to a Theory of Language.* Madison: University of Wisconsin Press.

McEnery, T. and Wilson, A. 1996. *Corpus Linguistics.* Edinburgh: EUP.

Pearson, J. 1998. *Terms in Contex* [Studies in Corpus Linguistics 1]. Amsterdam: John Benjamins.

Sapir, E. 1921. *Language.* New York: Harcourt, Brace, & World.

Saussure, F. de 1966 [orig. 1916]. *Course in General Linguistics,* translated by Wade Baskin. New York: McGraw-Hill.

Sinclair, J.McH. 1984. "Naturalness in language use". In *Lexis and Lexicography,* 96–104. Singapore: National University Press.

Sinclair, J.McH. 1991. "Shared knowledge". In J. Alatis (ed), *Georgetown University Round Table on Languages and Linguistics 1991,* 489–500. Washington, DC: Georgetown University Press.

Sinclair, J.McH. 1998. "Large corpus research and foreign language teaching". In R. de Beaugrande, M. Grosman, and B. Seidlhofer (eds), *Language Policy and Language Education in Emerging Nations: Focus on Slovenia and Croatia,* 79–86. Stamford, CT: Ablex.

SECTION 2

CHAPTER 2

Using small corpora to investigate learner needs
Two vocabulary research tools

Paul Nation

LALS, Victoria University of Wellington, New Zealand

Abstract

Corpus research has three essential requirements — a set of good research questions that can be answered by study of a corpus, a corpus to provide a source of data, and the computer programmes that can facilitate the task of organising the data from the corpus. This paper looks at such programmes and in particular describes two computer programmes that have been specially developed to address the needs of learners of English as a second or foreign language. It also looks at how teachers can use corpora based on the texts that learners will have to read, or based on writing produced by learners to investigate learners' vocabulary needs. This paper will also suggest several research questions that teachers could use to guide their investigation. It describes published and unpublished research that has addressed similar questions.

Introduction: Research questions and background

The two computer programmes that will be described in this paper, *VocabProfile* and *RANGE*, have been used to investigate the amount of low frequency and other types of vocabulary in different kinds of written input that second or foreign language learners may have to cope with, and to investigate the amount of different kinds of vocabulary in the written output produced by language learners.

When analysing reading texts, it is possible to use *VocabProfile* and *RANGE* to answer questions like the following.

- How large a vocabulary do you need to read newspapers?
- How large a vocabulary do you need to read novels?
- Do graded readers provide good conditions for vocabulary learning?
- Do you have to know the vocabulary introduced at a level in a graded reader scheme before you begin reading books at that level?
- What is the vocabulary load of an economics textbook?
- Is there a special purposes academic vocabulary which is important for reading academic texts?

When looking at learners' writing, it is possible to use *VocabProfile* and *RANGE* to answer questions like the following.

- Are learners using an appropriate variety of vocabulary in their written work?
- Is there a significant gap between learners' receptive and productive vocabulary?
- Is the vocabulary learners meet in their reading carried over into their written production?

The main idea lying behind some of the uses of these programmes is that the words in the vocabulary of a language are not created equal. Some words are much more important than others. The typical way of determining the importance of a word is by looking at its frequency and range of occurrence. That is, words that occur often in a wide range of language uses are much more generally useful for a language user to know than words which occur rarely and in a limited range of areas, particularly if these areas such as biology, computing, geography etc are not of immediate interest to the language user.

The words that occur often in a range of uses of the language are called high frequency words or general service words (West 1953). Typically the dividing line between high frequency and low frequency words in English is drawn at the 2000 word level. That is, it is generally considered there are around 2000 high frequency words. This dividing line is an arbitrary one but it is supported by a substantial amount of research. Table 1 shows how the coverage of vocabulary drops substantially beyond the most common 2000 word

Table 1: Vocabulary size and coverage (Carroll, Davies and Richman 1971)

Number of words%	Text coverage
86,741	100
43,831	99
12,448	95
5,000	89.4
4,000	87.6
3,000	85.2
→ 2,000	81.3
1,000	74.1
100	49
10	23.7

families in a corpus of 5,000,000 running words.

When we say that the high frequency vocabulary is important, its importance comes from its high probability of being met in a wide range of language uses. If a learner does not know it, then the learner will face the same vocabulary difficulties in all uses of the language. There are other ways of defining *important*, such as important for understanding the meaning of a particular text, but the way used here takes account of learners' long term use of the language.

There is plenty of evidence that generally learners learn high frequency vocabulary before they learn low frequency vocabulary (Read 1988). This is not surprising because language courses sensibly focus on high frequency vocabulary and there are many more opportunities in normal language use to meet high frequency vocabulary. For learners at an intermediate level and beyond, it will generally be the low frequency vocabulary that causes them difficulty. It is thus useful to be able to quickly analyze texts to see how much low frequency vocabulary they contain and what their low frequency vocabulary is. This can help a teacher decide if the text needs to be simplified, if it needs to be discarded and an easier one found, or if it is feasible to pre-teach some of the vocabulary. The computer programmes described in this article allow this analysis to be done.

One of the ways of making low frequency vocabulary more manageable is to increase the number of high frequency words. This can be done by taking a special purposes approach. That is, the language use goals of the learners are examined and then some research is done to see if there is a specialised vocabulary that is not in the most frequent 2000 words of the language but which is frequent and of wide range within the limited area of specialisation that the learners are interested in. The programmes described in this article are a useful means of doing such research.

One such specialised vocabulary that has been developed (using the *RANGE* programme) is an academic word list (Coxhead 2000). This is described in a little more detail later in this paper. Such vocabulary typically covers around 8.5% of the running words in academic texts (see Table 3). It is thus a very important learning goal for learners with academic purposes.

The most frequent 2000 words of English and the academic word list are available as word lists with the programmes described in this article.

The word lists which come with the programmes consist of base words and their closely related inflected and derived forms. They do not include collocations or lexical phrases, and the programmes are not capable of distinguishing different meanings of the same forms such as *row* (a lot of noise) and *row* (a line of objects or people), or *date* (the fruit) and *date* (a time). These are problems which could probably only be satisfactorily solved by marking up texts to tag such items. Only a small number of idiomatic collocations are frequent enough to get into the most frequent 2000 words of English (Nation 1999: 293). This is because the frequency of any collocation will be much less than the frequency of the individual items that make it up. The lists used in the programmes however do not include collocations.

Let us now look in detail at the two programmes.

VocabProfile and *RANGE*

VocabProfile and *RANGE* are freeware available at http://www.vuw.ac.nz/lals/. Detailed instructions about how to use the programmes are in a file called *instruct.wp* (or *instruct.dos*). They only run on PCs.

VocabProfile can be used to compare a text against vocabulary lists to see what words in the text are and are not in the lists, and to see what percentage of the items in the text are covered by the lists. It can also be used to compare the vocabulary of two texts to see how much of the same vocabulary they use and what vocabulary differences exist between them.

Specifically, *VocabProfile* shows which words in a text are covered by each of three user-created or ready-made word lists and which words are not covered by any of these lists. The available lists are described in detail below. It does this by comparing the words in a text with the words in the three lists, marks words in the text according to which word list or lists contain them, and produces various lists of the words from the texts.

In addition, *VocabProfile* provides a table which shows how much coverage of a text each of the three lists provides. For each word list, the programme shows how many word tokens (total running words), how many word types (different word forms), and how many word families, or *lemmas*, (groups containing different forms of a word) the text contains. (For information on word families see Bauer and Nation (1993).) It also provides similar statistics for words that are not contained in any of the lists. Both totals and percentages are given, as shown in Table 2, below. (In the 'word list' column, 'one', 'two', and 'three' refer to the three word lists.)

Table 2: *A word list table produced by VocabProfile*

Word list	Tokens/%	Types/%	Families
One	54/72.0	34/69.4	33
two	2/ 2.7	2/ 4.1	2
three	14/18.7	9/18.4	9
not in the lists	5/ 6.7	4/ 8.2	?????
Total	75	49	44

In the programme, word list one is called BASEWRD1.DAT, word list two is called BASEWRD2.DAT, and word list three BASEWRD3.DAT. The word count data in Table 2 refer to a short text which contained 75 running words (tokens). Fifty-four words in the text are in word list one and these 54 words make up 72% of the running words in the text. These 54 tokens are made up of 34 different words (types) from 33 word families.

In the three lists, *VocabProfile* also keeps a cumulative record of the frequency of items it meets in all the texts it is run on. Figure 1 shows the first items in word list one (BASEWRD1.DAT), showing word frequencies for a short text. Note that family members are indented under the head word for that word family.

A	1 4
AN	1 1
ABLE	0
ABLER	0
ABLEST	0
ABLY	0
UNABLE	0
ABOUT	6
ABOVE	3

Figure 1: Frequencies of the first few words in BASEWRD1.DAT

The programmes thus count the vocabulary used in a text and compare it with accompanying word lists which allow the vocabulary in the lists to be counted as word families.

What is needed to run VocabProfile?

To run *VocabProfile* on a text, three word lists are needed: They must be called BASEWRD1.DAT, BASEWRD2.DAT, BASEWRD3.DAT. They must be ASCII files. Any words can be put into these three lists as described below. If you want to use only one or two lists, you can just make one or two other files with the correct name (e.g. BASEWRD2.DAT) but with no words or a non-sense word in them in order to have the three lists which must be there for *VocabProfile* to run.

   VocabProfile will usually only run accurately on an ASCII (DOS) text file so it may be necessary to convert word processor files before using them. Word processing programmes are capable of doing this using the "save as" option.

The lists available for VocabProfile *and* RANGE
Three ready made lists are available. The first (BASEWRD1.DAT) includes the most frequent 1000 words of English. The second (BASEWRD2.DAT) includes the 2nd 1000 most frequent words, and the third (BASEWRD3.DAT) includes words not in the first 2,000 words of English but which are frequent in university texts from a wide range of subjects. All of these lists include the base forms of words and derived forms. The first 1000 words thus consist of around 4,000 forms. The sources of these lists are *A General Service List of*

English Words (West 1953) for the first 2000 words, and *An Academic Word List* (Coxhead 1998). The first thousand words of *A General Service List of English Words* are usually those in the list with a frequency higher than 332 occurrences per 5 million words, plus months, days of the week, numbers, titles (Mr, Mrs, Miss, Ms, Mister), and frequent greetings (Hello, Hi etc.).

The lists include both American and British spellings. Apostrophes are treated as spaces, so "I've" is counted as two items, as is "Jane's".

The word forms in the lists are grouped into word families under a headword. For example, the headword *aid* has the following family members *aided*, *aiding*, *aids*, and *unaided*. In the lists the family members have a Tab (indent) in front of them, as shown in Figure 1. The headword occurs just before the family members and has no Tab.

Preparing your own lists
You do not need to use the lists that are provided with the programmes. If, for example, you wish to look at the overlap between two texts, because you want to see how well one text prepares learners for a subsequent text, you can turn one of the texts into a word list by running the programme *WORD*, *VocabProfile*, or *RANGE*, edit it to make word families, and give it the name BASEWRD1.DAT, so that it becomes a base list that *VocabProfile* will use. You then make two other lists named BASEWRD2.DAT and BASEWRD3. DAT each with only a nonsense word in them, and run the programme with the other text as the input text.

To run *VocabProfile*, you type "VP". The computer will ask you to give the name of the data file you want to run *VocabProfile* over. Give the name of the data file (e.g. TEXT1.DOS) and hit the enter key. The data file is the file name of the text that you want to analyse. The computer will next ask you to give the name of the output file you want to send the results to. When you analyse your text with *VocabProfile*, you need a separate file for the results so that your original text remains unchanged. You can use any name for the output file, and you then can choose the options to get the kind of output you want.

You can choose to create a marked text if you want to see where the words in the lists occur in the text. The output, shown in Figure 2, will include a full copy of the text with the words marked according to the lists they occur in.

There are two numbers, separated by a vertical slash, following each headword in the family lists in the output. For example,

LEARN   4 | 1

The first figure is the total family members including the headword that occurred. In the example with *learn*, *learner* occurred twice in the text, *learning* once and *learn* once. The second figure is the number of times the actual form of the headword *learn* occurred.

The information produced by *VocabProfile* allows teachers to see how many and what words are not in the word lists and thus which might be unknown to their learners. Sometimes the table of tokens, types, and families is enough information to decide if a text will be too difficult, but it is wiser to look at the words not in the list as well, because many of these may be proper nouns or familiar words that could be considered as not adding to the vocabulary difficulty of the text.

RANGE

Another programme, *RANGE,* is used to compare the vocabulary of up to 32 different texts at the same time. This programme is useful when looking at a series of texts in a course book or a set of graded readers to see how much the vocabulary is repeated in different texts. For each word in the texts, the programme provides a range or distribution figure (how many texts the word occurs in), a headword frequency figure (the total number of times the actual headword type appears in all the texts), a family frequency figure (the total number of times the word and its family members occur in all the texts), and a frequency figure for each of the texts the word occurs in. It can be used to create word lists based on frequency and range, and can be used to discover shared and unique vocabulary in several pieces of writing.

What is needed to run RANGE?
To run the programme you need

1. the programme *Range.exe*,
2. the three base word lists (BASEWRD1.DAT, BASEWRD2.DAT, BASEWRD3.DAT),

RANGE can be used with the same word lists used by *VocabProfile*. This allows it to classify some of the words in the input files into word families. The programme will give different figures depending on whether the word lists are used or not. If the word lists are used, the figures will represent a mixture of families and types. All the words in the word lists are counted as families and the remainder are counted as types. If the word lists are not used, then all the words are counted as types, because it is the word lists that are used to make families.

Figure 3 shows some sample output from *RANGE*. In this example, the programme was run on four files (indo1.dos, indo2.dos, indo3.dos, indo4.dos). The output file was called 'results'. Notice the choices available in the options. Comments are included in brackets.

```
Comments included in brackets are not produced by the program but are added here to help
understand the example.


WORD LIST            TOKENS/%            TYPES/%         FAMILIES

one                  6464/85.1           650/74.1        432 (the first 1000 words)
two                   420/ 5.5           158/18.0        120 (the second 1000 words)
three                   8/ 0.1             3/ 0.3          3 (the Academic Word List)
not in the lists      706/ 9.3            66/ 7.5        ?????

Total                7598                877             555


(The following figures show how many words each list contains e.g. the AWL has 570 families and
these are made up of 3110 types)

Number of BASEWRD1.DAT types: 4125   Number of BASEWRD1.DAT families: 999
Number of BASEWRD2.DAT types: 3707   Number of BASEWRD2.DAT families: 986
Number of BASEWRD3.DAT types: 3110   Number of BASEWRD3.DAT families: 570

(Only a very small part of the output is provided here. The output has been sorted by frequency.
All the words shown here appear in all four input files and so have a range of 4. The is a single
member word family, so its family frequency and type frequency are the same - 333. The type
frequency of the word type A is 128. Its family frequency is 135 which means that the other
member of the family, an, occurred 7 times. F1, F2 etc refer to each of the four texts and the
family frequencies are given for each text.)

LIST OF FAMILY GROUPS

BASE ONE FAMILIES            RANGE TYFREQ FAFREQ    F1      F2      F3      F4
THE                            4    333    333      96      79      94      64
AND                            4    261    261      74      57      87      43
TO                             4    201    201      39      51      44      67
YOU                            4    154    177      33      39      44      61
HE                             4    151    247      98      51      54      44
SHE                            4    147    253      62      84      46      61
I                              4    142    215      51      45      36      83
A                              4    128    135      36      28      34      37
BUT                            4     83     83      16      28      21      18
IT                             4     83     83      28      13      17      25
...

(The following data is for some of the low frequency words)

TYPE                         RANGE  FREQ    F1      F2      F3      F4
SITA                           1     1      1       0       0       0
TANK                           1     1      0       0       1       0
TRUCKS                         1     1      0       1       0       0
TUTI                           1     1      1       0       0       0
VEGETABLE                      1     1      1       0       0       0
WELL-KNOWN                     1     1      0       0       0       1

(This is a list of types not families. Each type occurs only once in one of the four texts.)
```

Figure 3: Sample output from the *RANGE* program.
Comments included in brackets are not produced by the program but are added here to help understand the example.

This data on occurrences across texts, especially related texts, is valuable when making lists of useful words to focus on and when looking at what spaced repetitions are provided to help the incidental learning of words, as we shall see in some of the studies described below.

```
range.exe              (the programme)
basewrd1.dat           (the word lists)
basewrd2.dat
basewrd3.dat
indo1.dos
indo2.dos              (the files to be processed)
indo3.dos
indo4.dos
indo5.dos
indo6.dos
```

Figure 4: A sample directory for the RANGE programme

Research using *VocabProfile* and *RANGE*

There are now several studies which have used *VocabProfile* or *RANGE* to look at the vocabulary load of texts that learners may need to read.

Academic text and academic vocabulary

Studies of the vocabulary load of academic texts typically show that the most frequent 2,000 words of English cover around 80% of the running words, and the University Word List covers around 8.5% of the running words, making a total of 88.5% coverage by these two groups of words (Sutarsyah, Nation and Kennedy 1994).

Sutarsyah, Nation and Kennedy (1994) used *VocabProfile* to compare the vocabulary needed to read one complete economics text book with a collection of short academic texts on a variety of topics totaling the same length as the book. The texts were from a wide range of academic disciplines. Table 3 shows the results. In this table the word coverage is based in part on the *General Service List* (GSL) and the *University Word List* (UWL), both of which were mentioned earlier. The "1st 1,000" and "2nd 1,000" words are from the *General Service List*.

In Table 3, note that the economics text has a total vocabulary of 5,438 word families, while the collection of short academic texts contains 12,744 word families. Clearly, reading a continuous text on the same topic by the

Table 3: *Number of word families and percentage of coverage of the economics text and the general academic corpus by GSL and UWL*

Word level	Families in the economics text	Coverage of the economics text	Families in the general academic corpus	Coverage of the general academic corpus
1st 1,000 (GSL)	1,029	77.72%	1,095	74.11%
2nd 1,000 (GSL)	548	4.78%	796	4.32%
UWL	636	8.74%	811	8.40%
Others	3,225	8.77%	10,042	13.16%
Total	5,438	100%	12,744	100%

same author requires a much less diverse vocabulary. It is thus useful to focus on learners' specific disciplines as soon as they have control of the general academic vocabulary in order to keep a focus on the most useful vocabulary.

In a subsequent study, Coxhead (1998) used the *RANGE* programme to create an academic word list consisting of vocabulary that was frequent and wide ranging in academic texts, but which was not contained in the most frequent 2,000 words of English. Coxhead's corpus of academic texts consisted of four divisions of Arts, Commerce, Science, and Law. Each of these four divisions was divided into seven subject areas such as education, history, linguistics, and so on. *RANGE* was used to find the range and frequency of occurrence of words that were not among the 2,000 most frequent words. The resulting list is now available as BASEWRD3.DAT. Table 4 below shows the coverage of the sublists of this list.

This 570 word vocabulary provides very substantial coverage of academic text and is an important learning goal for learners with academic purposes.

Books written for teenagers

Hirsh and Nation (1992) used the *VocabProfile* programme[1] to look at the accessibility for second language learners of novels written for young native speakers. They found that if proper nouns are considered to be known, a vocabulary of the 2,000 most frequent words brought learners very close to the 95% coverage which is the minimum needed for adequate comprehension (Laufer 1989). Hirsh and Nation however considered that for reading for plea-

Table 4: Coverage of Coxhead's academic corpus by sublists of her Academic Word List (1998)

AWL sublist	Coverage of the Academic Corpus (%)
1 (60 families)	3.6%
2 (60 families)	1.8%
3 (60 families)	1.2%
4 (60 families)	0.9%
5 (60 families)	0.8%
6 (60 families)	0.6%
7 (60 families)	0.5%
8 (60 families)	0.3%
9 (60 families)	0.2%
10 (30 families)	0.1%
570 families	10.0%

sure, 98% coverage of the running words (1 unknown word in every 50 running words) was necessary. To achieve this coverage, learners would need a vocabulary size of around 5,000 word families.

Graded readers

Nation and Wang (1999) looked at forty-two books in a scheme of graded readers to see what conditions they provide for reading and vocabulary learning. The word lists were based on the vocabulary levels of the grading scheme. *VocabProfile* was used to measure how well the words from the preceding levels and current level covered the text. *RANGE* was used to investigate how often the words were repeated in individual books and groups of books. For most levels of the scheme studied, learners needed to know the vocabulary introduced at each level before they could read the books at that level comfortably. If they did not know these words, then they would know less than 95% of the running words in the books at that level and would have difficulty reading for pleasure. In terms of repetition, graded readers provide very good conditions for learning the high frequency vocabulary of English. The study also determined that to gain the best effects of repetition, learners needed to be reading about one graded reader per week, and should move through all the levels in the scheme, reading from three to five books at each level, preferably more at the later levels. This was calculated by relating the average gap between repetitions with the length of time that memory for a meeting with a word might remain in the learner's mind.

Vocabulary richness in learners' written production

The studies of the vocabulary richness of learners' writing (Laufer and Nation 1995; Laufer, 1994) have looked at the percentage of word types at various frequency levels. The most common measure used in these studies is the Lexical Frequency Profile, developed by Laufer and Nation (1995), which looks at the percentage of words beyond the most frequent 2,000 words (proper nouns and lexical errors are excluded from the compositions before they are processed by the *VocabProfile* programme using the existing 2,000 and academic word lists). The Lexical Frequency Profile has been shown to be a reliable and valid measure, and to change over time with instruction. Nation (2001) also suggests that teachers can use the learners' compositions with the words marked up according to their frequency level as a way of commenting on learners' vocabulary use in their writing.

Summary

The *VocabProfile* and *RANGE* programmes are useful ways of gathering information about learners' vocabulary needs. They allow texts to be compared with word lists based on word families and thus provide a way of measuring the vocabulary load or richness of texts. The results of these measures can then be compared with learners' vocabulary sizes to see what they need to focus on in their learning. The programmes put this kind of analysis well within the reach of teachers.

The most immediate use a teacher might make of the programmes is to look at texts that the learners are working with to see what low frequency words they contain and if there are too many of them. Learners' vocabulary size can be checked using the Vocabulary Levels Test (Nation 2001). This tests knowledge of the second 1000 high frequency words, the academic word list, and three low frequency word levels.

A teacher may also wish to check that the learners' course material is providing sufficient spaced repetition of target vocabulary. If it is not, then additional activities may need to be devised to reinforce such vocabulary.

If learners do some of their writing on the computer, it becomes very easy to see, using *VocabProfile*, if learners' receptive vocabulary knowledge (as measured by the Vocabulary Levels Test) is moving into productive use in their writing. If it is not, then it may be useful to encourage this move to productive use through the use of discussion activities before writing, or the use of outline sheets while writing.

Finally, the programmes can help in the preparation of material using a controlled vocabulary. In spite of the large numbers of graded readers available, there are still only a few with settings outside English speaking countries. Teachers are probably the best people to write such readers and the *VocabProfile* programme can be an easy way of checking on the control of vocabulary.

Note

1.   When running the programme, the proper nouns in the texts were made into a word list used by the programme.

References

Bauer, L. and Nation, I. S. P. 1993. "Word families". *International Journal of Lexicography* 6 (3):1–27.

Carroll, J. B., Davies, P. and Richman, B. 1971. *The American Heritage Word Frequency Book*. New York: Houghton Mifflin, Boston American Heritage.

Coxhead, A. 2000. "A new academic word list". *Tesol Quarterly* 34 (2):213–238.

Coxhead, A. 1998. "An academic word list". *Occasional Publication Number 18*, LALS, Wellington, New Zealand: Victoria University of Wellington.

Hirsh, D. and Nation, P. 1992. "What vocabulary size is needed to read unsimplified texts for pleasure?" *Reading in a Foreign Language* 8(2): 689–696.

Laufer, B. 1989. "What percentage of text-lexis is essential for comprehension?" In C. Lauren and M. Nordman (eds), *Special Language: From humans thinking to thinking machines*. Clevedon: Multilingual Matters.

Laufer, B. 1994. "The lexical profile of second language writing: Does it change over time?" *RELC Journal* 25(2):21–33.

Laufer, B. and Nation, P. 1995. "Vocabulary size and use: Lexical richness in L2 written production". *Applied Linguistics* 16(3):307–322.

Nation, I. S. P. 1990. *Teaching and Learning Vocabulary*. Rowley MA: Newbury House.

Nation, I. S. P. 2001. *Learning Vocabulary in Another Language*. Cambridge: Cambridge University Press.

Nation, I. S. P. and Wang, K. 1999. "Graded readers and vocabulary". *Reading in a Foreign Language* 12(2):355–380.

Read, J. 1988. "Measuring the vocabulary knowledge of second language learners". *RELC Journal* 19(2):12–25.

Sutarsyah, C., Nation, P. and Kennedy, G. 1994. "How useful is EAP vocabulary for ESP? A corpus based study". *RELC Journal* 25(2):34–50.

West, M. 1953. *A General Service List of English Words*. London: Longman, Green & Co.

CHAPTER 3

Comparing corpora and identifying key words, collocations, frequency distributions through the WordSmith Tools suite of computer programs

Mike Scott
University of Liverpool

Abstract

This chapter describes methods of carrying out research into small corpora, a method within reach of the language student, teacher or analyst working at home with a standard personal computer.

The *WordSmith Tools*[1] suite of software is described and illustrated. Like a Swiss army knife with its various components, this suite offers a number of different tools for different jobs.

The tool which is most akin to the standard large penknife blade is probably *Concord*, a tool which locates all references to any given word or phrase within our corpus, showing them in standard concordance lines with the search word centred and a variable amount of context at either side. This tool allows further examination of the company a given search word keeps (its collocates) to be studied, as well as dispersion plots — maps showing where in the texts the search words were found — and lists of recurring clusters or phrases.

A second major tool, perhaps the Swiss army knife's scissors, is *WordList*. As its name indicates, this creates word lists, ordering them by frequency and alphabetically. Word lists can be made of individual texts or of whole corpora. Word frequency information is very useful in identifying characteristics of a text or of a genre. Statistical information such as average sentence length is also generated.

The equivalent of the screwdriver is the *KeyWords* tool. This one uses the word lists just described, and compares them. The idea is quite simple: if a word is found to be much more frequent in one individual text than its frequency in a reference corpus would suggest, it is probably a "key word". The notion underlying this is therefore "outstandingness" based on comparison. In this tool, as in *WordList*, a number of detailed statistics are made available, but the chief interest of the tool lies in its ability to get at text "aboutness".

Other tools, which will not be described in detail, are: *Text Converter*, which allows the user to re-format their texts; *Splitter*, which makes it possible to split up large cdrom text files into their component texts; *Viewer* and *Aligner*, a utility which allows the user to examine the source texts and if necessary make a dual aligned text, i.e. one based on a translation, showing alternate sentences in two different languages.

Introduction

In order to work effectively with corpora large or small, the language student, teacher or researcher above all needs easy access to both the corpora themselves and suitable software. With the simple possibility of switching on and trying some idea out without having to book a seat in a distant laboratory, the chance of getting up in the middle of the night or on a Sunday afternoon, the language investigator can learn by trial and error, and store a mass of interim results on his or her pc without formality and in a relaxed state of mind.

It is with this need in mind that *WordSmith Tools* (Scott, 1996, 1997, 1999) was first designed and built. The software is intended to run on the kind of pc which many language students and researchers may possess in their own right, and to access corpora which they would build or obtain and store on their own hard drives.

A further important design consideration was the impossibility of predicting the uses to which the software would be put. In other words, the aim was to produce, as far as possible, tools which would be general purpose in nature as opposed to specific. A corkscrew would be an example of a specific tool, good at handling one job but only of any use for that one job. The designer of a corkscrew has taken a decision that a bottle is stoppered with a cork of such and such a diameter and the tool is designed to do one job, namely to pull the cork out, supremely well[2]. The designer of a pen-knife, on the other hand, can never predict what the user will use it for. The etymology of the name suggests the sharpening of quills for writing, but though pen-knives are in common use, nobody ever uses them for that purpose nowadays. The corkscrew is thus a prisoner of the wine-bottle technology, doomed to disappear if wine ever stops being distributed in conventional wine bottles. To return to language learning and language research, the one certainty is that learner and researcher purposes are unknown at any given time. Some may want word lists, others concordances, but others will need other forms of alteration and display of language data which have not yet been thought of.

An open design

These requirements implied a set of open constraints: standard equipment, standard texts, nothing language-specific, no pre-processing, "on the fly" handling. The software should run in a reasonably affordable amount of memory[3] on a standard pc (386 or greater) running under Windows 3.1 or greater[4]. At the same time, the software should be able to handle virtually any text or corpus[5] in more or less any language. Therefore no dictionary knowledge should be built into the system, though ideally users might be able to access specific lists of data, such as lists of lemma relationships like *be = was, were, am, are, is* etc. relating to a particular language if they wished. There should be no requirement that the text be tagged[6] or marked-up in any specific way, though it should be able to handle text with mark-up, separating out the mark-up from the text proper.

In this design, text operations should ideally be carried out on the fly[7], without any need to build or access large databases, as in indexed corpora. An indexed corpus is one which has been processed so that there is an index file on disk which already "knows" the position of each and every word in the corpus. Subsequent searches and word list operations are much quicker to carry out since the whole corpus has been pre-processed. This important advantage, however, is offset, in my opinion, by what one may dub the "tagset bind". A pre-indexed corpus will tend to stagnate, for the simple reason that the researcher will feel reluctant to re-index the corpus whenever s/he has corrected a spelling mistake in one text in the corpus, or when a text has been added or deleted from the corpus. In the same way, the danger of operating with a standard tagset, such as a set of part-of-speech (POS) tags marking various sorts of nouns, verbs, prepositions, etc., is that the system can become a prison. The tendency is to feel that since one has valuable POS information built into the corpus, therefore the obvious thing to do is to analyse the texts in terms of parts of speech. It is a double bind, actually, since one is not only likely to ignore other classifications (such as the speech acts, or the text segments) but one is also unlikely to wish to reform the classification system itself. Again, the one certainty is that linguists will not agree on a classification even of something as apparently primary as parts of speech.

These open design considerations are thus intended to enable those interested in language to carry out a varied and unpredictable set of operations as long as they have a number of texts available. An open design for general-purpose corpus analysis software thus implies freedom for the user to seek patterns which the designer could never imagine, and the ways of viewing data implicit in the now-conventional KWIC[8] concordance are bound to develop in the future. It is important to bear in mind, therefore, in the sections which follow, that the descriptions of corpus analysis which unfold are only those ones which have come to mind to date, and that new ways of looking at corpora are certain to evolve in the course of time.

The three main tools in the suite all produce lists of various kinds, as opposed to scatterplots, graphs, Venn diagrams etc. No doubt future incarnations will move away from the list as a basic structure, but for the present the matrix list has become the *WordSmith* default.

Concordance-derived analyses

The equivalent of the pen-knife in the Swiss army knife, the model to which *WordSmith* aspires, is *Concord*, which despite its name does not produce analyses of grammatical concord but concordances, lists of the occurrences of a given word or phrase in a corpus. These are extremely useful, since there is no other way of getting good examples of a morpheme, word, or phrase in context. For the word[9], a dictionary supplies a lot of valuable information, such as pronunciation, etymology, relevant grammatical information, meaning, and at most one or two examples of each meaning. A grammar has the purpose of exemplification as well as explanation but most words or phrases will not be exemplified. Therefore lexicographers and language students alike find concordances extremely useful in providing many examples. Examining these it becomes possible to find out not only what company the search-word keeps but also to gain an impression of frequency.

Cause has been shown (Stubbs, 1995) to be very often found in a context of negativity, (disease, accidents and so on), generating what John Sinclair has called a "semantic prosody" (Sinclair, 1991) — this can only be identified reliably by examining concordances. Another example comes from the advanced learner of English writing an academic paper and wishing to start with "this paper". Note that in English a paper may "present", "describe" and "argue" but not "complain" yet all these uses are figurative: there is no easy way to know which verbs typically collocate with *paper* or *article* in a given language except by consulting a concordance or a dictionary of collocations itself based on concordances.

Accordingly, in order to find out, a "nonce corpus" consisting of *MicroConcord Corpus Collection B* plus 65 academic papers written by staff in a range of disciplines at the University of Liverpool and forming the *LUDAL* (*Liverpool University Database of Academic Language*) corpus was put together. The search word was "article/paper" with a required context of *this* within two words to the left. Once the list had been pruned to include only cases where paper or article was the subject of a verb, the concordance shown in Figure 1 below was obtained.

It seems that an article or paper can readily *(attempt to) analyse, describe, examine, focus, highlight, indicate, include, look at, make (a case for), present, report, review, stem from, stimulate, suggest* and *outline*. Of these the commonest is *present* (4). It would be interesting to know which equivalents are found in academic corpora in other languages.

Or consider the case of the learner of English who says "the majority of people believe ..." because in his or her language the typical way of referring to "mostness" is by a noun phrase (*la plupart des gens, a maioria das pessoas,* etc.). A concordance of the *British National Corpus (BNC)* Sampler will show that while there are 66 occurrences of *most people* in 2,133,000 words there are only four instances of *the majority of people* (lines 14–17) and two of *the majority of the people* (31 and 34) in Figure 2 below.

Abraham Lincoln would probably agree that "the majority of (the) people" is perfectly grammatical (though his famous speech referred to all or some of the people), but it is clearly restricted in its usefulness. An expanded view of

Figure 1: A concordance of *paper* and *article* from the LUDAL corpus. (The original concordance displays the three words beginning with *this* in different colours, imitated here by different typeface styles.)

N			Concordance
1	ic Development.	THIS	**paper** *also* makes a very
2	eningococcal pili.	THIS	**paper** *also* describes a s
3	ecial character.	THIS	**article** *analyses* the con
4	Dench et al, 1987).	THIS	**article** *analyses* the ass
5	ese interactions.	THIS	**paper** *attempts* to highlig
6	ectious diseases.	THIS	**article** *attempts* to indica
7	the cell (10).	THIS	**paper** *describes* the clon
8	ABSTRACT	THIS	**paper** *examines* and co
9	SUMMARY	THIS	**paper** *focuses* on the co
10	z Szekeres (1972).	THIS	**paper** *includes* a derivati
11	ations. The task of	THIS	**paper** *is* to investigate th
12	a Fortran module.	THIS	**paper** *is* the result of so
13	ng together. While	THIS	**paper** *is* professedly con
14	early Homo taxon.	THIS	**paper** *is* an attempt to
15	are given.' Most of	THIS	**paper** *is* technical and in
16	collateral standard.	THIS	**paper** *looks* at a possibl
17	and assumptions.	THIS	**paper** *makes* no claim to
18	ex divisions [2].	THIS	**paper** *presents* fresh evi
19	to be written.	THIS	**paper** *presents* an oulin
20	ABSTRACT	THIS	**paper** *presents* fresh evi
21	ain uncertain.	THIS	**article** *presents* new evid
22	between taxa.	THIS	**paper** *reports* the results
23	Summary	THIS	**paper** *reports* the results
24	The second half of	THIS	**paper** *reviews* the theore
25	ion of this paper.	THIS	**paper** *stems* from the de
26	Abstract	THIS	**paper** *stimulates* the dis
27	ever the first part of	THIS	**article** *suggests* that t
28	ealth and Empire.	THIS	**article** *suggests* that the
29	cs and poetics.	THIS	**article**, *then*, is motivate
30	s are universal and	THIS	**paper** *will* outline them a
31	health perceptions.	THIS	**paper** *will* thus examine
32	and the final part of	THIS	**paper** *will* concentrate o

Figure 2: A concordance of *the majority of* from the *BNC* Sampler. (Different colours are represented by different typeface styles.)

N			Concordance	
1	in a pleasant evnironment. *	THE	**majority** of *colleagues* ar
2	to the Council of Ministers.	THE	**majority** of *EC* governme
3	it is sufficient to note that for	THE	**majority** of *economists*,
4	and the religious practices of	THE	**majority** of *Egyptians*. T
5	a family were better off than	THE	**majority** of *er* of families
6	nesday at 10.50 pm. Aren't	THE	**majority** of *fans* being sh
7	ite likely to find specimens of	THE	**majority** of *forms* of I, aq
8	bed3.1.2 Conventional bonds	THE	**majority** of *government* b
9	Road. Er as I say, it	THE	**majority** of *it* was soup,
10	ucester has cut the return on	THE	**majority** of *its* investment
11	een eighty nine and since by	THE	**majority** of *member* state
12	ly used method of increasing	THE	**majority** of *other* pool pla
13	ngress, time and time again,	THE	**majority** of *our* sponsored
14	Er I mean, I I would say that	THE	**majority** of *people* in this
15	here are exceptions. So that	THE	**majority** of *people* will be
16	inced were now satisfied that	THE	**majority** of *people* in Nort
17	with private cars has allowed	THE	**majority** of *people* to trav
18	. the one that goes nearest	THE	**majority** of *points*. One
19	of points. One goes nearest	THE	**majority** of *points*. Okay
20	ntral Clearing House: "	THE	**majority** of *recruits* to nu
21	ERC 6.4 SERC Grant While	THE	**majority** of *research* stude
22	of this chapter, namely that	THE	**majority** of *rural* inhabitant
23	I'll bet you'll find that	THE	**majority** of *shops* at the
24	Where shift overlaps permit	THE	**majority** of *staff* to be on
25	ry of the fire fighting jets and	THE	**majority** of *stock* may be
26	o;. This was certainly true of	THE	**majority** of *studies* before
27	certainly do yes, but the ma	THE	**majority** of *that* is done b
28	k had done enough to sccrurc	THE	**majority** of *the* points. T
29	logue is written as Cockney!	THE	**majority** of *the* writing is
30	rians — different from	THE	**majority** of *the* Romanian
31	er, generally though, they,	THE	**majority** of *the* people in
32	s should reflect the opinion of	THE	**majority** of *the* party me
33	ction). The first section lists	THE	**majority** of *the* laws we r
34	f er huge sections of the er of	THE	**majority** of *the* people er
35	one of the local chapels. Er	THE	**majority** of *the* local chap

Figure 2 *(continued)*

N			Concordance
36	st banished the city &equo;.	THE	**majority** of *the* camp foll
37	ll the hairs are in the wax so	THE	**majority** of *the* hair is out
38	blic who wish to drop in. For	THE	**majority** of *the* public the
39	al and the Ivory Coast spend	THE	**majority** of *their* time in h
40	spritually able to withstand.	THE	**majority** of *these* state c
41	ll 18-year-old school leavers.	THE	**majority** of *these* will hav
42	election suggests again that	THE	**majority** of *voters* in Nort

the relevant concordance lines (Figure 3 below) shows that *the majority of (the) people* is used in both speech and writing, but that four out of the six instances are followed by prepositional phrases such as "in Britain". Such prepositional phrase information is an example of colligation (Hoey, 1998) , the tendency of a given word or phrase to have a "grammatical prosody", a typical grammatical environment. The phrase may also be associated with a semantic prosody of surveys and statistics: more data are needed to check these initial findings.

Word list-derived analyses

A word list gives quite different information. It helps the language researcher identify the common words in a corpus, information which is useful for example when determining which lexical items to teach and which to ignore, or when the materials writer is attempting to ensure that new vocabulary is met more than once in a textbook.

This latter purpose is extremely difficult to meet. The reason is that a word list is a very strange object in its distribution. Typically, a small number of words will be of very high frequency, the most extreme case being *the* at around 6% of the running words in a corpus of English. At the other extreme there are always a very large number of word forms which occur once only. These are sometimes called *"hapax legomena"* (*hapaxes* for short).

Let us consider a word list based on the *BNC Sampler* (Table 1 below).

The most frequent 30 words in this list take up 35% of all the (over 2 million) running words in the corpus. It is also evident that these are function

Figure 3: An expanded view of the concordance lines in Figure 2 that contain the majority of (the) people.

N	Concordance
1	erson was pregnant or something. If there's a pregnant person in the house. Yes. There are exceptions. So that the majority of people will be subject to a forty percent deduction on their personal benefit and their personal rate.
2	ually vand still vulnerable. Yeah. Erm Erm well it doesn't make you feel very good. Er I mean, I I would say that the majority of people in this office, carry a lot of erm anxiety and pressure home with them. Mhm. Er just beca
3	cussed in Chapter 4), and second, the dramatic increase in accessibility for those with private cars has allowed the majority of people to travel much further distances to better and/or cheaper facilities (Rowley, 1971). Both the
4	many people, including politicians in the Republic, who had previously been unconvinced were now satisfied that the majority of people in Northern Ireland would not accept a united Ireland and wished to have another electio
5	use they have er access to the books for the various er designers of lighting fittings er, generally though, they, the majority of the people in the town er have come from er London boroughs and erm they view the same kind of
6	the er the er struggle of the Spanish people r really captured the imagination of er huge sections of the er of the majority of the people er er in Britain. And you'd got you'd got a tremendous buildup you know of er of en

words, in other words closed class items, with little lexical "content". Typically among the first content words in a word list are verbs like *know* (rank 48 in this list) , *said* (59) , *think* (76) and the first unambiguous noun is *year* (140). Hapaxes start at rank 28,340 (with the "word" *AAAAAGH !*) out of 44,101. That is, 36% of the whole list is comprised of words which occur once only. The same picture is obtained if one studies a word list based on 90 million words: in the case of the full *BNC's* written texts, the first hapax comes at rank 226,516 out of 377,384 (40% of that corpus being *hapax legomena*). It is quite noticeable that many of these hapaxes are proper nouns, examples from

Table 1: High frequency items

N	Word	Freq.	%	Cumulative %
1	THE	109,830	5.15	5.15
2	AND	54,759	2.57	7.72
3	OF	50,752	2.38	10.10
4	TO	49,538	2.32	12.42
5	A	42,436	1.99	14.41
6	I	38,974	1.83	16.23
7	IN	35,292	1.65	17.89
8	IT	34,308	1.61	19.50
9	YOU	30,700	1.44	20.94
10	THAT	30,208	1.42	22.35
11	S	27,873	1.31	23.66
12	IS	20,431	0.96	24.62
13	FOR	17,558	0.82	25.44
14	WAS	16,201	0.76	26.20
15	ON	15,436	0.72	26.92
16	N'T	14,407	0.68	27.60
17	WE	14,159	0.66	28.26
18	THEY	13,043	0.61	28.87
19	BE	12,791	0.60	29.47
20	HE	12,549	0.59	30.06
21	HAVE	12,345	0.58	30.64
22	WITH	11,784	0.55	31.19
23	DO	11,433	0.54	31.73
24	THIS	10,916	0.51	32.24
25	AS	10,841	0.51	32.75
26	ARE	10,681	0.50	33.25
27	BUT	10,652	0.50	33.75
28	AT	10,151	0.48	34.23
29	ER	9,765	0.46	34.68
30	NOT	9,649	0.45	35.14

the full BNC taken at random being *Mazankowski, Mazar, Mazarin, Mazaruni, Mazatl, Mazatzal.*

This means that approximately one third of a word list is taken up by words which occur once, and that approximately 30 highly frequent words take up one third of the texts in the corpus[10].

Implications for learning are quite serious: students cannot expect to see a whole lot of words more than once even if they read millions of words of text. The proper nouns probably do not matter in terms of learning, but there are still a lot of hapaxes which are not proper nouns: *lukewarm, lulls, lumber, lumbering, lumens, lumped, lunar, lunatics, lunge, lungfuls* for example.

Then there are words which do not crop up at all in the *BNC Sampler* but which do in the full *BNC: jangles, jangling, foetal. Dabble, dabbled, dabbles, dabbler, dabblers* and *dabbling* are all in the 90 million word list but only *dabbling* is in the 2 million word Sampler corpus, and it only comes once. If a learner has read 2 million words, which seems a lot in my experience of learners' reading habits, there will be a lot of items s/he will not have ever seen. *Jaundice* comes once only, *jaundiced* five times, which suggests that some items[11] are used primarily in a figurative sense. Word lists are thus seen to be strange objects; I do not think we have done more than scratch at the surface of the discoveries that are there to be made about them.

A further issue of interest to the language student or researcher is the notion that a content word may be consistent or inconsistent. By this I mean that some words are reliably to be found in a set of texts in a particular genre, whereas others are restricted in some way.

Table 2 below shows a fragment of a consistency analysis[12] based on 18 business reports written in English by Brazilian companies, which will help to make this clearer.

These are the first few items which occurred in 17 out of 18 reports. I have not shown those which occur in all 18 business reports because they include a good number of function words, but already this list shows some genre characteristics: the items which are consistent in that they occur in most of the reports. The number of times each one occurs in each text or overall is not shown here, as the measure of consistency is simply concerned with establishing that such lexical items can be expected to occur in most texts of a particular type. This has obvious implications for the language teacher and student.

Here are some which occurred in only a few of the texts (Table 3 below): These items reflect issues which were not the subject of the report except in three cases, and are therefore relatively inconsistent in the genre.

This leads to a further possibility, that of locating items which are unusual in their consistency. A consistent item is one which occurs in lots of texts, but a significantly consistent one is one which is unusual in so doing. Thus, we may well expect *the* and *this* and *of* and *was* to come in virtually every text in English, but may not expect *capital, company* and *costs* to do so. It is by using

Table 2: Consistency analysis (consistent items)

N	Word	Freq.	%
50	ALL	17	94.44
51	BALANCE	17	94.44
52	BETWEEN	17	94.44
53	CAPITAL	17	94.44
54	CHANGES	17	94.44
55	COMPANY	17	94.44
56	CONTINUED	17	94.44
57	CONTROL	17	94.44
58	COSTS	17	94.44
59	DEVELOPMENT	17	94.44
60	END	17	94.44
61	FINANCIAL	17	94.44
62	FIRST	17	94.44

Table 3: Consistency analysis (relatively inconsistent items)

N	Word	Freq.	%
2599	TURNOVER	3	16.67
2600	TWELVE	3	16.67
2601	ULTIMATE	3	16.67
2602	UNDERGONE	3	16.67
2603	UNDERSTANDING	3	16.67
2604	UNDERWAY	3	16.67
2605	UNDOUBTEDLY	3	16.67
2606	UNEMPLOYMENT	3	16.67
2607	UNMISTAKABLE	3	16.67
2608	UNSTABLE	3	16.67
2609	UNUSUAL	3	16.67
2610	USA	3	16.67

a technique developed for identifying key words, the subject of the next section, that it became possible to identify significant consistency.

"Significant Consistency Analysis" contrasts one Consistency List with another. In this case I contrasted a consistency list based on the 18 annual business reports in English produced by Brazilian companies, with 480 arbitrarily selected text files of similar average length from the *BNC* and *Guardian* newspaper.

The procedure works by contrasting the frequency of every word-type in a text or a consistency word list, with the frequency of the same word-type in some reference corpus or list. In this case 480 texts taken at random were used as a reference. Naturally, the item *the* will have occurred in all 18 business reports as well as in all 480 texts. Its frequency in terms of consistency is therefore 100% in each, and this item will therefore not be found to differ significantly in the comparison.

The comparison uses Dunning's Log Likelihood formula (Dunning 1993). The results are shown in Table 4 below. The first "Freq." column here gives the number of texts in which each item was found, an indication of consistency, ranging from 18 down to eight. The percentages in the "%" column beside it reflect these same numbers as percentages of the 18 reports. The next "Freq." column gives the consistency of the same word-types in the 480 texts used as a reference set. And the "%" column beside that represents the same number as a percentage. Thus, *program* occurred in 16 out of 18 business reports (88.89%) but only nine out of 480 other texts (1.88%). To understand the table, it is best to compare the percentage columns (e.g. 88.89% compared with only 1.88% in the case of *program*) where the differences are most easily seen. In a few cases (*CR$*, *favorable*, *capitalization*) the item was absent from the 480 texts entirely[13]. The last two columns give an indication of "keyness" (the product of the Log Likelihood procedure, with the highest numbers at the top), and the significance of the contrast in a statistical sense. All contrasts here are significant at a level lower than 0.0000001 (roughly interpretable to mean less than one chance in a million of error in claiming that each item is significantly consistent[14]).

It is also possible, using the same method, to find out which items are significantly *in*consistent. That is, items which one would otherwise expect to be found in most of the texts, but which are not in this particular genre. Accordingly, Table 5 provides a list of items which are unexpectedly inconsistent in the 18 business reports. Table 5 below shows the last 20 items: the most significantly inconsistent ones.

It is noticeable that amongst the items in Table 5 (in reverse order compared with Table 4 as the Keyness column shows) there are several which play a largely interpersonal role (*you*, *me*, *my*), two very general items (*thing*, *something*) and even the commonest reporting verb (*says*, *said*).

The business report, an extremely widespread and important genre, is still rather under-investigated (Harris & Bargiela, 1999); further research with a

Table 4: Significant Consistency Analysis for business reports

N	WORD	FREQ.	%	FREQ.	%	KEYNESS	P
1	PROGRAM	16	88.89	9	1.88	96.3	0.000000
2	CONSOLIDATED	16	88.89	15	3.13	86.1	0.000000
3	PROGRAMS	14	77.78	6	1.25	84.2	0.000000
4	US$	12	66.67	3	0.63	75.3	0.000000
5	MODERNIZATION	11	61.11	1	0.21	74.7	0.000000
6	BRAZILIAN	15	83.33	17	3.54	74.4	0.000000
7	STOCKHOLDERS	10	55.56	1	0.21	66.6	0.000000
8	CENTERS	10	55.56	1	0.21	66.6	0.000000
9	CR$	9	50.00	0	0.0	65.1	0.000000
10	AUDITING	11	61.11	5	1.04	61.8	0.000000
11	BRAZIL	15	83.33	31	6.46	60.7	0.000000
12	ACCORDANCE	15	83.33	31	6.46	60.7	0.000000
13	INTEGRATED	15	83.33	31	6.46	60.7	0.000000
14	PAULO	12	66.67	10	2.08	60.1	0.000000
15	TECHNOLOGICAL	14	77.78	23	4.79	59.8	0.000000
16	FAVORABLE	8	44.44	0	0.0	57.2	0.000000
17	CAPITALIZATION	8	44.44	0	0.0	57.2	0.000000
18	FISCAL	13	72.22	20	4.17	55.3	0.000000
19	AUDITORS	12	66.67	14	2.92	54.7	0.000000
20	EFFORTS	18	100.0	99	20.63	54.4	0.000000
21	INVESTMENTS	15	83.33	43	8.96	52.7	0.000000
22	CENTER	10	55.56	6	1.25	52.3	0.000000
23	COMPANY'S	16	88.89	59	12.29	51.7	0.000000
24	ADMINISTRATIVE	14	77.78	34	7.08	51.2	0.000000
25	SPECIALIZED	8	44.44	1	0.21	51.0	0.000000

larger sample is clearly needed to investigate to what extent it may manage to be more impersonal and precise than other genres, as these findings suggest. Nevertheless, even from this brief analysis, implications for language teaching and learning already begin to emerge, at the very least in terms of identification of core lexis.

Key words-derived analyses

The tool used for this was the "scissors" of the *WordSmith* army knife, *WordList*, which cuts up the text into its lexical components. In the next sec-

Table 5: Negative Significant Consistency Analysis for business reports

N	WORD	FREQ.	%	FREQ.	%	KEYNESS	P
268	MIGHT	2	11.11	375	78.13	35.4	0.000000
269	JUST	5	27.78	429	89.38	35.7	0.000000
270	THING	0		308	64.17	0.0	35.8	0.000000
271	LEAST	1	5.56	351	73.13	36.1	0.000000
272	IF	8	44.44	461	96.04	36.5	0.000000
273	MY	1	5.56	354	73.75	36.8	0.000000
274	SEE	3	16.67	405	84.38	38.3	0.000000
275	GOT	0		326	67.92	0.0	39.6	0.000000
276	ME	0		334	69.58	0.0	41.4	0.000000
277	SOMETHING	0		335	69.79	0.0	41.6	0.000000
278	SAYS	0		336	70.00	0.0	41.8	0.000000
279	HIM	1	5.56	374	77.92	42.2	0.000000
280	YOU	3	16.67	416	86.67	42.5	0.000000
281	SAID	3	16.67	417	86.88	42.9	0.000000
282	IT'S	0		342	71.25	0.0	43.3	0.000000
283	DON'T	0		352	73.33	0.0	45.8	0.000000
284	SAY	1	5.56	388	80.83	46.6	0.000000
285	LIKE	4	22.22	452	94.17	55.5	0.000000
286	TOO	2	11.11	429	89.38	55.7	0.000000
287	WHAT	4	22.22	457	95.21	59.8	0.000000

tion, I discuss the screwdriver in the set, *KeyWords*.

As the discussion of significant consistency above has shown, the words which are detected as "outstanding" are of various types. In terms of Halliday's (1973:99) well-established three meta-functions of language, most of the items (eg. *program*, *consolidated*, *stockholders*)are ideational, concerned with what Phillips (1989) terms "aboutness". Sometimes interpersonal key words crop up (*shall, I, you*) , and occasionally a key word is textual (*thing, it's*). Taken together, these items can help to characterise a set of texts or a single text in terms of both content and style.

The procedure for computing outstandingness described above is at the very heart of the *KeyWords* tool within the *WordSmith* suite, and indeed derived fairly recently from it. This tool, then, is one which is intended to identify key words in texts and plot them in a number of different ways. To illustrate this I shall take a text which was the major text in a 1998 study by Nélia Scott. It is a short novel by Clarice Lispector. Scott analysed this text in the original (Brazilian Portuguese) as well as the translation into English and goes into the work far deeper than space here permits me to tell. Suffice it to say that she was surprised to find that the text seemed easier to read in English than in the original, even though her own native language is Brazilian Portuguese. She wanted to investigate what had happened in the process of translation to make this so.

Let us begin with a list of the key words found in the translation (Table 6 below). The key words procedure relies on a reference corpus. In this case the whole of the BNC written corpus was used, namely 90 million words of mixed genres.

Table 6: Key Words in Hour of the Star

N	WORD	FREQ.	STAR. TXT %	FREQ.	WRITTEN. LST %	KEYNESS	P
1	MACABÉA	143	0.55	0		2,333.7	0.000000
2	SHE	645	2.48	318,234	0.35	1,425.9	0.000000
3	OLÍMPICO	74	0.28	0		1,207.4	0.000000
4	GLÓRIA	51	0.20	0		832.1	0.000000
5	I	615	2.36	514,122	0.57	829.5	0.000000
6	HER	453	1.74	312,040	0.34	746.9	0.000000
7	GIRL	117	0.45	13,481	0.01	571.2	0.000000
8	AM	114	0.44	24,335	0.03	422.8	0.000000
9	CARLOTA	21	0.08	2		329.0	0.000000
10	MY	174	0.67	129,018	0.14	265.3	0.000000
11	MACABÉA'S	16	0.06	0		261.0	0.000000
12	MADAME	33	0.13	1,028		245.0	0.000000
13	HERSELF	63	0.24	16,833	0.02	207.2	0.000000
14	STORY	55	0.21	12,931	0.01	193.9	0.000000
15	ME	138	0.53	111,440	0.12	192.0	0.000000
16	THAT	506	1.94	899,287	0.99	188.1	0.000000
17	MYSELF	45	0.17	10,907	0.01	156.1	0.000000
18	NEVER	76	0.29	48,918	0.05	132.9	0.000000
19	BANG	20	0.08	1,101		126.2	0.000000
20	CARLOTA'S	7	0.03	0		114.2	0.000000
21	ALAGOAS	8	0.03	8		108.3	0.000000
22	MACA	7	0.03	1		108.2	0.000000
23	BACKWOODS	9	0.03	25		107.5	0.000000
24	AUNT	22	0.08	2,921		101.3	0.000000
25	PARIAÍBA	6	0.02	0		97.9	0.000000

Simply "eye-balling" the list of the top 25 key words in this 90-page novel gives some idea as to its "aboutness". The main characters are Macabéia, her boyfriend Olímpico, her workmate Glória, and Madame Carlota who runs a brothel. Macabéia and Olímpico come from Alagoas and Paraíba, states in the "backwoods" of North-Eastern Brazil. However, much of the novel — a structurally interesting and often perplexing novel — is concerned with the author's querying of her own role. A distinction is made between the writer (Lispector) and the narrator, who seems to be a man. Much of the early part of the novel deals with the purpose of the novel itself, and the reason for writing about a non-entity, a failure, who achieves nothing in the story and dies rather pointlessly near the end.

In view of this, items of especial interest to the student of literature are interpersonal *I*, *my*, *me*, the names, and possibly *story*. A plot (Figure 4) will help to illuminate this.

Figure 4 below is a key words plot, in which the left and right margins represent the beginning and end of the story. It has been ordered in terms of each key word's first mention in the text.

Of especial interest to the literature student is the prevalence at the beginning and end of *I*, *am*, *myself* and *my* (when either Lispector or the narrator has the floor) — the story is arguably a novel about the writing of literature. Then there is the mention, delayed until about half way through, of the chief characters, Macabéia, Olímpico, etc. Before that time we have mention of *she* and *girl* but Macabéia has not yet been named. But the most interesting item is actually the item *never*. In the original, the word *não* (meaning no, not, -n't) was found to be key. Scott (1998) was surprised to find this, and much of her work dealt with trying to analyse the patterns of negativity in the original and the translation, where she found that a number of negatives had been omitted, or reformulated as positive (e.g. *don't forget* becoming *remember*). Even so, *never* is still a key item in the translated version, and as the plot above shows, is distributed fairly evenly through the text.

Scott points out that literary effects may operate at a variety of levels, conscious and sub-conscious, so that the writer, the translator and the readers may or may not realise how effects are achieved. If this is so, some effects may get missed out in the process of translation, and it is very possible that this feature of negativity is one which a machine can detect although the human translator is unlikely to notice the prevalence of simple negative adverbs such as *não*.

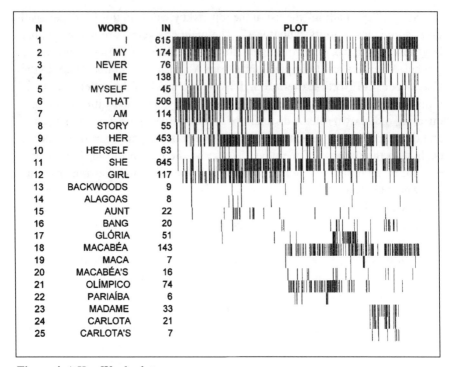

N	WORD	IN
1	I	615
2	MY	174
3	NEVER	76
4	ME	138
5	MYSELF	45
6	THAT	506
7	AM	114
8	STORY	55
9	HER	453
10	HERSELF	63
11	SHE	645
12	GIRL	117
13	BACKWOODS	9
14	ALAGOAS	8
15	AUNT	22
16	BANG	20
17	GLÓRIA	51
18	MACABÉA	143
19	MACA	7
20	MACABÉA'S	16
21	OLÍMPICO	74
22	PARIAÍBA	6
23	MADAME	33
24	CARLOTA	21
25	CARLOTA'S	7

Figure 4: A Key Words plot

Conclusions

This chapter has attempted to show how a number of software tools can help to illuminate language for the language student, the teacher, the researcher.
I hope it has become clear that through concordances it is possible to "get at the parts the others cannot reach", complementing the dictionary and grammar book. Word lists enable us to explore the range of items students may need to know, and locate genre-specific items too. (See also chapter 5.) Key words can help in a number of ways, many of which (text retrieval, investigation of plagiarism, text structure study[15], analysis of stereotype[16]) go well beyond what it has been possible to discuss here, where our example has been literary.
One last thought. The computer and its software are only tools. It is up to us to use our creativity in deciding what to do with them. The fact that it is not possi-

ble to predict what we may each choose to find out, lends a fascination to our observation of the new findings and display procedures which are beginning to emerge.

Notes

1. Mike Scott, Oxford University Press, 1999 (version 3.0). Further details at http://www.liv.ac.uk/~ms2928/homepage.html

2. Not that many corkscrews do this job particularly easily! One also wonders why designers of corkscrews do not generally seem to have considered it useful to be able to re-insert the cork after the bottle has been partly used.

3. At the time the main design constraints for *WordSmith* were laid down, around 1992–3, 4 MB of RAM was considered a generous amount. At the time of this writing, 1999, an ordinary cheap pc will be built with 64 MB — in a few years' time no doubt this will seem extremely restrictive.

4. At the time of writing, a new version is being prepared which will operate under Windows 95, 98, NT and their successors. The choice of Windows as an operating system, and the IBM PC as the machine base is consequent on the decision to produce software for the average language investigator to use on a Sunday afternoon. As technology changes it has now become much more usual for such users to have access to Windows 95 or better.

5. *WordSmith Tools* handles up to 20 million words with relative ease — in English. (In highly inflected languages such as Lithuanian, or agglutinative languages like Finnish, there are so many different word forms, and these can easily be 25 or 30 letters long, that pc memory can choke on 20 million words, when building a word list.) With a corpus such as the *BNC*, containing 100 million words, the 16-bit versions (1–3) of *WordSmith* start to cough and splutter. When building a cluster word list — a word list based on repeated clusters of 2, 3 or up to 8 words, *WordSmith* gets apoplectic after only a few million words. This is because of the "on the fly" processing requirement.

6. Marked up text is text which has extra information built into it with *tags*, e.g. "We<pronoun> like<verb> spaghetti<noun>.<end of sentence>"

7. Such is the development of the technology as well as corpus methods, that I remember Jeremy Clear of Cobuild expressing scepticism regarding "on the fly" processing, as recently as the beginning of the 1990s, when Tim Johns and I were designing *WordSmith Tools'* predecessor, *MicroConcord* (Oxford University Press, 1993). Jeremy's belief at that time, like most other corpus pioneers, was that the only rational way to proceed was by pre-indexing one's corpus. In 1992 he acknowledged that *MicroConcord* was able to process millions of words of text seeking instances of a given word or phrase and find instances in a matter of a very few seconds.

8. Key Word In Context. An unfortunate but established name — in fact what is normally

meant is SWIC (search-word in context) or NIC (node in context), since the search-word or phrase being concordanced is not necessarily "key" in the usual senses of that word.

9. Though not always the phrase or morpheme. It can also be hard to find a derived form such as *took*, not listed or cross-referenced in the large two-volume *Shorter Oxford English Dictionary*, for example.

10. In other words, a word list has an unusual shape compared say to the symmetrical normal curve, for example plotting people's heights, where most people are in the middle and a few are at either extreme. Here a few are extremely frequent but a very large proportion are hapaxes.

11. Another example is *torrents* which is more frequent than *torrent*. This fact made the *Cobuild* lexicographers decide to change their definition for a subsequent edition of the dictionary (Gwyneth Fox, 1993 paper at University of Liverpool).

12. Consistency is a function which *WordSmith* can compute automatically. It measures the number of text files each word-type is encountered in, across the corpus. It does this by using previously prepared word lists, building a "master list" of all word types, and checking each word list to see whether each word type is found or not. The "Simple Consistency" function does not therefore report how many occurrences there are in any given text file, merely presence or absence. It then sorts the word types in frequency order and presents results as in Table 2.

13. Partly because of spelling differences between US and British English.

14. There are well known problems (Dunning, 1993 and Stubbs 1995), in making claims of this sort. They relate to the strange structure of word lists, and the danger of making statistical claims on repeated measures, which is certainly the case here. I do not wish to imply rigorous proof by the explanation I have given above, but am attempting merely to explain a difficult concept in fairly simple language. Note also that Tables 4 and 5 have only the first six decimal zeroes shown. After them there may have been more before any non-zero numbers.

15. Scott, 2000.

16. Scott, 1997.

References

Barbara, L. and Scott, M. 1999. "Homing in on a genre: Invitations for bids". In S. Harris and F. Bargiela (eds), *Writing Business*. Harlow: Longman.

BNC Consortium, 1999. *British National Corpus Sampler*. Distributed by Humanities Computing Unit, Oxford University.

Dunning, T. 1993. "Accurate methods for the statistics of surprise and coincidence". *Computational Linguistics* 19 (1): 61–74.

Harris, S. and Bargiela, F. (eds). 1999. *Writing Business*. Harlow: Longman.

Hoey, M. 1998. "'Introducing applied linguistics': 25 years on". Plenary paper in the 32nd BAAL Annual Meeting: "Language and Literacies", University of Manchester, September 1998.

MicroConcord Corpus Collection B, 1993. Oxford: OUP. (A collection of approximately 1 million words of academic text in Arts, Belief and Religion, Medicine, Science and Social Science. Originally sold to accompany *MicroConcord* (Scott, M. and Johns, T. 1993).)

Phillips, M. 1989. *Lexical structure of text* [Discourse Analysis Monographs 12]. Birmingham: University of Birmingham.

Scott, M. and Johns, T. 1993. *MicroConcord*. Oxford: OUP. (No longer in press but freely downloadable from http://www.liv.ac.uk/~ms2928/homepage.html.)

Scott, M. 1996, 1997, 1999. (versions 1.0, 2.0, 3.0), *WordSmith Tools*. Oxford: OUP.

Scott, M. 1997. "PC analysis of key words — and key key words". *System* 25 (1): 1–13.

Scott, M. 2000, "Reverberations of an echo". In B. Lewandowska-Tomaszczyk and P.J. Melia (eds), *PALC'99 Practical Applications in Language Corpora*, Frankfurt: Peter Lang.

Scott, N. 1998. Normalisation and Readers' Expectations: A study of literary translation with reference to Lispector's *A Hora da Estrela*. Ph.D thesis, University of Liverpool.

Sinclair, J. McH., 1991. *Corpus, Concordance, Collocation*. Oxford: OUP.

Stubbs, M. 1995. "Collocations and semantic profiles: On the cause of the trouble with quantitative methods. *Functions of Language* (2)1:1–33.

SECTION 3

CHAPTER 4

Concordancing as a tool in course design[1]

John Flowerdew
City University of Hong Kong

Abstract

Computerized text analysis programs (concordancers) are now available for use on personal computers. Drawing upon experimental work done at Sultan Qaboos University, Sultanate of Oman, this paper shows how such programs can be used as a tool in course design. The starting point is a corpus of written and/or spoken text from the target communicative situation. From this data-base computer text-processing can provide criteria for: (a) the selection and grading of items for the syllabus, and (b) the authentic contextualization of these items in learning materials.

Introduction

Computerized text analysis, or concordancing, programs (Sinclair, 1986, 1991) are now becoming widely available for use on personal computers. A concordancer usually consists of two programs: a word frequency program, to provide data on the number of instances of all words in a corpus of text, and the concordancing program proper, to find all instances of a given word in a corpus and to present these instances in their immediate linguistic context (The Appendix shows what a concordance actually looks like). This paper will show how such programs can be applied to a specialized corpus of language and used in specific purpose course design.

The potential for computer-assisted corpus analysis, or concordancing, in language teaching and learning has been the focus of attention on the part of teachers and researchers for some time now. The best documented work in this area is that of Professor John Sinclair and his colleagues at the University of Birmingham, under the auspices of the *Collins Cobuild English Project* (Sinclair, 1991). The *Cobuild* project employed a corpus running into several million words and its application has been in the area of dictionaries (Sinclair, 1987), grammars (Collins/University of Birmingham, 1990) and main course ELT syllabuses (Sinclair and Renouf, 1988; Willis and Willis, 1988).

In parallel to this *Cobuild* work, concordancing techniques have also been applied in the classroom, both for materials production (Johns, 1989; Tribble, 1990) and for use as a learning tool by students themselves (Tribble, 1990; Stevens, 1991). For these direct classroom applications much smaller corpora have been used.

This paper presents a further application of small corpus concordancing, but this time in the field of ESP course design. The *Cobuild lexical syllabus* (Willis and Willis, 1988), the only publicly available application of concordancing to course design developed so far, was based on the full *Cobuild* corpus, as it was a "general" English syllabus and therefore needed to sample a wide cross-section of registers and genres. It is the contention here, however, that where a course is designed for a particular specific purpose a much smaller corpus of language, drawn from the given specific purpose area, is more appropriate. This paper will demonstrate the potential of this approach by means of a case study of a course developed in the Language Centre at Sultan Qaboos University (SQU) , Sultanate of Oman.

Background

In the foundation course for science students at the English-medium SQU, science and English are taught in parallel, the English course taking its material in large part from the science course. The function of the English course is two-fold: first, to help students cope on a day to day basis with the communicative demands which are put on them in their science classes, and second, to foster the ongoing development of their communicative competence in English within their area of studies.

To fulfil these twin aims, a decision was made that the language presented in the English course should be developed around the language and communicative activities students are exposed to in Science. By developing a corpus of language used in the science course, it was possible to provide systematically selected and graded input to the communicative activities developed in the English course, which corresponded to the actual language students were exposed to in their science.

It may be felt that the corpus-derived language input approach just outlined suggests a "product-based" orientation, when a "process-based" orientation would be more in keeping with current thinking on syllabus/course design (Breene, 1987; White, 1988). However, it is emphasized that the procedure forms but one part of the course design procedure (it is a tool) and is not meant to produce the complete syllabus or course [2]. The overall organizing principle of the English course at SQU, based around communicative activities associated with the study of science, was task-, and hence process-based. Tasks were used in a similar way to that proposed by Hutchinson and Waters (1987), with input from the concordancing introduced in what Hutchinson and Waters refer to as a "language focus" stage, leading up to the task [3]. This procedure is illustrated in a later section of the paper, "Using the data from the analysis: An example".

Corpus and analysis

For the first ten weeks of their studies students receive approximately twenty five hours of lectures in biology, supported by very short readings. A corpus was created consisting of transcriptions of these lectures (one set, but given by different lecturers) and readings. The corpus, which consisted of 104,483 words, was thus made up of the actual language students were exposed to in their study of science. The corpus was analyzed by means of a frequency/concordancing program developed at SQU by David Poulton, chief technician in the Language Centre. However, similar programs are available commercially (e.g. *Longman mini-concordancer, Oxford Micro-OCP, TACT, 1.2.*). The analysis of the data is presented under two main headings: word frequency and concordancing.

Word frequency

Total word count
The total of 104,483 words in the corpus breaks down into 4,232 separate items. In order to be able to make valid comparisons with other word counts, it

is necessary to explain how this figure is arrived at.

Computerized word counts are less discriminatory than other traditional types, such as those based on dictionaries, for example, and therefore the total number of items tends to be larger. In particular, computerized counts include all derived forms of a given word as separate items. Thus, where the dictionary includes *convince, convincing, convincingly, convincible,* under one single item, or head-word, the computer counts these as separate items. Derived forms have been estimated to make up over 50% of word entries in dictionaries (Goulden, Nation and Read, 1990). In addition, computerized counts include singular and plural of nouns and inflected verb forms as separate items, where these are included under single head-words in dictionaries. These items make up some ten per-cent of the present corpus. On the other hand, one area where computerized counts are more parsimonious than dictionary-based counts is in the treatment of homographs, words with the same spelling, but different meanings. As far as the computer is concerned, words with the same spelling represent one item. In dictionaries, however, where a single word has two unrelated meanings, these count as two separate entries, or head words. In a recently published word count, Goulden, Nation and Read (1990) estimate that homographs account for some 5% of total items.

Taking the above distorting factors into account — i.e. derived forms (+50%), plurals (+10%) and homographs (-5%) — in order to provide a valid comparison with other published word counts, the total number of items for the specialized corpus should be reduced by some 55%, to a figure of less than 2,000 words.

Such a small number of words is a very realistic target for teaching. To make a comparison with the vocabulary knowledge of the average native speaker, Goulden, Nation and Read (1990) estimated the average educated native speaker to have a vocabulary of around 17,000 base words, eight and a half times our total of less than 2,000. In terms of a potential objective for teaching, therefore, our specialized corpus word count represents a consider-able refinement *vis-à-vis* a general word list. Instead of having to select for course design, as would a general English course, from among the 17,000-odd words known by the average educated native speaker, the ESP course can limit its focus to the much smaller 2,000-odd words in the specialist corpus. Of course, all language courses are based on a limited vocabulary objective inso-far as they do not include the complete 17,000 words known by the average native speaker. Renouf, for example, in an analysis of nine major EFL courses (cited in Sinclair and Renouf, 1988), showed that in the first book of each series the number of different word forms varies from 1,156 to 3,963 (a number not far off our total of 4,232 forms). A decision must therefore have been made to include only a fraction of the words known by the average native speaker. However, the great power of the corpus-based word list is in that the course designer can be sure that the words selected are the most useful (i.e. the most frequently used). Of course, there are other well established criteria for vocabulary selection in addition to frequency, such as *disponibilité* (or *coverage*), *teachability*, and *classroom needs* (Halliday, McIntosh and Strevens, 1964, Carter, 1987). The course designer may want to modify application of the frequency according to such criteria. In addition, the question of the need for receptive vs. productive and spoken vs. written usage of vocabulary (the latter, which, incidentally, the concordancer can identify) needs to be addressed.

Frequency data as criteria for syllabus selection and grading
The previous section has shown the power of frequency data in helping to provide an *overall total* for the number of vocabulary items to be incorporated into a course. Another important application of the word frequency data in course design is in establishing the *relative importance* of vocabulary items and thereby providing criteria for syllabus selection and grading.

Table 1 below shows relative frequency of items in the corpus. There is an inverse relation between frequency of occurrence and number of items occurring with a given frequency. Thus, while there are 1417 items occurring only once, there are only 549 items occurring twice, 356 items occurring three times, 256 items occurring four times, etc.; until by the time we reach ten occurrences there are only 72 items occurring this number of times.

This data offers a very powerful tool in the hands of the course designer, each level of frequency offering a potential cut-off point for selection and grading of items (the number of words targeted by the syllabus designer, of course, depending on entry level of learners and time available for teaching/learning). Table 2 below shows how progressive exclusion of the lower frequency items radically reduces the number of target lexical items. By excluding single occurrence items, for example, the number of target items is immediately reduced from 4,232 to 2,815 (by over a third)[4]. By excluding items occurring 2 or less times, the target is further reduced to 2,266 (by nearly a half). By excluding items occurring 10 or less times, the target shrinks to 975

Table 1: Relative frequency of items*

Number of occurrences of items	Number of items occurring this many times
1	1417
2	549
3	356
4	256
5	184
6	142
7	99
8	99
9	83
10	72

*Total words = 104,483, total items = 4,232.

Table 2: Total items, progressively excluding low frequency items

Total items	4,232
Less single occurrence items	2,815
Less 2 or less occurrences	2,266
Less 3 or less occurrences	1,912
Less 4 or less occurrences	1,654
Less 5 or less occurrences	1,470
Less 10 or less occurrences	975
less 20 or less occurrences	602

(less than a quarter of the total). By the time items occurring 20 times or less are excluded we are left with only 602 words (less than a seventh). As mentioned above, criteria other than frequency, of course, may also enter into the selection procedure.

Frequency of specialist corpus vs frequency of general corpora
Purely as far as word frequency is concerned (and ignoring for the moment the role of word frequency as a necessary condition for concordancing), in order for there to be particular value in creating a specialist corpus, it must be demonstrated that the specialist corpus has a different make up to a general corpus; otherwise an already available general frequency list could be used to the same end. We will now consider this question.

A large percentage of the most frequently occurring items of the specialist corpus are grammatical, or form, words, as opposed to lexical, or content, words. The ten most frequent items in the specialist corpus , for example, are all grammatical words. In this respect it is true that the corpus is very much like any other, be it an ESP corpus or a "general" one. The *Cobuild general corpus*, for example, also has grammatical words as its ten most frequent items (see Table 3).

Table 3: The ten most frequent items in the specialist corpus and in *Cobuild*

Specialist corpus			Cobuild
the	=	8315 (8.7%)	the
and	=	3099 (3.2%)	of
of	=	3014 (3.1%)	and
is	=	2886 (3.0%)	to
a	=	2429 (2.5%)	a
in	=	2225 (2.3%)	in
are	=	1785 (1.9%)	that
to	=	1709 (1.8%)	I
it	=	1366 (1.4%)	it
this	=	1356 (1.4%)	was

Given this overall similarity, however, differences in the ordering of certain grammatical items are nevertheless considerable. In *Cobuild*, for example, *was* is the tenth most frequent item[5], whereas it is only fiftieth in the specialist corpus, indicating perhaps the greater use of past narrative in general usage than in descriptive science . Certainly, the lower frequency of the past form in the specialist corpus has possible implications for work on tenses in course design. To take another example, in *Cobuild* the word *so* is not a high frequency item (it does not appear in the top 200 items printed in Sinclair and Renouf (1988)), but in the specialist corpus it is very frequent, occurring in thirteenth position. This might be accounted for by the greater use of cause and effect markers in academic discourse, a hypothesis which, if corroborated by the concordancer, needs to be taken into account in course design.

Turning now to lexical items, there is considerable variation between *Cobuild* and the specialist biology corpus. For example, none of the top twenty nouns in *Cobuild* occurs among the top twenty nouns of our specialist corpus (Table 4).

Table 4: Top twenty nouns in Cobuild and in biology

Top twenty nouns in *Cobuild*–	time, people, way, man, years, work, world, thing, day, children, life, men, fact, house, kind, year, place, home, sort, end.
Top twenty nouns in biology –	cell, cells, water, membrane, food, plant, root, molecules, plants, wall, energy, concentration, organisms, cytoplasm, animal, stem, structure, body, part, animals.

As further support for the use of the specialist corpus, it should be pointed out that even where items are common to both general and the specialist corpus, the items in the specialist corpus may have particular uses, a possibility which will be corroborated when these items are concordanced (see the section below on concordancing).

Technical vs. sub-technical vocabulary

As a further counter to the use of the specialist corpus, it might have been predicted that many of the lexical items particular to the specialist corpus would be technical words and would not need to be incorporated into an ESP syllabus, as they would be explained by the content teacher. However, this is not the case. With the nouns cited in Table 4 above, for example, *cytoplasm* is the only word clearly falling into the "technical" category (although a case might also be made for *cell*, *membrane*, and *molecule*). If the majority of these items are not technical words, neither are they "general", or common-core; rather they might be classed as semi, or sub-technical; that is to say they are words in general usage, but which have a special meaning within the technical area (Inman, 1978). *Wall, energy, concentration, structure, body,* and *animal,* clearly fit into this category. Because these words are not likely to be glossed by the content teacher their sub-technical meanings are clearly the domain of the ESP teacher.

Items conspicuous by their low frequency or absence

A significant point about the specific purpose corpus *vis-à-vis* a general corpus is that some items which might have been predicted to be high frequency are conspicuous by their low frequency or total absence. Given that the corpus is an academic one, it might have been predicted, for example, that the full range of logical connectors would be well represented. However, as Table 5 shows, whilst a small group of connectors are very frequently used — *so* (1183), *then* (266), *first* (103), *next* (72) [6]–others are less common — *however* (13), *therefore* (11), *thus* (8), *finally* (8), *as a result* (4), — and others do not appear at all — *what is more, furthermore, nonetheless, nevertheless, hence, consequently, in conclusion, in contrast, after that* [7]. As well as telling course designers, therefore, which items to include in a syllabus, the frequency list also tells them which items not to include.

Frequency and functional/notional selection and grading
Table 5: Connectors

Important connectors:
    so (1183), then (266), first (103), next (72)

Less important connectors:
    however (13), therefore (11), thus (8), finally (8), as a result (4)

Connectors not appearing at all:
    what is more, whatsmore, furthermore, nonetheless, nevertheless, hence, consequently, in conclusion, in contrast, after that

---

An important application of the frequency list for course design is in deriving intuitions about functional and notional areas which might be important for the syllabus. For example, frequent occurrences of *called* (414), *call* (57), *means* (172), and *mean* (31), identify defining, or naming, as an important function, worthy of inclusion in a syllabus. Other examples of important functional/notional areas, as identified by various lexical items used to realize them, are listed in Table 6 below. That these items are indeed used with these particular functional/notional uses has to be corroborated by concordancing (see below).

Frequency in the evaluation and revision of currently used syllabuses and materials
As well as its important role in the design of new courses, frequency data can also be extremely useful in the evaluation and revision of existing courses.

    With the availability now of optical scanners, a complete set of materials can very easily be fed onto a word-processor and a frequency list created of the

Table 6: Indicators of functional/notional areas

Naming or defining:
    called (414), call (57), means (172), mean (31)

Referring back:
    remember (155)

Checking / topic changing:
    okay (252), right (194), now (561), well (175)

Boosting and down-toning:
    just (263), very (490), quite (108), really (77)

Spatial location:
    in (2238), on (481), around (161), between (159), ùùacross (87), below (15),
    beneath (7)

---

vocabulary items contained therein. If this frequency list is then compared with that of the authentic corpus, discrepancies can serve as a basis for evaluation and revision.

Concordancing

Whilst frequency data, as we have seen, tell us which items to select for a syllabus, concordances tell us how these items are actually used. This information is useful in three main areas of course design: (1) for the syllabus, (2) for providing instances of use for direct incorporation into instructional materials, and (3) for the evaluation of current syllabuses and materials.

Concordancing for syllabus design
Concordancing has a number of applications for syllabus design. First, given that any item may have a number of different uses, concordancing can identify which uses of items to teach (and, by extension, which uses not to teach). The concordance of *well*, for example (partly reproduced in the Appendix) allows us to identify three important uses of this item in the corpus (dictionaries contain many more) — as an adverb (as in *show up well*), as a conjunct (as in *as well as causing some diseases*), and, importantly for ESP students needing lecture comprehension skills, as a discourse marker (as in *well, I think this might be interesting*). Concordancing of *or* identifies two main uses of this item in the corpus (dictionaries, again, have many more) — "exclusive or" (as in *the*

thorax is pushed to one side or the other) and to introduce a synonym or para-phrase (as in *side roots or lateral roots, produce new cells or grow*). Concordancing thus reduces those uses of a given item to be presented for learning to those which actually occur in the corpus, eliminating time-consum-ing attention to other uses pointed to by dictionaries and reference grammars.

A second application of concordancing for syllabus design is in showing the syntactic patterns in which words occur. In this respect, incidentally, much published instructional material is shown up to be inauthentic. For example, concordancing shows that the connector, *then*, rarely occurs as sentence initial (as it is often taught [e.g. Bates and Dudley-Evans, 1976]), but is more usually found between subject and verb:

the viruses then do the same
these goblet cells then secrete mucus
the cells then expand

— or between auxiliary and main verb:

the liquid is then discharged
classes which are then divided
it can then put down more layers

Similarly, spatial prepositions are most often used to introduce post-modifying phrases (reduced relative clauses), as in:

the lysosome in the cytoplasm of most cells
the membranes around the sap vacuole
the microtubules just below the plasma membrane

Compare this with course books which prefer to teach prepositions in their role as adjuncts, by means of statements such as *The circle is at the top, The square is under the circle* (e.g. Bates and Dudley-Evans, 1976).

A third application of concordancing for syllabus design has already been referred to in the above section on frequency. This is in corroborating intu-itions derived from the frequency list on important functional and notional areas which might be included in a syllabus (Table 6). Some of these items are fairly transparent in their function — e.g. *in, on, across*, etc., as indicators of spatial location — , and therefore do not really need corroboration as to their function. Others, however, are less transparent and do need corroboration by the concordancer. For example, the discourse markers used to check or indicate topic change — *okay, right, now, well*–all have other possible functions; for example, *okay* could be used to agree to a request, *right* could be used to evaluate a student comment. It is only by looking at authentic instances of use, as provided by the concordancer, that the analyst/course designer can be sure of the true functions of items such as these.

Concordancing for providing instances of use for direct incorporation into instructional materials

Any of the examples cited as means of identifying areas for inclusion in the syllabus could also be incorporated directly into the teaching materials developed to promote the syllabus. High face validity is given to an ESP course if the learning materials contain actual examples of use which are drawn from the content area and which the learner is likely to have come across, or will be likely to come across, in their specific area studies. In teaching post modification, therefore, learners are more likely to see the relevance of phrases drawn from the corpus such as the following:

> *the lysosome in the cytoplasm of most cells*
> *the membranes around the sap vacuole*
> *the microtubules just below the plasma membrane*
> *animals with a small surface/volume ratio*

than they are the type of phrases more usually employed to teach this grammatical construction, such as, *the girl in the corner, the little boy down the lane, the man with the beard*, etc.

Similarly, in teaching discourse markers, the authentic instances of their use provided by the concordancer can be presented directly to learners.

> *… okay, any questions?*
> *… okay, don't worry*
> *… now, a good example of a glycoprotein is …*
> *… now, any cell that is very active …*
> *… well, I think this might be interesting …*
> *… well, maybe if I think out the question…*

In addition to high face validity, the use of authentic examples in materials, of course, ensures that an accurate representation of actual use is presented to the learner. With fabricated examples, however closely modeled they may be on authentic instances of use, there is always a danger that learners will be presented with a distorted picture of actual use.

Concordancing for the evaluation of current syllabuses and materials.
As well as being a powerful tool in the development of a syllabus and materials, as with raw frequency data, concordancing can also fulfil an important role in the evaluation of a course, once it has been developed. To illustrate how this type of evaluation might apply we will take two areas where concordancing has revealed a discrepancy between published materials and our specialist corpus.

The first of these examples concerns the teaching of definitions. Many commercially available course books teach learners to express definitions by means of a formula such as *X is/can be defined as ...* (e.g. Allen and Widdowson, 1974; Master, 1986). In the corpus, however, there is only one instance of the lexical items *define*; on the other hand, there are 417 instances of the lexical item *called*, used in a defining function. Clearly, the commercially available materials, in presenting an inauthentic formula are doing a disservice to learners and need to be replaced by materials presenting a more accurate model of how definitions are expressed.

Our second area concerns the tendency of published materials to present idealized patterns in their teaching of syntax. We have already referred to the teaching of connectors as sentence initial, while the corpus reveals that they are more often found between subject and verb. As another example, published materials have a tendency to teach the passive as a simple subject + auxiliary + past participle construction (*The work was finished, The cake was eaten*, etc.) (Ewer and Latorre, 1969; Allen and Widdowson, 1976; Master, 1986). Many instances in the corpus, however, contain an adverbial between the auxiliary and past participle (*Water is actively passed., The nerve cells are also linked together., The viruses are then released.*). Many other examples of the distorted picture of syntax presented by published teaching materials could be cited, based upon the corpus.

Using the data from the analysis: An example

A number of examples of how the data is used in course design have been given already in the above sections. Although this paper is primarily aimed at showing the potential of concordancing as a tool in course design in general (albeit by means of a case study of SQU), in order to see what a syllabus/set of materials employing concordancing might look like, this section will show how the data has been used in the production of a unit of teaching material[8]. It is emphasized that this is only one way of using the concordancing technique. Concordancing can play a role in the design of other types of courses/elements of courses.

The unit in question is taken from the writing component of the SQU course. The syllabus for this unit is built upon three objectives: a task objective, a vocabulary objective and a grammar objective, as follows:

Task objective
To write a cohesive paragraph from diagrams, tables and prior knowledge describing structure and function (biology topic)

Vocabulary objective
Productive knowledge of 15 verbs used in describing structure and the interrelationship of parts (e.g. *enclose*, *suspend*, *surround*, *contain*, *separate*)

Grammar objective
To be aware of the relationship between transitivity and the passive voice. To be able to judge when and when not to use the passive voice, with and without an explicit agent.

The task objective (writing a paragraph) is derived primarily from needs analysis, although concordaning does play a role in helping to identify the importance of the language functions of structure and function. The vocabulary and grammar leading up to the task, on the other hand, are derived primarily through concordancing. The verbs listed under the vocabulary objective are drawn from the frequency list, their use in describing structure being corroberated by means of concordancing. The grammar objective derives from an analysis of the concordances of the structure verbs, which demonstrate that such verbs vary in transitivity and therefore in their susceptibility to passivization.

The unit begins with an "input section", which presents a text on the structure of the eye. Information transfer and text labelling exercises help to familiarize learners with the text and draw attention to the language associated with structure and function. A "vocabulary" section presents instances of use of the structure verbs from the input text or the corpus (derived by means of the concordancer), which are compared with more "everyday", made-up examples, supported by visuals. A grammar section follows, again making use of examples from the input text or the corpus, and presenting and practising the relationship between transitivity and the passive. The unit culminates in a task which requires students to write a paragraph about the biological species *hydra* (something studied in the biology course), based upon a table and diagram. At this stage students make use of the language from the input and vocabulary and grammar sections (which have been derived from the corpus) in negotiating the production of an authentic piece of English.

The degree to which the students make use of the language presented leading up to the task varies. More proficient students tend to be more creative and are able to deviate more from what is presented. Less proficient students, on the other hand, tend to rely more on what they have been taught. Students at all levels, however, experience has shown, make some use of the language presented and hence benefit from the use of the concordancing from which this language is derived.

Conclusion

This paper has shown how computerized text analysis can assist in the design and evaluation of an ESP course. The only necessary conditions for such a procedure are possession of the relatively simple frequency and concordancing programs and a corpus of language drawn from the specific area of the targeted students. Armed with these, course designers can ensure that the language they present in their courses corresponds as closely as possible to the language that is actually required by learners in their specific purpose area. Although the technique itself is product focussed, this paper has shown how concordancing can contribute equally well to both process- and product-oriented approaches to course design.

Notes

1. This paper originally appeared in *System* 21(2):231–244, 1993 and is a revised version of a paper originally presented at the 24th Annual TESOL Convention. San Francisco, March, 1990. I should like to acknowledge the helpful comments of Lynne Flowerdew and Martha Pennington on an earlier draft.

2. One anonymous reviewer of a previous version of this paper expressed the concern that teachers and course designers might simply use the frequency data from concordancing and "use the lists in class to walk students through". This certaily is not the approach envisaged here, as will be made clear in the course of this paper.

3.   Some might argue that this overt focus on language in a task-based approach is inappropri-
     ate (c.f. Breen and Candlin, 1980; Prabhu, 1987), because, as Nunan (1989) (cited in
     Loschky and Bley-Vroman, 1990:163) has put it, learners attention, in the performance of a
     task, "is principally focused on meaning rather than form". However, there are signs that this
     view is losing ground (Nunan, 1989), with a growing awareness of the role instruction can
     play in the acquisition of grammar (see Loschky and Bley-Vroman (1990) for review).
     Further, even in a meaning focussed approach such as that promoted by Breen and Candlin
     and Prabhu, learners will require units of meaning (lexical and grammatical items) with
     which to negotiate. In addition, there are a number of practical reasons for such an approach
     in the present context. First, the students come from an educational background based upon
     a traditional lock-step approach to learning, with much emphasis on rote; they thus appreci-
     ate something concrete to hold on to. Second, in post-course questionnaires the students
     repeatedly asked for more "grammar". Third, the large body of teachers involved in the
     course also requested a focus on language, as well as tasks. Fourth, language drawn from the
     science course had high face-validity with students. And fifth, the language presented in the
     lead-up to the tasks, experience demonstrated, was useful in the performance of the tasks.

4.   Bear in mind with all frequency data quoted that to make a valid comparison with published
     frequency lists, as outlined in the previous section, account needs to be taken of the different
     treatment of derivatives, plurals, inflected verb forms and homographs, and that numbers
     cosequently need to be approximately halved.

5.   Frequency data relating to *Cobuild* are taken from Sinclair and Renouf (1988).

6.   Bracketed numbers refer to the number of instances of a word in the corpus.

7.   This may be related to the fact that most of the corpus consists of spoken (albeit academic)
     language, where the range of connectors is narrower than in the written mode.

8.   The unit in question was written by James Scott. For reasons of space and to highlight the
     role of concordancing, the description which follows is simplified. The unit is in fact more
     complex than as described and other pedagogical factors enter into its format besides those
     mentioned.

References

Allen, J. P. B. and Widdowson, H. G. 1974. *English in Focus: English in physical sci-
    ence*. London: OUP.
Bates, M. and Dudley-Evans, T. 1976. *Nucleus: General science*. London: Longman.
Breen, M. P. 1987. "Contemporary paradigms in syllabus design". (2 Parts). *Language
    Teaching* 20(2):81–92; 20(3):157–174.
Breen, M. P. and Candlin, C. 1980. The essentials of a communicative curriculum in
    language teaching. *Applied Linguistics* 1(2):89–112.
Carter, R. 1987. "Vocabulary and second/foreign language teaching". *Language

Teaching 20(1):3–16.

Collins/University of Birmingham. 1990. *Collins Cobuild English Grammar*. London: Collins.

Ewer, J. G. and Latorre, G. 1969. *A Course in Basic Scientific English*. London: Longman.

Goulden, R., Nation, P. and Read, J. 1990. "How large can a receptive vocabulary be?" *Applied Linguistics* 11(4):341–363.

Halliday, M. A. K., McIntosh, A. and Strevens, P. D. 1964. *The Linguistic Sciences and Language Teaching*. London: Longman.

Hutchinson, T. and Waters, A. 1987. *English for Specific Purposes: A learning centred approach*. Cambridge: CUP.

Inman, M. 1978. "Lexical analysis of scientific and technical prose". In L.Trimble, M. Todd-Trimble, and K. Drobnic (eds), *ESP: Science and technology*, 242–256. Portland WA: English Language Institute, Oregon State University.

Johns, T. 1989. "Whence and whither classroom concordancing?" In Bongaerts et al. (eds), *Computer Applications in Language Learning*. Dordrecht: Foris.

Loschky, L. and Bley-Vroman, R. 1990. "Creating structure-based communication tasks for second language development". *University of Hawai'i Working Papers in ESL* 9(1):161–212.

Master, P. E. 1986. *Science, Medicine and Technology: English grammar and technical writing*. Englewood Cliffs NJ: Prentice-Hall.

Nunan, D. 1989. *Designing Tasks for the Communicative Classroom*. Cambridge: CUP.

Prabhu, N. 1987. *Second Language Pedagogy*. Oxford: OUP.

Sinclair, J. McH. 1986. Basic computer processing of long texts. In G. Leech, and C. N. Candlin, (eds), *Computers in English Language Teaching and Research*. London: Longman.

Sinclair, J. McH. (ed), 1987. *Collins COBUILD English Language Dictionary*. London: Collins.

Sinclair, J. 1991. *Corpus, Concordance, Collocation*. Oxford: OUP.

Sinclair, J. Mc.H. and Renouf, A. 1988. "A lexical syllabus for language learning". In R. Carter and M. McCarthy (eds), *Vocabulary and Language Teaching*. London: Longman.

Stevens, V. 1991. "Classroom concordancing: Vocabulary materials derived from relevant, authentic text". *English for Specific Purposes Journal* 10:35–46.

Tribble, C. 1990. "Using concordancing in an academic writing programme". Paper presented at 24th Annual TESOL Convention. San Francisco, March, 1990.

Willis, J. and Willis, D. 1988. *The Collins Cobuild English Course*. London: Collins.

Appendix

Analysis

Two programs were used to analyze the data: a word frequency program, to provide data on the number of instances of all words in the corpus, and a concordancing program, to find all instances of a given word and to present these instances in their immediate linguistic context. The lists show how data analysis is printed out. The first list shows part of the frequency listing in numerical order, while the second list shows part of the frequency data in alphabetical order. The third list shows part of a concordance for the word *well*.

First page of word frequency count in numerical order

the 8315	some 330	that's 166
and 3099	with 329	also 164
of 3014	food 314	outside 164
is 2886	other 312	look 163
a 2429	about 310	around 161
in 2225	plant 309	know 161
are 1785	not 297	between 159
to 1709	through 292	part 159
it 1366	yes 274	remember 155
this 1356	different 267	animals 154
you 1347	then 266	enzymes 153
which 1195	root 264	way 152
so 1183	just 263	xylem 150
cell 1110	okay 252	don't 149
that 999	an 247	system 149
cells 861	two 243	example 148
they 846	many 223	going 146
can 836	inside 219	nucleus 140
here 814	molecules 217	tissue 140
have 764	no 214	got 139
these 729	plants 209	their 136
there 712	wall 207	how 134
we 637	them 205	get 132
what 575	up 205	down 131
one 572	another 202	leaves 128

now 561
or 537
be 507
water 505
for 493
very 490
on 481
from 473
but 469
it's 459
by 429
called 414
if 412
all 408
i 395
has 391
like 390
into 375
as 372
at 371
do 371
membrane 371
because 364
see 341
will 339

energy 199
right 194
would 194
organisms 190
concentration 189
out 189
cytoplasm 188
when 186
go 184
same 183
animal 182
where 182
more 181
stem 180
structure 178
small 177
well 175
body 172
found 172
its 172
made 172
means 172
think 170
make 168
living 166

surface 126
oxygen 123
something 123
function 122
leaf 122
bacteria 119
name 119
material 117
roots 117
only 115
much 114
organism 114
can't 113
may 113
does 111
put 111
mitochondria 110
vacuole 109
quite 108
each 107
sieve 107
things 107
important 106
species 106
good 104

First page of word frequency count in alphabetical order

a 2429
abbreviation 2
abdulla 2
abdulrahman 1
ability 1
able 54
about 310
above 17
absence 1
absent 7
absolutely 3
absorb 24

adhesive 1
adjacent 7
adjectival 1
adjective 4
adjectives 2
adopted 1
adrenal 1
adult 3
advanced 1
advantage 2
afar 1
affect 4

allow 11
allowed 1
allowing 2
allows 3
almost 11
almuwadi 1
aloes 1
along 26
alongside 2
alphabetical 1
already 19
alright 37

absorbed 15
absorbent 1
absorbing 8
absorbs 2
absorption 16
abundant 1
accepted 1
accessory 1
accident 1
accompanies 1
according 5
accurate 1
acetates 1
ache 1
achieve 1
acid 36
acids 49
across 87
act 10
acted 1
actin 2
acting 5
action 1
activated 1
active 40
actively 6
activities 13
activity 5
acts 9
actual 7
actually 32
adaptations 3
add 8
added 9
adding 5
addition 13
additional 2
adenosine 7
adenosine-triphosphate 1

affects 2
affinity 1
afraid 3
africa 1
after 27
afternoon 5
afterwards 1
again 85
against 10
aggregation 3
ago 2
agricultural 1
agriculture 3
ah 1
ahead 1
ahmed 3
aiding 1
aids 4
air 38
airplane 1
airport 1
akaryote 4
akaryotes 2
akaryotic 5
akhdar 10
akhdar's 2
alabri 1
alanine 1
albattoshi 1
albusaidy 2
alcohol 4
aleikum 2
alfairzy 1
algae 2
alhamdulilah 1
alharthy 2
ali 2
alive 18
all 408

also 164
alternately 2
although 26
altogether 1
alwadi 1
alwahibi 2
always 23
alyahai 1
alyia 1
    al-khuwair 2
am 37
america 4
americans 1
amino 59
aminoplasts 8
ammonia 2
amoeba 4
among 1
amongst 1
amount 18
amounts 3
amphibians 1
an 247
anatomy 4
anchor 4
anchorage 3
anchoring 3
ancient 1
and 3099
anemone 3
angiosperms 1
angle 4
angles 2
angular 4
    animal 182
animalia 11
animals 154
anions 1
annelid 1

Part of a concordance for *well*

uoles / you know what these are/	**well**	actually to be precise / leave out
w these words can be adjectives as	**well**	/ akarytotic / prokaryotic / and euk
own food / how do they do it / yes	**well**	alright / we've heart lots of usefu
sensitive / it has to reproduce as	**well**	/ and for this reason hydra has got
anules under normal conditions as	**well**	/ and so you could asdd them here on
rom the bacteria / so it can grow	**well**	/ and the bacteria has a nice place
here are various other families as	**well**	/and within the lumbricidae there
phloem / these need some water as	**well**	and water can move out through the
vacuole might contain solutes as	**well**	as water / so that it's rather like
all because it contains protein as	**well**	as carbohydrate / it's called a pap
very useful kind of organisms as	**well**	as being / as well as causing some d
f organisms as well as being / as	**well**	as causing some disease / now there
found in animals and in plants as	**well**	as a very similar substance is foun
s another difference / not so / as	**well**	as the length yes yes / yes / in l
hey have a cellulose cell wall as	**well**	as / I don't know if you know that e
e things are in the plant cell as	**well**	as the animal cell / now you can se
hates / sulphates / potassium / as	**well**	as another / and these are the are
of the functions of the xylem / as	**well**	as conducting / is to give strengtrh
ignin / so the xylem supports / as	**well**	as its main function which is to co
before in any chemistry classes /	**well**	at school / yeh / the smell of bad
so that here we have / somewhere	**well**	at the moment there's one and a hal
r has as concentration gradient as	**well**	but it cannot pass through the memb
so this is a the sieve element as	**well**	but this one here is maybe cut ther
membrane is in the plant cell as	**well**	/ but on the outside of the membrane
ma which doesn't shown up quite so	**well**	but we can see one or two other thi
what else / the stem needs it as	**well**	/ but why else do the leaves need wa
the root / okay / any questions /	**well**	call them the root cap cells / okay
u got the idea secretory but where	**well**	can somebody tell me better what is
carrot which / other roots do as	**well**	/ can you think of any other root wh
tem / the roots and the flowers as	**well**	/ collenchyma parenchyma and sclere
discharged through the cytoproct /	**well**	contractile vacuoles / these are us
`t think people have studied hydra	**well**	enough to know / if there are races
n is / a finger-like projection /	**well**	finger-like projections of the cell
cant / it lubricates the surface/	**well**	glycoprotein on the surface of the
is outside again from the phloem/	**well**	/ have a look / we'll have a look a
is the function of the nucleus /	**well**	/ heredity it contains what does it
no one knows how many there are /	**well**	/ hold your horses / there are a hug
ena has a flagellum / i don't think	**well**	hydra does have cilia but it's not
a / in fact it's an interesting /	**well**	i think this might be interesting to

cells nerve cells that's five and	**well**	i will write these down and add the
's the answer to question thirteen	**well**	i think the you the safest thing to
eif halak / alhamdulilah / zain /	**well**	i am very pleased to see you all aga
e looking at plant anatomy / right	**well**	i think you seem to have remembered
do you have them with you now / oh	**well**	/ i think we'll just leave it at th
ne cell isn't it and …. / right	**well**	i think we can finish off there for
t get the light from the sun very	**well**	/ if the pressure in the cells
t to ask a special question now /	**well**	/ if there are any qwuestions later p
parts other types of molecules as	**well**	in the cell wall / and some of these
s through these pits very easily /	**well**	in the root as well the water can
any questions about this / okay /	**well**	in your readings there is another wo
then is secreted from the cell /	**well**	it depends on the actual substance
eventually what will happen to /	**well**	it won't explode or blow up but the
t its eyes from outside stimulus)	**well**	it protects its eyes because it has

CHAPTER 5

Using a small corpus to obtain data for teaching a genre

Alex Henry

University of Brunei Darussalam

Robert L. Roseberry

University of Brunei Darussalam

Abstract

A small corpus of texts from a single genre can be analysed, in part
with computer assistance, to provide linguistic information useful in
language teaching. This paper outlines the steps in this process and
applies them to a small corpus of introductions to guest speakers with
comparisons to a similar corpus of letters of application. The importance of *move registers* (Henry and Roseberry 1996) — the language
of the purpose-oriented segments of *genres*–is stressed; and it is
shown how the resulting linguistic information can be developed into
effective language teaching materials, supplemented by computerised, hyperlinked pages of organised data, drawn directly from the
corpus.

Introduction

The analysis of a genre based on data obtained from a small corpus of texts has
become a widely used method of obtaining information about language use.
Such genre analyses have derived information about academic genres (eg.
Swales 1981, Dudley-Evans 1986, Hopkins and Dudley-Evans 1988, Henry
and Roseberry 1999, Thompson, 1994, Swales 1996), as well as about English

genres in professional settings (eg. Bhatia 1993, Henry and Roseberry 1996, 1997, and forthcoming).

In addition to language description, the concept of *genre* has also influenced language teaching in terms of approach, methodology and materials production (Bhatia 1991, Swales and Feak 1994, Weissberg and Buker 1990). The overall aim of a genre approach to language teaching is to make learners aware of the relationship between the communicative purpose of a genre, the context, and language chosen to achieve the purpose. In the final section of this chapter we include sample language teaching materials, based on a genre analysis and show ways in which small corpus information can be made accessible to language students in ways that can accelerate the language learning process. We begin by presenting a genre analysis based on a small corpus of texts of the genre *introductions to guest speakers*. We show, step by step, how such an analysis can be carried out easily by a teacher or student.

Background

We begin by defining some important terms. The term *genre*, for example, has a long history and many diverse meanings spanning a number of fields. With regard to language, the various meanings of the term can be found in the overviews of deBeaugrande (1993) and Leckie-Tarry (1993). The most commonly accepted definition of genre in the field of language learning at present, however, is the one put forward by Swales (1990) and Bhatia (1993). These writers have stressed that a genre is, first of all, a cultural and interpersonal event making use of language. For example, a letter of application and a religious sermon are both interpersonal events using language, and they are recognized as such in the cultures that make use of them. In other cultures, letters of application and sermons may not be known. Miller (1984: 165) stressed this aspect of a genre when she wrote that learning a genre implied learning how to "participate in the actions of a community".

Swales and Bhatia also stress, however, that a genre has a recognizable form or structure that is related to its social purpose. Everyone familiar with the culture of letters of application or sermons can easily recognize these. And both Swales and Bhatia, following Hasan (1984, 1989), have shown that this generic structure is made up of what Hasan called *elements of text structure*, or simply *elements*, but now more commonly called *moves* of the genre. Each

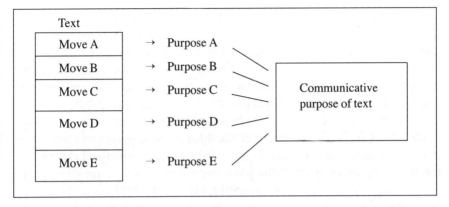

Figure 3: An expanded view of the concordance lines in Figure 2 that contain the majority of (the) people.

move attempts to fulfill a partial purpose of the genre, and all the moves together answer the genre's total purpose as shown in Figure 1 above.

To take an example, two of the moves in a letter of application are *referring to a job advertisement* and *offering candidature* (cf. Henry and Roseberry forthcoming). These are two of the things that a job applicant can do in such a letter to contribute to the total purpose of the letter, which is to secure a job interview or the job itself.

In a study of the genre of service encounters, Hasan (1985, 1989) noted that these moves can sometimes appear in slightly different orderings, although most genres have a somewhat fixed and recognizable ordering of moves. And she further pointed out that some moves are obligatory, while others are optional. In our example, *referring to a job advertisement* and *offering candidature* can appear in either order in a letter of application. Furthermore, *offering candidature* is a move common to all the letters of application in the corpus we created and is thus an obligatory move in this genre. On the other hand, *referring to a job advertisement* appeared in fewer than 50% of the texts in our corpus and must therefore be considered an optional move (cf. Henry and Roseberry forthcoming).

Just as the term *genre* has had a number of meanings assigned to it, so too has the corresponding term *register* been hard to pin down. Once again, deBeaugrande (1993) and Leckie-Tarry (1993) provide useful overviews of the various meanings of these terms. For our purposes, we use the term *register* to refer to the language patterns associated with a genre. These include word choices, phrasing, idioms, cohesive devices, and others. Grammar choices such as tense, aspect, voice, and so on, are also included in register. Since a genre is defined as a linguistic event, there is a sense in which our definitions of register and genre overlap. In this chapter, we will use the term *genre* when we are stressing the social or formal characteristics of the text, and *register* when we are stressing the language patterns that are used to realize it.

This definition of genre, as we have presented it, turns out to be a very powerful one for language description and hence for language teaching. One important example is that it allows us to make a clear distinction between, on the one hand, genres, which fulfill particular purposes, and, on the other hand, what we call *modes of discourse* (narrative, exposition, description, instruction and argumentation). Modes thematise certain kinds of information (Ghadessy 1995) by placing certain information prominently at the beginnings of clauses. Let us take as an example *narrative*, which according to Virtanen (1992), holds a unique position among the modes of discourse (*text types* in her terminology) as somehow being more "basic" than the others. Narrative in this sense is considered by some writers to be a genre (cf. Biber 1988). However, it is excluded by the definition of genre given above. It is not a social or cultural event reflecting a purpose, and it does not have a recognizable move structure. Narrative, however, can be the predominant mode of a number of well defined genres, including stories, anecdotes, fairy tales, personal accounts, and so on.[1]

There is, in fact, a definite relationship between modes of discourse and genre. Within a genre framework, a speaker or writer often has a choice as to how to accomplish a particular move. The choices available are called *strategies* (cf. Bhatia 1993: 30–32) and different strategies are often strongly associated with particular modes of discourse. To see this more clearly, consider an example from the *letter of application* genre. Perhaps the most important obligatory move of this genre is what we call *promoting the candidate*. There turn out to be several strategies that candidates can adopt to promote themselves. They can *list skills and abilities*, they can *state how these skills were obtained*, they can *list qualifications*, and so on (cf. Henry and Roseberry, forthcoming). In the first of these, *listing skills and abilities*, it is likely that the present tense will be used and that exposition will be the preferred mode, with the candidate being thematized repeatedly as *I*. Typical sentences include *I am a technical writer* and *I am very skilled in customising computer software*. On the other hand, if the candidate *states how the skills and abilities were obtained*, we find the past tense together with a narrative mode in which adverbials of time will be more often thematized, eg. *In 1989, during my time with X,* etc.

Many of the moves of most genres appear to have only a single strategy. In the *letter of application* genre, for example, only two of the eleven moves have multiple strategies available to the writer. For this reason, we have preferred to refer to the language choices at this level as *move registers* (cf. Henry and Roseberry 1996). But this should not obscure the fact that the language choices are actually made at the level of the strategies.

There has been at least one attempt to identify the language variation across sections of a genre, namely Biber and Finegan's (1994) study of medical research articles, but sections of articles as identified by section-headings are not intrinsic purpose-oriented parts of a text, whereas moves, by definition, are. Sections are divisions established by convention. Each such division may consist, in turn, of several moves, each with its own language patterns (cf. Dudley-Evans 1986).

The importance of move registers, rather than sections, for language teaching cannot be too greatly stressed. Here is where all linguistic choices reside. Attempts to teach the language of an entire genre or of sections of it divided by headings are apt to impede the language learning process, especially in those cases where language choices can vary greatly from one move to another. Unless students are shown clearly how language conjoins with purpose and how purpose is related to moves, it is not likely that the student will easily learn how to make appropriate language choices for the different moves of a genre. To take a simple example from the genre *brief tourist information text,* the word *take* appears almost exclusively in the move that describes the available facilities and activities of the tourist destination and is used almost exclusively as an imperative and with exclusively idiomatic meanings (*take a boat ride...*, *take a relaxing swim...*). We have identified hundreds of similar lexico-grammatical variations across the moves of several genres (cf. Henry and Roseberry, 1996, 1997, and forthcoming). This work has provided further confirmation of Sinclair's observation that words have their own grammar (1991), and, therefore, lexis and grammar must be learned together.

The Study

Our selection of the genre *introductions to guest speakers* was based on several considerations. First, introducing a guest speaker is an important social activity resulting in a clearly recognisable genre, especially in academic, government, and business settings. All our students at the University of Brunei Darussalam will, during their undergraduate and professional careers, attend many of these events and, on occasion, be required to deliver such introductions. A second reason for choosing this genre is that it is a spoken one. Our previous work has focused exclusively on written genres for special purpose English courses, and we wished to demonstrate that a spoken genre could be analysed almost as easily as a written one. Finally, for clarity of presentation, we wanted to select a genre that was reasonably brief, contained a small number of moves, and yet demonstrated all the typical variations associated with moves, strategies, and move registers.

For comparison, a second genre, *letters of application*, was chosen (cf. Henry and Roseberry forthcoming). Both *letters of application* and *introductions to guest speakers* attempt to promote an individual in various ways, and we were interested in noting any similarities and differences in the language they use to do this. We believed that this kind of information could be useful in teaching the language patterns of the two genres.

Aims

The aims of this study were to determine the optional and obligatory moves of the genres, the strategies of the moves if present, and the allowable move order, and to identify the important linguistic features of each of the moves and strategies. In addition, the study aimed to compare and contrast any moves and strategies common to both genres.

Methods and Procedures

In this section we will describe the method that we used in this and in previous genre analyses (Henry and Roseberry 1997, 1998, and forthcoming). In addition, we explain the rationale behind each of the steps.

The first step in the procedure was to select suitable data for analysis. Our corpus of *letters of application* consisted of 40 letters from several sources: a South East Asian university English department, a British university science department, the personnel department of a British horticultural company, and a

United States legal firm. Applicants from the USA, Britain, Australia, Canada, and New Zealand were applying for academic, secretarial, administrative and senior management posts (Henry and Roseberry forthcoming).

Our corpus of *introductions to speakers*, being of a spoken genre, involved a different method of collection. Our university keeps a videotaped record of all guest lectures and the introductions to the speakers, so it was easy to locate a large repository of spoken texts of this genre. We selected in a quasi-random fashion about 15 videotapes, and a research assistant was hired to help us transcribe the introductions. In order to get a "feel" for the genre we attended and tape-recorded some introductions to guest lectures that were given in the university during the early stages of our study, and we added their transcriptions to our collection, bringing the total to 20. We included introductions made by native speakers of several languages, including English, Chinese, and Malay; but all introductions were given in English. We were aware that we might find cultural differences among the language groups, and we were thus on the look-out for any such discrepancies. If significant discrepancies had been found among these groups, it would have been necessary either to restrict our study to one group, and provide more texts from that group, or to increase the number of texts of all three groups in order to obtain sufficient data for a comparison. In the event, this turned out not to be an issue.

We decided that we would limit our analysis to language and text structure and ignore paralinguistic information, such as stress, intonation, and so on. However, if this kind of information is wanted for a particular study, several systems of transcription exist for the purpose of capturing the relevant paralinguistic features on paper (cf. Schriffrin 1994: 422–433). Capturing this kind of information is a more time-consuming process, of course, and the transcriber requires some training in order to be able to make useful transcriptions.

When we had collected 20 examples of the genre we carried out our initial analysis, reading and comparing similar parts of the texts, and we decided that this genre had indeed a relatively simple move structure as there were no significant move variations from text to text. We thus decided that these 20 speeches would provide enough data for our purposes and so, after removing all names and any other information likely to identify the participants, we created our corpus.

The second step was to identify the moves and create move corpora. Small corpus analysis, like large corpus analysis, relies heavily on computer assistance to manipulate data and capture patterns that would otherwise be difficult or impossible to spot. But unlike large corpus analysis, it also relies heavily on expert judgements, based on whole-corpus reading and study. In most cases, the corpus is short enough that it can be read and studied in its entirety. In the present study, we laid out the transcribed data and studied it. Each researcher, independently of the other, identified a set of moves that characterised the texts in the corpus. Each of us marked these moves on copies of the texts and exchanged marked texts so that the move markings could be confirmed or contested by the other researcher.

Once a consensus was reached on the identities and purposes of the moves, we were ready to move to the third step, the creation on a computer word-processor of small corpora of each of the moves. From the file of the corpus of 20 texts a separate file was made for each move. This was done by copying from each example in the corpus only the text of a specific move and pasting it into a file for that move. These sub-corpora of the whole genre corpus are called *move corpora* and it is from them that we derive the important *move register* language information alluded to earlier and that we believe is so crucial in the teaching and learning of the language of a genre.

In the final stage of the procedure, we analysed, with the aid of a computerised concordancing programme, important words found in the whole corpus and in each of the move corpora. The identification of important words is based both on information from a computer programme, and by careful study by the researcher. Several such programmes for PCs are available, and a few are described in some detail in Kennedy (1998, chapter 4). The one that we used in our analysis is the *WordSmith* suite of programmes for text analysis (Scott 1996). The function and operation of this suite of programmes are described in some detail in chapter 3 of this book. *WordSmith* provides two important types of information to help us select words for more detailed analysis: word frequency and word distribution. Clearly, if a word appears frequently throughout the texts in a corpus of a genre, and if the word is well distributed throughout the texts, the word and its associated grammar patterns are important for the learning of the genre. The WordList programme of *WordSmith* was used to provide a list of word types (all the different words in the text), sorted by frequency in descending order. By studying these lists for each of the corpora, we see not only what the most frequently used words in the corpus are, but we also note any discrepancies among the various move corpora and any differences that may exist between these and a word-frequency list derived from a large corpus, such as the *Cobuild* frequency list given by Sinclair (1991: 143).

Significant variations in these lists are the first indication we have of special-ized uses of words and their associated grammar patterns from one move regis-ter to another. The second type of information provided by *WordSmith* con-cerns distribution. A word that is much more likely to appear in one genre than in many other genres is an obvious learning target for students of that genre. To find such words, called *key words*, *WordSmith* makes use of statistical proce-dures such as the Chi-square test, to measure the extent to which a word appears in a corpus significantly more frequently than one would expect by chance alone. Although there are limitations to the use of Chi-square and other tests for this type of analysis, they do provide valuable information for our pur-poses.

The computer can provide information regarding word frequencies, and identify key words based on statistical analysis of distribution, but word fre-quency and word distribution are not necessarily reliable indicators of the importance of certain words, and so, much work has to be done by the researcher to identify other words from within the word lists that might be sig-nificant for the genre. This work consists of identifying two categories of words: the first concerns words found in an important part of a text, and the second concerns groups of words related by semantic class. An example of the first category is words found in the central idea or thesis statement of an acade-mic essay. The thesis statement of an essay corresponds to the macro-proposi-tion in van Dijk and Kintsch's (1983) terms and they showed that the under-standing of the macro-proposition was crucial in understanding the whole text. The words in the thesis statement of an academic essay will, therefore, carry much more interpretive weight in terms of understanding the whole essay than words occurring in the body of the essay. Thus, depending on placement, a word that appears only once in a text may, in some cases, be much more crucial to comprehension than a word that appears 10 or 15 times elsewhere in the same text.

The second class of words which may be of low frequency is words belonging to a semantic class which is important to the genre. These are words that are related to each other by meaning. Synonyms, hyponyms, antonyms, and so on, comprise the semantic classes (cf. Leech 1981: 92–109). A seman-tic class of words may be strongly present in a move of a genre, and yet it may be that no word in that class appears more than once in the corpus. In our work on brief tourist information texts (Henry and Roseberry 1996), we showed that the location move of such texts consists primarily of one of three possible phrase frames (cf. Becker 1975, Nattinger and DeCarrico 1992, Pawley and Syder 1983), each containing a slot for *place name.*

(a)   PLACE NAME + static verb + prepositional phrase (location)
          (*Damai Beach is about 20 km from Kuching.*)

(b)   participle + prepositional phrase (location) + PLACE NAME ...
          (*Situated approximately halfway between Sydney and Brisbane,*
          Coff's Harbour....)

(c)   Adverbial phrase (location) + PLACE NAME ...
          (*Less than 27 km from Bandar Seri Begawan, Muara Beach...*)

Thus the name of the tourist destination, already mentioned at or near the beginning of the text, frequently appears again in the location move. However, since most of the texts in the corpus were about different tourist destinations, each of the place names had a frequency of only 1 or 2 on the word frequency lists and might have been overlooked without a careful analysis by the researchers.

In addition to frequency lists, the researcher can also use the computer program to calculate a list of *key words*, which are words that appear in a text with greater frequency than one would expect from chance occurrence alone. Using information from both the frequency list and the key words list, the researcher can now identify words that appear to be particularly important in the text or part of the text being analysed. To see how these words are used in their cotexts, the computer can now be used to provide lists of cotext lines with the chosen word in the middle. These lines, popularly misnamed *key words in context*, or KWIC lines, actually have nothing to do with key words, but merely show whatever words the researcher has selected. (For more on frequency lists, key word lists, and KWIC lists, see chapter 3.)

Results and discussion

Unfortunately space does not allow a full description of the two genres but we are able to present the moves and strategies identified, their definitions and the allowable move order. This will be followed by examples of the kinds of linguistic information we can obtain from the above procedure. We will also show relevant comparisons between similar moves of the two genres.

Moves, allowable move order and strategies

After some discussion, we agreed that the 20 texts consisted largely of six moves that could be labelled *getting the audience's attention, giving background to the talk, introducing the speaker, promoting the speaker, previewing the talk/event*, and *calling on the speaker*. The definitions of the six moves identified and their frequencies are given in Table 1.

Table 1: The moves, definitions, and frequencies of the moves

Move (no. of introductions containing move)	Definition
Getting the Audience's Attention (14)	The introducer indicates it is time to start.
Giving Background to the Talk (2)	The introducer provides information or opinion as to the importance of the talk or the subject of the talk.
Introducing the Speaker (19)	The introducer names the speaker.
Promoting the Speaker (19)	The introducer presents the speaker's credentials.
Previewing the Talk/Event (10)	The introducer gives details of the talk or of the whole event.
Calling on the Speaker (19)	The introducer invites the speaker to start.

An example of most of these moves is shown in the introduction in Figure 2, below.

If we consider the frequencies of each of the moves, as shown in Table 1, above, it would appear that none of the moves was obligatory. However, it would seem obvious that for the genre to have the purpose of introducing a guest speaker, then the speaker has to be introduced. The fact that one of the speeches appears to lack this move suggests that members of an audience would have judged this text to be less effective than the other texts in the corpus. In fact, this same speech was the only one to lack the promotion move.

Similarly, the move *inviting the speaker to begin* was only realised linguistically in 19 of the 20 speeches. In the remaining speech it is likely that the *invitation* was performed paralinguistically, perhaps with a smile or a nod of the head. Leaving aside these two speeches it would seem that a paradigm

Attention:	Good afternoon ladies and gentlemen. A very warm welcome to this our fourth public lecture of the year.
Introducing:	I'm very pleased to introduce our speaker today, Professor X.
Promoting:	For the last 30 years Prof X has been in the Department of Y at Z University in Scotland. He recently retired from Z and is now visiting professor at A.
	During his time at Z University he had two main fields of interest: language testing and sociolinguistics. His interest in sociolinguistics may have been prompted by his stated desire to escape language testing into a more respectable field. This partial escape produced valuable contributions to the debates on English as an international language and to the role of the native speaker in applied linguistics.
	Thankfully his escape from language testing was largely unsuccessful as he came to realize that testing far from being on the periphery of applied linguistics was in fact not only in the mainstream but also of great importance throughout the world. This realisation led to the publication of the book *Principles of B* in 1990.
	In addition to *Principles of B*, his contribution to language testing and project evaluation has been immense. Interestingly, Professor X identified perhaps the only type of test validity that most of us pay any attention to: face validity. He has also been involved in the evaluation of communicative language teaching projects, the most famous being, of course, the C project. X has also been heavily involved in the validation of national and international language tests such as IELTS.
Previewing:	Today he is going to talk on a subject which is of great relevance to all of us concerned with language teaching `An evaluation of an extensive reading programme'.
Calling on:	Ladies and Gentlemen Professor X.

Figure 2: Introducing Professor X.

speech from our corpus would consist of three obligatory moves *introducing the speaker, promoting the speaker* and *calling on the speaker*. These are the three moves that have the most to contribute to the overall purpose of the genre.

The remaining three moves would appear to be optional. If the introducer has the *audience's attention* then this move would not be required. If however, the introducer did not have the *audience's attention*, then this move would become obligatory for an effective speech to take place. *Giving background information* was only found in two speeches and in the first case the background information consisted of telling the audience that the seminar about to be presented was the first in a series. In the second case the introducer gave his/her own opinion about what was required to effect change in teacher behaviour and it appears from this introduction that the event was meant to produce answers to this question. In the last of the optional moves *previewing the talk/event* the most common detail given was the title of the talk which appeared in seven of the speeches in the corpus. *Stating the relevance of the talk* was found in two speeches while the *structure of the event* in terms of how long the speaker will speak and how long will be given over to questions from the audience appeared in one speech, as did *stating the subject area of the talk* as opposed to the actual title.

In all texts in the corpus, both the obligatory moves and the optional moves, wherever they appeared, occurred in the same order. It is conceivable that an effective introduction could have one or more of the moves in a different order, and perhaps a larger sampling would have shown this. But it does seem that the stated order (Table 1) is the preferred one.

Identification of moves and strategies arises most readily out of combined analyses and discussions among researchers. An example of the type of discussion that arose concerned the first move. One of the researchers suggested that

Table 2: Strategies of the moves *getting the audience's attention* and *promoting the speaker*

Move	Strategies
getting the audience's attention	welcoming, greeting the audience calling the gathering to order
promoting the speaker	listing relevant skills and abilities stating how skills and abilities were obtained listing qualifications naming present job listing publications

Table 3: Moves of the *letter of application* and their definitions
(Henry and Roseberry forthcoming)

Move	Definition
Opening (O)	The writer identifies the target and invites the target to read the letter.
Referring to a Job Advertisement (AD)	The writer refers to the advertisement in which the position was named and described.
Offering Candidature (CA)	The writer states an interest in applying for the position.
Stating Reasons for Applying (RA)	The writer gives reasons for wanting the position.
Stating Availability (A)	The writer indicates when he or she would be able to take up the position.
Promoting the Candidate (P)	The writer presents selected information demonstrating qualifications and abilities relevant to the desired position.
Stipulating Terms and Conditions of Employment (TC)	The writer indicates expectations regarding salary, working hours, and other relevant contractual matters.
Enclosing Documents (EN)	The writer lists documents enclosed with the letter.
Polite Ending (PE)	The writer ends the letter in a way intended to procure a favourable response.
Signing Off (SO)	The writer signs his or her name in a respectful manner, thus claiming ownership of the letter.

the *attention* move might instead have the purpose of *greeting the audience*. This argument was supported by the fact that at least one of the introducers seemed quite clearly to be greeting the audience by expressing genuine pleasure at seeing them. In the end it was agreed that the main purpose of the move was to get attention. One way to describe this move might be to assign *greeting* to the status of a strategy that might optionally be included within the move, depending on the introducer's personality, mood, and/or relationship with the audience.

Of the six moves only two were thought to have more than one strategy and these are listed in Table 2 above.

In our study of the *letter of application* (Henry and Roseberry forthcoming), we found ten moves, as shown in Table 3 above.

Of these, five moves are obligatory: *opening, polite ending,* and *signing off,* which are common to all business letters, and *offering candidature* and *promoting the candidate* (Henry and Roseberry forthcoming). Table 4 shows the strategies of the *promotion* move.

Table 4: Strategies of the promotion move, letters of application, giving the number of letters in the corpus of 40 in which the strategy was found
(Henry and Roseberry forthcoming)

---

listing skills, abilities (34)
stating how skills, abilities were obtained (21)
listing qualifications (12)
naming present job (12)
predicting success (5)
listing publications (2)
giving reasons for leaving present job (2)
demonstrating knowledge of target position (1)

We see that, in addition to the five strategies of *promoting* in *introductions,* shown in Table 2, three others: *predicting success, giving reasons for leaving present job,* and *demonstrating knowledge of target position* are used by writers of *letters of application* (Henry and Roseberry forthcoming). It is easy to see why these are irrelevant and inappropriate in *introductions.* Clearly, the purpose of the promotions move here is quite different from that of the *promotions* move in *letters of application.* As a result, the two moves are realised differently in the two genres. *Letters of application* are written by a person for himself or herself. *Introductions* are written for someone else.

Another difference in strategies between the *promotion* moves in the two genres is the degree to which the individual strategies are separated from each other. In *letters of application* (as in all planned, written genres that we have studied), one strategy is usually completed before another strategy is begun. We have found that moves are sometimes split, but strategies rarely are. However, the *promotion* strategies are frequently inserted into the *introductions* that we examined. For instance, some skills may be mentioned, then a few words on how they were obtained, then a mention of a degree or qualification, then more skills, etc. The patterning is more chronological than in *letters*

Table 5: Frequency lists for the twenty-five most frequent word types in the *introductions to guest speakers* corpus, the six move corpora, with the *Cobuild* corpus given for comparison (Sinclair 1991:143.)

Whole Corpus	Attention	Background	Introducing	Promoting	Previewing	Calling on	COBUILD
the 269	the 10	the 10	the 14	the 23	to 201	to 14	11 the 309497
of 209	and 9	in 9	to 7	of 17	and 177	and 11	7 of 155044
and 187	gentlemen 8	this 8	is 6	in 13	the 152	prof 11	7 and 153801
in 176	ladies 8	and 8	speaker 5	and 11	is 149	I 10	6 to 137056
to 135	good 7	change 7	in 5	to 10	of 82	without 9	6 a 129928
is 85	morning 6	of 6	of 5	a 10	on 64	gentlemen 8	5 in 100138
a 82	to 5	teacher 5	I 4	he 8	a 64	his 6	5 that 67042
he 74	of 4	to 4	our 4	is 8	he 59	ladies 5	5 I 64849
I 68	afternoon 3	is 3	a 3	education 8	this 50	the 5	5 it 61379
education 55	from 3	will 3	from 3	I 7	us 49	ado 5	4 was 54722
his 55	session 3	a 3	introduce 2	has 7	in 48	further 4	4 is 49186
has 50	welcome 3	an 3	Prof. 2	his 7	morning 46	now 4	4 he 42057
for 49	a 2	approach 2	we 2	for 7	talk 43	so 4	4 for 40857
this 42	departments 2	first 2	have 2	as 6	we 36	address 4	3 you 37477
from 40	deputy 2	for 2	this 2	university 6	will 33	call 4	3 on 35951
with 40	friends 2	kind 2	today 2	with 6	an 32	invite 3	3 with 35844
as 39	headmasters 2	our 2	and 2	at 5	be 28	on 3	3 as 34755
on 37	principals 2	paradigm 2	Dr 2	from 5	for 28	would 3	3 , 30952
university 34	this 2	session 2	but 2	language 4	going 27	you 3	3 be 29799
prof 32	about 1	task 1	great 1	was 4	his 26	all 3	2 had 29592
language 31	Brunei 1	among 1	he 1	been 4	language 22	David 3	2 but 29572
at 29	chairman 1	any 1	my 1	research 4	prof 22	deliver 3	2 they 29512
that 27	colleagues 1	as 1	on 1	also 4	teaching 21	Dr. 3	2 at 28958
been 26	committee 1	be 1	pleasure 1	on 4	today 21	Ellerton 3	2 his 26491
have 26	different 1	by 1	with 1	teaching 4	by 21	friend 2	2 have 26113

of application, and suggests a narrative approach. The relatively relaxed and informal way in which most *introductions* are planned and delivered may be the reason for this approach. Such an approach in a *letter of application* would make a poor impression on many employers, which probably explains the greater care taken in that genre to present information in a more structured way.

Word frequencies

Table 5 shows the first several words in the frequency word lists for our whole corpus, the six move corpora, and the *Cobuild* corpus, used here as a control (Sinclair 1991: 143). Frequency lists, such as these, give us our first indication of how language is patterned in the various move registers. To take one example, let us examine the frequency list for the corpus of the move *calling on the speaker*. We immediately notice several anomalies. The word *the*, which is typically the most frequent word in large corpora and in most small corpora as well, is quite far down the list here. This may suggest, among other things, that direct address and/or fixed phrases predominate in this move. Noticing the frequencies of *ladies*, *gentlemen*, *I*, *call*, *ado* and so on would confirm this hypothesis. Because this move corpus is so small, we can easily examine it, without computer assistance, to learn that one of the preferred lexical phrases for this move is the following:

> So (ladies and gentleman),
> without further ado, I would (now) like to $\{ \begin{matrix} \text{call (now) on} \\ \text{invite} \end{matrix} \}$ x to deliver ...

(Parentheses indicate syntagmatic variation, while brackets indicate paradigmatic variation.) Most move corpora are longer and more complex than this one, however, and other computer tools may be helpful in revealing otherwise hidden patterns.

For comparison, Table 6 repeats the frequency list of the *promotion* move of *introductions* (from Table 5, above) and contrasts this with the corresponding list from *letters of application* (Henry and Roseberry forthcoming). It is not surprising that *promotion* in *letters of application* makes greater use of *I*, *my*, *experience*, and *skills*, among others, than the third-person oriented *promotion* move in *introductions to speakers*. Some other differences may be accounted for by the broader subject matter of *letters of application*.

Table 6: The 25 most frequent words in the *promotion* moves of *introductions to guest speakers* and *letters of application*

Promotion Move			
Introductions		*Letters*	
the	201	and	257
of	177	the	223
in	152	I	211
and	149	in	206
to	82	of	205
a	64	a	122
he	64	to	116
is	59	my	86
education	50	have	80
I	49	as	75
has	48	for	72
his	46	at	53
for	43	with	51
as	36	English	49
university	33	an	40
with	32	experience	37
at	28	am	36
from	28	teaching	34
language	27	was	34
was	26	university	29
been	22	language	28
research	22	on	28
also	21	that	28
on	21	skills	26
teaching	21	this	25

Key words

Another important tool that can shed light on the way words are used in move registers is a key words analysis. As previously mentioned, key words are words that appear in a text or a part of a text with a frequency greater than chance occurrence alone would suggest. Key words are usually found by comparing the target corpus with a much larger corpus to see if the words in the target corpus occur with significantly different frequencies than they do in the

Table 7: Key words for *listing skills and experience*

world	cultural	worked
fact	editor	both
involved	projects	appointed
interests	third	foundation
learning	around	general
field	experience	politics
main	journal	problems
being	management	served

Table 8: Pairs of nouns, verbs and adjectives in the *promotion* move of *letters of application*

Nouns	Verbs	Adjectives
ability and tenacity	assess and implement	adaptable and able
administration and development	identify and solve	interesting and meaningful manner
announcers and newsreaders	meet and exceed	internal and external
background and experience	motivate and communicate well with	applied and theoretical
skills and knowledge	set up and operate	

larger corpus. There is a problem inherent in this method of key word analysis, however. Any corpus, large or small, is a collection of examples of one or more genres or parts of genres. The large multi-million word corpora usually contain examples of several genres. Since there is no way of knowing what constitutes a "normal" mix of genres in a language, we prefer not to use large corpora in our key word analyses. Furthermore, since we are mainly interested in the ways in which the different move registers vary with respect to each other, it is only necessary to compare each move register with the entire corpus. Using a method that we devised for this purpose (See Appendix), we obtained a list of key words for the promotion move strategy *listing relevant skills and experience* (Table 7, above).

The words in this table are listed from greater to lesser "keyness", though all the words in the table appear with noticeably greater frequency in this strategy than anywhere else in the corpus. We will have more to say about some of these words in a later section.

One striking difference in word use between the *promotion* moves of the two genres involves the unexpectedly high frequency of the word *and* in the *letters*, as shown in Table 6. A remarkably common feature here, missing almost entirely from the *introductions*, is binary phrases such as those listed in Table 8, above (Henry and Roseberry forthcoming).

KWIC lists

Armed with word frequency lists and key word lists, we can now examine the lexico-grammar of important and interesting words in the several move corpora. When the move corpus is small enough, this task can be accomplished merely by reading and studying it. In the case of longer corpora, computer assistance may be required, and this is usually in the form of KWIC lists, mentioned earlier.

As an example, let us focus on the word *interests*, identified as a key word in the *listing relevant skills and abilities* strategy and shown in Table 7, above. Figure 3, below, shows a *WordSmith* KWIC list for the words *interest* and *interests* in this strategy. The list contains seven numbered lines – one for each appearance of *interest* or *interests* – and is sorted alphabetically by the first word to the right of the given word. Different sortings make it easier to see common patterns of collocation. In this case we note that *are* follows the word in more than half of the instances given. Looking to the left of the selected word, we note that *main* collocates with it in more than half the given instances. The numbers in the second column are tags, showing which text contains the given line. We can thus see easily that these usages are well distributed across the 20 texts of the corpus, with only two instances occurring in the same text (#4).

By way of contrast, Figure 4 shows a KWIC list of *interest / interests* in the *promotion* move of the *letters of application* (Henry and Roseberry forthcoming).

Although *letters of application* is a larger corpus than *introductions to guest speakers*, there are fewer uses of *interest(s)*. Unlike introducers, applicants are usually more concerned with proven skills and experience than with interests (Table 6). Because of the small set of examples here, it is not possible to generalise about different patterns of use of *interest* between the two genres. However, it is likely that the frequent use of *I* in the *letters* precludes the use of the verb *be* after *interest*, although this verb is commonly found in the *introductions* (Figure 3).

1	12>	ited Kingdom. His main research **interests** are language teach
2	14>	orate levels. His main academic **interests** are language polic
3	9>	ew years ago. His main research **interests** are (…) as medium
4	11>	is of (…)'. <11> Her research **interests** are in the area of
5	4>	sting and sociolinguistics. His **interest** in sociolinguistics
6	7>	tion. <7> Her special fields of **interests** include linguistic
7	4>	rsity he had two main fields of **interest** language testing an

Figure 3: A *WordSmith* KWIC list of *interest/interests* in the strategy *listing relevant skills and abilities*, in the *promotion* move of *introductions to guest speakers*

1	in Brunei. I also have a wider **interest** in the standard of Engli
2	ays a week and I took a special **interest** in the needs of ESL/EFL
3	valent to a Masters. I found my **interest** in literacy skills conti
4	round and experience will be of **interest** to you. I have a B.A. In

Figure 4: A *WordSmith* KWIC list of *interest/interests* in the strategy *listing relevant skills and abilities,* in the *promotion* move of *letters of application*

Linguistic features of the promotion moves

We now look in some detail at strategies of the promotion move of our two corpora and present some of the linguistic information derived from the methods and tools described above. We will then use some of this information to contrast the two genres.

Listing relevant skills and abilities

The context in which these speeches are delivered and the fact that many of the speakers had academic titles means that, unlike in the letter of application, overly explicit description of the speakers' specific skills and abilities is unnecessary. If someone is a professor, for example, it is understood that that person has research, teaching and administrative skills. This does not mean, however, that the claims made are in any way modest, as shown by the presence of another small group of low frequency words and phrases which include: *actively (sought after), immense (contribution), illustrious (academic record), outstanding (work), numerous (references), well known, at the fore-*

front of, known all over the world. Most of these descriptive words and phrases would be hard to include in a letter of application without breaking what is known as the "Modesty Maxim" (Leech, 1983).

The more modest way of highlighting particular skills and abilites in an academic setting would seem to be through the word *interests.* Unlike the general meaning of the word — a rather casual desire to find out about something — in the educational setting the meanings of this word range from *has considerable expertise in X* to *is doing research in X.* The most frequent collocate of *interest* is *main,* and these words normally appear together in this strategy in the following lexical phrase frame, derived from the KWIC information in Figure 3, above:

$$X\text{'s (main)} \left\{ \begin{array}{l} \text{research} \\ \text{academic} \end{array} \right\} \text{interests} \left\{ \begin{array}{l} \text{include} \\ \text{are (in the area of)} \end{array} \right\} Y$$

The word partnership of *main* and *interests* occurs four times in this strategy. This highlights again the importance of move or strategy registers. The word *main* occurs five times in the whole corpus in 146th position, and five times in 105th position in the narrower promotion corpus. As we saw in Table 7, above, these words are also key words in this strategy. From the language learning perspective, the knowledge of the use and usage of such words is very important to the teacher wishing to teach the strategy *listing relevant skills and abilities.*

Apart from the syntactic pattern described above, the other choices available have no obvious common syntactic pattern. Two examples are *Many of you are familiar with his poetry* and *It is impossible to open a book about bilingualism without finding numerous references to X.* In the last section of this chapter we show how language learners can discover such structures for themselves.

In contrast, the same strategy in *letters of application* yields the following lexical phrases, not commonly found in the *introductions*:

I (also) have + (adj) experience in + NP (and NP)
I am + NP
I am + adjective / participle
I + consider + NP + (Adj) + (to be + NP)
I + feel + that + clause
(I + verb + that) I + modal + (adv) + verb + NP

The first-person orientation is evident and selects many of the language patterns here.

Stating how skills and abilities were obtained

This strategy emphasises how the speakers acquired their expertise and is found in 12 introductions. The most striking linguistic feature of this strategy is the choice of tense: simple past tense in narrative mode, or present perfect or present perfect continuous in expository mode. As expected with these tenses a time marker or preposition of time is often present. Examples include: *X was involved with language teaching and teacher education in the United Kingdom, For the last 30 years X has been in the Department of. . .*, and *X has been working in a number of places around the world*. The most common verb is *be + involved* which occurred in this strategy in four of the speeches in both the simple past and in the present perfect. Other verbs used all indicate involvement such as, *to be* (+ *active, an adviser*), *work, teach, manage, train, served, have* (+ *experience*).

An interesting discourse pattern found in this strategy is generalisation-example which is found in three speeches. A very clear example is *He has been active in various professional associations. He was the founding president of … .*

In the *letters of application*, this strategy is characterised by verbs indicating participation in important activities (*involved, developed, designed, monitored*), and time expressions such as *for the last X years, since 19XX, during 19XX, during my career*, and *during that time*.

Listing qualifications

This strategy is found in eight of the speeches. Of interest is the large number of different verbs found in this corpus most of which are of low frequency in the whole corpus of introductions. These verbs include two in the present tense *have* and *hold*, and six in the simple past tense *graduated, obtained, received, earned, was* and *did*. This group represents one of the semantic classes mentioned earlier which consist of low frequency but important words. As we found in our study of the *letter of application*, the choice of tense depends on whether the speaker wishes to give the date of graduation. One interesting example of rather informal speech, used by a native speaker of English, is *and [he] went and did another [MA] in Indiana.* It is unlikely that *went and did* would be an effective way of listing qualifications in a letter of application.

In our corpus of *letters of application*, this strategy was used for academic qualifications only. A larger corpus would no doubt make reference to other kinds of qualifications. Typical examples here include, *I have a bachelor of Science degree in X, I hold a PhD in X, I am a graduate of X.* Aside from the first-person orientation, the language here resembles that of the corresponding strategy of the *introductions*.

Naming present job

This strategy was found in 11 of the speeches. The most popular choice of tense was the present with seven occurences in the simple present and two in the continuous form. These tenses were often accompanied by *now* or *currently* as in *He is currently a visiting professor*, and *He is now occupying the position of Acting Director.* It is this strategy which accounts for three of the four occurrences of the word *currently* in the *promotion* move corpus. The present perfect and simple past passive were each used once with the time markers *since 1996*, and *in 1991* respectively.

Again, in this strategy, the language of *letters of application* is similar, barring the first-person orientation.

Listing publications

In an academic context a scholar's eminence is usually in proportion the the number of scholarly works he or she has published. It is, therefore, not surprising to find this strategy in 11 speeches. Another example of an important semantic class is found in the adverbs *widely* and *extensively*. Their frequency in the whole corpus is 2 and 1, respectively, but they each appear once in this strategy filling an important slot in verb phrases as in *X has published widely*, *X has written extensively.* These words are important in fulfilling the purpose of the genre to establish the credentials of the speaker in an educational setting. Only two structures occur more than once: the first case being present twice *X is the author of...*; and the second structure three times *X has written / published / edited.* These three would however, be a useful starting point in the classroom.

This strategy was not commonly used in the *letters of application*, possibly because it applies largely to academic positions only and most of the relevant information would be contained in the curriculum vitae.

Applications to Language Teaching

Having made the case for the need for a narrow-angled analysis of the language at the level of the move or, where they exist, at the level of the strategy, we would now like to describe a language teaching methodology which has been proved empirically to be effective in an academic setting with young adult learners. We would like to make clear however, that the methodology and exercises described below would need to be modified considerably to suit younger learners.

Information from a genre analysis, such as the one described in this chapter, can form the basis for two kinds of teaching materials: lessons, and source materials, which students can use as a source of more data. We have developed lessons for several genres and have created computer-based source materials for two of these. To illustrate this section, we will use examples from the lesson and source materials for teaching *letters of application*. We have chosen these materials because they provide a model for creating similar materials for other genres, including *introductions to guest speakers*, and because our students have used them successfully for several semesters.

Lesson materials

Our genre-based lessons are presented in four parts: (1) Introducing the genre, (2) Reading and analysing the moves, (3) Learning the language of moves, and (4) Constructing the genre.

The first section, introducing the genre, begins with background information on the genre, placing the genre in a social and cultural framework. It explains who the users of the genre are: who produces it and who receives it. The purpose of the genre is stressed, and a class discussion focuses on whether members of the class are familiar with the genre and whether or not it is commonly used in the local culture. Many of our Bruneian students, for example, seem to be aware of the fact that the *letter of application*, though not a well defined genre in the local culture, is becoming increasingly important for success in job hunting.

Table 9: The moves and their descriptions for the genre letter of application (Henry and Roseberry forthcoming)

Move	Definition
Opening	The writer identifies the target and invites the target to read the letter.
Referring to a Job Advertisement	The writer refers to the advertisement in which the position was named and described.
Offering Candidature	The writer states an interest in applying for the position.
Stating Reasons for Applying	The writer gives reasons for wanting the position.
Stating Availability	The writer indicates when he or she would be able to take up the position.
Promoting the Candidate	The writer presents selected information demonstrating qualifications and abilities relevant to the desired position.
Stipulating Terms and Conditions of Employment	The writer indicates expectations regarding salary, working hours, and other relevant contractual matters.
Enclosing Documents	The writer lists documents enclosed with the letter.
Polite Ending	The writer ends the letter in a way intended to procure a favourable response.
Signing Off	The writer signs his or her name in a respectful manner, thus claiming ownership of the letter.

In the next part of the lesson, students are led to recognise the moves by being shown a table of moves, such as Table 9, above, followed by a marked example of the genre.

Students who are already familiar with the process of move analysis are encouraged to work in groups and discover the moves for themselves. The move descriptions in Table 9 are given only to students who are just becoming familiar with the genre approach.

Students are then asked to mark several other example texts themselves, and a class discussion follows this exercise. Sometimes there are disagreements about where one move ends and another begins, or about whether a certain move exists at all in a given example. These matters are discussed in class, and students learn that there may be somewhat different interpretations of what is going on in a particular example text.

Students then attempt to determine whether there is any pattern in the organisation of the moves and whether some moves might be optional. The three or four example texts are chosen to facilitate this task without recourse to the larger corpus. After studying the example texts and performing their own move analyses on them, students are able to determine the order of the moves, and whether a move is likely to be obligatory or not, by completing a table such as shown in Figure 5, below, in which the data for one text is provided for guidance.

Moves	Text 1	Text 2	Text 3	Text 4
Opening	1			
Referring to a Job Advertisement	3			
Offering Candidature	2			
Stating Reasons for Applying	5			
Stating Availability	–			
Promoting the Candidate	4			
Stipulating Terms and Conditions of Employment	–			
Enclosing Documents	6			
Polite Ending	7			
Signing Off	8			

Fig. 5: An exercise table enabling students to discover move order

Next, students are asked to examine the ways in which the producers of the texts accomplished the moves. It is at this stage that the students first begin to become sensitised to the strategies of the moves and how they work. By using statements of the form, "This writer does move X by VERBing ...", students can discover the strategies for themselves. For example, "This writer refers to a job advertisement by giving the name and date of the newspaper".

Familiar now with the moves and strategies of the genre, students are in a position, first to analyse and improve the moves and strategies of a faulty example of the genre, and then to collect real examples and analyse them critically. Up to this point in the lesson, attention has focused on the social and cultural purpose, the form and the content of texts in the genre, rather than on the language of the genre moves.

In Part 3 of the lesson, the language of each move of the genre is examined in detail. Exercises are in the form of language awareness activities, and students work in groups, analysing a number of examples according to a set of questions designed to focus their attention on relevant linguistic points. Such questions as "What tense is most common?", "How is politeness shown?", "What words reappear often?" and so on, are designed to aid the students in their task. At every stage in the lesson, tables are provided for students to fill in with the missing information. In the earlier stages, some information is provided for guidance, as in Figure 6, below, which gives a partially complete table, designed to elicit language patterns which students may discover by studying the strategy *listing skills and experience* in the move *promoting the candidate*.

Promoting the candidate: Listing skills and experience	
Text 1	I have excellent verbal and written communication skills.
Text 2	
Text 3	...a graduate in Business Studies from Stanford University
Text 4	

Fig. 6: An exercise table enabling students to discover the language patterns of a move strategy

Gradually, at this stage in the lesson, students are asked to begin to write their own example of the genre, in this case a *letter of application*. They may do this move by move, as they study the language of each move, or they may write the whole text in a rough draft and review it move by move as they become more familiar with the kinds of words and structures commonly used.

In the final part of the lesson, the students finish creating a draft of their text and then, through a process of peer critiquing, develop the draft into a presentable text.

Source materials

In chapter 13 of this volume, Lynne Flowerdew notes the pedagogical advantages of getting students to work with the raw corpus data as a way of increasing their awareness and competence. She points out, however, that many students find working with the computer output to be a stumbling block – an additional source of confusion to be added to the difficulties caused by an imperfect command of the target language. Faced with this problem, we have tried to find ways to help our own students make efficient use of the corpus data as an aid in learning a genre.

We discovered, by working with our students on this problem, that two principles must be followed if the use of raw corpus data is to be helpful, rather than confusing, to language learners. First, the data must be organised in some way for them. Although we can help our students discover patterns during supervised lesson periods, we cannot expect the students to find such patterns without guidance. Secondly, the data must be invisible unless and until it is needed. We found that giving our students a thick compendium of the hundreds of language patterns that we had extracted from a corpus analysis had the effect of intimidating them to such an extent as to make learning the genre seem to be an impossible task. This was the case even when we directed the students' attention to only that part of the compendium that was needed for the purpose at hand.

The embodiment of both of these principles turned out to be a computerized branching program, of the kind that was popularly used in CALL programs in the eighties. Today, no specialized software is required to create a branching algorithm of this kind, since the standard word processing programs allow text pages to be saved in HTML code, which can be hyperlinked to create whatever kind of branching patterns are required. Internet sites are created in this way, but the same method can be used to create a hyperlinked set of pages on a single computer or a local network. We employed this technique to create sets of hyperlinked branching texts, containing patterns of raw corpus data, demonstrated through the examples given below.

We begin with the raw data, which we have extracted using the method of analysis described in this chapter. The information is divided by move and strategy, and language patterns in each strategy are grouped as lexical phrases and other patterns useful in language learning. The completed compendium may run to dozens of pages in length, depending on the complexity of the genre. We term these compendia *Language Pattern Dictionaries*, and there is one for each genre that we have analysed for teaching purposes. Small portions of the *Language Pattern Dictionaries* for the *description* move of *brief tourist information texts* and the *promotion* move of the *letter of application* genre are given below in Figure 7 and Figure 8, respectively.

A.6.1.1.3 Post-modification of the Noun Phrase	
in [the] (noun: often "world")	the largest flower **in the world**, …clear waters **in the world**, most beautiful waters **in the world**, some of the finest beaches **in the world**, the biggest **in the Alps**, the loveliest suburban gardens **in New Zealand**, the Alps **in the south**, white sandy beaches **in the north**, unique wildlife **in the lush outway rain-forests**…
(verb+ed) [by/with, etc.]	sugar-spun sand — **kissed by the Caribbean**…, Five-acre island **filled with quaint shops**, areas **set aside for public**…, Sandakan Mosque, **built on the**…, 100 miles of coastline **surrounded by**… enchanting harbor **lined with**…, colourful homes **snuggled along the hilltops**…
that (+ clause)	prominent feature **that makes the face**…, streets **that reflect**…, the gentle river **that meanders through**…, sculptured coastlines **that stretch beyond**…

Figure 7: A small segment of the *Language Pattern Dictionary* for the *description* move of the *brief tourist information* genre

It should be stressed that information from the *Language Pattern Dictionaries*, as shown in Figures 7 and 8, is not given to students in this form. Instead, it is then divided into manageable chunks and displayed as a series of pages, linked by HTML hyperlinks, in exactly the same way as an Internet web site is constructed. The resulting branching algorithm is structured according to the design shown in Figure 9, below. Selecting the program causes the opening menu to appear, represented here by the top box in Figure 9. The student then chooses from the menu selection, thus causing a screen in the next level of the hierarchy to appear, and so on. There are several hundred screens of language information available to the students, but the branching program allows the student to find only the information that is desired, leaving the rest invisible.

Assume for example that a student is writing a draft of a *letter of application* and wants to get more information about how actual writers of such letters

D.4.1.Most frequent words used in this strategy: and, in, I, of
D.4.2. Collocations and Clusters:

| I: | clusters: | I have a, **I** also have |
| | collocations: | I am, **I** would, **I** consider myself, **I** have |

I have: I have…background, **I have**…strong commitment, **I have** (extensive, wide, practical) experience in, **I have** experience using, **I have** a good understanding of, **I have** an undergraduate degree, **I have** a BSc degree, **I have** two degrees, **I have** an MA, **I have** both ESP/EAP experience, **I have** the full range of academic and professional qualifications, **I have** a wide range of duties, **I have** intermediate/advanced skills, **I have** a B.A., **I have** excellent verbal and written communication skills.

I am: I am a technical writer, **I am** very skilled with, **I am** (fully) computer literate, **I am** technically very competent in, **I am** experienced in writing, **I am** a career educator, **I am** a graduate in, **I am** (was) responsible for, **I am** a CPC holder and a member of, **I am** an experienced distribution manager, **I am** I.T. literate, **I am** responsible for all contract matters, **I am** familiar with, **I am** fully adapted to, **I am** an American teacher of English, **I am** a good teacher who…

I (verb)   I **possess** the ability, **I consider** myself to be an overachiever, **I feel** that I possess the ability, **I** most recently **functioned**, **I consider** myself adaptable…

Figure 8: A small segment of the *Language Pattern Dictionary* for the *giving qualifications* strategy of the *promotion* move of *letters of application*

give their qualifications in the *promotion* move. The student would select "Letter of Application" from the genre menu at the top of the hierarchy (the first page to appear on the computer screen). The "Letter of Application" menu now appears, from which the student selects the move "Promoting the

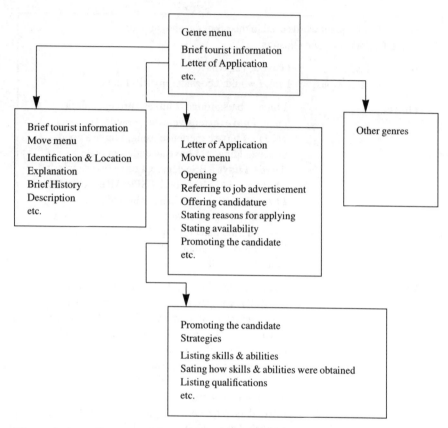

Figure 9: A small portion of the branching algorithm used to display the *Language Pattern Dictionary* source materials

Candidate". Since this move can be accomplished through several strategies, a menu of these strategies now appears, and the student may select the desired one: "Listing qualifications".

If the student chooses "Listing qualifications" in the bottom screen of Figure 9, above, the following screen (Figure 10) appears, showing the student the several most common patterns and usages, from the *Language Pattern Dictionary*, found in actual examples of this strategy, as written by job applicants whose letters were judged to be good examples of the genre. All language information is taken directly from the small corpora, via the *Language Pattern Dictionary*, and is pre-arranged for students' convenience and ease of use.

Listing Qualifications

A time phrase is sometimes used with graduated, completed, or obtained:

I graduated from X in 1995 with a degree in...

I completed an MA in English in 1995 at X...

In 1980 I obtained the Diploma in Teaching...

If no time phrase is used, the verbs have, hold, or am are used as follows:

I have: I have an undergraduate degree..., I have a BSc degree...,
            I have two degrees..., I have an MA..., I have a B.A....

I hold: I hold a [name of degree]...

I am: I am a graduate in..., I am a CPC holder and a member of...

My is used frequently in this strategy:

My [name of degree]..., ...my qualifications (relevant to this position)
include...

Promotion Strategies I Move Menu I Genre Menu

Figure 10: One computer screen displaying language information from the *listing qualifications* strategy of the *promoting the candidate* move in the genre *letter of application*.

The last line on the screen (Figure 10) contains the hyperlinks, which allow the student to return to previous screens, containing menus of further choices. Many of the pages contain further links, showing the student additional language information or further examples.

The computerised version of the *Language Pattern Dictionaries* is most effectively used together with exercises in the third and fourth parts of the genre lesson, in which the students are beginning to discover the language patterns of the genre and are practicing creating their own example texts. Several of the exercises in those parts of each lesson are marked with Compac Disc icons, reminding the students that those exercises should be carried out with reference to the relevant parts of the computerised *Language Pattern Dictionary* for that genre. Students use the computer laboratory or their own computers at home, drawing on the computerised materials as a resource while studying and writing examples of the genre.

Using materials of this kind, students are quickly and easily able to find needed language information from the small corpus. The information is arranged in ways that enable students to find the important patterns without difficulty. Students have commented that they find these materials both easy to use and interesting

Conclusion

In this paper we have shown how language patterns can vary greatly from one strategy or move of a genre to another, between two genres as a whole, and even between very similar moves of two genres. We have outlined a procedure for analysing the moves and strategies of a genre, using a small corpus of texts to derive information useful in teaching the genre. And we have demonstrated how three different strands of language teaching can be combined to make learning more effective. A genre framework allows us to make clear to language learners how communicative purpose, language, and context interact to form text. Small corpus analysis allows us to obtain important, detailed information about how this purpose is realised in language. Finally, the principles of language awareness combined with the data processing and storage capabilities of computer software allow us to present this valuable linguistic information to learners in a meaningful context.

Note

1. This confusion arises from the use of narrative (uncountable) and narratives(s) (countable). The former is a mode of discourse. The latter includes, among others, the genres listed here.

References

Becker, J. 1975. "The phrasal lexicon". In R. Schank and B. Nash-Webber (eds), *Theoretical Issues in Natural Language Processing*, 70–73. Boston: Bolt, Beranek and Newman.

Bhatia, V. K. 1991. "A genre-based approach to ESP materials development". *World Englishes* 10 (2): 1–14.

Bhatia, V. K. 1993. *Analysing Genre: Language use in professional settings*. London:

Longman.

Biber, D. 1988. *Variation Across Speech and Writing*. Cambridge: CUP.

Biber, D. and Finegan, E. 1994. "Intra-textual variation within medical research articles". In N. Oostdijk and P. de Haan (eds), *Corpus-Based Research into Language*, 201–221. Amsterdam: Rodopi.

Beaugrande, R. de. 1993. "'Register' in discourse studies: A concept in search of a theory". In M. Ghadessy (ed), *Register Analysis: Theory and practice*, 7–25. London: Pinter.

Dudley-Evans, T. 1986. "Genre analysis: An investigation of the introduction and discussion sections of Msc dissertations". In M. Coulthard, (ed), *Talking About Text*, 128–145 Birmingham: English Language Research, Birmingham University.

Ghadessy, M. 1995. "Thematic development and its relationship to registers and genres". In M. Ghadessy (ed), *Thematic Development in English Text*, 129–146. London: Pinter.

Hasan, R. 1984. "Coherence and cohesive harmony". In Flood, J. (ed), *Understanding Reading Comprehension*, 181–219. International Reading Association, Delaware.

Hasan, R. 1989. "The structure of a text". In M. A. K. Halliday and R. Hasan, *Language, Context, and Text: Aspects of Language in a Social-Semiotic Perspective*, 52–69. Oxford: OUP.

Henry, A. and Roseberry, R. L. 1996. "A corpus-based investigation of the language and linguistic patterns of one genre and the implications for language teaching". *Research in the Teaching of English* 30: 472–489.

Henry, A. and Roseberry, R. L. 1997. "An investigation of the functions, strategies and linguistic features of the introductions and conclusions of essays". *System* 25: 479–495.

Henry, A. and Roseberry, R. L. 1998. "An evaluation of a genre-based approach to the teaching of EAP/ESP writing". *TESOL Quarterly*, Brief Reports and Summaries 32 (1):147–156.

Henry, A. and Roseberry, R. L. 1999. "Raising awareness of the generic structure and linguistic features of essay introductions". *Language Awareness* 8(3/4):190–200.

Henry, A. and Roseberry, R. L. Forthcoming. "A narrow-angled corpus analysis of moves and strategies of the genre: 'letter of application'". *English for Specific Purposes*.

Hopkins, A. and Dudley-Evans, T. 1988. "A genre-based investigation of the discussion sections in articles and dissertations". *English for Specific Purposes*, 7: 113–122.

Kennedy, G. 1998. *An Introduction to Corpus Linguistics*. London: Longman.

Leckie-Tarry, H. 1993. "The specification of a text: Register, genre and language teaching". In Ghadessy, M. (ed), *Register Analysis: Theory and Practice*, 26–42. London: Pinter.

Leech, G. 1981. *Semantics: The study of meaning*. (2nd ed.). Harmondsworth: Penguin.

Leech, G. 1983. *Principles of Pragmatics*. London: Longman.

Miller, C. R. 1984. "Genre as social action". *Quarterly Journal of Speech*. 70: 151–167.

Nattinger, J. R. and DeCarrico. J. S. 1992. *Lexical Phrases and Language Teaching*. Oxford: OUP.

Pawley, A. and Syder, F. 1983. "Two puzzles for linguistic theory: Nativelike selection and nativelike fluency". In J. Richards and R. Schmidt, *Language and Communication*, 191–226. London: Longman.

Schriffrin, D. 1994. *Approaches to Discourse*. Oxford: Blackwell.

Scott, M. 1996. *WordSmith Tools* [Computer program]. Oxford: OUP. (http://www.oup.co.uk/elt/software/wsmith).

Sinclair, J. McH. 1991. *Corpus, Concordance, Collocation*. Oxford: OUP.

Swales, J. M. 1981. *Aspects of Article Introductions*. Aston ESP Research Report No.1, Language Studies Unit, University of Aston in Birmingham, Birmingham, UK.

Swales, J. M. 1990. *Genre Analysis: English in academic and research settings*. Cambridge: CUP.

Swales, J. M. 1996. "Occluded genres in the academy: The case of the letter of submission". In E. Ventola and A. Mauranen (eds), *Academic Writing: Intercultural and textual issues*, 45–58. Amsterdam: John Benjamins.

Swales, J. M. and Feak, C. B. 1994. *Academic Writing for Graduate Students: A course for non-native speakers of English*. Ann Arbor: University of Michigan Press.

Thompson, S. 1994. "Frameworks and contexts: A genre-based approach to analysing lecture introductions". *English for Specific Purposes*. 13:171–186.

van Dijk, T., and Kintsch, W. 1983. *Strategies of Discourse Comprehension*. London: Harcourt Brace Jovanovich.

Virtanen, T. 1992. "Issues of text typology: Narrative – a 'basic' type of text?" *Text* 12(2): 293–310.

Weissberg, R. and Buker, S. 1990. *Writing up Research: Experimental report writing for students of English*. Englewood Cliffs NJ: Prentice Hall.

Appendix

A procedure for identifying key words in the moves of a genre

1. A text analysis program is used to prepare two lists: (a) a list of all words in the given move sub-corpus and the number of times each occurs, and (b)

a list of all words in the whole corpus and the number of times each occurs. Words in these lists have the following format:

(a) move sub-corpus list		(b) whole corpus list	
PROGRESS	4	PROGRESS	13
RAISE	1	RAISE	5
SAY	5	REMINDER	5
		SAY	21

2. A word processor is used to combine these two lists and then remove the words that are not in both corpora. This is done by converting the lists to tables and sorting by frequency. This yields a list of all words in the given move sub-corpus only, each followed by the number of occurrences in the move sub-corpus and the number of occurrences in the entire corpus. (At the end of this Appendix the steps for doing this using WordPerfect are given.) Words in this list have the following format:

combined list		
PROGRESS	4	13
RAISE	1	5
SAY	5	21

3. These data are then pasted into a computerized spreadsheet. The following columns are defined:

A   contains the list of words (from step 2, above);

B   contains the number of occurrences of the word in the given move sub-corpus (from step 2, above);

C   contains the total number of occurrences in the whole corpus (from step 2, above);

D   equals the proportion of occurrences within the move sub-corpus (the value in B divided by that in C);

E   is the total number of words in the whole corpus (non-variant);

F   is the total number of words in the given move across all texts (the move sub-corpus), (non-variant);

G   is set equal to the value in F divided by the value in E (the proportionate size of the move sub-corpus in relation to the whole corpus), (non-variant);

H   is set equal to the value in D divided by the value in G (the keyness index, equal to 1 for a randomly distributed word);

I   is the number of different texts in the corpus in which this word appears in the given move;

J   is the ratio of the data in I divided by the data in B (a measure of the spread of the word across different texts in the given move).

Table A1, below, is a small excerpt from a spreadsheet that was created in this way. (Note that the data in E and F, and therefore their ratio G, are invariable.)

Table A1: Portion of a spreadsheet created according to the words/move procedure

	A	B	C	D	E	F	G	H	I	J
1	PROGRESS	4	13	0.31	39477	1596	0.04	7.61	1	0.25
2	RAISE	1	5	0.20	39477	1596	0.04	4.95	1	1.00
3	SAY	5	21	0.24	39477	1596	0.04	5.89	4	0.80
4	SEES	1	1	1.00	39477	1596	0.04	24.73	1	1.00
5	SOCIAL	5	22	0.23	39477	1596	0.04	5.62	4	0.80
6	MENTAL	3	3	1.00	39477	1596	0.04	24.73	2	0.67
7	LIVE	5	20	0.25	39477	1596	0.04	6.18	2	0.40
8	RETARDATION	2	2	1.00	39477	1596	0.04	24.73	2	1.00
9	RULE	2	2	1.00	39477	1596	0.04	24.73	1	0.50
10	SKILLS	4	7	0.57	39477	1596	0.04	14.13	1	0.25
11	SORT	2	6	0.33	39477	1596	0.04	8.24	1	0.50
12	SUCH	2	75	0.03	39477	1596	0.04	0.66	2	1.00
13	VALUES	2	6	0.33	39477	1596	0.04	8.24	2	1.00
14	WHOLE	1	2	0.50	39477	1596	0.04	12.73	1	1.00

4. Selection criteria can now be applied to the word table:

(a) Since words that appear only infrequently in the whole corpus cannot spread enough throughout the corpus to demonstrate a pattern of attachment to moves, all such words are removed from the analysis. This may be done by deleting all words for which the value in column C is 1 or 2. These are the words that appear only once or twice in the whole corpus. (Applying this selection criterion to the table above causes the removal of *sees*, *retardation*, *rule*, and *whole*.)

(b) Of the remaining words, those that are unable to show a pattern of spread throughout the move sub-corpus are now removed. Such words may occur too infrequently within the move sub-corpus to suggest a pattern, or they may gravitate too strongly to a single text and thus be more a property of the text than of the move as a whole.

There are two criteria in our procedure that can be used for identifying and removing such words: (i) If the number in column I equals 1, the word appears in only one text in the move sub-corpus and is removed from analysis. (Applying this criterion removes *progress*, *raise*, *skills*, and *sort* from the remaining words in Table A1.) (ii) A word may be highly concentrated in a very few texts in the move sub-corpus. This could indicate that the word is related to a common topic shared by these texts. Such words will have a low value in column J, which measures the ratio of number of texts in which the word appears in the given move to the number of occurrences of the word in that move sub-corpus. For example, if a word appears in the move sub-corpus four times, but in a single text, J will equal 0.25. The same value of J will be obtained if the word appears 16 times in 4 texts or 160 times in 40 texts. Obviously, then, the J value is useful as a selection criterion only if the total number of texts (column I) is a relatively small proportion of the number of texts in the corpus.

In the example corpus from which Table A1 was derived there are 42 texts. Thus all the I numbers in Table 1 are small in proportion to the whole corpus. We may thus judiciously remove all remaining words for which the J values are less than, say, 0.50. (The only remaining word in Table 1 affected by applying this selection criterion is *live*. Examining this word more closely, we note that it is used 20 times in the whole corpus and five times in the given move sub-corpus. But all these occurrences are confined to a mere two texts out of the 42 that comprise the move sub-corpus. It is clear, therefore, that this word has a special affinity for the two texts in which it appears and not for the move sub-corpus as a whole. It is very likely related to the topic of these texts or results from the personal style of the writer or writers of the texts. We may safely remove it from our analysis.)

(c) We are now in a position to remove all words that do not appear in the given move sub-corpus considerably more frequently than chance alone would dictate. This can be accomplished by deleting all words for which the value in column H is less than approximately 5. H is the number that indicates the keyness of the word. It is the ratio of D, which measures the proportion of the occurrences of the word within the given move sub-corpus, and G, which is the proportionate size of the move sub-corpus as a fraction of the whole corpus. In our example, column G indicates that the sub-corpus of the target move is 4% of the size of the whole corpus. Therefore, we would expect that 4% of the occurrences of a randomly distributed word in the whole corpus would occur within the target move sub-corpus, giving H the value of 1 for such a word. (Applying this criterion to the remaining words in Table 1 causes the removal of *such*. This word's two appearances in the move sub-corpus are not far off from what one would expect from a random distribution of the word throughout the whole corpus.)

Application of these criteria thus reduces Table A1 to the following (Table A2):

Table A2: Words remaining from Table A1 after the selection criteria are applied

	A	B	C	D	E	F	G	H	I	J
3	SAY	5	21	0.24	39477	1596	0.04	5.89	4	0.80
5	SOCIAL	5	22	0.23	39477	1596	0.04	5.62	4	0.80
6	MENTAL	3	3	1.00	39477	1596	0.04	24.73	2	0.67
13	VALUES	2	6	0.33	39477	1596	0.04	8.24	2	1.00

We therefore conclude that these four words are the only ones from the original list (Table A1) that are likely to bear a close relationship with the given move. We can conclude this for the following reasons: (a) they occur with some frequency both in the total corpus and in the given move sub-corpus, (b) they exhibit a tendency to spread through the move sub-corpus, and (c) their appearance in the given move sub-corpus is considerably greater than what would be expected if they were randomly distributed.

Carrying out steps 1–3 using WordPerfect and a spreadsheet programme.

The merging of the two word lists, as described here, can be accomplished by any full-featured word processor as well as by some text analysis programs. We give below the precise steps for carrying out this part of the procedure using WordPerfect 3.0 for Macintosh computers. These steps can be modified for use with other word processors:

1. Use a text analysis program (such as *WordSmith Tools*) to prepare the two lists as described in the text. Each list should have the format [TAB]WORD[TAB]99[TAB]99[TAB][Hrt], where "99" stands for a number and Hrt is a hard return. It may be necessary to use the column function of the word processor to put the lists into this format, if the text analyzer does not automatically do so.
2. Put * after each item in the move sub-corpus list: Find: [TAB][Hrt]; Replace with [TAB]*[Hrt]; Change all. Save. Close.
3. Use "Insert File" to add this list to the bottom of the corpus list.
4. Sort: Select All: Tools…Sort: Key 1 Alphanumeric Field 1 Word 1: Key 2 Alphanumeric Field 3 Word 1: Descending Order: Begin.
5. Find *[Hrt]; Replace with [TAB].
6. Select All: Tools…Sort: Key 1 Alphanumeric Field 4 Word 1: Descending Order: Begin
7. Scan down the list. Remove all words at the bottom which appear only once in a line. These words will appear together as a large block and can be deleted easily. ([Shift][end] selects to the bottom of a file.)
8. Find [TAB][TAB]; Replace with [TAB].
9. Select All: Table: Text to Table: Tab Delimited: OK.
10. Click on Column 3 (the second appearance of the word): Table: Delete: Delete 1 column: OK. (Repeat this procedure for each unwanted column. The final table should contain three columns: the word and two numbers.)
11. Select all cells in the table: Table: Table to text: Tab Delimited: OK.
12. Select All: Tools…Sort: Key 1 Alphanumeric Field 1 Word 1: Ascending: Begin.
13. Paste data into a spreadsheet.

CHAPTER 6

Small corpora and language variation
Reflexivity across genres

Marina Bondi

University of Modena and Reggio Emilia, Italy

Abstract:

This chapter explores ways in which small corpora can be used to study language variation across genres within a given discourse area. Focusing on academic genres and on the field of economics, the chapter shows that different features can be studied, ranging from a variety of functional units to specific lexico-grammatical patterns. The examples discussed all centre on the representation of speech and thought in forms of self-projection or other-projection, with a view to the dialogic and argumentative features of academic discourse. The analysis is based on small corpora consisting of abstracts and introductory chapters of textbooks. After a brief overview of the forms and functions of reported argument, the chapter focuses on the different roles meta-argumentative expressions play across the genres and provides a closer analysis of specific lexical items (*show; agree/disagree*). The final section focuses on the pedagogical implications of the study.

Introduction

The notion of genre, as a recognisable communicative event characterised by a set of communicative purposes[1] (Swales 1990), has been extremely influential in many areas of language pedagogy. A genre-based approach has been developed in ESP/EAP (Swales 1990, Bhatia 1993), as well as in North-American writing studies (Freedman and Medway 1994, Berkenkotter and Huckin 1995, Grabe and Kaplan 1996) and in systemic functional studies, where a major role is played by a genre-based literacy pedagogy (Christie 1989, 1992, 1997, Martin 1993, Christie and Martin eds. 1997, Paltridge 1997). Special attention has been paid to genre in studies of register (Ghadessy ed. 1988, 1993) and of scientific discourse (Halliday 1988, Halliday and Martin 1993, Martin and Veel eds. 1998). Genre-based studies of scientific discourse have often concentrated on textual structures with obligatory and optional elements (Halliday and Hasan 1989). The study of academic discourse in particular has focused on the most highly conventionalised genres and therefore on research-based genres like the research article (Swales 1990, Bhatia 1993), where textual structures can somewhat be related to the procedures of scientific inquiry, in terms of purpose, methods and materials, results, discussion and conclusions. More recently, a variety of studies have been carried out on scientific genres, often combining linguistic and rhetorical analysis (Berkenkotter and Huckin 1995) and showing significant variation across specific knowledge areas (MacDonald 1992, 1994). Parallel to a closer look at language features is an attempt to relate textual structures to social and cultural factors that may influence the use of language, as in the North-American genre studies of Bazerman (1988), Bazerman and Paradis (eds. 1991), Myers (1990, 1992, 1994) and Freedman and Medway (eds. 1994).

The analysis of academic discourse has often paid particular attention to "metadiscourse", that is discourse that refers to the evolving text rather than to the subject matter: e.g. *we can use a numerical example to help clarify*....[2] Studies of metadiscourse have proliferated in the eighties and nineties and numerous typologies and classifications have been produced, both in the field of literacy studies and in the analysis of oral discourse.[3] The issue links to the notion of reflexivity, introduced in semantics by Lyons (1977: 5) as the capacity of natural languages "for referring to, or describing, themselves", which has recently come to the attention of a variety of approaches to linguistics and anthropology (see for example Lucy 1993), as well as in discourse studies of reporting expressions and evaluation (Tadros 1993, Caldas-Coulthard 1994, Thompson and Ye 1991, Hunston 1994, Thomas and Hawes 1994, Hunston and Thompson 2000). From a lexical point of view, a number of categories will play a major role. Some of these, like referring expressions (*verba dicendi* with their nominalisations) have been a key issue in metapragmatic studies of illocution and in studies on reflexivity (Verschueren 1985, 1989, 1995; Lucy 1993). Reporting expressions may allow writers to detach themselves from the proposition by attributing it to others, thus creating a variety of discourse planes. As we will see more clearly, projection[4] does not necessarily imply detachment from "others": writers can even detach themselves from their own propositions in forms of self-projection, which provide advance or retrospective reference to their own discourse (*as I hope to show below, as defined above etc*). Though not necessarily related to variation in field, the lexicogrammar of projection finds its place in EAP programmes for a number of reasons. First, it plays a major role in the description and analysis of academic discourse, especially because it reflects the inherently discursive nature of science. Second, its role in making the reading process more efficient is also very important for the student-reader as such: forms of self-projection offer readers frameworks to support their reading, while forms of other-projection help the reader identify the writer's position as to the proposition reported and as to the debate within the scientific community.

Our specific language focus will be on meta-argumentative expressions and the role they play in a variety of types of economics discourse in English. Meta-argumentative expressions are defined by Stati (1998: 54) as nouns referring to argumentative roles (like *Claim, Concession, Objection, Proof,* etc.)[5] and verbs used to introduce an argumentative proposition or to report argumentative processes realised by another person. These include both forms of self-projection (*In chapter 8 we show...*) and forms of other-projection (*Keynes believes.....*) (See Bondi 1998b: 93).

Meta-argumentative expressions play a major role in genres where the representation of scientific argument is in focus. This is the case for example with abstracts and introductory chapters of economics textbooks (almost invariably devoted to a presentation of economics with its epistemological problems and its "tool kit"). Comparative analysis of small corpora focusing on different genres within the same discourse area allows for consideration of lexico-grammatical variation within the framework of genre studies. Specific language features or areas can thus be focused upon and studied against the background of textual structures. An analysis of the forms and functions of meta-argumentative expressions could reveal the role they play in the definition of the genre (or subgenre) under consideration.

Taking the discourse of economics as a case in point, this study focuses on comparative analysis of meta-argumentative expressions in two small corpora of abstracts and textbook chapters. The analysis centres on the role played by reference to discursive procedures in textbooks and abstracts. In particular, with reference to textbooks, the study investigates whether the representation of scientific discourse can be shown to be a key issue in the genre and to play a leading role in introductory chapters (Bondi 1997b, 1998a, 1998b) by explicitly introducing the student-reader to the conventions of the scientific community. With reference to abstracts, the role played by the representation of discursive procedures can help to show that abstracts do not simply reproduce the main points made in an article, but actually represent the sequence of argumentative procedures adopted in the text.[6]

The chapter starts with a brief presentation of the corpora used for the study and provides a general overview of meta-argumentative expressions and of the categories that can be used for their analysis. The analysis will then proceed to highlight the main features of meta-argumentative expressions in general as identified in the small corpora, before illustrating more detailed quantitative analysis of specific lexical items across the data. The final section before the conclusion will focus on the pedagogical implications of the study.

Materials and methods

The paper is based on the analysis of meta-argumentative nominal and verbal expressions in two small machine-readable corpora:

– a corpus of 10 introductory chapters of economics textbooks published in English[7] (consisting of about 71000 words)
– a corpus of 456 economics abstracts taken from the first issue of *Econlit*, 1997, the electronic version of the standard abstracting journal in economics (*JEL*) (consisting of about 47000 words).

The study has focused on expressions used in textbooks and abstracts in order to represent argumentative activity within scientific procedures. Of course most reporting expressions may textually realise forms of reported argument. Not all of them, however, refer to some element of argumentativity: a verb like *say* is a potential — and often actual — operator for the projection of reported discourse, but it does not in itself refer to argumentativity. A verb like *show*, on the other hand, when used to refer to a verbal process, does indeed imply that a

Claim is made and that there is a Justification of the Claim(s) made, whether this is then made explicit or not. A verb like *state*, finally, though less explicitly argumentative does indeed signal a pragmatic function of the verbal activity referred to that is often associated with a Claim. This paper concentrates on the latter two types of meta-argumentative expressions i.e. expressions that more or less explicitly refer to argumentative procedures, either by denoting the speech event as argumentative (*state*) or by specifically identifying argumentative roles (*show*).

The corpora have been analysed using *Wordsmith Tools* (Scott 1996), and in particular studying frequency lists, key-words and concordances. Key-words are identified by the program on a mechanical basis by comparing patterns of frequency in two texts or corpora. A word is said to be a "positive key-word" if it occurs more often than would be expected by chance in comparison with a reference corpus. It is said to be a "negative key-word" if it occurs less often.[8] For this study, key-words have been identifie for both corpora in relation to a wider corpus of chapters on micro- and macro-economic issues used as a comparative database.[9]

Exploration of frequency lists and key-words helped me identify a list of meta-argumentative expressions that were foregrounded for various reasons in the quantitative data. These were subjected to closer scrutiny. In particular I studied all the occurrences of the lexical basis in their context in order to investigate two major issues:

1. *The object of the metasemiosis*, one of Silverstein's (1993) dimensions of metapragmatic-pragmatic functional relationship: here, rather than distinguishing, as Silverstein does, between metasemantics and metapragmatics, I have tried to classify expressions according to the role they played in identifying the problem and in identifying argumentative roles (according to Stati's (1994) major distinction between active and passive argumentative roles[10]);

2. Patterns of syntactic foregrounding in the two genres. Attention has been paid to the relative proportion of nominal and verbal references to argumentative procedures. Concordances have then been studied to work out a variety of quantitative data; here we focus on the thematic relevance given to verbs by attributing them main clause position. The grammatical subjects of main verb occurrences have been studied and classified according to Gosden's (1993) categories of functional roles:

- *participant* domain (ranging from more internal, writer-oriented, to more external, community-oriented);
- *discourse* domain (including discourse event, macro- and micro-entities, and interactive discourse);
- *hypothesized/objectivized* domain (references to viewpoint and to hypothesized entities or relations);
- *real world* domain (Gosden 1993: 65–67).[11]

An overview of the analysis

Key-words and frequencies

A brief look at key-words, as defined by Scott (1996), allows a preliminary consideration of the difference between introductory chapters and main chapters in the textbooks of my corpus. The tables below show selective data of positive (and negative) keywords divided according to two categories:

- discourse participants and products (potential argumentative voices)
- meta-argumentative expressions (references to argumentative procedure and features).

Let us start with discourse participants and products (potential argumentative voices). A brief consideration of Table 1a, below, shows the key role played in introductory chapters by the representation of the discipline itself, through references to the discipline and its sectors or nature (*economics, macroeconomics, microeconomics, science*), to the scientist as such (*economists, economist, scientists*), to a few paradigmatic cases (*Smith* and *Marx*), to the cognitive tools of research (*model, models, theory, theories, graphs* but also more general terms like *issues, topics, questions*), as well as products and procedures of scientific research like *statements, questions, judgements, predictions, forecasts*. Then there are a few words like *you* and *book* which clearly highlight the anticipatory function of introductory chapters. On the other hand there are references to cognitive tools like *factor, figure, curve*, which are identified as negative key-words and thus shown to be interestingly absent from introductory chapters when compared to the wider corpus.

References to cognitive tools, on the other hand, figure most prominently in the keywords of abstracts, as can be seen from Table 1b below. Here, as could be expected, we find that all positive keywords can be accounted for in terms of the research process, again identifying participants (*authors, author, Nash, Pareto, Bertrand, co-authors*), products (*paper, results, literature, data, papers, studies, essay, findings, research*), cognitive tools (*model, models, theorem, approach*). Negative keywords, on the other hand, may be clearly referred to features of textbooks in general, with their frequent reference to discourse participants as *we* (both inclusive and exclusive *we*) and their frequent recourse to expository procedures based on example and illustration (especially through graphs, with curves and points).

Further information could be gathered from the frequency lists of the two corpora. If we study frequencies above 0.02%, for example, we will find a further set of potential subjects of argumentative projection. When considering discourse participants, we will see that writer-oriented *we* features in both corpora, but introductory chapters will foreground another "founding father" (Keynes), while abstracts will give prominence to the collective nature of writing by foregrounding *co-authors* . When considering discourse units, we will once more find common elements (like *example*) and differentiating elements, reflecting the specific needs of the two genres. Expressions like *chapter, part, table, figure, diagram, definition* and *approach* are frequent in introductory textbooks, thus reflecting their need to refer to micro-textual units and to theoretical premises, whereas words like *study, outline, introduction, overview* and *research* are frequent in abstracts, where they are meant to capture the essence of the abstracted article.

If we now move on to our main focus, meta-pragmatic expressions, again we may see that there are common lexical elements. Some belong to the widest area of meta-argumentative expressions, like *issues* (which shows in both corpora a similar degree of keyness). Many refer to argumentative procedures, mostly to the semantic area of active roles (Claim and Justification), like *statements, assumptions, implications, show, prove....* others to the semantic area of passive roles, or roles with a passive component, like *agree, disagree*, used to represent dialogic interaction between argumentative voices. These are only key-words in textbook introductions, where they play a major role in the representation of debate within the disciplinary area. In abstracts, on the other hand, divergence of opinions or points of view may be related to lexical elements like *discusses* or *reviews*, which presuppose a plurality of voices as their object.[12]

Table 1a: Discourse participants and products in introductory chapters
(neg. key-words in italics)

Word		Frequence (%)	Frequence in reference corpus (%)	Keyness
1	ECONOMICS	352 (0.49%)	42 (0.02%)	671.2
4	ECONOMISTS	221 (0.31%)	86 (0.05%)	262.1
8	YOU	175 (0.24%)	94 (0.06%)	160.1
12	BOOK	68 (0.10%)	8	127.6
15	STATEMENTS	49 (0.07%)	2	104.7
16	QUESTIONS	86 (0.12%)	32 (0.02%)	103.7
22	MODELS	41 (0.06%)	1	89.8
24	ECONOMIST	55 (0.08%)	12	85.8
27	ISSUES	59 (0.08%)	18 (0.01%)	79.2
37	MACROECONOMICS	37 (0.05%)	6	62.9
41	SMITH	32 (0.04%)	4	57.8
43	MICROECONOMICS	29 (0.04%)	3	54.2
56	MODEL	60 (0.08%)	36 (0.02%)	48.1
60	SCIENCE	27 (0.04%)		46.3
62	THEORY	66 (0.09%)	45 (0.03%)	45.9
79	JUDGMENTS	21 (0.03%)	2	39.0
80	THEORIES	25 (0.03%)	5	38.9
85	PREDICTIONS	20 (0.03%)	2	36.7
97	MARX	14 (0.02%)	0	33.2
103	QUESTION	63 (0.09%)	54 (0.03%)	31.7
120	GRAPHS	12 (0.02%)	0	28.5
121	SCIENTISTS	19 (0.03%)	4	28.4
124	STATEMENT	30 (0.04%)	15	27.8
152	FORECASTS	16 (0.02%)	3	24.6
189	*FACTOR*	*6*	*199 (.12%)*	*69.0*
192	*FIGURE*	*39 (0.05%)*	*356 (0.21%)*	*73.3*
208	*CURVE*	*19 (.03%)*	*659 (.39%)*	*233.7*

The most important lexicalisations of argumentative procedures, however,
also had to be studied in frequency lists. Special use was made of *lemmatisation*, the possibility offered by the programme to store several entries together:
e.g. *show*, *shows*, *showing*, *showed* as members of the same lemma. Since references to argumentative procedures can be realised both nominally (*the argu-*

Table 1b: Discourse participants and products in abstracts
(neg. key-words in italics)

Word		Frequence (%)	Frequence in reference corpus (%)	Keyness
2	PAPER	196 (0.42%)	27 (0.02%)	570.9
3	MODEL	179 (0.38%)	36 (0.02%)	475.6
4	AUTHORS	112 (0.24%)	0	399.2
7	RESULTS	100 (0.21%)	29 (0.02%)	233.1
13	MODELS	48 (0.10%)	1	163.1
16	AUTHOR	38 (0.08%)	0	132.4
20	ARTICLE	36 (0.08%)	1	119.9
21	NASH	34 (0.07%)	1	112.7
39	LITERATURE	23 (0.05%)	0	82.9
43	DATA	66 (0.14%)	51 (0.03%)	80.8
51	PAPERS	20 (0.04%)	0	72.1
89	THEOREM	14 (0.03%)	0	50.5
134	STUDIES	26 (0.06%)	15	39.5
174	PARETO	16 (0.03%)	6	33.7
175	APPROACH	32 (0.07%)	28 (0.02%)	33.4
192	ESSAY	9 (0.02%)	0	32.4
237	BERTRAND	8 (0.02%)	0	28.8
246	FINDINGS	9 (0.02%)	1	27.4
201	CO-AUTHORS	9 (0.02%)	0	32.4
291	RESEARCH	17 (0.04%)	10	24.6
321	POINT	21 (0.04%)	270 (0.16%)	37.0
330	*EXAMPLE*	*16 (0.03%)*	*256 (0.15%)*	*41.0*
333	*WE*	*158 (0.33%)*	*969 (0.57%)*	*43.3*
367	*CURVE*	*3*	*659 (0.39%)*	*180.5*

ment is . . .) and verbally (*we argue that . . .*), the decision was taken to create lemmas that grouped together all the lexical entries that had the same lexical basis, whether nominal or verbal. The procedure helped us identify the most frequent lemmas in both corpora. Some frequencies are reported in Table 3 below.

The lemmas that are more frequent in introductory chapters include both items like *assume/assumption* which do not show great variation across genres, and items like *(dis)agree/agreement*, which do. The lexical items which

Table 2a: Meta-argumentative expressions in introductory chapters

Word		Freq.	%	Frequence in reference corpus	%	Keyness
15	STATEMENTS	49	(0.07%)	2		104.7
16	QUESTIONS	86	(0.12%)	32	(0.02%)	103.7
36	ASSUMPTIONS	49	(0.07%)	16		63.0
54	DISAGREE	25	(0.03%)	2		48.3
79	JUDGMENTS	21	(0.03%)	2		39.0
85	PREDICTIONS	20	(0.03%)	2		36.7
103	QUESTION	63	(0.09%)	54	(0.03%)	31.7
105	PREDICT	15	(0.02%)	1		31.5
114	AGREE	20	(0.03%)	4		30.6
115	DISAGREEMENT	20	(0.03%)	4		30.6
118	DISPUTES	12	(0.02%)	0		28.5

show higher frequencies in textbooks are fewer and not all of them represent scientific procedures in the same way as they are represented in abstracts. Lemmas like *think, suppose/supposition* and *dispute*, which play a minor but significant role in the representation of argumentative procedures in introductory textbook chapters occur with no significant frequency in abstracts. It is also obvious that equal frequencies do not necessarily imply any similarity in lexico-grammatical patterns, as we will see when analysing *argue/argument* below.

References to argumentative procedures were investigated on a lexical basis, considering both verbal and nominal forms. The investigation focused on variation in meanings and in morpho-syntactic patterns. The analysis of meta-argumentative expressions in terms of the object of the metasemiosis shows that they can be grouped according to whether they refer to:

–   problem identification (*examine, consider, investigate/ investigation*);
–   argument as an interactive event implying a multiplicity of opinions (*argue, discuss, disputes, questions*);
–   active roles (*claim/counter-claim, show, find, think, explain/ explanation, state/ statement, assume/ assumption, imply/ implication, suppose, predict, indicate*);
–   passive roles (*agree, disagree, objection*).

Table 2b: Meta-argumentative expressions in abstracts

Word		Freq.	%	Frequence in reference corpus	%	Keyness
17	EXAMINES	40	(0.08%)	2		129.2
22	STATE	63	(0.13%)	32	(0.02%)	108.5
26	DISCUSSES	30	(0.06%)	0		103.6
29	CONSIDERS	31	(0.07%)	2		97.0
49	IMPLICATIONS	28	(0.06%)	5		73.7
50	ANALYZES	20	(0.04%)	0		712.1
69	ESTIMATES	34	(0.07%)	17	(0.01%)	578.0
81	SHOW	59	(0.13%)	60	(0.04%)	52.7
98	REVIEWS	13	(0.03%)	0		46.8
103	PROVE	14	(0.03%)	1		45.2
134	STUDIES	26	(0.06%)	15		39.5
135	EVIDENCE	30	(0.06%)	21	(0.01%)	39.1
137	PROPOSED	26	(0.06%)	16		37.6
139	ANALYZED	13	(0.03%)	2		37.2
151	EXAMINED	15	(0.03%)	4		36.6
194	ASSESSES	9	(0.02%)	0		32.4
195	INVESTIGATES	9	(0.02%)	0		32.4
205	ARGUES	10	(0.02%)	1		31.0
214	INVESTIGATE	15	(0.03%)	6		30.5
222	ESTIMATION	12	(0.03%)	3		30.0

Most lexical items examined did not show any significant variation in meanings across genres, apart from *argue*. The occurrences highlight both basic meanings of the lexical unit: argument can be a set of statements supporting an opinion (the "claim+justification" meaning) and a disagreement over a specific issue. Abstracts invariably use the various lexicalisations in the sense of supporting an opinion, whereas textbooks actualise both meanings: 28% (13/45) of the occurrences realise the "disagreement" sense of the word. The reference to disagreement often encapsulates more specific occurrences introducing a variety of positions with their justifications and thus offers an interrelated view of the two basic meanings.

Patterns of syntactic foregrounding and collocation, on the other hand, show a few dominant trends. Analysis of nominal and verbal forms indicates

Table 3: Frequencies of main meta-argumentative lemmas

Lemmas	Introduction Chapters %	Abstracts %
Analyse/analysis	0.13	0.28
Argue/argument	0.06	0.06
assume/assumption	0.13	0.12
Consider/consideration	0.07	0.17
(Dis)agree/agreement	0.13	0.04
Discuss/discussion	0.07	0.13
Dispute	0.03	-
Estimate/estimation	0.01	0.17
Examine/examination	0.05	0.17
Explain/explanation	0.10	0.06
Find/findings	0.11	0.12
Imply/implication	0.04	0.11
Indicate/indication	0.01	0.05
Predict/prediction	0.07	0.04
Show	0.14	0.28
Suggest/suggestion	0.03	0.07
Suppose/supposition	0.03	-
Think/thought	0.07	-

that textbooks are characterised by a higher degree of nominalisation. This may be related to the fact that nominalisation turns argumentative procedures into objects of scientific exposition and thus suits the main pedagogic functions of introductory chapters. Patterns of syntactic foregrounding also confirm that textbooks tend to thematise discourse participants, whereas abstracts tend to prefer subjects that refer to human agents. The trends can be illustrated through a few examples.

An analysis of the occurrences of the lemma *show*, including only verbal forms like *show, shows, showed, shown, showing*, reveals very clearly the patterns of grammatical foregrounding. The process is systematically thematised in abstracts, where it is not only very frequent, but also mostly given main clause position: in 92% of the occurrences (120/131). The percentage is much lower in textbooks where 74% (72/97) of the occurrences have main clause position. The most striking variation, however, can be noticed in the functional role of grammatical subjects (Table 4 below). Textbooks offer a more varied

Table 4: Show: Main clause subjects

	Reference	Introductory Chapters	Total	Abstracts	Total
participant domain	authors: external internal empty theme	we (19) he [Smith] (1) economists (1)	21/72 (29%)	authors/author (24) we (17) they (10) I (1) he (1) my paper (1)	54/120 (45%)
discourse domain	external d. units empty d. theme micro-unit macro-unit event/ process	studies (1) theories (1) figure (5) table (7) exhibit (3) production possibility frontier (8) points (5) picture (1) items (1) numbers (1) section (1) example (2) argument (1) evidence (1) book (1) analysis (1) result (1)	41/72 (57%)	anaphoric it (4) article (2) paper (8) analysis (1) note (1) literature (1) tables (1) example (1)	19/120 (15%)
hypothesized / objectivized domain	hypothetical entity empty theme (propositions) viewpoint	experience (1) observation (1) combination (1) possibility (2)	5/72 (7%)	anticipatory it (24) result/s (6) anaphoric they (3) analysis (2) simulations (2) effects (2) expression (1) statistics (1) formulation (1) rate (1) equilibrium (1) conjecture (1)	45/120 (37%)

Table 4 (*continued*)

		Reference	Introductory Chapters	Total	Abstracts	Total
real world domain (Phenomenal)	entity process		standards (1) cost (1) countries (1) price increase (1) percentage changes (1)	5/72 (7%)	firm (1) a coalition structure (1)	2/120 (2%)

pattern of subjects, with a clear preference for discourse products and in particular for formal representations as "showing". In abstracts, the preference clearly goes to participant domain (*we show, authors show*) and to the objectivized, hypothesised world (*results show, or it is shown that...*)

The case of *examine*, on the other hand, can be taken to show how the nominal and verbal forms *(examination, examine)* follow the general trend. Nominalisation shows up more frequently in textbooks (3/39, i.e. 8%) than in abstracts (3/81, i.e. 4%). The verbal element is often foregrounded by main clause position in abstracts (64/78, i.e. 82%), whereas in textbooks it is more often found in subclauses (*setting up experiments to examine, analyse sth. by examining sth. else*) (23/33, i.e. 70%). The analysis of the few main clause subjects is presented in Table 5 below. The data shows a reversed trend in terms of preferred subjects: there is in fact a clear preference for participant domain (*we examine*) in textbooks, whereas abstracts prefer discourse domain subjects (*the paper examines*).

A further set of problems could be illustrated by considering *agree/disagree* (*agree, disagree, agreement, disagreement*). The textbook corpus presents 89 occurrences of *agree/disagree*, 33 in the semantic area of "agreement" and 56 of "disagreement". Thirty eight of the 89 occurrences are nominal — 10 occurrences of *agreement* (as against 23 occurrences of its verbal form) and 28 of *disagreement* (as against 30 occurrences of the verb *to disagree*), all of them acting as projecting frameworks. Once again then nominalisation is fairly high (43%) and it plays a central role in structuring the sentence. The corpus of abstracts presents a much lower number of occurrences of the lexical items (22). There is a single occurrence of *disagreement*, only in its nominal form, 16 nominal forms of *agreement* and 5 of the verb *to agree*. All nominal forms, however, have nothing to do with agreement as an argumentative procedure

Table 5: Examine – main clause subjects

Domain	Reference	Textbooks	Total (%)	Abstracts	Total (%)
participant domain	authors: external internal empty theme	we (6) macroeconom- ics (1)	7/10 (70%)	a western authority (1) proper nouns (3) authors/author (3) we (4) they (2) government official (1)	14/64 (22%)
discourse domain	external d. units empty d. theme micro-unit macro-unit event/ process	chapter 5 (1)	1/10 (10%)	anaphoric it (2) article (3) paper/s (19) ellipsis (7) study (4) analysis (1) review (1) sections (1)	38/64 (59%)
hypothesized / objectivized domain	hypothetical entity empty theme (propositions) viewpoint	statistics (1) experiments (1)	2/10 (20%)	details (1) forms (1) characterizations (1) growth (1) behavior (1) approaches (1) disadvantages (1) prospects and problems (1) characteristics (1) properties (1) relationship (1), factors (1)	12/64 (19%)
real world domain (phenomenal)	entity process				

and simply refer to the world that is the object of the discipline: most of them refer to legal documents or to examples of situations in the light of game theory and they are therefore never used in order to represent the activity of the abstracted paper itself. The same can be said of the five instances of the verb *to agree*, which are not thematised and belong to the world of the data of the papers or to their assumptions.

This is quite clearly a lexical set which shows very different patterns in the

MARINA BONDI

Table 6: Agree/disagree (9 agree + 19 disagree)

Domain	Reference	Lexical items a/d	Total
participant domain	authors: external internal empty theme	we (2/2) physicists(0/1) doctors(0/1) economists (5/7) people (1/2) they (economists) (0/3)	24/28 (86%)
discourse domain	external d. units empty d. theme micro-unit macro-unit event/ process		
hypothesized / objectivized domain	hypothetical entity empty theme (propositions) viewpoint		
real world domain (Phenomenal)	entity process	they (1/1) people(0/1) teachers (0/1)	4/28 (14%)

two corpora. In abstracts the occurrences do not play any major role in the representation of scientific procedures at all, whereas in textbooks they have been seen to be key-words, highly frequent expressions and mostly associated with the discipline itself or with economists in general (about two thirds of the occurrences are). *Agreement* and *disagreement*, then — which are analytically very useful categories in describing argument — turn out to be often introduced as representative of scientific dialogue in textbooks but certainly realised by other means in abstracts, where they are basically only used to refer to the world of economic agents.

Table 6 above shows the functional role of the subjects of the relatively few main verb forms found in the textbook corpus. Abstracts have a single example of the verb in main clause position (with a real world subject: *Three Atlantic provinces*).

Reflexivity across genres

Textbooks: Introductory Chapters

From the point of view of language variation and register studies, textbooks seem to share some of the most interesting features that Christie (1997) has studied in pedagogic discourse, in particular the notion of the different registers operating within them: the regulative and the instructive, which she adopts from Bernstein (1990). The first order or regulative register refers to sets of language choices which are principally involved in establishing goals for teaching-learning activities, and with fostering and maintaining the direction of the activities until the achievement of the goals. The second order or instructional register refers to language choices in which the knowledge and associated skills being taught are realised. (Christie 1997: 136). A powerful methodology Christie derives from Bernstein is the focus on the relationship between the two registers, where the regulative (pedagogic discourse) is seen as "projecting" the instructional discourse of knowledge. The relation between the two registers is thus seen as metaphorically modelled on that of projection at the level of the clause complex (Halliday 1985, 1994: 219). In projection, something said or thought is "reinstated" through some other discourse; in this case, the discourse of economics as a science is reinstated for the purposes of the pedagogic activity.

Introductory chapters are normally devoted to a presentation of the discipline and its methodology. The identification of problem areas and the representation of scientific procedures play a major role in this process of gradually drawing a map of the discipline. A study of the language resources involved in this process identifies an admittedly fuzzy set of lexicalisations of cognitive and verbal processes — many of which representing science as argument — that may be taken as key-words in the representation of scientific discourse.

Extracts below provide examples of this reflexive activity. Many of their lexical items refer to scientific procedures by identifying theoretical-cognitive constructs (like *theories, evidence, assumptions, problems, implications*) or discursive constructs (like *questions, definitions, enumeration*).

Example 1 provides an example of a topic identification move. It is perhaps the most extreme example of a long series of moves by which introductory chapters identify economic problems often presenting them in the form of questions. The chapter section — under the heading of *Economic issues* — opens with a series of 18 questions, which are then explicitly referred to in what follows:

(1)   These are a few of the questions with which economists concern
       themselves, and on which the theories of economics are designed to
       shed some light. Such a list may give you a better idea of the scope
       of economics than could be obtained at this stage from an enumera-
       tion of the common textbook definitions. (Lipsey, chapter 1)

These problem identification moves often lead on to more explicit discussions
of the argumentative nature of a question, as we can see in example (2), which
explicitly tackles a methodological issue — the *ceteris paribus* assumption.
The extract provides an example of how topic identification can be followed
by methodological statements about economic theoretical argument, which is
presented as based on assumptions, rather than evidence, etc.

(2)   Questions in economics often concern the effects of one change on
       people's behavior or on the outcome of the economy. For example,
       we discuss theoretically the extent to which a consumer buys more
       or less of something when he or she becomes richer. When we do
       this, we assume that there is no change in the prices of anything
       that is bought, so that we can isolate the effects of the increase in
       income. Economists use the *ceteris paribus* assumption when they
       are examining a problem theoretically; that is, when they are not
       using evidence from a real world situation. The difficulty of doing
       controlled experiments in economics implies that this assumption
       often cannot be used when we are assessing the implications of
       information on what people have actually been observed doing.
       (Craven, chapter 1)

Example 3, on the other hand, illustrates moves in which, rather than providing
a picture of how economists argue or should argue, we are offered examples of
specific ways of arguing, through a stylised representation of debate within the
discipline. Notice the variety of reporting expressions (*according to, attacked,
said*) as well as of expressions referring to argument evaluation: *conclusions
have stood up remarkably well, one stood out in its simplicity.*

(3)   According to Smith, the best policy is *laissez-faire* — leave it
       alone. Government intervention usually makes things worse. For
       example, [...]. Smith's work has been refined and modified during
       the past 200 years, but many of his laissez-faire conclusions have
       stood up remarkably well. For example, there is still a very strong

economic argument against high tariffs on imported goods. In recent decades one of the principal areas of international co-operation has been the negotiation of lower tariffs.

A century and a half after the appearance of Smith's *Wealth of Nations* (that is, during the Great Depression of the 1930s), John Maynard Keynes wrote his *General Theory of Employment, Interest and Money* (also known, more simply, as the *General Theory*). In this book Keynes (which rhymes with Danes) attacked the laissez-faire tradition of economics. The government, said Keynes, has the duty to put the unemployed back to work. Of the several ways in which this could be done, one stood out in its simplicity. By building public works, such as roads, post offices, and dams, the government could directly provide jobs, and thus provide a cure for the Depression. (Wonnacot, chapter 1)

References to argumentative procedures are clearly set on a secondary discourse plan. The relationship of meta-argumentative expressions to the communicative event they refer to is what Silverstein (1993) would call "mutual calibration". The next example on the other hand exemplifies cases of "reflexive calibration", in which the textualised event coincides with the communicative event in progress. Example 4 is representative of a great number of cases, frequent in introductory chapters as well as in main chapters, where the argumentative procedures in focus are rather those established in the book itself. The reader is asked to make assumptions, and the figures are there to *show* things.

(4)   Assume for simplicity that a country produces only two goods, food and cloth. Figure 1 shows the different combinations of these two commodities which can be produced. The vertical axis measures the quantity of food in tonnes and the horizontal axis measures the quantity of cloth in metres. The straight line AB is the production possibility frontier. It shows that when all resources are efficiently employed in the production of food, OA tonnes can be produced and when all resources are employed in the production of cloth, OB metres can be produced. All points on the production possibility frontier represent combinations of food and cloth which the country can just produce when all its resources are employed. [...]

The production possibility frontier thus provides us with an illustration of the problem of scarcity and choice facing a country when deciding what goods and services to produce. The analysis of production is dealt with in greater detail in Chapter 2. (Baumol, chapter 1)

Abstracts

The representation of scientific procedures — and of argumentative procedures in particular — also plays a major role in abstracts. The lexicalisations of scientific procedures can even be seen as *constitutive* in the definition of abstracts as a genre. Many studies of the relationship between an abstract and the abstracted article focus on how abstracts represent the structure and content of the article itself in a multiple semiotic process in which words are used to represent verbal objects. Abstracts are meant to represent perhaps the most important activity carried out within the community: scientific argument/exposition in research articles. The article itself and its textual structure become objects to be represented, perhaps with a specific emphasis.

In a historical survey of the development of abstracts in economics (Bondi 1997a) I have found that their *representationality*, i.e. syntactic foregrounding of metadiscursive references to the original article and its procedures, can be seen as a distinctive feature in the development of abstracts (as a genre) in contemporary scientific discourse. Representationality can be identified with an increasing use of metadiscursive references in general, or specifically with a writing style which increasingly foregrounds discourse procedures by giving them main-clause position and which thematises discourse products and producers rather than discourse objects: *the results show..., we analyse...* rather than *inflation is seen...* The increasing focus on metadiscursive features of abstracts suggests a growing awareness of the nature and characteristics of the genre, as well as of the role it now plays within the scientific community. The pervasiveness of the genre in contemporary scientific discourse, as well as its growing importance in a world where scientific production has increased to otherwise unmanageable limits, emphasise the need for more detailed analyses of the different subgenres of abstracts, of their language features and of their variation across disciplines.

The basically metalinguistic nature of the genre is clearly marked by its typical structures, by the recurrent pattern of main clauses centred around mental or verbal processes and by the thematisation of discourse products or procedures. Extracts 5 and 6 offer examples of abstracts of empirical research papers, where common expressions are used in slightly different contexts (*this paper offers a model /a simple model is proposed*), then there are references to data and to the testing of a theory or of a hypothesis: in one case *the results show*, and in the other the authors (*we*) show and *results are explained*.

(5)   *This paper offers a model* of the allocation of funds in Chinese state-owned enterprises (SOE) and *provides an empirical test of the theory using* firm-level *data. The paper explains* why bank loans and grants coexist with self-financing, which SOEs take out loans, and why subsidies on loan interest payments exist. *The model is based on* heterogeneous SOEs, asymmetric information, sales taxes, and quota requirements. *The results show* that reforms of enterprise finance must come as a package, *suggesting* that the interlocking nature of reform measures should be considered in deciding the direction of further policy modification. (*Econlit* 1997).

(6)   A *simple model* of political popularity, as recorded by opinion polls of voting intentions, *is proposed. We show* that, as a consequence of aggregating heterogeneous poll responses under certain *assumptions* about the evolution of individual opinions, the time series of poll *data should exhibit* long memory characteristics. In an *analysis* of the monthly Gallup *data* on party support in the UK, *we confirm* that the series have long memory and further *show* them to be virtually pure 'fractional noise' processes. *An explanation* of the latter *result* is *offered. We study* the role of economic *indicators* in *predicting* swings in support, *perform event analyses* and *use our estimates to generate post-sample forecasts* to April 1997. (*Econlit* 1997).

Examples 7 and 8 present a different structure, which is not unusual in economics discourse. They do not simply reveal the "internal structure" of argument — its internal consistency — but also its interactive patterns. Example 8 does it very clearly, by referring to an external discourse event: a theory produced by some other article. The analysis of this "counter-discourse" occupies all the opening sequence of the abstract which then proceeds to juxtapose the writers' claim:

(7)   *Piccione and Rubinstein argue* that a seemingly paradoxical form
        of time inconsistency can arise in games of imperfect recall. *Their
        argument depends on* calculating the expected value of a game
        from the standpoint of a player in the middle of play. *We claim* that
        this concept is not well defined in games with absentmindedness
        (where two nodes on a path can be in the same information set)
        without additional *assumptions*. *We show* that, under some reason-
        able *assumptions*, no time inconsistency arises. *Different assump-
        tions* will *validate* Piccione and Rubinstein's calculations, but
        these are such as to remove the appearance of paradox. (*Econlit*
        1997).

Example 8 shows a similar pattern, although there is no explicit attribution of
the rejected hypothesis to any external authority: the article's analysis is simply contrasted with what evidence would imply:

(8)   *This article investigates* the forecast value of U.S. interventions in
        the foreign exchange market, which have become increasingly
        rare in the last seven years. *Evidence* of superior forecasting skill
        would imply that U.S. monetary authorities typically act with bet-
        ter information than the market and that intervention could alter
        foreign exchange traders' expectations about rates. *However, the
        analysis* presented here *shows* that this was not the case for recent
        interventions (May 1, 1990 – March 19, 1997), and that official
        transactions by U.S. monetary authorities do *not* seem to improve
        the efficiency with which the foreign exchange market obtains
        information. (*Econlit* 1997).

Comparative discussion

Table 7 below reviews some of the main differences we have noticed.
Textbooks are particularly interested in representing the argumentative procedures of the community: the focus of their representation is on *what* economists think or should think, in forms of both self- and other- projection (intended to offer the reader a map of the text and a map of the discipline). Their meta-
argumentative activity centres on generic reference (often introduced by general verbs like *think*) and nominalisation, with its capacity for representing
argumentative procedures as things. Meta-argumentative expressions high-

Table 7: Review of differences between introductory chapters and abstracts

Features	Introductory Chapters	Abstracts
Dominant macro-function:	Ideational: representation of the procedures in the community	Textual: Representation of the abstracted article
Focus of the representation on:	what economists think or should think	how researchers go about their research
Reference	Generic	Specific
Pragmatic status	Both factual and non-factual Both self- and other-projection	Factual projection of abstracted article
Nominalisation	High	Low
Thematisation	Low	Very high
Structures highlighted	Moves like: – problem identification – representation of methodological tools – guiding the reader through the argument	Textual patterns: – based on structure of inquiry (problem - method- results-conclusion) – based on argumentative dialogue (discourse and counter-discourse)

light moves like: identifying a problem, presenting methodological tools, representing debate within the discipline, guiding the reader through argument.

As far as abstracts are concerned, their representationality has a high degree of syntactic foregrounding. Their syntactic patterns clearly identify two well defined semantic areas: the area of scientific procedures and that of scientific objects, identified by opposition. Their metalinguistic activity is clearly focused on specific reference, and specifically on reference to the abstracted paper, rather than to the variety of situations that textbooks reflect. The focus of their representation is on *how* researchers go about their research. Two standards patterns can be highlighted in their textual structures: patterns based on the structure of inquiry (identification of the problem — methods — results — conclusions); patterns based on argumentative dialogue, with discourse and counter-discourse. This pattern is explicitly discussed in textbooks, but more clearly exemplified in abstracts, often signalled by connectors, negatives, parallel structures, etc.

Pedagogic implications

Throughout this paper I have emphasised the usefulness of a corpus-based approach for studying how academic writers combine the linguistic resources available to them. I have also shown the need to consider the complex network of options that are available to writers against the background of accepted genres and contextual features. The methodology adopted for the analysis has combined internal study with comparative examination across genres. Comparison is the foundation of any study of language varieties and it is certainly essential to genre analysis. It is only by comparing textbooks to other genres, like research article or abstracts, that we can actually substantiate any claim as to what characterises a textbook. The study has also shown how relatively straightforward computer-based analytical techniques can provide real data on which current models of language description and production can be tested. The implications of this kind of work in the field of foreign language teaching deserve a few conclusive remarks.

The general development of corpus linguistics (Ajimer and Altenberg 1991, Sinclair 1991, Svartvik 1992, McEnery and Wilson 1996, Thomas and Short 1996, Biber, Conrad and Reppen 1998, Kennedy 1998) cannot be ignored by anyone with an interest in language study. Corpus linguistics in general has drawn attention to features of language description that have great relevance for the teacher. It has offered language teachers and students grammars that are descriptively more adequate. It has drawn attention to the notion of a probabilistic grammar (Halliday 1991) and to lexical patterns, as well as emphasising the idea that lexis and grammar cannot be totally separate domains (Sinclair 1987, 1991). A wide range of studies has focused, for example, on the implications of corpus linguistics for the development of both grammatical (Mindt 1996) and lexical syllabuses (Sinclair and Renouf 1988, Willis 1990).

Foreign language teachers' main interest, however, lies in small corpora of specialised texts that can be easily compiled and analysed. As shown for example by Henry and Roseberry (1996), the small-scale analysis of specialised corpora has a more direct bearing on the needs of a language teacher than the large corpora that are now available for large-scale language research. The greatest potential for the teacher is in accessible tools which can be used to discover the properties of corpora that they themselves have selected. Word frequency lists, concordance programs, collocation analysis, as well as tagging and parsing software[13] can be shown to offer the teacher tools for self-development and for more effective materials and course design.

Comparing moves across genres, our analysis has shown patterns of variation that were not considered by many EAP teaching materials and general descriptions of the discourse of economics. Further research on other features might bring to light other less visible patterns, which may be of use to students, teachers and researchers. This analysis has also supported the claim for a genre-based approach to the language syllabus (Swales 1990, Bhatia 1993, Dudley-Evans and St.John 1998) and for students' exposure to a variety of genres. Though focused on a few language features and their relationship to some specific moves, the analysis has provided an example of the qualitative if not quantitative role played by language variation across genres in the field of economics discourse. ESP and EAP language materials based on an inadequate range of genres do not only misrepresent the rhetoric and the communicative purposes of the special interest area, but they also offer a partial representation of how some key concepts find their verbal expression in the variety of genres that make up the discourse areas that may be relevant to the students' curricula.

The implications of corpus-based studies in the field of language teaching, however, are not limited to providing teachers with adequate descriptions, samples and examples of the language they teach. Corpus-based research has also offered teachers a wealth of suggestions on how to use computer-based techniques in the language classroom (Johns 1986, Johns and King 1991, Tribble and Jones 1990, Murison-Bowie 1993) in forms of data-driven, inductive learning. More recently, attention has been drawn to the need to start from the pedagogic context, making sure that the patterns highlighted by corpus work emerge from contexts that facilitate learning and that combine analysis with communicative use of language in problem solving tasks (Aston 1995, 1997; Gavioli 1997).

The most important implications of corpus-based activities, however, seem to me those that can be included within the area of learning about language. Language awareness — irrespective of the role we think it might play as part of learning language — can play an important role in developing critical skills. Students of economics, for example, could become much better readers by developing an awareness of the forms and functions of different meta-argumentative expressions and by learning to understand the different role they play in the different genres, according to the different communicative purposes and to the different "tenors" of the interaction. Student-conducted corpus work can be explored as one of the many methodological choices open to the teacher in the field of language awareness.

The corpora used for this study, for example, were compiled for the needs of students of economics learning English as a foreign language in Italy. The corpora provided material for language focus work on the structure of abstracts (Worksheet 1 in the Appendix). Students were offered sets of abstracts and asked to:

a. underline or circle the subjects and verbs of the main clauses;
b. classify them according to given parameters;
c. identify the dominant verbal forms in frequency lists;
d. identify the most frequent subjects in the concordance of a verbal form (*show*) and check on concordances of near synonyms whether the verbs were actually found associated with the same subjects.

Students could then be given parallel sets of examples or concordances with gapped elements to check whether they were able to recognise the missing elements through a process of hypothesis formulation and testing.

The same corpora were also used with undergraduates specialising in English for a sequence of activities on meta-argumentative expressions across genres combining internal analysis (Worksheet 1) with comparative analysis (Worksheet 2). Students were asked to collect a brief corpus of examples of uses of meta-argumentative expressions (*show, examine/examination* and *discuss/discussion)* in the textbook corpus. A first attempt was made to classify them according to some given dictionary definitions. Discussion over the results of the first exploration led to some disagreement and therefore to a critical questioning of the given models.

Students then observed that some areas of meanings largely dominated their corpus because we were dealing with examples of academic discourse. A clearer focus on textual genre, on the role of meta-argument in its definition then led students to notice that these were probably involved in different moves. Examples of different functions of reflexive moves were offered for preliminary consideration; on the basis of the classification offered, students were then asked to identify the functions realised in a further set of examples.

Concordances showing the different nominal and verbal patterns in the two genres considered (introductory textbook chapter and abstract) were used to highlight the different patterns in the same expressions that had been studied in the textbook corpus. Analysis of a few examples from the corpus led to the identification of the two basic textual structures of economics abstracts: those based on the process of inquiry and those based on argumentative dialogue. Closer group study of other full texts helped students identify the structures, classify the examples and reconstruct a wider picture of the options open to the writer of an abstract when trying to represent discursive procedures in articles.

Comparison across genres was then explored by focusing on collocation. Students were first asked to study references to potential argumentative voices in the two corpora. Working on the concordances of these items, they were asked to find meta-argumentative expressions in the list of collocates produced by *Wordsmith Tools* (Scott 1996) and thus led to notice how collocation differed. Closer analysis of concordances of meta-argumentative expressions focused on the functional roles of main clause subjects and further highlighted variation across genres.

A particularly rewarding extension activity on this issue was based on a study of the occurrences of meta-argumentative expressions in a collection of abstracts from academic journals in a variety of disciplines. Significant differences were noticed for example when comparing the data in economics abstracts with small corpora of abstracts in management sciences and in literature, which showed a much greater incidence of thematisation of "real world" subjects and different patterns in personal and impersonal forms.

Having the relevant corpus in machine-readable form or having access to computerised corpora proved to be very helpful both as a starting point and as an extension to these reflective activities, providing wider and easily collectible sets of examples. We could in fact work on a systematic collection of instances of many relevant units and study their immediate context in concordances of varying dimensions.

These simple techniques of corpus analysis allow students to work with real data and train them in fundamental learning and analytical skills. In the sequence of activities above, for example, they have practised the basic skills of language awareness in a typical sequence:

a. Noticing language features and validating existing representations of knowledge;
b. Selecting data and working at their classification;
c. Formulating and testing hypotheses.

An attitude of inquiry towards language constitutes the necessary basis for developing language awareness and for fostering autonomous language improvement. Research-based activities of language analysis do indeed involve learning strategies of various kinds: cognitive (inference, induction, deduction, grouping, etc.), metacognitive (planning, checking, testing, monitoring etc.) and social/affective (cooperation, questioning for clarification, etc.).

The general aim of a language awareness component becomes even more important in teacher education (see also Bondi 1999). Its aim is not simply to structure student teachers' knowledge about the language, but more widely to develop an autonomous and research-based approach to self-development and to teaching practice, with reference to both the content and the methodology of EFL teaching. Student teachers should be trained to design and compile their own reference corpora, in order to learn how to select language samples that may be suitable for teaching within a given framework. This can be done by involving the students in the creation, as well as analysis, of data-bases for given teaching situations. In this kind of activity it is always important to emphasise that there can be nothing definitive about it: it might be better to explicitly reject any claim for exhaustivity, by asking student teachers to work on a couple of genres or subgenres only. What really matters is the confidence students gain by being able to work out their own analysis and the skills they develop, not the product itself. Corpus-based reflection activities are not meant to produce neat descriptions, but to develop the students' awareness and power of observation, as well as their learning skills and strategies.

Notes

1 "A genre comprises a class of communicative events, the members of which share some set of communicative purposes. These purposes are recognised by the expert members of the parent discourse community, and thereby constitute the rationale for the genre. This rationale shapes the schematic structures of the discourse and influences and constrains choice of content and style. Communicative purpose is both a privileged criterion and one that operates to keep the scope of a genre as here conceived narrowly focused on comparable rhetorical action. In addition to purpose, exemplars of a genre exhibit various patterns of similarity in terms of structure, style, content and intended audience." (Swales, 1990: 68).

2 In a wider sense we can regard as metadiscourse all the expressions that writers use to help readers organise, classify and evaluate propositions in the text. We would therefore include connectors, rhetorical questions, recapitulation of information from a previous place in the text, etc.

3 Vande Kopple (1985) provides one of the best known classifications on the basis of a major distinction between textual and interpersonal metadiscourse. Textual metadiscourse

includes text connectives, code glosses used to help readers grasp the meanings of expressions, action markers (or illocution markers) specifying the discourse act performed by the author and "narrators" used to let the reader know who said something. Interpersonal metadiscourse includes modality markers attitude markers and commentary used to draw readers into dialogue with the author. Revisions of the schema can be found in Crismore (1989), Crismore et al. (1993) and Hyland (1998, 1999),

4   "Projection" is the term used by Halliday (1985: 196) to refer to the general notion of the logical-semantic relationship whereby discourse can instate a locution or an idea in forms of representation of linguistic representation. Projection is thus a cover term for all forms of representation of speech and thought, whether quotes (direct speech) or reports (indirect speech).

5   Argumentative roles may be defined with Stati (1990:16) as "la fonction, offensive ou défensive, que la phrase est capable d'exercer dans le mécanisme de la persuasion: preuve, rectification, conclusion, etc." This may be distinguished from the illocutionary force of a speech act, although both functions pertain to the area of pragmalinguistics, and — in their reflexive dimension — to metapragmatics (see Verschueren, 1995; Lucy, 1993: 11–21 and Silverstein, 1993: 33–35). In classifying argumentative roles, Stati (1990) considers the following categories: a) "assentiment, confirmation, adhésion"; b) "justification, preuve"; c) "concession"; d) "rectification"; e) "objection"; f) "contestation, désaccord, dissentiment"; g) "critique, accusation, reproche" (65–85).

6   On the "representationality" of abstracts, see Bondi (1997a). Genre studies of the structure of abstracts can be found in Swales (1990), Bhatia (1993), Kaplan et al. (1994) Santos (1996) and Hyland (2000): 63–84).

7   Baumol, W.J. and A.S. Blinder, *Economics. Principles and Policy*, 4th Edition, Orlando, Harcourt Brace Jovanovich, 1988; Begg, D., S. Fischer and R. Dornbusch, *Economics*. British Edition, Maidenhead, McGraw-Hill, 1983; Craven, J., *Introduction to Economics*, 2nd Edition, Blackwell, Oxford, 1990; Dolan, E.G. and D.E. Linsey, *Economics*, 5th Edition, NY, Holt, Reinhart and Winston, 1988; Fischer, S. and R. Dornbusch, *Economics*, NY, McGraw-Hill, 1983; Hardwick, P., B. Kahn and J. Langmead, *An Introduction to Modern Economics*, 3rd Edition, London, Longman, 1990; Lipsey, R., *An Introduction to Positive Economics*, 7th Edition, London, Weidenfeld and Nicholson, 1989; Samuelson, P.A. and W.H. Nordhaus, *Economics*, 14th Edition, NY, McGraw-Hill, 1992; Stanlake, G.F., *Introductory Economics*, 5th Edition, London Longman, 1989; Wonnacot, P. and R. Wonnacot, *Economics*, 2nd Edition, NY, McGraw-Hill, 1982.

8   For more information on the statistical tools used to determine key-ness see Scott (1996) and Scott, this volume.

9   The reference corpus amounts to nearly 170,000 words. It consists of 20 full chapters from the textbooks considered for the small corpus of introductory chapters. Two chapters have been selected from each textbook, one on micro-economics issues, with a view to representing the widest range of topics.

10   Particular attention has been paid by Stati (1994) to a distinction between *active* moves "which essentially tend (a) to convince the addressee to accept (adopt, share...) a certain opinion or (b) to determine him to assume a certain behaviour" (1994: 259) — typically

Claim and *Justification* — and *passive* moves, which are "related to the effects of the active moves, i.e. with the process of 'being persuaded'. By uttering a sentence which plays a passive role the arguer: (a) accepts or rejects the partner's argumentation, and in doing so, he proves the success or the failure of the partner's move, or (b) he expresses his wish (his availability / willingness) to be convinced by his partner"(1994: 259). Stati proposes a tentative inventory divided into two sets: Passive moves (*Agreement; Confirmation; Acknowledgement; Concession, Disagreement; Request for explication; Request for support; Conjecture;*) and Moves including a passive component (*Antithesis; Rectification; Objection*).

11   This last category has been interpreted as roughly coinciding with MacDonald's (1992) "Phenomenal". This might be a more adequate denomination for a discipline like economics, which often deals with hypothetical rather than factual worlds. This feature of economics — discussed for example in Bondi (1996) — suggests using at least inverted commas in referring to a world as 'real'.

12   Direct comparison of the two corpora also produces a set of key-words but it is more problematic for a number of reasons. This confirms most of the trends I have already noticed and adds material for further comments, for example: the higher degree of key-ness of nominal element (*statements, questions*) in textbooks as against the key-ness of verbal expressions (*considers, examines, discusses, state*) in abstracts. The key-ness of nouns referring to expository procedures like example in textbooks is set against the keyness of references to research constructs like data and results in abstracts.

13   For an introduction to the basic techniques see Sinclair (1991) and Barnbrook (1996).

References

Aijmer, K. and Altenberg, B. 1991. *English Corpus Linguistics. Studies in honour of Jan Svartvik*. London: Longman.

Aston, G. 1995. "Corpora in language pedagogy: Matching theory and practice". In G. Cook and B. Seidlhofer (eds), *Principles and Practice in Applied Linguistics. Studies in honour of H. G. Widdowson*, 257–270. Oxford: OUP.

Aston, G. 1997. "Enriching the learning environment: Corpora in ELT". In A. Wichmann, S. Fligelstone, T. McEnery and G. Knowles (eds), *Teaching and Language Corpora*, 51–64. London: Longman.

Barnbrook, G. 1996. *Language and Computers. A practical introduction to computer analysis of language*. Edinburgh: EUP.

Bazerman, C. 1988. *Shaping Written Knowledge*. Madison WI: The University of Wisconsin Press.

Bazerman, C. and Paradis, J. (eds), 1991. *Textual Dynamics of the Professions*. Madison, WI: The University of Wisconsin Press.

Berkenkotter, C. and Huckin, T. 1995. *Genre Knowledge in Disciplinary Communication. Cognition/culture/power*. Hillsdale NJ: Lawrence Erlbaum

Associates.

Bernstein, B. 1990. *The Structuring of Pedagogic Discourse. Class, codes, and control* (Vol. IV). London: Routledge.

Bhatia, V. K. 1993. *Analysing Genre. Language use in professional settings.* London: Longman.

Biber, D., Conrad, S. and Reppen, R. 1998. *Corpus Linguistics. Investigating language structure and use.* Cambridge: CUP.

Bondi, M. 1996. "Language variations across genres. Quantifiers and worlds of reference in (and around) economics textbooks". *Asp (Anglais de Specialité).* Université de Bordeaux 2, Bordeaux: Geras Editeur, 33–53.

Bondi, M. 1997a. "The rise of abstracts. Development of the genre in the discourse of economics". In E. Barisone and G. Hughes (eds), *Textus*, X:329–352.

Bondi, M 1997b. "Reported argument in economics textbooks. A meta-pragmatics of argumentative dialogue". In B. Caron (ed), *Proceedings of the 16th International Congress of Linguistics.* Amsterdam: Elsevier Science.

Bondi, M. 1998a. "Dialogues within discourse communities in economics textbooks". In S. Čmejrková, J. Hoffmannová, O. Müllerová and J. Svetlá, (eds), *Dialoganalyse VI.* 229–238. Tübingen: Niemeyer.

Bondi, M. 1998b, "Libri di testo e argomentazione riportata. Esempi di metapragmatica nell' inglese degli economisti". In M. Bondi (ed), *Forms of Argumentative Discourse. Per un'analisi linguistica dell'argomentare.* 85–107. Bologna: CLUEB.

Bondi, M. 1999. "Language Awareness and EFL teacher education". In P. Faber, W. Gewehr, M. Jimenez Raya, and A. Peck (eds), *English Teacher Education in Europe. New trends and developments.* Frankfurt: Peter Laing.

Caldas-Coulthard, C. R. 1994. "On reporting reporting: the representation of speech in factual and factional narratives". In M. Coulthard (ed), *Advances in Written Text Analysis*, 295–308. London: Routledge.

Caron, B. 1997. *Proceedings of the 16th International Congress of Linguists.* Paris, 20–25 July 1997. Amsterdam: Elsevier Science.

Carter, R. and McCarthy, M. (eds), 1988. *Vocabulary and Language Teaching.* London: Longman.

Christie, F. 1989. *Language Education.* Oxford: OUP.

Christie, F. 1992. "Literacy in Australia". *Annual Review of Applied Linguistics.* 12 (1): 42–55.

Christie, F. 1997. "Curriculum macrogenres as form". In F. Christie and J. Martin (eds), *Genre and Institutions. Social Processes in the Workplace and School*, 133–160. London and Washington: Cassell.

Čmejrková, S. and Stícha, F. (eds), 1994. *The Syntax of Sentence and Text.* Amsterdam: John Benjamins.

Crismore, A. 1989. *Talking with Readers. Metadiscourse as rhetorical act.* New York: Peter Lang.

Crismore, A., Markkanen, R., and Steffensen, M. 1993. "Metadiscourse in persuasive writing: A study of texts written by American and Finnish university students". *Written Communication.* 10 (1): 39–71.

Dudley-Evans, A. 1994. "Genre analysis: an approach to text analysis for ESP". In M. Coulthard (ed), *Advances in Written Text Analysis,* 219–228. London: Routledge.

Dudley-Evans, A. and St.John, M. J. 1998. *Developments in English for Specific Purposes.* Cambridge: CUP.

Eid, M. and Iverson, G. (eds), 1993. *Principles and Prediction. The analysis of natural language.* Amsterdam: John Benjamins.

Freedman, A. and Medway, P. (eds), 1994. *Genre and the New Rhetoric.* London: Taylor and Francis.

Gavioli, L. 1997. "Exploring texts through the concordancer: Guiding the learner". In A. Wichmann, S.Fligelstone, T. McEnery and G. Knowles (eds), *Teaching and Lanaguage Corpora,* 83–99. London: Longman.

Ghadessy, M. (ed),1988. *Registers of Written English. Situational factors and linguistic features.* London: Pinter.

Ghadessy, M. (ed), 1993. *Register Analysis. Theory and practice.* London: Pinter.

Gosden, H. 1993. "Discourse functions of subject in scientific research articles". *Applied Linguistics* 14 (1): 56–75.

Grabe, W. and Kaplan, R. 1996. *Theory and Practice of Writing.* London: Longman.

Halliday, M. A. K. 1985. *An Introduction to Functional Grammar.* London: Arnold.

Halliday, M. A. K. 1988. "On the language of physical science". In M. Ghadessy (ed), *Registers of Written English. Situational factors and linguistic features,* 162–178. London: Pinter.

Halliday, M. A. K. 1991. "Corpus studies and probabilistic grammar". In K. Aijmer and B. Altenberg (eds), *English Corpus Linguistics. Studies in honour of Jan Svartvik,* 30–43. London: Longman.

Halliday, M. A. K. and Hasan, R. 1989. *Language Context and Text. Aspects of language in a socio-semiotic perspective.* 2nd edition. Oxford: OUP.

Halliday, M. A. K. and Martin, J. R. 1993. *Writing Science. Literacy and discursive power.* London: Falmer.

Henry, A. and Roseberry, R. 1996. "A corpus-based investigation of the language and linguistic patterns of one genre and the implications for language teaching". *Research in the Teaching of English.* 30: 472–492.

Hoey, M. (ed), 1993. *Data, Description, Discourse. Papers on the English language in honour of John McH. Sinclair on his sixtieth birthday.* London: Harper Collins.

Hunston, S. 1994. "Evaluation and organization in a sample of written academic discourse". In M. Coulthard (ed), *Advances in Written English,* 191–218. London:

Routledge.

Hunston, S. and Thompson, G. 2000. *Evaluation in Text. Authorial stance and the construction of discourse.* Oxford: OUP.

Hyland, K. 1998. *Hedging in Scientific Research Articles.* Amsterdam: John Benjamins.

Hyland, K. 1999. "Talking to students: Metadiscourse in introductory coursebooks". *English for Specific Purposes.* 18 (1): 3–26.

Hyland, K. 2000. *Disciplinary Discourses. Social Interactions in Academic Writing.* London: Longman.

Jacoby, S. 1987. "References to other researchers in literary research articles". *ELR Journal.* 1. 33–78.

Johns, T. 1986. "Micro-concord, a language learner's research tool". *System* 14(2): 151–162.

Johns, T. and King, P. (eds), 1991. "Classroom concordancing". *English Language Research Journal* 4. Birmingham University.

Jordan, R. R. 1997. *English for Academic Purposes. A guide and resource book for teachers.* Cambridge: CUP.

Kaplan, R. B., Cantor, S., Kamhi-Stein, L. D., Shiotani, Y. and Boyd Zimmerman, C. 1994. "On Abstract Writing". *Text.* 14 (3): 401–426.

Kennedy, G. 1998. *An Introduction to Corpus Linguistics.* London: Longman.

Kiefer, F. and Verschueren, J. (eds), 1988. "Metapragmatic terms". Special issue of *Acta Linguistica Hungarica.* 38: 1–289.

Klamer, A. 1990. "The textbook presentation of economic discourse". In W. J.Samuels (ed), *Economics as Discourse,* 129–154. Boston: Kluwer Academic Publishers.

Klamer, A., McCloskey, D. and Solow, R. (eds), 1988. *The Consequences of Economic Rhetoric.* Cambridge: CUP.

Lucy, J. 1993. "Reflexive language and the human disciplines". In J. Lucy (ed), *Reflexive Language. Reported Speech and Metapragmatics,* 9–32. Cambridge: CUP.

Lyons, J. 1977. *Semantics.* Cambridge: CUP.

MacDonald, S. P.1992. "A method for analyzing sentence-level differences in disciplinary knowledge making". *Written Communication.* IX(4): 533–569.

MacDonald, S. P. 1994. *Professional Academic Writing in the Humanities and the Social Sciences.* Carbondale and Edwardsville: Southern Illinois University Press.

Martin, J. R. 1989. *Factual Writing: Exploring and challenging social reality.* Oxford: OUP.

Martin, J. R. 1992. *English Text: System and structure.* Amsterdam: John Benjamins.

Martin, J. R. 1993. "Genre and literacy: Modelling context in educational linguistics". *Annual Review of Applied Linguistics* 13: 141–72.

Martin, J. R. 1997. "Analysing genre: Functional parameters". In F. Christie and J.

Martin (eds), *Genre and Institutions. Social processes in the workplace and school,* 3–37. London: Cassell.

Martin, J. R. and Veel, R. (eds), 1998. *Reading Science: Critical and functional perspectives on discourses of science.* London: Routledge.

McEnery, T. and Wilson, A. 1996. *Corpus Linguistics.* Edinburgh: EUP.

Mindt, D. 1996. "English corpus linguistics and the foreign language teaching syllabus". In J. Thomas and M. Short (eds), *Using Corpora for Language Research,* 232–247. London: Longman.

Murison-Bowie, S. 1993. *Micro-Concord Manual: An introduction to the practices and principles of concordancing in language teaching.* Oxford: OUP.

Murison-Bowie, S. 1996. "Linguistic corpora and language teaching". *Annual Review of Applied Linguistics* 16: 182–199.

Myers, G. 1990. *Writing Biology. Texts in the social construction of scientific knowledge.* Madison, WI: University of Wisconsin Press.

Myers, G. 1992. "Textbooks and the sociology of scientific knowledge". *English for Specific Purposes* 11: 3–17.

Myers, G. 1994. "Narratives of science and nature in popularizing molecular genetics". In M. Coulthard (ed), *Advances in Written English,* 179–190. London: Routledge.

Paltridge, B. 1997. *Genre, Frames and Writing in Research Settings.* Amsterdam: John Benjamins.

Santos, M. B. 1996. "The textual organization of research paper abstracts in applied linguistics". *Text.* 16(4): 481–499.

Scott, M. 1996 *Wordsmith Tools.* Oxford: OUP.

Silverstein, M.1993. "Metapragmatic discourse and metapragmatic function". In J. Lucy (ed), *Reflexive Language. Reported speech and metapragmatics,* 33–58. Cambridge: CUP.

Sinclair, J. McH. 1991. *Corpus, Concordance, Collocation.* Oxford: OUP.

Sinclair, J. McH.1995. "Corpus typology — A framework for classification". In G. Melchem and B. Warren, (eds), *Studies in Anglistics* [Acta Universitas Stockholmientis LXXXV]. 17–33.

Sinclair, J. McH. and Renouf, A. 1988. "A lexical syllabus for language learning". In R. Carter and M. McCarthy, M. (eds), *Vocabulary and Language Teaching,* 140–160. London: Longman.

Stati, S. 1998. "Il lessico dell'argomentazione". In M. Bondi (ed), *Forms of Argumentative Discourse. Per un'analisi linguistica dell'argomentare,* 51–56. Bologna: CLUEB.

Stati, S. 1994. "'Passive' moves in argumentation". In S. Cmejrková, and F. Stícha (eds), *The Syntax of Sentence and Text,* 259–271. Amsterdam: John Benjamins.

Stubbs, M. 1996. *Text and Corpus Analysis. Computer-assisted studies of language and culture.* Oxford: Blackwell.

Svartvik, J. (ed), 1992. *Directions in Corpus Linguistics*. Berlin: Mouton.

Swales, J. 1990. *Genre Analysis. English in academic and research settings.* Cambridge: CUP.

Swales, J. 1994. "The role of the textbook in EAP writing research". *English for Specific Purposes* 28: 3–18.

Swales, J. M., Ahmad, U. K., Chang, Y. Y., Chavez, D., Dressen, D., and Seymour, R. 1998. "Consider this: The role of imperatives in scholarly writing". *Applied Linguistics* 19(1): 97–121.

Tadros, A. 1993. "The pragmatics of text averral and text attribution in academic texts". In M. Hoey (ed), *Data, Description, Discourse. Papers on the English language in honour of John McH Sinclair on his sixtieth birthday*, 98–114. London: Harper Collins.

Thomas, J. and Short, M. (eds), 1996. *Using Corpora for Language Research*. London: Longman.

Thomas, S. and Hawes, T. P. 1994. "Reporting verbs in medical journal articles". *English for Specific Purposes* 13(2): 129–148.

Thompson, G. and Ye, Y. Y. 1991. "Evaluation in the reporting verbs used in academic papers". *Applied Linguistics* 12(4): 365–82.

Tribble, C. and Jones, G. 1990. *Concordances in the Classroom. A resource book for teachers*. London: Longman.

Vande Kopple, W. and Crismore, A. 1990. "Readers' reactions to hedges in a science textbook". *Linguistics and Education.* 2: 303–322.

Vande Kopple, W. J. 1985. "Some exploratory discourse on metadiscourse". *College Composition and Communication.* 36: 82–93.

Verschueren, J. 1985. *What People Say they Do with Words: Prolegomena to an empirical-conceptual approach to linguistic action.* Norwood: Ablex.

Verschueren, J. 1989. "Language on language". *IPrA Papers in Pragmatics.* 3(2): 1–14.

Verschueren, J. 1995. "Metapragmatics". In J. Verschueren, J. Ola-Östman, and J. Bommaert, (eds), *IPrA Handbook of Pragmatics*, 367–371. Amsterdam: John Benjamins.

Verschueren, J., Ola-Östman, J. and Bommaert, J. (eds), 1995. *IPrA Handbook of Pragmatics*. Amsterdam: John Benjamins.

Willis, J. D. 1990. *The Lexical Syllabus. A new approach to language teaching.* London: Collins.

Appendix

Sample teaching materials

Worksheet 1. Internal analysis
(corpus access restricted to the teacher)

1. Study the abstracts you have collected and:
   i.   underline the subjects of the main clauses
   ii. circle main verbs.

2. Work in groups. Different groups will work on (i) and (ii). Then appoint someone to report to the whole class.
   (i) Study the verbs you have underlined above and discuss in your group whether they refer to:
      a.   relational processes or states
      b.   verbal or mental processes
      c.   material processes

   (ii) Study the subjects you have underlined and discuss in your group whether they refer to:
      a.   discourse participants (*we*, *the authors*, etc.)
      b.   discourse units (*this paper, the next section, the conclusions*, etc.)
      c.   hypothesised entities or relations (*the model, the approach*, etc.)
      d.   real world entities or processes.

3. Study the following frequency list, compiled by selecting the most frequent verbal forms found in a corpus of abstracts from *Econlit* (excluding modals). What types of verbs are dominant according to the categories listed above?

N	Word	Freq.	%
12	are	384	0.82
20	be	185	0.39
28	has	113	0.24
33	have	99	0.21
74	show	59	0.13
120	based	40	0.08
121	been	40	0.08

N	Word	Freq.	%
122	examines	40	0.08
124	use	40	0.08
137	shown	37	0.08
154	presents	35	0.07
163	estimates	34	0.07
164	expected	34	0.07
165	find	34	0.07
182	study	33	0.07
190	provides	32	0.07
192	considers	31	0.07

4. Here are concordances of the verbal forms (simple present) of *show* and *claim* (main clause only).

   i. Study the concordance of *show* and underline the subjects of main clauses. Which of the categories listed above do you think is dominant?

   ii. Check on the concordances of *argue* if the verb can be freely used with subjects referring to both discourse participants and discourse units. Underline the specific subjects and compare.

N	Concordance (SHOW) [Note: Only the first 20 lines are shown below]
1	tion he releases back to the market. The authors **show** that the equilibrium price as a function of the
2	quilibrium. AB: In this paper, the authors **show** that a noncooperative game with a finite set
3	if it exists, of the original problem. We also **show** that the optimal consumption and
4	polls of voting intentions, is proposed. We **show** that, as a consequence of aggregating hete
5	and markets, and global links. Most tables **show** indicators for a recent year and an earlier ye
6	weakly dominated by another pure strategy. We **show** the existence of the least and the greatest
7	ex ante and ex post payments. The authors **show** that optimal ex ante payments are inversely
8	in the presence of a structural break. We first **show** that the CFR should not be ignored in the
9	model for the Soviet economy. Simulations **show** that farm marketings would have been subst
10	some equilibrium payoffs in some games. We **show** that appropriate one-shot public communic
11	over institutions. AB: The authors **show** that the core of a continuous convex game
12	permajority voting at any level tau>.5286 they **show** that the probability of Condorcet cycles
13	the optimal ownership patterns. The authors **show** how ownership by voucher funds depends o
14	zero in the limit as well. However, the authors **show** by the construction of two examples that
15	lly be made to factor levels. The authors then **show** two specific model classes and exploit their
16	between financial and labor systems, we first **show** that the American type of financial and labor

N	Concordance (SHOW)
17	and production sets of the economy. They also **show** that if there are a finite number of types,
18	and a horizon of arbitrary length. The authors **show** that the optimal investment strategy follows
19	ive' real estate firms. Novel comparative statics **show** that debt value May increase for a given incr
20	and a pollution abatement subsidy. We **show** that total pollution may be increasing in the

N	Concordance (ARGUE)
1	Ruggiero et al- (1997) **argue** that the 'Pythagorean Theorem' is an inappr
2	s with Frictions' (Summer 1994). AB: We **argue** that in extensive decision problems (extens
3	February 27, 1997. AB: In this paper, we **argue** that it is essential to incorporate bounded
4	On the basis of existing evidence, the authors **argue** that these conditions held for many Chinese
5	quilibrium. AB: Piccione and Rubinstein **argue** that a seemingly paradoxical form of time in
6	AB: M. Jensen and K. Murphy (1990) **argue** that the observed pay-performance sensitivi
7	markets to fail. While this is true, the authors **argue** this failure is due to the structure of the Arr
8	dox of the absentminded driver." AB: We **argue** that a notion of constrained time consisten
9	in a civilian Southern population. The authors **argue** that the decline in heights was caused by s

Worksheet 2. Comparative analysis
(corpus access given to both teacher and students)

1. Work in small groups. Focus on one of the following meta-argumentative expressions (metadiscursive references to argument).
    – *show*
    – *discuss/discussion*
    – *examine/examination*
    – *argue/argument*
    – *agree/disagree/agreement/disagreement*

    Extract the concordances of the various forms from the corpus of introductory chapters of economics textbooks.

2. Check the appropriate dictionary entries in your dictionary.

    Which meanings do your concordances exemplify? Are there any definitions that are not exemplified?

    If not all meanings are exemplified, what do you think is the reason for this? Discuss within your groups.

Then report to the whole class.

3. Meta-argumentative expressions are often used in textbooks in moves like
   a. problem identification
   b. representation of methodological tools
   c. representation of debate within the discipline
   d. activities guiding the reader through argument

Working within your groups, find examples of the moves above in your concordances. You may need to consider the wider context.

Then report to the whole class.

3. Extract concordances of the same lexical items from the corpus of abstracts and compare:

   i. Do the two sets of concordances offer a different view of the meanings of the lexical elements you are studying?
   ii. Do they offer a different proportion of the nominal and verbal forms?

4. Consider the lexical elements chosen by your group within the context of the full abstract.

Find examples of abstracts that may be representative of the different textual patterns:
   a. abstracts based on the structure of inquiry (problem; method; results; conclusions);
   b. abstracts based on argumentative dialogue (discourse and counter-discourse).

Report to the class.

5. Extract the concordances of the items listed below in one of the two corpora and find out which meta-argumentative expressions collocate with them by using the automatic function of the programme.

Fill in the appropriate column. Discuss with the class and complete the chart.

Introductory	Chapters	Abstracts	
We		We	
You		Author(s)	
Economist(s)		Paper(s)	
Figure/Table/Exhibit		Result(s)	
Models(s)		Model(s)	

6. Study the concordances of *show* in one of the two corpora. Identify main clauses and fill in the table below with examples of main clause subjects under the appropriate heading:
    a. discourse participants (*we, the authors*, etc.)
    b. discourse units (*this paper, the next section, the conclusions*,etc.)
    c. hypothesised entities or relations (*the model, the approach*, etc.)
    d. real world entities or processes.

    What is the dominant category in your corpus?

    Report to the class and fill in the chart with data from the other groups.

Domain	Reference	Introductory chapters	Abstracts
Discourse participants	Authors: External Internal Empty theme		
Discourse units	External d. units Empty d. theme Micro-unit Macro-unit		
Hypothesized entities	Hypothetical entity Empty theme Viewpoint		
Real World Entity	Phenomena Process		

CHAPTER 7

Investigating and Teaching Genres Using the World Wide Web

Vincent B Y Ooi

National University of Singapore

Abstract

Computer-mediated communication afforded by the World Wide Web can shape new and existing genres/ sublanguages. Communication of this nature is reflected in electronic texts that are readily available and can be judiciously sampled to form the basis of concrete, directly observable linguistic evidence. Such principled bodies of data (or corpora) can then be studied for their lexico-grammatical patterning and genre-specific properties. The central means of doing the study of such language data is to employ a corpus linguistic methodology, which includes subjecting the texts to a quantitative analysis using readily available software and from which the human analyst can interpret the results. In this chapter, a corpus linguistic methodology is demonstrated through an investigation of the genre of personal advertisements on the Web. The study of such a genre can help bring out a more direct comparison of (i) the language preferred by men and women and (ii) the cultural backgrounds shaping these preferred linguistic choices. This chapter suggests that corpus creation for language study need not be restricted to the professional corpus linguist but can also be done judiciously by the teacher and the student of language. It also indicates that the Web, containing its myriad texts and discourses, has become indispensable to language study; many complete e-texts are readily available for linguistic analysis without the need for labour-intensive efforts to key or scan them in. Linguistic software for measuring electronic textuality is also increasing in sophistication and availability.

Introduction: the influence of the Internet on corpus linguistic research

In this millennium, the Internet / World Wide Web has become indispensable as a way of life to many computer-literate people. In turn, the widespread use of the Web (as it is known) raises many new issues, including whether the traditional ways in which we write, speak (and even) think are undergoing a change. In this connection, Jones (1999:2) claims that the Internet has become "not only a technology but an engine of social change, one that has modified work habits, education, social relations generally, and maybe most important, our hopes and dreams." In this chapter, I would like to investigate the language of these "social relations", "hopes and dreams" with regard to personal advertisements on the Net, as it is popularly called. Because the Net is changing the way research is conducted (Jones 1999; Rodrigues 1997; Woodward 1997), I would like — in keeping with the theme of this book — to explore what the Internet has to offer for the creation of small corpora for language teaching and study.

For working purposes, the Internet, as the "Information Superhighway", is a worldwide network of networks.[1] In this chapter, I use it interchangeably with the term "World Wide Web", which is the portion of the Internet accessible when one clicks on Internet browsers (or "windows" to the Internet) such as *Microsoft Internet Explorer* or *Netscape Communicator*. The World Wide Web (otherwise known as "WWW" or the "Web") contains links that, at the click of a button, allow the user to surf to text, audio files, graphic images or even video (and download them). These hypertext links, as they are known, are markers of unique virtual addresses all over the world, and form the basis of the World Wide Web.

At first glance, the WWW represents a monumental electronic resource that is amenable to the theory and practice of *corpus linguistics*. There are various definitions of *corpus linguistics*, but the one I have used most until now is "the study of language on the basis of textual or acoustic (speech) corpora", and which "almost always involves the computer in some phase of storage, processing and analysis of this data" (Ooi, 1994:2). With the rapid explosion of the Internet and the World Wide Web, this definition might be modified to one involving the computer for the study of language involving (the interaction between) computer text, audio or video files which are maximally representative of the linguistic phenomenon in question. Underlying this definition, the Web is the immediate electronic resource that comes to mind, since the corpus can be easily obtained in electronic form. Of course, it is a truism to say that the corpus has to be in electronic form before it can be subjected to any analysis using the computer. Further, while texts in printed form can nowadays be scanned in *en masse* (with some post-editing, of course), I would argue that computer-mediated communication (as afforded by the Web) is likely to give rise to distinctive language patterning. Thus, the voice (telephone) personal advertisements/personal classifieds on a printed magazine will be a variant, but can be distinguished from the genre of personal advertisements of a web site dedicated to this purpose. This is because the web site concerned might constrain the user with certain parameters of information not found in printed personal advertisements. On the other hand, responses via e-mail do not usually necessitate an additional expense (unlike expensive telephone chat lines), and the users are free to convey more information about themselves in subsequent e-mail messages to each other; such responses are stored in a database residing on the web site concerned. A further difference between a web site and a printed magazine is that the web site traverses national barriers, and is accessible to a global audience of "personal dream seekers", as it were, at the click of a button. The web site also gets continually updated and information is disseminated at a faster rate. Thus, because of such different modes of communication, it is interesting to investigate whether the dynamics of the Web can engender different language patterning.

"Small" vs. "large" corpora

The practice of collecting electronic data for some particular linguistic purpose need not be restricted to the professional corpus linguist, who usually favours the collection of a large corpus. In any case, the optimal size of a representative corpus varies over time. In 1961, the first and largest electronic corpus was judged to be of the order of a million words (e.g. the *BROWN* corpus of 1 million words of American English); in 1987 the *Collins-COBUILD* database was the largest in existence at over 20 million words; in 1999, the same database has expanded to over 330 million words. What hope does this hold for the use of small corpora? In Ooi (1998), I mentioned that the stress on size or quantity for a corpus does not necessarily mean that all types of computer corpora gathered must be large, since there are some genres of texts restricted in scope and size. For instance, a corpus of Old English texts can never be of the order of a hundred million words, simply because it is restricted to the set of texts which have survived from the Old English period. Leech (1991:10-12) therefore rightly warns that "to focus merely on size...[in defining something as worthy of the enterprise of corpus linguistics] is naive", although he is in favour, of course, of having large corpora. So, defining corpus linguistics as "the branch of linguistics that is concerned with the study of language use by means of large text corpora" (Oostdijk, 1991:preface) begs the question of what is "large". It also neglects the inclusion of the computer by which the word "large" has been made possible (through the expansion of hardware storage) and applicable (through considerable success in using probabilistic methods of analysis). However, Oostdijk is also right in focusing on the "large" aspect of language data gathering for professional corpus linguists. Corpus linguistic projects will tend to be concerned with analysing and processing vast amounts of (textual) data, simply because large quantities of text are needed for a number of reasons. The different motivations for focusing on large quantities of text include (1) building probabilistic systems for natural language processing which require reliable large training datasets; (2) providing more and different textual examples, and (3) simply hoping to capture the linguistic phenomenon in question in a more adequate manner.

Corpus representativeness and the language genre

Whether large or small, the guiding principle involved in calling some collection of machine-readable texts a corpus is that it is "designed or required for a particular representative[2] function" (Leech 1991:11). Atkins et al (1992:1) distinguish four types of text collection, which may be summarised as follows:

- *Archive:* a repository of readable electronic texts not linked in any coordinated way, e.g. the Oxford Text Archive
- *Electronic text library* (or ETL, Fr. 'textothèque'): a collection of electronic texts in standardized format with certain conventions relating to content,

etc., but without rigorous selectional constraints.

- *Corpus:* a subset of an ETL, built according to explicit design criteria for a specific purpose, e.g. the Corpus Révolutionnaire (Bibliothèque Beaubourg, Paris), the Cobuild Corpus, the Longman/Lancaster corpus, the Oxford Pilot corpus.
- *Subcorpus:* a subset of a corpus, either a static component of a complex corpus or a dynamic selection from a corpus during on-line analysis.

A corpus can thus be designed to serve as a resource for general purposes, or for a more specialised function such as being a resource that is maximally representative of a particular language genre, or language specific to a particular domain, e.g. the language of law. If a corpus is collected for a particular genre, it need not be large. This is because the major properties of the genre can be known after a certain *threshold* of words instantiating specialised language is reached. For instance, the *PROLEX Corpus* (cf. Webster 1984) stands at only c. 65000 words, but exemplifies a more specialised corpus which has been compiled to offer insights into the form and function of business English. I am not, however, suggesting that all such thresholds should be set at 65000 words. It depends on the genre concerned, and the optimal size can be reached only when the collection of more texts does not shed any more light on its lexico-grammatical or discourse patterning.

A *genre*, as "an instance of a successful achievement of a specific communicative purpose using conventionalised knowledge of linguistic and discourse resources" (Bhatia 1993:16) can be more precisely determined after going through most or all of the following steps (as suggested by Bhatia, 1993:22-34):

1. The first step is the placing the texts concerned in a situational context and, based on one's prior knowledge and other internal clues in the text, intuitively assessing whether the texts belong together as a group;
2. The second step involves surveying existing literature which involves identifying materials relevant to a specific genre. This is also undertaken by consulting practitioners, guidebooks and manuals;
3. The third step involves refining the situation or context by defining the writer, the audience and the linguistic traditions associated with the genre;
4. The fourth step is the selection of the corpus. The right kind and size of corpus to be analysed is seen against what makes it distinct from other genres;

5. The fifth step involves the study of the institutional context where the methodology, rules and conventions governing the use of language in the particular setting are used;
6. The sixth step calls for the analyst to decide on the levels to carry out the analysis;
7. The seventh step involves a study of the lexico-grammatical features and the statistics associated with the language variety.

For Bhatia (1993:25), empirical evidence is necessary to "confirm or disprove some of the intuitive and impressionistic statements that we all tend to make about high or low incidence of certain lexico-grammatical features."

Such empirical evidence, captured in a corpus, can either extend or contradict one's intuitions about language. The corpus, as a snapshot of the language, measures the central and typical aspects of language. Thus, the corpus tends to represent the *language of probability* (i.e. some words and grammatical structures are preferred over others), instead of the *language of possibility* (favoured in traditional methods of doing linguistics, i.e. a sentence is either grammatical or it is not).[3] Of course, both perspectives complement each other in the study of language. In addition, on the Web, *snapshots* of the language afforded by the corpus take place from time to time, in the sense that the data gets updated at a regular pace. Thus, the Web is (continually) amenable to the study of contemporary language.

Investigating the genre of personal advertisements

Let us now apply the principles mentioned in the preceding sections to a case study. Suppose a teacher wishes to ask her/his students to investigate whether men and women in both the U.S. and Singapore differ in writing personal advertisements on the Net. This is not an unreasonable question to ask, since it is said that

> one discernible and consistent impact of technology on social organizations is the attenuation of social linkages. Inch by inch, the network of face-to-face contacts of the primordial village has been thinned out and dissolved as more and more rarified threads link us to people farther and farther away (O'Donnell 1998:175).

Such an exercise would involve finding out the way(s) in which people in different cultures communicate electronically on the same topic, including how the respective genders perceive themselves and their expectations of the opposite sex, if any. In order to begin, one types in various keywords such as "personal ads", "personal advertisements", "personal classifieds" on a search engine (which includes www.excite.com, www.hotbot.com, www.altavista. com, etc.) in an Internet browser (such as Netscape or Internet Explorer). There are a number of websites that the search reveals, including http://www.webpersonals.com., http://www.lovecity.com and http://www.kiss. com. Such websites can be divided into three basic sub-sites, depending on one's sexual orientation: Men+Men, Men+Women and Women+Women. Since our current exercise concerns (among others) the relationship between men and women, there are three types of relationship postulated: "Romance" (for serious relationships), "Dating" (for those who wish to start out as friends first) and "Intimate" (for those wanting a more physical and casual relationship). Websites of this nature are also able to group people by their country of origin, as well as by other parameters such as gender and age.

In order to research the topic postulated at the beginning of this section, there are 12 possibilities to consider and the respective data files to gather:

1. Men into Romance, from Singapore (file: mr_spore.txt)
2. Men into Romance, from the U.S. (file: mr_us.txt)
3. Women into Romance, from Singapore (file: wr_spore.txt)
4. Women into Romance, from the U.S. (file: wr_us.txt)
5. Men into Dating, from Singapore (file: md_spore.txt)
6. Men into Dating, from the U.S. (file: md_us.txt)
7. Women into Dating, from Singapore (file: wd_spore.txt)
8. Women into Dating, from the U.S. (file: wd_us.txt)
9. Men into Intimate Relationships, from Singapore (file: mi_spore.txt)
10. Men into Intimate Relationships, from the U.S. (file: mi_us.txt)
11. Women into Intimate Relationships, from Singapore (file: wi_spore.txt)
12. Women into Intimate Relationships, from the U.S. (file: wi_us.txt)

Data files

How much text should be collected? As an arbitrary guide, let us require 10 different "advertisers" for each file and suppose that each file is reasonably "balanced" in terms of the number of words, although it is difficult to control for this factor (since each advertiser will differ in being succinct or verbose). In addition, the files would (as far as possible) include those advertisers who mention their expectations of a mate or date in their advertisement. Twelve small files were collected, representing the twelve categories given above. (See Appendix I for representative sample texts and respective data file sizes indicated in bytes.)

An impressionistic analysis is that the tenor of discourse is informal (e.g. *u* instead of *You*) and the mode of discourse is that these texts are written somewhat as if they are spoken (e.g. shorter sentences and less redrafting of the text). Also, as the files are collected, one's impression is that the advertisers from the U.S. on the whole tend to have slightly longer (and perhaps more explicit) descriptions of themselves and their potential partners. Compared with the U.S. files, the Singapore ones are slightly smaller in the number of bytes respectively. As a result, one has to bear in mind that the results might be affected because of this slight disparity in the different file sizes.

Analysing the data using WordSmith Tools

In order to have a more precise linguistic description, the files are first subjected to analysis using *WordSmith Tools* (Version 3.0), a suite of lexical analysis tools developed by Mike Scott (currently at http://www.liv.ac.uk/~ms2928/ homepage.html; see also Chapter 3, this volume). Possibly the most used tools are both the Concordancer (showing the collocates or words that tend to occur to both the left and right sides of the word in question), and the WordLister (showing an alphabetical list of words as well as a wordlist sorted in order of descending frequency).

Word frequency profiles by gender and country of origin
Appendix II shows the frequency results (in terms of descending raw frequency count) that were obtained. From these word frequency rankings, the perceptive reader will notice that I have omitted words that occur only once. The main reason for doing so is to economize on space, because of the phenomenon of *hapax legomena* in which nearly half of the words in a corpus will occur only once. Besides space constraints, this cue is also taken from Sinclair (1996:81) who says that "in gathering and organizing corpus evidence, the first focus is on repeated events rather than single occurrences…a language pattern

— however defined — has to occur a minimum of twice."

In any case (whether one prefers to have the entire wordlist, including words which occur only once), word frequency profiles do give the teacher and student a strong indication of the ways in which language is used in this genre. Firstly, the profiles give an idea of the words that are most and least frequently occurring in each of the Romance, Dating and Personal Sections. They also indicate that the mode of discourse here is closer to speech: in a spoken corpus. A piece of evidence is that the pronouns *I* and *you* typically occur more frequently than the corresponding wordforms in a written corpus (where the most frequent words are typically the function words *the, of, and, a,* etc). Also, the notion of appropriateness is important here, since sexually explicit words such as *foreplay, threesomes* and *oral sex* (found in the Intimacy Section) are not acceptable for the Dating and Romance Sections. Neither is a phrase such as *no-strings attached* acceptable in the Romance Section, since the notion is the very antithesis of what this section is about. However, a word such as *caring* would be acceptable for all three sections. The student needs to be sensitive to these pieces of information in order to generate a text that will guarantee him/her a good response!

Word frequency profiles by gender (Do males and females differ in their expectations of each other?)
By itself, WordSmith Tools does not distinguish between the parts of speech — noun, verb, adjective, adverb etc. Hence, these basic word frequency profiles can be improved further through the use of a *part-of-speech tagger* that can automatically annotate these raw text files to a high degree of accuracy (see Ooi 1998:135; Garside and Smith 1997). Once each raw text file is tagged, it is possible to set *WordSmith Tools* to generate these word frequency profiles again with, say, *good* tagged as *good_JJ* ("JJ" indicating adjective) and *needs* tagged as *needs_NN2* ("NN2" indicating plural noun). More importantly, search techniques can be used to extract linguistic generalizations such as the most common adjectives used by men, compared with those for women.

Therefore, as part of our exercise, the *CLAWS* hybrid grammatical tagger (see Garside & Smith 1997:102) is used to annotate the 12 files discussed iearlier. *CLAWS (Constituent Likelihood Automatic Word-tagging System)*, developed at Lancaster University, is a tagger which "chooses the most likely sequence of tags by calculating the probability of all possible sequences of tags, and then choosing the sequence with the highest probability" (Garside & Smith

Table 1: Top 25 words corresponding to different word-classes used by both U.S. and Singapore men

Noun		Verb		Adjective		Adverb	
life_nn1	31	is_vbz	86	good_jj	28	just_rr	36
woman_nn1	26	am_vbm	78	old_jj	15	really_rr	29
person_nn1	23	be_vbi	53	important_jj	14	also_rr	19
time_nnt1	23	looking_vvg	53	willing_jj	14	out_rp	19
love_nn1	22	have_vh0	43	great_jj	13	when_rrq	15
sex_nn1	20	will_vm	34	attractive_jj	12	there_rl	14
fun_nn1	19	like_vv0	33	fit_jj	9	up_rp	14
women_nn2	18	do_vd0	32	new_jj	9	very_rg	14
guy_nn1	17	are_vbr	31	single_jj	9	here_rl	11
lady_nn1	16	can_vm	31	honest_jj	8	so_rr	11
friends_nn2	15	would_vm	30	nice_jj	8	still_rr	10
body_nn1	13	love_vv0	23	special_jj	8	too_rg	9
humor_nn1	12	meet_vvi	22	beautiful_jj	7	basically_rr	8
relationship_nn1	12	like_vvi	19	hot_jj	7	never_rr	8
things_nn2	12	have_vhi	16	blue_jj	6	on_rp	8
hair_nn1	11	enjoy_vv0	15	brown_jj	6	please_rr	8
sense_nn1	11	want_vv0	15	free_jj	6	soon_rr	8
honesty_nn1	10	share_vvi	14	open_jj	6	always_rr	7
people_nn	10	think_vv0	14	possible_jj	6	back_rp	7
eyes_nn2	9	find_vvi	13	quiet_jj	6	enough_rr	7
man_nn1	9	happens_vvz	12	tall_jj	6	how_rrq	7
friend_nn1	8	see_vvi	12	afraid_jj	5	now_rt	7
work_nn1	8	get_vvi	11	long_jj	5	down_rp	6
years_nnt2	8	hoping_vvg	11	passionate_jj	5	more_rgr	6
fantasy_nn1	7	know_vvi	11	romantic_jj	5	ever_rr	5

(Key4: nn1=singular common noun; nn2=plural common noun; vbr=present tenseform of BE (*are*); vbz= present tense –s form of BE (is); vd0=finite base form of the verb DO (*do*); vhi= infinitive have; vh0=finite base form of HAVE (*have*); vhi=infinitive *have*; vm= modal auxiliary (e.g. *can, will, could*); vv0=base form of lexical verb; vvg= -*ing* form of lexical verb (e.g. *giving, working*); vvi=infinitive of lexical verb (e.g. [*to*] *give*, [*will*] *work*); vvz= -*s* form of lexical verb (e.g. *gives, works* etc); jj=general adjective; jjt= general superlative adjective (e.g. *oldest, best, biggest*); jk=catenative adjective (e.g. able in *be able* to); rg=degree adverb (e.g. *very, so, too*); rgr=comparative degree adverb (*more, less*); rl=locative adverb (e.g. *alongside, forward*); rp=prepositional adverb or particle (e.g. *in, up, about*); rr=general adverb (*soon, quickly, perhaps*); rrq= wh- general adverb (*where, when, why, how*); rrr=comparative general adverb (e.g. *better, longer*); rt=nominal adverb of time (e.g. *now, tomorrow*).

1997:103). The tagger, like others, operates in the UNIX environment and is said to achieve 96 to 97 per cent accuracy rate and an error rate of only 1.5. Alternatively, if the UNIX environment seems unfamiliar, it is currently possible either to try out Lancaster University's tagging service or use the WWW on-

Table 2: Top 25 words corresponding to different word-classes used by both U.S. and Singapore women

Noun		Verb		Adjective		Adverb	
life_nn1	35	is_vbz	98	good_jj	40	just_rr	37
man_nn1	33	am_vbm	66	attractive_jj	19	also_rr	32
person_nn1	31	be_vbi	62	important_jj	13	really_rr	31
friends_nn2	22	looking_vvg	58	new_jj	13	out_rp	25
things_nn2	22	are_vbr	46	great_jj	10	very_rg	25
time_nnt1	20	would_vm	38	nice_jj	10	when_rrq	16
woman_nn1	19	have_vh0	33	single_jj	10	then_rt	11
sense_nn1	18	do_vd0	32	willing_jj	10	never_rr	10
eyes_nn2	14	can_vm	26	intelligent_jj	9	up_rp	10
love_nn1	14	love_vv0	26	married_jj	8	basically_rr	9
guy_nn1	13	like_vv0	23	romantic_jj	8	how_rrq	9
humor_nn1	13	want_vv0	20	sensitive_jj	8	please_rr	9
way_nn1	13	find_vvi	19	serious_jj	8	as_rg	8
relationship_nn1	12	meet_vvi	18	free_jj	7	now_rt	8
sex_nn1	11	will_vm	17	honest_jj	7	there_rl	8
friend_nn1	10	like_vvi	16	interested_jj	7	too_rg	8
humour_nn1	10	think_vv0	16	long_jj	7	well_rr	8
lady_nn1	10	has_vhz	15	old_jj	7	here_rl	7
people_nn	10	does_vdz	14	right_jj	7	more_rrr	7
movies_nn2	9	happens_vvz	14	wonderful_jj	7	only_rr	7
smile_nn1	9	share_vvi	13	special_jj	6	pretty_rg	7
hair_nn1	8	get_vvi	12	able_jk	5	so_rg	7
dreams_nn2	7	hoping_vvg	12	best_jjt	5	still_rr	7
fun_nn1	7	being_vbg	11	chinese_jj	5	together_rl	7
idea_nn1	7	enjoy_vv0	11	compassionate_jj	5	down_rp	6

See Table 1 for the Key to these tags; see also Garside 1987:256-60.

line demo service (currently at http://www.comp.lancs.ac.uk/computing/research/ucrel/claws/) for 300 words at any one time. In the future, a Windows version which becomes commercially available will also make the program more accessible to people who are more used to working with icons than commands.

In the present instance, the UNIX tagger is run on these 12 files and the output sorted using both *WordSmith Tools* and simple UNIX commands (such as *grep* and *awk,* powerful utilities which search and manipulate strings) to produce tables of the top 10 tagged words for four major parts of speech (noun, verb, adjective, adverb) by men and women, as shown in Tables 1 and 2 above.

The reader is invited to interpret the rankings of these tables, which serve a useful but rather limited purpose. The usefulness of these tables is that they provide an averaging of the words and notions that most and least concern the men and women in this sampling (assuming, of course, that the sampling is representative). However, the limitation of these tables is that, without the context of significant collocates (or words which tend to co-occur), one cannot quite access the intended meanings. Nevertheless, an interpretation is that, where nouns are concerned, men and women are both rightly most concerned about living the life that they want and inviting the other to share it; they are also concerned about such matters as time, relationships, love and sex. Men tend to be more concerned about having *fun* and *sex* than women, who seem keener on getting to make friends (first). The noun *sense* is also certainly more valued by women, although we are not sure of the sense (pardon the pun!) in which it is used. Where verbs are concerned, the student might generally wish to distinguish between different types of verbs, including verbs of knowing (e.g. *know, think*), verbs of doing (e.g. *run, walk*), verbs of sensing (e.g. *see, hear*), and verbs of relations (e.g. *is, are*). From the tables, an important verb that characterises this genre is *looking* (meaning *searching*). Where adjectives are concerned, both men and women share similar ways in describing themselves and their ideal partner. However, adjectives such as *intelligent, romantic* and *sensitive* have higher rankings in Table 2 than Table 1 (before). The adverbs used by both men and women are also strikingly similar, but men tend to intensify matters less than women (e.g. compare *very* and *never*).

Word Frequency Profiles by Country of Origin (Do Singaporeans and Americans prefer different modes of writing?)
Using the method established in the preceding section, two similar tables can be generated to look at the words used by Singaporeans and Americans, as indicated in Tables 3 and 4 respectively (below).

The reader is also invited to interpret Tables 3 and 4. Where nouns are concerned, it seems significant that *lady* ranks more highly in Table 3 than in Table 4; there is perhaps a perception associated with this word which merits further investigation. In Table 4, the term *humor* certainly ranks higher than it would in Table 3 (Incidentally, note that in Singapore, British spellings are generally preferred to American ones). Also, perhaps predictably, a word that distinguishes the U.S. profile from the Singapore one is *Chinese* which occurs more frequently in Table 3. Where verbs are concerned, *looking* again figures quite prominently in the rankings of both tables. However, it is interesting that there is the preferred use of the verb *share* in Table 3, with its noticeable absence in

Table 3: Top 25 words corresponding to different word-classes used by Singaporean men and women

Noun		Verb		Adjective		Adverb	
life_nn1	33	is_vbz	74	good_jj	30	really_rr	26
person_nn1	30	am_vbm	64	important_jj	13	just_rr	24
lady_nn1	19	are_vbr	52	willing_jj	13	out_rp	22
time_nnt1	19	looking_vvg	50	new_jj	12	also_rr	15
love_nn1	18	be_vbi	47	old_jj	11	up_rp	14
sex_nn1	16	will_vm	33	nice_jj	10	when_rrq	14
friends_nn2	15	can_vm	29	attractive_jj	8	there_rl	12
guy_nn1	13	do_vd0	27	passionate_jj	7	still_rr	11
woman_nn1	13	like_vv0	26	able_jk	6	very_rg	11
chinese_nn1	12	have_vh0	24	fit_jj	6	basically_rr	8
friend_nn1	12	love_vv0	23	fun_jj	6	course_rr22	8
things_nn2	12	would_vm	22	intelligent_jj	6	how_rrq	8
people_nn	11	meet_vvi	19	mature_jj	6	of_rr21	8
humour_nn1	10	share_vvi	18	serious_jj	6	well_rr	8
man_nn1	10	like_vvi	15	single_jj	6	back_rp	7
body_nn1	9	think_vv0	13	tall_jj	6	here_rl	7
years_nnt2	9	want_vv0	13	wild_jj	6	always_rr	6
fantasy_nn1	8	find_vvi	12	young_jj	6	more_rrr	6
fun_nn1	8	happens_vvz	12	chinese_jj	5	most_rgt	6
mail_nn1	8	have_vhi	12	hot_jj	5	never_rr	6
music_nn1	8	enjoy_vv0	10	interested_jj	5	only_rr	6
ladies_nn2	7	does_vdz	9	intimate_jj	5	please_rr	6
relationship_nn1	7	drop_vvi	9	sincere_jj	5	all_rr	5
sense_nn1	7	go_vvi	9	comfortable_jj	4	am_ra	5
sports_nn2	7	hoping_vvg	9	free_jj	4	on_rp	5

Table 4. Where adjectives are concerned, the terms *attractive* and *great* seem to be preferred descriptive strategies among U.S. men and women, but they do not seem to be significantly used among Singaporeans. Adverbs also seem more frequent among the U.S. personal advertisers, compared with their Singaporean counterparts.

Lexical and grammatical collocations (or the company that words keep)
The preceding two sections indicate that words cannot be studied in isolation; a word is best studied when one considers the "company" (as it were) that it keeps.This dictum, attributed to the British linguist J.R. Firth (Firth 1957), can best be applied when one has access to a KWIC (Keyword-in-Context) concordance listing of the word/expression concerned. Such a listing allows one to

Table 4: Top 25 words corresponding to different word-classes used by U.S. men and women

Noun		Verb		Adjective		Adverb	
lifxe_nn1	33	is_vbz	110	good_jj	38	just_rr	49
man_nn1	32	am_vbm	80	attractive_jj	23	also_rr	36
woman_nn1	32	be_vbi	68	great_jj	20	really_rr	34
humor_nn1	24	looking_vvg	61	important_jj	14	very_rg	28
person_nn1	24	have_vh0	52	honest_jj	13	out_rp	22
time_nnt1	24	would_vm	46	single_jj	13	when_rrq	17
friends_nn2	22	do_vd0	37	old_jj	11	so_rr	13
sense_nn1	22	like_vv0	30	willing_jj	11	never_rr	12
things_nn2	22	can_vm	28	new_jj	10	here_rl	11
eyes_nn2	19	love_vv0	26	romantic_jj	10	now_rt	11
fun_nn1	18	are_vbr	25	special_jj	10	please_rr	11
love_nn1	18	want_vv0	22	beautiful_jj	9	too_rg	11
guy_nn1	17	meet_vvi	21	free_jj	9	then_rt	10
hair_nn1	17	find_vvi	20	long_jj	9	there_rl	10
relationship_nn1	17	like_vvi	20	blue_jj	8	up_rp	10
women_nn2	17	has_vhz	18	married_jj	8	basically_rr	9
sex_nn1	15	have_vhi	18	nice_jj	8	so_rg	9
honesty_nn1	12	will_vm	18	afraid_jj	7	down_rp	8
way_nn1	11	think_vv0	17	fit_jj	7	how_rrq	8
body_nn1	10	enjoy_vv0	16	open_jj	7	on_rp	7
people_nn	9	get_vvi	15	possible_jj	7	always_rr	6
dreams_nn2	8	happens_vvz	14	sensitive_jj	7	as_rg	6
games_nn2	8	hoping_vvg	14	brown_jj	6	soon_rr	6
movies_nn2	8	know_vv0	14	confident_jj	6	still_rr	6
heart_nn1	7	let_vm21	14	dark_jj	6	together_r	6

see all instances of the word/expression on the vertical axis and the company it keeps on the horizontal axis (using a span of approximately four words to each side—left and right—of the word/expression). In other words, a word/lexical item should not only be studied in relation to other words (paradigmatic relations, in terms of synonymy, antonomy, etc) but also related to its significant cotext for syntagmatic relations.This significant cotext refers to collocation, the habitual co-occurrence of a group of words, or the combination of words that have a "mutual expectancy" (Jackson and Amvela 2000:92).

Focusing on word relations does not mean that a frequency list of single lexical items is unimportant; however, the usefulness of such a list is that it is "never more than a set of hints or clues to the nature of a text" (Sinclair 1991:31). The way forward beyond the single word frequency list is to focus instead on *multi-word items* in our study of language. Such a perspective accords well with Sinclair (1996:82) who thinks that "the notion of a linguistic item can be extended, at least for English, so that units of meaning are expected to be largely phrasal." Not dissimilar to this view is Mel'cuk (1995:169), who claims that "people do not speak in words; they speak in *phrasemes*" (including very frequent collocations, idioms and fixed phrases).

If we accept that much of language consists of patterning longer than the single lexical item, then such extended units of meaning should be the main objects of our linguistic investigation. In this respect, *WordSmith Tools* is a program that is becomingly increasingly sophisticated for handling collocations (by means of its *Concord* feature). Thus, to extend the lead in Section 4.2.2 concerning the preference of *sense* by women (i.e. whether they want their men to have, say, *common sense*) the following concordance (Figure 1) is obtained:

Conordance
ken... A gentleman's charm and a **sense of humor**. A clean slate w/p
is confident and honest. I like a **sense of humour** in a person. Ope
elling errors, and have a sarcastic **sense of humor**. Must be able to
e. You are fun yet serious, with a **sense of humour**, that energy to
ny, and likes to have fun. I like a **sense of humor** in a person. Frien
faithfulness. I really like a great **sense of humor** in a person. I'm l
et to know someone with a good **sense of humor**, a degree of intelligence
ood-natured, loves sex, and has a **sense of humor**. He has to be cre
to keep my mind off of my work! **sense of humor** very important. Mu
ortable for both of us. Guys with a **sense of humour**, good conversation
one on one relationship. I love a **sense of humor** and someone that
njoy people who have a wonderful **sense of humour**, practice safe sex
-old vegetarian gal with a quirky **sense of humor** and a love of learn
est when I'm with my children. My **sense of humor** is really important
who's eloquent, intelligent, with a **sense of humour**, compassionate

Figure 1: Edited concordance listing of *sense of humour* used by U.S. and Singaporean women

Figure 1 above shows that, instead of our earlier expectation of *common sense*, it is the set phrase *sense of humour* that is valued by women in their men. Collocating with this phrase to its left are adjectives such *great, wonderful, sarcastic, quirky* and *good*. The preferred verbs collocating to the left of this phrase include *like* and *love*. To the right of this phrase, an important prepositional phrase is *in a person*. Such linguistic facts are important in order for the learner to master such discourse in a native-like manner.

As another illustration, let us turn again to the word frequency profiles listed in Tables 1 and 2 in which the adjective *old* (listed as *old_JJ*) seems unusually high on the list in Table 1. To examine this in further detail, the following concordances (Figures 2 and 3 below) are generated for both men and women respectively:

Conordance
Moi: 6'2", good looking 30 yr **old** WM who wants serious physical
ilk about them. NO6 32 year **old** San Francisco resident. 6'1", 175
eet an intellegent, 18-26 year- **old** proportional Caucasian female in
tive black man. 5'9" 30 years **old,** fit (muscular). Just a down to ear
nde hair, blue eyes, 47 years **old** trim build. I like tennis almost an
ful ladies out there... 29 year **old** chinese male would like to meet
ried??? I think I'm somewhat **old,** fashioned in the values I desire in
e-mail me. NO4 I'm 22 years **old** and I live in the Sacramento area
gards. NO3 I AM 30 YEARS **OLD** SINGLE GUY,I love to exercise
r mails. NO9 I'm a 29 years **old** Chinese with an athletic/lean and
o find her. Now I grew up with **OLD** fashion values and sex before
San Francisco. I'm 38 years **old,** but I look like I'm in my mid twe

Figure 2: Edited concordance listing of *old* used by U.S. & Singaporean men

Conordance
All endowed. NO5 I'm 33 years **old** chinese girl and I'm looking for
what happens! NO4 A 30 years **old** asian lady looking for serious re
NO2 I am a "kid" in a 47-year- **old** body who has a combination of
r mature man from 30-38 years **old.** You must not be married or att
ad-lib version of me: I'm a 23-yr- **old** vegetarian gal with a quirky se
t happens! NO9 I am 29 years **old,** very pretty, blonde hair and blu
preferably between 25 - 35 yrs **old,** and will respect a beautiful, qu

Figure 3: Edited concordance listing of *old* used by U.S. & Singaporean women

The word *old* does not occur in isolation, but tends to be part of a phraseme that has a frame which is somewhat like X-*year(s)-old*-(adjp)/ (noun phrase premodifier) H (of noun phrase); in other instances, it functions as part of the collocational frame *old*-X(noun/adjective). Also, as expected, men generally have no qualms about revealing their age, which may be given as part of their vital statistics (the other two being height and weight) for the respondent to have a clearer idea of the what the advertiser looks like. However, by comparison, Figure 3 shows more or less the total number of lines concerning women who are either willing to reveal their age or require a specific age range in their men. Hence, the age-old stereotype that women are generally reluctant to reveal their age does seem to hold true.

Conordance
Most people go to the bars **looking for** a mate. Not me! I don
play golf. I'm definitely not **looking to** get married, and if u ar
nships together. NO9 I am **looking for** somebody who can st
07 I enjoy SEX a lot!!!! I am **looking for** something different to
t, so phone sex is what I am **looking for** – at the moment at le
ally discriminating. NO5 I'm **looking to** meet someone within t
kids, spic-n-span (no d/d), **looking for** a discreet relationship[
u're taken care of as well)!! **Looking for** one person for multipl
To stay that way -- I'm just **looking to** fill some unmet needs
are things that just are. I am **looking for** a gentle/man who re
rl living in the big city who is **looking for** her prince charming.

Figure 4: Edited concordance listing of *looking for/ to*, used by U.S. & Singaporean women

Conordance
picture, N10 hi there,I'm **looking for** that special woman tha
felt about love. What I am **looking for** is to share sweet and p
70 cm tall and 65 kg. I am **looking for** some real open and ho
aiting, and here is what I'm **looking for**. I'm interested in an in
them andf a lot more with. **looking for** that attractive lady with
other. Are you the one I'm **looking for**? Desire a girl between
s well as, in a Tuxedo. I'm **looking for** someone to talk with,p
ly. Quite good looking. I'm **looking for** someone special that
shy, thoughtful guy whose **looking for** a female who also ha
s, enjoy keeping fit and am **looking for** someone to go out wi

Figure 5: Edited concordance listing of *looking for*, used by U.S. & Singaporean men

Let us now look at the verb *looking* (or rather predominantly *looking for*) which is so prominent in all four tables (cf Figures 4 and 5 above). The object of *looking for* represents the desired "hope" or "dream": *someone special, that special woman, a discreet relationship*, or *prince charming* (sic). The most common auxiliary (*am*) indicates the primacy of the present time, which is used for this search of some future fulfilment by the advertiser.

With a tagged corpus and the various perspectives afforded by WordSmith Tools, the possibilities of grammatical study are increased tremendously. Let us turn to Figure 6 as a demonstration of this claim.

Conordance		File
_VVI out_RP and_CC	*see_VVI live_JJ bands_NN2 ._.* movies_NN2	2/h/md_us.h
d_VM like_VVI to_TO	*find_VVI cycling_JJ buddies_NN2* and _CC te	/md_spore.h
JJ ,_, willing_JJ to_TO	*try_VVI new_JJ things_NN2* and_CC see_V	~2/h/mi_us.h
IS1 hope_VV0 to_TO	*find_VVI new_JJ penpals_NN2* from_II all_R	/wd_spore.h
PIS1 likeVV0 to_TO	*try_VVI new_JJ things_NN2 ._.* variations_N	h/wi_spore.h
_ RR love_VV0 to_TO	*explore_VVI new_JJ places_NN2* and_CC ex	2/h/wd_us.h
PIS1 love_VV0to_TO	*try_VVI new_JJ things_NN2 ._.* ^I_PPIS1 c	!w/h/wi_us.h

Figure 6: Edited concordance listing of the pattern VVI+JJ+NN2, from the entire corpus

The grammatical pattern VVI (infinitive of lexical verb), JJ (general adjective), and NN2 (plural noun) is extracted from the entire tagged corpus; the correspondingly longer pattern of VVO+TO (infinitive marker) +VVI+JJ+NN2 can also be studied separately. The phrase *willing/love to try new things* interestingly coincides in the files 'mi_us' (U.S. men into Intimate Relations), 'wi_spore' (Singaporean women into Intimate Relations) and 'wi_us' (U.S. women into Intimate Relations) such that it is no mere chance that this euphemistic phrase typically characterises this sub-genre (of intimate relations). The advertiser is seeking someone who also wants to try out sexual experimentation, the referent of (*new*) *things*. The term *new,* however, takes on quite a different meaning in the files 'wd_spore' (Singaporean women into Dating) and 'wd_us' (U.S. women into dating) with their more innocent collocates *penpals* and *places* respectively. Grammatical tagging therefore allows for their corresponding grammatical patterns to be extracted, and such annotation has been undervalued as a pedagogical tool until now.

Teaching Genres

What I have sketched in the preceding sections relates to a linguistic investigation of a genre, illustrated by the application of a corpus-based methodology to the language of personal advertisements. Although pedagogical issues are implied in the preceding sections, in this section, I would like to a little more explicit about the kinds of questions that the instructor can suggest to the student. Depending on the level of sophistication (elementary to advanced), the instructor could construct project exercises and study questions along the following lines:

(i)   (elementary skill: computational) Surf the web using a search engine such as Altavista for "personal advertisements", "dating", "friendship", romantic links" etc. What sites can you find?

(ii)   (intermediate skill: linguistic, conceptual) Identify the topic that you wish to investigate. Is it (i) The Language of Romance; (ii) The Language of Dating; (iii) The Language of Intimacy? What hypothesis / hypotheses can you expect of the language of each of these topics?

(iii)   (intermediate skill: linguistic, conceptual) Can you group these three categories in (ii) into a broader one entitled The Language of Desire? (N.B.: It would be helpful to fix the sexual orientation that you wish to investigate, i.e. a comparison between straight Men and Women, or a comparison between Gay Men, or a comparison between Gay Women.) In addition, if you study the language of men and women (are they from your country of origin?), you might like to sub-divide your corpus into one for men and another for women. In your hypothesis, do you expect men and women to speak and write differently? Alternatively, do you wish to compare between the language of men and women from different cultures? For instance, you could compare and contrast European women and Asian women in terms of the following parameters: (a) interests and hobbies (e.g. frequency of music, reading, traveling, cooking, movies, shopping); (b) values (such as frequency of references to religion and monogamy, the frequency of words such as *sex, wild, kiss, intimacy, spiritual, affection, cuddling* etc); (c) personal qualities sought after (e.g. *good, intelligent, humorous* etc)

(iv)   (intermediate to advanced skill: linguistic, computational, conceptual) Gather a corpus large enough to help you answer the questions you have identified in (ii). In your project entitled "A corpus-based study of personal advertisements", how large should your corpus be and what corpus-based methodology will you use?

(v)   (intermediate to advanced skill: computational, linguistic) Use the annotation software CLAWS to tag your corpus. After tagging the corpus, take about 5 paragraphs, selected at random, and calculate the percentage of accuracy that CLAWS gives you.

(vi)   (elementary to intermediate skill: computational) Run the WordSmith Tools software on this tagged corpus (N.B.: remember to define the underscore sign "_" as part of the word, otherwise WordSmith Tools will count the tag separately from the word). Use the Concord Feature to sort out the nouns, verbs, adjectives, adverbs, determiners, prepositions etc. from one another.

(vii)   (intermediate to advanced skill: linguistic, analytical, interpretative) By using *WordSmith* to analyse the tagged corpus, you might like to relate the features to following parameters in your study: (a) length & difficulty of words; (b) personal pronouns used; (c) emotive verbs like *like, love* and *enjoy*; (d) nouns relating to personal appearance, eg.
        Hair eyes, nose, mouth, ears, teeth, complexion, face, lips (in order to see whether men and/or women are particular about a particular body feature; (e) adjectives relating to personal qualities, e.g. *honest, romantic, tender, cheerful* etc.; (f) potential partner's attitude to *child children* etc What can you generalize about the Language of Personal Advertisements?

(viii) (intermediate to advanced skill: linguistic, conceptual) What are the limitations of your approach, and what further improvements can you envisage for future studies of this kind?

(ix)   (elementary to advanced skill: presentation, oral competence, expository) Give a 40-minute presentation on "The language of personal advertisements on the Web"; or "Using the web to understand the language of personal advertisements"; or "A linguistic analysis of the language of personal advertisements" using *Powerpoint* or a web presentation tool such as *Microsoft Frontpage*.

Doubtless, the instructor can demonstrate her/his creativity in setting challenging questions, but I trust this section has indicated that the skills tested can (and will) include computational, linguistic, conceptual, argumentative, and presentational ones.

Conclusion

In this chapter, I have suggested how the language of personal classifieds might be investigated using a corpus-linguistic methodology. The suggested methodology for a small corpus includes judicious sampling of electronic texts of a genre (of which many computer-mediated ones are found on the Web), analysing these texts using *WordSmith Tools*, and annotating them with a part-of-speech tagger such as *CLAWS*. Of course, such a methodology can be extended by means of annotating the corpus for other useful linguistic information (including syntactic and semantic tagging—see Garside et al. 1997). With the widespread availability of the Web and more sophisticated linguistic tools which continue to come to the fore, the student of language in the 21st century is likely to do more self-directed learning in creating and analysing her/his own small representative corpus. Exciting challenges for corpus linguistics based on the study of the Web also lie ahead, as Web technologies for Internet Relay Chats (IRC), on-line discussion groups, and M(ulti) U(ser) D(omains) continue to engender new modes of communication.

Notes

1. For an introduction to the Internet and the World Wide Web, see Dry and Aristar (1998).
2. The term *representative* as applied to a corpus is problematic. See Summers (1993, 1996) and Biber (1993) for a detailed treatment.
3. For a more detailed treatment of *language as probability* and *language as possibility*, see Kennedy (1998:270-273).
4. The version of the tagset used here is the *CLAWS7* tagset (see Garside et al. 1997:257–260 for the entire listing).

References

Atkins, B. T. S., Clear, J. and Ostler, N. 1992. "Corpus design criteria". *Literary and Linguistic Computing*. (7) 1: 1–16.
Bhatia, V. 1993. *Analysing Genre: Language use in professional settings*. London:

Longman.

Biber, D. 1993. "Representativeness in corpus design". *Literary and Linguistic Computing* 8 (4): 243–257.

Biber, D., Johansson, S., Conrad, S., and Finegan, E. 1999. *Longman Grammar of Spoken and Written English*. London: Pearson Education.

Dry, H. A., and Aristar, A. R. 1998. "The Internet: An introduction". In J. M.Lawler and H. A.Dry (eds), *Using Computers in Linguistics: A Practical Guide*, 26–61. London: Routledge.

Firth, J. R. 1957. "A synopsis of linguistic theory, 1930–1955". *Studies in Linguistic Analysis*, [Special Volume], 1–32. Philological Society.

Garside, R. and Smith, N. 1997. "A hybrid grammatical tagger: CLAWS4". In R. Garside, G. Leech and A. McEnery (eds), *Corpus Annotation: Linguistic information from computer text corpora*, 102–121. London: Addison Wesley Longman.

Garside, R., Leech, G.and McEnery, A. (eds), 1997. *Corpus Annotation: Linguistic information from computer text corpora*. London: Addison Wesley Longman.

Jackson, H. and Amvela, E. Z. 2000. *Words, Meaning and Vocabulary*. London: Cassell.

Jones, S. (ed), 1999. *Doing Internet Research: Critical issues and methods for examining the net*. London: Sage.

Kennedy, G. 1998. *An Introduction to Corpus Linguistics*. London: Addison Wesley Longman.

Leech, G.1991. "The state of the art in corpus linguistics". In K.Aijmer and B. Altenberg (eds), *English Corpus Linguistics: Studies in honour of Jan Svartvik*, 8–29. Harlow: Longman.

Mel'cuk, I. 1995. "Phrasemes in language and phraseology in linguistics". In M. Everaert, E. J. van der Linden, A. Schenk, R. Schreuder (eds), *Idioms: Structural and psychological perspectives*, 167–232. Hillsdale NJ: Lawrence Erlbaum.

Mitra, A. and Cohen, E. 1999. "Analyzing the Web". In S. Jones (ed), *Doing Internet Research: Critical issues and methods for examining the net*, 179–202. London: Sage.

O'Donnell, J. J. 1998. *Avatars of the Word: From papyrus to cyberspace*. Cambridge MA: Harvard University Press.

Ooi, V. B. Y. 1994. "Corpus linguistics". *SAAL Quarterly* 28: 2–4.

Ooi, V. B. Y. 1998. *Computer Corpus Lexicography*. Edinburgh: EUP.

Oostdijk, N. 1991. *Corpus Linguistics and the Automatic Analysis of English*. Amsterdam: Rodopi.

Rodrigues, D. 1997.*The Research Paper and the World Wide Web*. Englewood Cliffs NJ: Prentice-Hall.

Sinclair, J. McH. 1991. *Corpus, Concordance, Collocation*. Oxford: OUP.

Sinclair, J. McH. 1996. "The search for units of meaning". *Textus* IX: 75–106.

Summers, D. 1993. "Longman Lancaster English Language Corpus: Criteria and design". *International Journal of Lexicography* 6 (3): 181–208.

Summers, D. 1996. "Computer lexicography-the importance of representativeness in relation to frequency". In J. Thomas and M. Short (eds), *Using Corpora for Language Research: Studies in honour of Geoffrey Leech*, 260–306. London: Longman.

Webster, J. 1984. "The PROLEX project". In R. R. K. Hartmann (ed), *LEXeter '83 Proceedings*, 435–40. Tübingen: Max Niemeyer Verlag,

Woodward, J. A. 1997. *Writing Research Papers: Investigating Resources in Cyberspace*. Lincolnwood: NTC.

Appendix I

Data file categories, size of each in bytes, and a representative sample text of each:

1. Men into Romance, from Singapore (file: mr_spore.txt) 5614 bytes

Sample text: I am a Singapore male looking for a gal to spend my life with. I know that it is difficult but I will try. Looks is not important to me, what is more important, is that both of us will care for and trust each other. Do drop me an email and see what happens…

2. Men into Romance, from the U.S. (file: mr_us.txt) 6690 bytes

Sample text: hi there, i'm looking for that special woman that is loving, caring, honest and is fun to be with,she needs to like children and know how to treat a man with respect, i don't play games and i expect the same in return, i like traveling, dining out, cuddling, walking, camping, candelight diners and just having fun. i'm a very honest person, sweet and lovable, 33, 6'0 ,155, brown hair, green eyes. if you would like to know more just ask.

3. Women into Romance, from Singapore (file: wr_spore.txt) 5964 bytes

Sample text: I am an attractive Singaporean Chinese who is longing to meet a nice caucasian male. Ideally, he is attractive (in my eyes only), patient and kind with good humour. He need not impress me with his status, wealth, knowledge, etc. Just be his real self. As for me, I enjoy everything in life. I hope with the right chemistry, my man will help me appreciate this life better. If you are warm like the sun, write soon. I am waiting – patiently of course!

4. Women into Romance, from the U.S. (file: wr_us.txt) 8908 bytes

Sample text: What is it that makes you special? Is it the way you smile or the way you laugh? Is it how you notice the littlest things – the goofy things? Or is it the way you stand for what you believe in? Maybe it's all those things, maybe it's something all too unique to just you? The man of my dreams is tall with a generous eyes, a kind smile, a sincere and loving spirit. A sense of humor in a person is a must – the ability to laugh with life is priceless. I'm looking for romantic best friend to share my life with. What are you looking for?

5. Men into Dating, from Singapore (file: md_spore.txt) 6079 bytes

Sample text: I shall not go on blabbering abt myself. Let's just say that I'm in my 20s, enjoy keeping fit and am looking for someone to go out with and have fun. That someone should be 19–35, doesn't smoke, and most importantly she's in Singapore, either working or a resident there.

6. Men into Dating, from the U.S. (file: md_us.txt) 7038 bytes

Sample text: Hi ! I am looking for an average looking woman in Pennsylvania. I am 6' 1 280 and look like an offensive tackle. I would prefer a non-barbie type of lady, someone who likes to be treated special. I like all women, small to large. I am gentle, brown hair and light mustache and handsome. i have a terrific sense of humor and so must you. I like to read and play golf and hang out with my dog. I like movies on my satellite dish. Basically, i have been a loner the last few years and am getting a bit restless. If you would like to chat, send me a message and i will respond to all. There is a lot more to say, so message me and we shall talk. My pic will be online soon and you can view the merchandise, so to speak. Let's face it, there has to be that initial attraction.. See ya..

7. Women into Dating, from Singapore (file: wd_spore.txt) 5278 bytes

Sample text: Does getting physical usually mean you're in love? How come guys simply don't say the words... I'm an expressive person, I feel good at 30, Malay (with a Chinese look, they say) and I enjoy a good challenge in life. You are fun yet serious, with a sense of humour, that energy to write voraciously and that spirit to move, inspire, change.

8. Women into Dating, from the U.S. (file: wd_us.txt) 7038 bytes

Sample text: Hmmm... I'm not sure what to say.. and that doesn't happen too often… I live in High Point and I'd like to get to know someone with a good sense of humor, a degree of intelligence, who does not play golf. I'm definitely not looking to get married, and if u are married yourself, please don't waste your time or mine.

9. Men into Intimate Relationships, from Singapore (file: mi_spore.txt) 6311 bytes

Sample text: Hi there, i'm a chinese guy in my early 30's and i'm looking for ladies age between 21–36 for no-strings attached affair. if u enjoy long foreplay like i do and if u are a lady with high sex drive, pls drop us a note and well… lets see if we are comfortable with each another and let the fun begin…. hope to hear from u ladies soon.

10. Men into Intimate Relationships, from the U.S. (file: mi_us.txt) 5788 bytes

Sample text: I am a good looking young business owner in the pac northwest. In great shape, I feel as though I have a lot to offer. I am looking for a woman who is very sensual and sexual, for erotic chat, and long bouts of sexy fun. I travel frequently, so if you would like to get together just email me and we can have fun. Please leave youre email address in youre response.

11. Women into Intimate Relationships, from Singapore (file: wi_spore.txt) 5689 bytes

Sample text: hello guys, Im rather new to this, but i'd really like to meet some well built, decent looking guy for some discrete passionate fun and games. I am into role playing, acting out fantasies, strip teasing (both ways), oral (both ways) and anything else that is safe. As my nick implies, I like to try new things, variations, locations etc. Lets discuss. Email me and lets see how things can hot up.Im interested in chinese guys, preferable muscular and well endowed.

12. Women into Intimate Relationships, from the U.S. (file: wi_us.txt) 9111 bytes

Sample text: I am in need of a man who is good-natured, loves sex, and has a sense of humor. He has to be creative and not be afraid to have sex outside the privacy of a bedroom. I am open to performing before a video camera as I like to expose my body.I do drink occasionally but do not smoke or will not tolerate anyone who does. I am disease free and my partner should be likewise. I am also bi-sexual, so if any ladies out there want to chime in, I'd be glad to entertain you – let's make it a threesome, shall we?? Please send me a pic if interested…

Appendix II

Word Frequency Profiles by Gender and Country of Origin. For each category, the most frequent words are given with their raw count in parentheses. The lists are edited slightly.

1. Men into Romance, from Singapore (file: mr_spore.txt)

I (52), and (30), the (19), love (18), me (17), I'm (15), like (11), you (11), looking (9), someone (9), life (7), important (6), mail (6), good (5), share (5), caring (4), have (5), her (4), know (4), person (4), she (4), time (4), fun (3), find (3), kind (3), loving (3), sweetheart (3), sports (3),care (2), enjoy (2), anyone (2), fit (2), friendship (2), gal (2), games (2), guy (2), ladies (2), lady (2), passionate (2), partner (2), tanned (2), together (2), welcome (2), surfing (2), sweet (2).

2. Men into Romance, from the U.S. (file: mr_us.txt)

I (46), and (35), the (25), I'm (24), you (16), like (13), have (12), looking (9), someone (9), woman (9), life (8), me (8), my (8), know (7), enjoy (6), fun (6), great (6), say (6), share (6), good (5), humor (5), person (5), special (5), guy (4), relationship (4), sense (4), think (4), times (4), activities (3), attractive (3), caring (3), friends (3), her (3), love (3), quiet (3), children (2), give (2), complete (2), honest (2), honesty (2), listener (2), loving (2), sensual (2), sincere (2), romantic (2), search (2).

3. Women into Romance, from Singapore (file: wr_spore.txt)

and (41), I (31), the (22), I'm (21), me (21), my (11), looking (11), person (10); you (9), have (8), like (8), love (8), life (6), share (6), nice (5), someone (5), enjoy (4), family (4), good (4), humour (4), attractive (3), caring (3), intelligent (3), loves (3), music (3), relationship (3), romantic (3), serious (3), travel (3), Caucasian (2), Chinese (2), communicating (2), company (2), conversation (2), Eurasian (2), fair (2), feel (2), financially (2), great (2), guy (2), Jesus (2), loving (2), passionate (2), sensitive (2), preferred (2) Singaporean (2), special (2), stable (2), understanding (2).

4. Women into Romance, from the U.S. (file: wr_us.txt)

I (1971), and (63), the (51), my (35), you (35), I'm (32), me (20), looking (13), like (12), have (11), life (9), love (9), smile (8), someone (8), knew (7), man (6), think (6), person (6), anyone (5), dreams (5), guy (5), honest (5), hoping

(5), wonderful (5), children (4), compassionate (4), friends (4), good (4), great (4), humor (4), make (4), alone (3), believe (3), gentleman (3), important (3), relationship (3), romantic (3), special (3), woman (3), want (3), afraid (2), attractive (2, beautiful (2), disease (2), friend (2), flowers (2), enjoy (2), company (2), lady (2), loving (2), meet (2), soulmate (2), prefer (2).

5. Men into Dating, from Singapore (file: md_spore.txt)

I (61), and (60), my (22), me (21), you (20), the (19), am (18), I'm (15), have (12), like (9), love (9), friend (6), life (5), meet (5), we (5), friends (4), lady (4), person (4), say (4), share (4), someone (4), think (4), trust (4), contact (3), find (3), fun (3), good (3), her (3), hoping (3), kind (3), learn (3), let's (3), party (3), people (3), times (3), want (3), build (2), clubbing (2), enjoy (2), fit (2), girl (2), guy (2), drinks (2), interesting (2), jogging (2), know (2), look (2), loves (2), passionate (2), please (2), music (2), relationship (2), romance (2), willing (2).

6. Men into Dating, from the U.S. (file: md_us.txt)

and (51), I (50), I'm (29), the (27), my (19), am (11), good (11), like (11), you (11), love (10), someone (9), friends (8), looking (8), me (8), attractive (6), have (6), humor (6), man (6), time (6), find (5), meet (5), person (5), think (5), want (5), important (5), know (4), life (4), say (4), sense (4), woman (4), basically (3), enjoy (3), friend (3), funny (3), let's (3), men (3), happens (3), sensitive (3), old (3), together (3), blonde (2), creative (2), caring (2), friendship (2), goodlooking (2), golf (2), honesty (2), interested (2), living (2), look (2), professional (2), simple (2), outdoors (2), spend (2).

7. Women into Dating, from Singapore (file: wd_spore.txt)

and (31), I (20), the (20), you (17), good (13), I'm (12), me (11), like (10), life (7), looking (7), someone (6), person (5), am (4), meet (4), friends (3), humour (3), movies (3), really (3), serious (3), say (3), times (3), want (3), woman (3), write (3), attractive (2), Chinese (2), eloquent (2), energy (2), friendship (2), enjoy (2), equal (2), fit (2), intelligent (2), love (2), man (2), people (2), pleasures (2), professional (2), share (2), sincere (2), single (2), smile (2), sports (2), thoughts (2), time (2), travelling (2), writing (2), years (2), working (2), we'll (2), you'll (2).

8. Women into Dating, from the U.S. (file: wd_us.txt)

and (82), I (70), the (47), I'm (41), my (31), you (28), good (24), like (21), me (19), am (15), looking (15), someone (15), love (12), friends (11), life (11), person (10), really (10), get (9), have (9), meet (9), attractive (8), know (8), want (8), find (7), say (7), woman (7), humor (6), idea (6), includes (6), enjoy (5), friend (5), important (5), movies (5), times (5), basically (4), friendship (4), hoping (4), let's (4), men (4), professional (4), old (4), sensitive (4), serious (4), together (4), caring (3), creative (3), funny (3), gal (3), need (3), single (3), tired (3), people (3), you'll (3), you're (3), Chinese (2), eloquent (2), equal (2), family (2), financially (2), goodlooking (2), guys (2), hate (2), honesty (2), humorous (2), intelligent (2), laugh (2), looks (2), loves (2), male (2), pretty (2), relationship (2), qualities (2), romance (2), possess (2), simple (2), sincere (2), take (2), values (2), workaholic (2), writing (2), yourself (2).

9. Men into Intimate Relationships, from Singapore (file: mi_spore.txt)

and (54), I (50), you (32), I'm (25), me (18), the (17), sex (14), love (10), really (9), fantasy (8), looking (7), body (6), lady (6), guy (5), look (5), meet (5), piercing (5), person (5), willing (5), Chinese (5), drive (4), gals (4), her (4), ladies (4), tattoo (4), think (4), time (4), want (4), woman (4), basically (3), deliver (3), happens (3), horny (3), let's (3), life (3), male (3), message (3), open-minded (3), please (3), night (3), tall (3), try (3), type (3), whip (3), wild (3), affair (2), attached (2), bra (2), bed (2), fantasize (2), give (2), good (2), physique (2), quickies (2), relationship (2), safe (2), string (2), strings (2), undress (2), women (2), wonder (2).

10. Men into Intimate Relationships, from the U.S. (file: mi_us.txt)

I (44), and (40), the (15), am (13), looking (13), you (12), be (11), have (11), with (11), I'm (8), like (8), fun (6), old (6), it (6), women (6), enjoy (5), know (5), sex (5), someone (5), woman (5), attractive (4), free (4), good (4), great (4), looks (4), man (4), open (4), enjoys (3), hair (3), long (3), please (3), pleasure (3), person (3), try (3), want (3), wants (3), willing (3), attached (2), caring (2), clean (2), disease (2), email (2), erotic (2), foreplay (2), games (2), giving (2), humor (2), huge (2), interest (2), interested (2), love (2), new (2), partner (2), perfect (2), pleasant (2), relationship (2), romantic (2), safe (2), sensual (2), sexually (2), sexual (2), she (2), years (2), young (2), you're (2).

11. Women into Intimate Relationships, from Singapore (file: wi_spore.txt)

and (39), you (32), I (21), the (21), me (12), am (11), looking (10), her (9), like (9), Chinese (7), guys (7), fun (5), someone (5), woman (5), friends (4), good (4), I'm (4), life (4), she (4), try (4), want (4), contact (3), enjoys (3), girl (3), interested (3), intimate (3), lady (3), let's (3), love (3), mature (3), need (3), new (3), really (3), share (3), strong (3), tell (3), think (3), work (3), young (3), attached (2), attractive (2), believe (2),comfortable (2),decent (2), disease (2), games (2), happens (2), humour (2), intimacy (2), meeting (2), playing (2), pretty (2), safe (2), seek (2), sex (2), sexually (2), single (2), ways (2).

12. Women into Intimate Relationships, from the U.S. (file: wi_us.txt)

I (68), and (61), the (38), me (22), I'm (20), my (20), am (14), love (13), man (13), have (12), like (11), looking (11), sex (9), good (7), really (7), very (7), want (7), feel (6), married (6), need (6), please (6), someone (6), attractive (5), find (5), make (5), person (5), smile (5), woman (5), attached (4), eyes (4), know (4), relationship (4), sense (4), sense (4), wet (4), willing (4), better (3), confident (3), dark (3), humor (3), important (3), life (3), pretty (3), romantic (3), submissive (3), appearance (2), assertive (2), attention (2), basically (2), consider (2), discreet (2), educated (2), explore (2), bi (2), explore (2), fantasize (2), discreet (2), intelligent (2), kisses (2), laugh (2), loves (2), men (2), needs (2), new (2), look (2), prefer (2), preferably (2), oral (2), passion (2), sexy (2), single (2), soft (2), sweet (2), threesome (2), try (2), warm (2), write (2), wanted (2), wants (2).

SECTION IV

CHAPTER 8

Classroom Use of a Systemic Functional Small Learner Corpus

Peter H. Ragan

Embry-Riddle Aeronautical University

Abstract

Language researchers and teachers have begun to use small corpora as a viable means of conducting practical classroom-centered research and meeting specific language teaching needs. While corpus analysis typically focuses on discrete lexical items and their patterning in texts produced by native speakers, this paper combines the use of a small corpus with a systemic functional perspective to investigate texts written by language learners. Following a description of the considerations that serve as background for such a study, the paper describes the compilation and annotation of a small learner corpus for features of discourse and wording using a Hallidayan model of language. It describes the classroom investigation of this corpus comprised of sets of instructions written by university-level ESL students, and suggests the usefulness of a small learner corpus in improving language proficiency and promoting language awareness.

Introduction

If accessibility and relevance are pertinent criteria, the use of corpora in English language teaching can be seen as having made significant progress over the last decade. The availability of concordancing software and more powerful personal computers, and growing interest in classroom-based action research combine to make applications of small corpora an attractive and realistic undertaking for instructors in the English language classroom. A growing number of articles document the utility of corpus investigations in developing course materials and promoting language awareness for teaching and training purposes. What is less familiar, however, and of interest to a classroom instructor, is the classroom use of small corpora comprised of texts written by English language learners. There remain a number of preliminary issues in this regard which warrant closer scrutiny to help instructors appreciate the scope and benefits of a small learner corpus as a classroom-based language learning tool. Then, there are the considerations of the actual application of a small corpus in the classroom.

This paper first gives background and considerations for the use of a small learner corpus in key areas of sampling and analysis pertinent to the would-be classroom instructor-investigator. These are the size of the corpus to be developed, the target population whose texts are of interest, the text types to be studied, and the manner in which the language data are to be treated. The use of a systemic functional perspective on language to annotate the texts is justified as a means to promote language awareness of the relation between the features of discourse and wording that are realized in a text used in a particular social context. There follows the description of an example of preparing and investigating a model small learner corpus comprised of sets of instructions written by university native speakers and learners of English.

Corpus size and target population

Can a small learner corpus be representative of what people do with language? A classroom instructor may well wonder whether a collection of student-written essays or texts of other types is even large enough to constitute a useful, effective language sample. Biber addresses the major issues of "representativeness" in linguistic corpus design, which he submits "refers to the extent to which a sample includes the full range of variability in a population" (1993:243). Corpus size is, of course, a relative matter. What is considered large today may not be so tomorrow, for most of the largest corpora are growing larger every day. In principle, corpus size ranges from two or more texts to hundreds of millions of words in many texts. These corpora may be general or specialized; they may be static, that is, collected and archived, or dynamic, that is, added to on a regular basis. It is the very large dynamic corpora such as the *Collins COBUILD Bank of English* which earn the title of "monitor corpus". The worth of a small learner corpus is unlikely to be measured in terms of adequacy of breadth of sample as determined by measures of statistical significance; hence, a more specific interpretation of representativeness should be applied to it.

The notion that bigger is better with regard to corpus size derives from the mistaken belief of much early corpus linguistics that all or somehow enough of the sentences of natural language could be collected to give a full picture of language use. Moreover, the increasing reliance by language researchers on quantification and significance testing of findings based on language data contributes to a misplaced anxiety over the validity and reliability of intuitive deductions based on small samples of language. Indeed, Owen (1996) has suggested that research in corpus linguistics has led to a denial of the value of the intuition of language instructors. However, there will remain a need for an instructor's intuition in a small learner corpus that addresses a limited range of the variability of language use in a limited population and is used to develop student intuitions about language. Johansson contrasts the broad quantitative investigations invited by very large corpora with the "delicate, qualitative studies of the small, carefully-constructed corpus which samples from a variety of text types...and can be subjected to total accountability, forcing researchers to see what they might otherwise overlook" (cited in Granger 1992:67). The accessibility of the small learner corpus to students whose texts make up the corpus and to the instructor who manages its application to teaching activities makes it an ideal tool for mediation between the empirical and the intuitive, and thereby between description and prescription.

Classroom instructors may consider the small learner corpus of two groups of 25 student-written texts described in this paper of little import in comparison with a collection of published or otherwise public texts. There is also the pressing question of what to do with the errors of features of wording and discourse inevitably characteristic of student-written texts. However, all collections of authentic language in use have much in common, whether they be a corpus of everyday essays or a seemingly more esoteric use of text such as the collection of everyday spoken exchanges between air traffic controllers and pilots featured in the *Air Traffic Control Corpus* of the Linguistic Data

Consortium (1996). Errors are more of an assurance of the realities of use than a problem, for what many language users attempt and are supposed to do with language, and what they actually do are readily apparent and usefully displayed within in the concordance of a corpus. The pleasantly amusing or terribly disastrous non-standard utterance of a pilot responding to an air traffic controller with something other than the expected phraseology of the language of the air may not be any more surprising (Ragan 1999) than the inappropriate sentence of a student writer. Nonetheless, there are valid reasons why both instances warrant detection, analysis and some manner of remediation. Certainly, for the classroom instructor, being able to create a list of unacceptable and acceptable features of language, and to document his or her own students' response to a writing task with a few strokes of the computer keyboard is appropriate motivation to develop a small learner corpus.

A corpus that is appropriate in size for the classroom, following the definition offered for a small corpus in this volume, should be one that can be easily and effectively created, maintained, and used by an individual, such as a teacher. This classroom tool is not intended to meet Biber's requirement that "a corpus must be 'representative' in order to be appropriately used as the basis for generalizations concerning language as a whole" (1993:243). In the classroom the small corpus only represents itself in providing specific information and a basis for generalizations concerning the limited range of the variety of language being produced and studied by a small number of students.

Biber feels that developing a comprehensive picture of the target population and a sophisticated sampling methodology are more important than ensuring an adequate sample size in assuring the representativeness of a large corpus (1993:243). The utility of a homogenous small learner corpus does not depend on these features, which are important considerations of large collections of learner texts, such as the *Longman Corpus of Learners' English (LCLE)* of some ten million words in a variety of text types written by learners of English at more than eight levels of proficiency from over 160 different language backgrounds (Warren 1992). Perhaps the largest corpus of a single group of learners will be the planned five million words of the *Hong Kong University of Science and Technology (HKUST) Corpus*, which is restricted to the collection of the writing of Chinese English learners (Milton and Tong 1991). There is also the dynamic *International Corpus of Learner English (ICLE)*, comprised of growing subcorpora of essays written by advanced adult EFL learners from a number of countries around the world. Granger stresses the importance of comparability for the *ICLE* to minimize different levels of language ability, tasks, and the like in the investigation of learner language (1994:26).

Comparability is more readily controlled in a small learner corpus, which, whether static or dynamic, is likely to comprise all of the texts produced by the population of interest to the instructor. That is, it presents rather than represents the work of students, for instance, in one or more sections of a course. The small learner corpus is usually created to provide new perspectives on language for the students who have provided the language; accordingly, the instructor teaching the course develops the corpus to meet their specific needs. The size of the sample is less important than the preparation and tailoring of the language product and its subsequent corpus application to draw attention to an individual or group profile of learner language use.

Text types and corpus annotation

Are there any special considerations to be made in determining which text and what manner of annotation should be chosen for a small learner corpus? In fact, the use of a small learner corpus offers the opportunity to take advantage of text types and annotation schemes that facilitate the growth of students' language awareness. Biber notes that another concern of representativeness is "the range of text types in a language and…the range of linguistic distributions in a language"1993:243). A small learner corpus does well to focus on a limited, more specific type of text. For teaching purposes, the small learner corpus effectively investigates texts that rely upon the smaller range of linguistic features associated with more specialized text types. This is the sort of enquiry Chris Kennedy suggests can be justified for use in the classroom to promote language awareness by learning about language (1995). His description of the utility of analyzing the "little" texts that make up the holiday postcard genre rests on the linkage between language and context that allows movement "from linguistic features to the semantic and social reasons for their presence" (1995:164). He illustrates how a small corpus of 100 postcards, using a Hallidayan model of analysis, can be used selectively for an empirical investigation of student hypotheses originating in sociocultural intuitions about language use. Idiosyncratic texts, then, such as Kennedy's postcards, job application letters, encyclopedia articles, scientific abstracts, and instructions, are promising choices for the compilation of small learner corpora since the gener-alizations to be drawn from their investigation are predictably drawn from a limited pool of language features, and yet promote language awareness and are transferable to the study of other text types. Accordingly, the interpretation of how language use is to be limited in the classroom and how the texts are to be analyzed in the small learner corpus requires careful consideration.

The concepts of sublanguage and register are informative with regard to the choice of text type as well as suggestive of the manner in which corpus annotation may be undertaken. McEnery and Wilson (1996) introduce tools of corpus manipulation and explore corpora as finite bodies of language use through a case study comparing large corpora as exceptional tools for the study of constrained and unconstrained uses of language. They remind us how sub-languages (q.v. Kittredge and Lehrburger 1982) are hypothesized to be a genre representing a "constrained subset of natural language" as they are a "version of a natural language which does not display all of the creativity of natural lan-guage" (1996:148). The perspective of language deficit and restricted semantic domains associated with sublanguage, however, play down the creative poten-tial of language to realize meaning in response to the personal interaction between communicants, the organization of the message being communicated, and its content in particular contexts of use. When students and their instructor compile and use a corpus to study a more specialized text type, i.e., one being used in a limited social context, their attention is readily drawn to features of discourse and wording.

Language awareness is promoted by drawing on the intuition that we use language for some purpose in any given situation, and that its use and usage respond to the demands of the situation. While our university learner students bring with them from their native language a sense of language variation, i.e., of this text-in-context relationship, they lack awareness of the features of English discourse and wording that can appropriately and correctly realize it; ELT instructors, for their part, often lack a model of language capable of demonstrating and describing this connection. The concept of "register" as "the name given to a variety of language according to its use" (Halliday, McIntosh, and Strevens 1964:87) has been developed by Halliday and Hasan (1985) and others to provide a conceptual framework that closely describes the situational demands on language. Register is a semantic concept which relates the situational, extra-linguistic context in which language is used to the lan-guage usage itself. Here language "use" is meant as the application of language to fulfill a discursive purpose, while language "usage" refers to the wording, or conflation of lexis and grammar, that realizes that use. Halliday explains that "grammar and vocabulary are not two different things", as "they are simply different ways of regarding the same phenomenon". He argues that "the study of discourse ...cannot properly be separated from the study of grammar that lies behind it" (1944:366).

Yet discourse and wording are rarely investigated together. This is true in corpus linguistics as well as language studies more generally. McEnery and Wilson (1996:52) note how infrequently aspects of language at the level of text and discourse have been annotated in corpora, not only because of the demanding manual annotation this requires, but also the context-dependence of the text and the associated propensity for dispute between different linguists over their interpretation. Pery-Woodley, reporting on contrasting discourse studies, writes in support of broadening contrastive analysis, which typically has been restricted to predicting or explaining L2 learners' structural errors on the basis of L1 interference, to "throw light on what texts are and how they function" (1990:143). She argues that contrastive studies have been directed at sentence syntax, "in accordance with dominant thinking in linguistics, (where) both pedagogical and descriptive contrastive studies have tended until recently to be exclusively concerned with language systems as opposed to language use" (1990:143). As McEnery and Wilson perceptively point out, the missing link here between discourse and wording is the context-dependence of texts. A language instructor, however, is less interested in the outcome of theoretical linguistic disputes over how to characterize the connection between language "use", and "usage", than in the productive application of language description in the classroom.

Holborow (1991:24) has addressed this issue of context in her useful article on "Linking language and situation: a course for advanced learners". She asserts that understanding the appropriacy of text with regard to the situation in which it is used is a problem. It is particularly acute for advanced learners. Her response to this need was to develop a course which goes beyond the typical genre-based approach that presents the student with a variety of text types, and concentrates on the writing of surface discourse features of texts such as formal letters, academic articles, and the like. Her course consisted of examining the language-situation relationship, providing a framework of analysis, and producing texts appropriate to their situation. The theoretical framework involved the approach of Halliday, Hasan and others focussing on "register", "situational features", "language varieties" and their "social contexts", and "speech acts". She concluded that talking about language and situation as well as producing and practicing it were important for nonnative speakers to bring out their awareness of language variation and provide support for the contention that a model of language should be a way of improving practice.

Despite the variety of corpora in terms of size and text-type, most corpora typically share the characteristic of being samples of language in use, that is, authentic text operating in some social context. It is not surprising, then, that interest in small corpora first developed among researchers and teachers in schools and universities, where students are being prepared to communicate meaning in discipline-specific domains of language. Nor is it unexpected that student-written learner texts are now also coming under scrutiny in large and small corpora as the basis of much language teaching is the identification of features of language that are "at risk", that is, which learners are unaware of, have trouble encoding, or do not respond to as being valued by the readers of their texts. A small learner corpus which has been compiled for use in the classroom should be comprised of texts with features that are sufficiently varied to provide a picture of use and usage that can be transferred to other writing applications. The texts should challenge students and require a response to the writing situation such that measures of their use and usage, and the errors made in their production, can be used to assess language proficiency practically in terms of the success with which the texts carried out their purpose.

One way to address these needs is for students to write in response to a situation that gives them relatively fewer options from which to choose features of discourse and wording; that is, they are called on to produce a limited register employing a more specialized or restricted range of language features. Halliday and Hasan refer to the language of closed registers as "restricted language" (1985:39), giving examples such as the English that comprises the International Language of the Air, the language of many games, the bidding system in bridge, and the restricted language of menus. A limited use of English requires that decisions be made about how language usage, i.e., lexis and grammar, relates to language use in order to meet the specific needs of academic and vocational environments. The text type chosen for the small learner corpus exemplified in this paper was a set of instructions. The manner of analysis of these sets of instructions in the corpus was crucial in promoting student awareness of the interaction of discourse, wording, and situation.

A corpus comes into its own when its features are systematically characterized, whether this be the product of a time-consuming manual tagging or annotation, an automatic computer parsing or some combination of the two. Biber further describes a representative corpus as "a principled collection of text stored on a computer" (1996:115). This characteristic applies to a small learner corpus, which becomes principled through the application of the analytical framework chosen to describe its collected texts. The success and utility of this analysis is crucial for students as well as the investigator-instructor since it organizes the investigation, discussion and application of the results of the analysis in the classroom. This is the type of linguistic corpus annotation described by McEnery and Wilson as "problem-oriented tagging", in which the annotation is oriented towards a particular research, or in this case, pedagogical goal (1996:57). Since the small learner corpus exemplified here was intended to relate the discourse and wording of texts produced in a particular social context calling for sets of instructions, the semantically based features of systemic functional lexicogrammar developed by Halliday and his colleagues was chosen rather than the traditional grammar terminology used to identify surface syntactic representations in most corpora.[1] For example, the "tagset", or the terms employed to label features of grammar in the corpus, used for the *International Corpus of English (ICE)* is based on the terminology of *A Comprehensive Grammar of the English Language* (Quirk et al. 1985) to provide familiar tags with clear and precise definitions (Greenbaum 1993); however, these tags do not address the semantic and functional nature of language described from a situational perspective.

The small learner corpus of interest here was annotated for selected features of discourse and wording, which are listed in Table 1 below. The discourse features follow descriptions found in Halliday (1978) and Halliday and Hasan (1985), while features of wording are those described in Halliday (1994). The "register" of the texts in this corpus is a semantic description of their social context of communication. "Field", "tenor", and "mode" are the three interlinking elements of this context. "Field" refers to what is happening, the nature of the social interaction taking place. In this classroom activity, the "field" was the making of a design using coloured wooden blocks. The second element is the "tenor" — the relationship between instructor and student, i.e., between expert and novice, which guides the interaction. The final element is the "mode", comprised of channel — the visual and aural presentation of instructions via a televised videotape, and rhetorical mode or text type — a task-oriented procedural text, a set of instructions for the temporal and spatial manipulation of wooden blocks. Associated with the text type is the organizational concept of "generic structure potential" (GSP) applied to a set of instructions. GSP is defined as the total range of optional and obligatory elements and their order in the text structure appropriate to a text type, and is realized as discursive features of text.

The "wording" refers to the lexicogrammar of the texts, i.e., the conflation, or concurrent encoding, of lexis and grammar as the realization of the register at clause level. The semantic notion of field is realized in the text as experiential, or content, wording. Tone is realized as interpersonal, or exchange, wording. The mode of the text is realized in the text as thematic, or message, wording. The manual annotation of the text by the instructor ensures reliability of the marking as there was only one person doing it, and allows for selectivity of the features of discourse and wording used to annotate depending on the instructor's perception of student proficiency and need.

The annotation of errors of discourse and wording is the key to the combination of description and prescription that benefits student language awareness in the classroom, in particular with regard to evaluation of the success of their use of language. There is much scope for analysis and interpretation here, and intuition comes into play. Moreover, some errors leave no trace when a useful but optional feature of meaning is omitted for want of proficiency; alternatively, the error is apparent as an omission of an obligatory feature of meaning. The analysis of a small learner corpus enables an instructor to consider more carefully the under- and over-representation of errors as well as correctly encoded features in different parts of the text; comparisons may be made with native-speaker (NS) texts, written by learners as well but operating at a different proficiency level, to determine linguistic strengths and weaknesses of the non-native-speaker (NNS) group.

Because of its size and the likelihood that it will be manually annotated, a small learner corpus promotes an effective error analysis. This analysis provides the opportunity for the instructor-investigator to support intuitions about the students writing with empirical data. Granger reports that a major issue for a large machine-read learner corpus like the *ICLE* is the danger of "over-normalization", which refers to the excessive correction of the "substantial number of errors and certainly all those words and word sequences which might affect the performance of tagger and parser" (1992:61). This involves the analyst in the subjective task of identifying an error and correcting it. She indicates that in the *ICLE* an effort is made to normalize the bare minimum of

(1)	You are going to make a design using coloured blocks.
(2)	This design will have four sides.
(3)	The opposite sides will be equal in length.
(4)	Take one red and one white block.
(5)	Put their long sides together so that they match up evenly.
(6)	Line up the red block against the right side of the white block.
(7)	Place them flat in the middle of the table with their short sides facing you.
(8)	Take a black block from the remaining unused blocks.
(9)	Put one of its long sides against the sides of the white and red blocks closest to you.
(10)	Take another white block from the unused blocks.
(11)	Place one of its long sides against the side of the black block closest to you.
(12)	Now take the remaining black block.
(13)	Line up one of its long sides against the right side of the red block in your design.
(14)	Now take the last block, which is yellow.
(15)	Place it in the open right corner of your design.
(16)	One of its long sides should be placed against the short sides of a black and a white block.
(17)	Its short side farthest from you should be up against the short side of a black block.
(18)	Now let's check your design.
(19)	We will start from the farthest left corner of the design and proceed to the right.
(20)	The three blocks, in order, are white, red, and black.
(21)	The remaining three blocks are, from left to right, black over white, and then yellow.
(22)	Together, these six blocks form a design with four sides.
(23)	Its longest side is the length of two blocks.
(24)	Its shortest side is the width of three blocks.
(25)	The design is a red, white, black, and yellow rectangle.

Figure 1: The original set of instructions. The sentences have been numbered for ease of reference. The original text has no numbers.

assumes the use of a balanced set of angled brackets, <and>, to enclose references within a text. Here they apply to categories that are extended portions of text. The markers are diacritics, letters and/or symbols used to distinguish

Table 1: *OCP* format references and markers

category	format reference
student number	\<s \>
generic structure element	\<p \>
− orientation	\<p 1 – 3\>
− procedure	\<p 2\>
− recapitulation	\<p 3\>
clause type	\<c 1 – 5\>
− paratactic	\<c 1 – 2\>
− simple clause	\<c 3\>
− hypotactic clause	\<c 4 – 5\>

category	markers
generic structure and logical component	¢ 1 – 6
− isolating	¢ 1 – 2
− placing	¢ 3 – 4
− other	¢ 5 – 6
theme	{0 – 10
− no topical theme	{0
− simple theme (subject)	{1
− simple theme (predicator)	{2
− simple theme (circumstance}	{3
− multiple theme (other)	{4 – 6
− multiple theme (subject)	{7
− multiple theme (predicator)	{8
− multiple theme (circumstance	{9
− other	{10
mood	#1 – 8
− proposal	#1 – 3
− proposition	#4 – 6
− non-finite verb	#7
− complement	#8
transitivity	\$, %, or #°
process	\$1 – 11
− material	\$1 – 2
− relational	\$3 – 8
− existential	\$9
− other	\$10 – 11
participants	%1 – 8

Table 1 *(continued)*

– actor or goal	%1 – 2
– carrier, attribute, identified, identifier	%3 – 6
– existent	%7
– other	%8
circumstantial adjuncts	° 1 – 8
– c. adjunct (adverbial)	° 1 – 4
– c. adjunct (prepositional phrase)	° 5 – 8
other features	&1 – 9
errors	E 1 – 3
– omission	E1
– commission	E2
– other	E3

words when they cannot be distinguished in any other way. Markers here apply to words and groups of words, i.e., limited portions of text. Figures 2 and 3 below show an annotated text from student 3 of the NS group and student 2 from the NNS group, respectively.

After annotation, the *OCP* software was used to search for, retrieve and print out the selected features of interest. *OCP* was given commands to identify specific features that are realizations, that is, encodings, of the text structure of discourse that can be identified as relevant to sets of instructions as well as principal features of wording. For example, "orientation", "procedure" and "recapitulation" elements can be realized as part of the generic structure of a set of instructions. While "orientation" and/or "recapitulation" are optional within the generic structure of a set of instructions, their sequence is ordered; a "procedure" element, however, is obligatory in keeping with the purpose of the text type. An "orientation" is defined here as one or more clauses that introduce the procedure of making the design and which precede the first specific instruction for the movement of one or more blocks. The beginning "orientation" in the annotated text of Figure 2 is indicated by the format reference <p 1> and begins with the text "You will now make…", and ends with the text "…with the coloured blocks." This is followed by the format reference <p 2>, which is the beginning of the "procedure" element.

One of the benefits of a systemic functional analysis is the identification and relation of features of discourse and wording that are conflated, that is, realized concurrently at different levels of the realization of meaning in the

FILE: MP1AV-3 OCPTEXT A1 VM/SP —
CONVERSATIONAL MONITOR SYSTEM
<s 3>
<p 1><c 3>1. You{1%1 will#1 now02 make$1 a rectangle%2 + whose&4 opposite sides are equal in + length with the coloured blocksE3.
<p 2><c 1> 2. First{302, take#3$1 a¢1 white and a red block%2 + <c 2> and{5 join{8#3$1 the(3 longer sides%2 of the + two blocks&2 with the red block07 on the right side&3 + of the white block&9.
<c 3>Put{2#3$1 them%2 flat¢501 on the table01.
<c 3>The width{1%3 of¢4 the two blocks&2 should#5 have$5 one side%4 + closest to you&3 and + one side farthest&3.
<c 1>3. Then{6 take{8#3$1 a¢1 black block%2 from the remainingE205 + of the coloured blocks&2 +
<c 12>and{5 join{8#3$1 its¢3 longer side%2 + to the right side05 + of the red block&9,<c 5> which{5{7%5 is#4$6 + also¢404 the longer side%6 of the red block&2.
<c 3> 4. Now{4, take{8#3$1 a¢1 yellow block%2 from the remainingE205 + of the coloured blocks&2.
<c 3>Join{2#3$1 the shorter¢3 side%2 or width of the yellow block&2 + to the width05 of the + black block&2 that&4 is closest to you.
<c 3>You{1%5 will#2 now02¢4 have$8 the yellow block%6 + directly below the black block05.
<c 3> 5. Finally{6, take{8#3$1 the¢1 remainingE2%2 of the two + coloured blocks&2, that is&8 the + white and the black blocks.
<c 3>Place{2#3$1 the longer¢3 side%2 of the black block&2 + directly below the widths05 + of the yellow and red blocks&2 that&4 are closest to you.
<c 1>Then{6 take{8#3$l the¢1 white block%2<c 2> + and{5 join{8#3$1 its¢3 longest side%2 to the black05 + which&4 you have just put down.
<p 3><c 3>6. Now{4 you{7%3 will#5 have$5 a rectangle%4 + with its opposite sides07 equal&3.
<c 3>The rectangle{1%5 is#4 made up$6 + of red, black, white and yellow blocks%6.<c><p >

Figure 2: Annotated text of student 3 of the NS group

language. For example, features of wording in the textual component such as the realization of a "topical theme" in the simple, or head, clause of each sentence of text can be identified throughout a set of instructions. A "theme" is

---

FILE: LP1AV-2 OCPTEXT A1 VM/SP —
CONVERSATIONAL M0NITOR SYSTEM
<s 2>
  <p 2><c 1> First{302, take#3$1 the¢1 white block%2 <c 12> +
  placeE1{2#3$1 along¢3 the long side05 of the red block&2 + <c 5>in
  such a way that{5 the¢4 joiningE3 short side{7 + of the white and
  redE1 block&2.
  <c 1>Second{302, take#3$1 the¢1 unused black block%2 + <c
  2>placeE1{2#3$lE3 against¢3 the joiningE3 width + side05 of the
  white and red block&2.
  <c 3>Third{302, place#3$1 the¢3 unuse white blockE3 + long side%2
  against the black block05.
  <c 4>Then{6 take{8#3$1 the¢1 remaining black block%2 + <c 5>to
  place{0#7$1 the¢3 long side%2 against the + red block05.
  <c 4>Finally{6, take{8#3$1 the¢1 remaining yellow block%2 + <c 6>to
  placedE2{0#7$lE3 in the empty space05 <p 3> + <c 7>to
  form{0#7$1 a four sideE3 rectangle shape%2 whichE2&4 the short
  side is facing you. <c ><p >

Figure 3: Annotated text of student 2 of the NNS group

defined as the point of departure or what the message is about, and is realized
by the first "topical element" — "participant", "process" or "circumstantial
adjunct" — in the clause. In Figure 2, the word "put" of "Put them flat on the
table" on the sixth line of the text has been marked with {2#3$1. It is a "simple
theme", encoded as a "predicator" — {2. "Put" also realizes an unmodulated
"proposal" with regard to mood — #3. It realizes a "material process" in terms
of "transitivity" — $1, and falls within the "procedure" element of the generic
structure <p 2>, which began four lines above with the word "First". *OCP* can
combine analysis of features such as these, and then produce an index, list or
concordance of them with or without frequencies for all the instances of the
features of interest, singly or in combination, in single or multiple texts of the
corpus.

The texts of Figures 2 and 3 have been marked extensively for a broad
range of features of discourse and wording. It is possible that an instructor may
choose to mark fewer features, thereby spending less time in annotation and
using the small learner corpus to focus on a limited number of features of the
language production of groups or classes of students. These might be features

identified by the instructor as specifically relevant to the students' language proficiency needs with regard to the discourse and wording demands of the text type of interest. The instructor, for example, might wish to annotate texts for separate or combined identification and retrieval of elements of the logical component such as the relation between clauses; of the interpersonal component such as distinctions between proposal and proposition, and mood and residue; of the participants, process and circumstance realized in the experiential component, and so forth.

Investigating the corpus

The twenty-five NNS remedial students who wrote sets of instructions were in two different sections of their required academic English course. They had undergone 12 years of comprehensive, traditional English study in Singaporean primary and secondary schools. Their first encounter with a corpus and with features of the systemic functional model of language took place with their undertaking the task based language learning activity of communicating sets of instructions as part of their remedial English course. The production of lists, indexes and concordances by OCP culled from selected features of the texts they and the NS students had written, became the stimulus for classroom analysis and discussion of the writing of sets of instructions. The features described here have been chosen to illustrate how quantified data can be used to identify characteristics of the writing of learners and open discussion about use and usage with reference to the situation, in particular the rhetorical mode, or text type, as it is realized here as sets of instructions. Many classroom instructors have some familiarity with lists of lexical items found in a concordance; instead, the emphasis here is to exemplify the occurrence of words and strings identified as functional units of wording and discourse.

A quantitative perspective: investigating frequency data

A noteworthy characteristic of a specialized corpus is that on comparison it will yield quantitative evidence of how it differs from other special uses of language as well as from general corpora in terms of features of discourse and wording. It will, to a greater or lesser degree, not only be different from corpora of other text-types, but will also disclose differences that exist between it and a NS corpus comprised of the same specialized text type. Given the availability of a similar NS corpus, I opened discussion of the texts by selecting features enumerated by OCP that bring out more general characteristics of the text type and point to general differences between learner and native speaker texts in the corpus. These selections stimulated student interest and led to qualitative investigations of texts conducted by presenting students with specific instances of language in a concordance or list. Examples of such data are shown in Table 2.

Table 2: Frequency of words, clauses, generic structure elements, and total errors with averages per text

group/element	words (average)	clauses (average)	no. of elements (average)	errors (average)
NS				
– orientation	261 (10.4)	30 (1.2)	15 (0.6)	
– procedure	4761 (190.4)	406 (16.2)	25 (1)	
– recapitulation	1253 (50.1)	93 (3.7)	23 (0.9)	
– total	6275 (251)	529 (21.2)	63 (2.5)	25 (1)
NNS				
– orientation	274 (11)	27 (1.1)	11 (0.4)	
– procedure	4205 (168)	384 (15.4)	25 (1)	
– recapitulation	854 (34.2)	27 (1.1)	21 (0.8)	
– total	5333 (213.3)	481 (19.2)	57 (2.3)	125 (5)

As results of the analysis of the 50 texts of this corpus, these data were not subjected to statistical tests of significance. Instead, they were shared with the NNS students and became starting points for discussion of how the sets of instructions written by NS and NNS differed. In this case, the NNS learners noted that they that had written somewhat fewer words overall than the NS group, more notably in the "recapitulation", where they also had written many fewer clauses than the NS group. They had written somewhat fewer "orientations" and "recapitulations". They questioned the significance of the difference in number of errors and how useful the optional "orientation" and "recapitulation" elements were in their texts. This led to speculation about how useful their instructions would be if given to someone to follow without an accompanying video to watch. This was later tried out following discussion of the corpus data.

At this point I prepared a concordance of particular features or combination of features that had proven of interest in discussion of the introductory data. This could be, for instance, all the clauses in "orientation" elements, to introduce students to the wording of discursive or lexicogrammatical features in an element whose purpose is to prepare the reader for the ensuing instructions. While errors are often of greatest interest to the students at the beginning of the investigation, I found it better to delay scrutiny of these items pending study of the encoding of the specific lexicogrammatical features students may be having difficulty encoding. A concordance may then be produced which displays errors in combination or proximity with features which have since become familiar and are of particular interest, such as the "themes" of clauses or the "predicators" of proposals.

A further example of quantified data that proved stimulating to the NNS students and exemplifies the value of the use of a small learner corpus in the classroom involved presenting data about the wording of experiential meaning, namely, the content function of process, and interpersonal meaning, namely, the content function of modality. I did this again in association with their occurrence in elements of the generic structure. This combines discursive and lexicogrammatical features which highlight the interaction of use and usage in this particular academic situation of use.

Table 3 shows data for the wording of content in terms of the "transitivity structure" of the clause, in terms of "process". "Process" is the wording that refers to what is going on, such as "doing", "being", and "saying", and is typically realized by a verbal group. Data are shown here for the two types most likely to be realized in a set of instructions dealing with the movement of concrete objects. The first is "material process", which expresses "doing" involving an "actor participant" extending the process to a "goal participant". "Then take a black block" is an example of a "material process" clause written by student 3 of the NS group (see line 9 of Figure 2 above). The second is "relational process", which expresses "being" involving an "identifying" or "attributive" relationship between two participants. "Now you will have a rectangle…opposite sides equal." is an example of a "relational process" clause written by student 3 of the NS group (see the fourth from the last line of Figure 2 above).

Also given in Table 3 are data for the wording of content in terms of the mood structure of the clause. A basic semantic concept here, which serves nicely to introduce mood structure to students, is the distinction between two of the primary speech functions, "propositions" and "proposals". "Propositions" are realised as statements and questions, having to do with exchange of information, while "proposals" are realised as offers and commands, having to do with the exchange of goods and services. The example of "material process" in the preceding paragraph is, of course, realised in a clause that is a command or "proposal". The example of "relational process", in turn, is realised in a clause that is a statement or "proposition".

Table 3: Frequency of features of process and mood in elements of the generic structure

	(orientation, procedure, recapitulation) NS	NNS
Material process	381 (21, 336, 24)	347 (16, 298, 33)
Relational process	135 (10, 69, 56)	120 (8, 76, 36)
Proposals	281 (5, 272, 4)	237 (2, 234, 1)
Propositions	196 (12, 114, 70)	194 (20, 121, 53)

Without doing any statistical analysis, students quickly focussed on how both NS and NNS groups wrote more proposals than propositions. Moreover, they saw that "proposals" seem closely correlated with "material process", and "propositions" with "relational process". After being cautioned about the differences in the frequencies of words and elements of the generic structure encoded by both groups, students were able to figure out independently that "material process" dominates in the writing of the "procedure" elements by a ratio of more than 4 to 1 for both groups, and "proposals" occur approximately twice as frequently as "propositions" in the procedure. This natural discovery of the clarity gained by the use of ratios interestingly follows the use of proportional statistics in many corpus investigations where ratios are found by dividing the number of occurrences of a type by the number of tokens in the entire sample.

As I described and exemplified the differences in "process" and "speech" function, students drew conclusions about the text type and features of discourse and wording. Their observations were significant and important, for they have everything to do with the purpose of sets of instructions, and made it clear that the students had become aware that usage is related to use. In other words, they saw that particular features of wording do go hand in hand with particular features of discourse. This particular investigation of data from a small learner corpus, made possible by a functional grammar, gave most of the students their first, clear evidence of the relation between wording, discourse, and text type. It was the classroom confirmation of their intuition that what one does with language must somehow be connected with the words one writes. It was clear that there is a role for intuition in corpus investigation. At my discretion, I was able to choose other data which would help focus students' attention on the relation between situation, discourse, and wording while improving language proficiency.

A qualitative perspective: investigating a group profile and individual texts

After a number of interactions with corpus data such as these over the course of a semester, it proved useful for students to turn to individual texts for a more qualitative investigation of discourse and wording. This was done in two steps,

(1)	1. You will now make a rectangle whose opposite sides are equal in length with the coloured blocks.
(2)	2. First, take a white and a red block and join the longer sides of the two blocks with the red block on the right side of the white block.
(3)	Put them flat on the table.
(4)	The width of the 2 blocks should have one side closest to you and one side farthest.
(5)	3. Then take a black block from the remaining of the coloured blocks and join its longer side to the right side of the red block, which is also the longer side of the red block.
(6)	4. Now, take a yellow block from the remaining of the coloured blocks.
(7)	Join the shorter side or width of the yellow block to the width of the black block that is closest to you.
(8)	You will now have the yellow block directly below the black block.
(9)	5. Finally, take the remaining of the 2 coloured blocks, that is the white and the black blocks.
(10)	Place the longer side of the black block directly below the widths of the yellow and red blocks that are closest to you.
(11)	Then take the white block and join its longest side to the black which you have just put down.
(12)	6. Now you will have a rectangle with its opposite sides equal.
(13)	The rectangle is made up of red, black, white and yellow blocks.

Figure 4: Unmarked set of instructions written by student 3 of the NS group. The numbers in parentheses have been added to number sentences.

starting with the identification and investigation of a text to represent the group, and culminating with students working on their own text. Because the small learner corpus responsively analyses variation in the writing of the students, it may be used to facilitate this progression from a quantitative to a more qualitative perspective. Again, selective use of the data can contribute to an overview of how the group has written their sets of instructions. While the process of selection of a text needn't be overly rigorous, it usefully relies on comparison between the NS and NNS groups, but can take place with reference to the NNS data alone. A profile was developed by looking at key features that investigation of the corpus data had led my students and me to realize are important to the description of a typical text written by a NNS student.

Through comparison of numerous data derived from the NS and NNS texts, the NNS students and I selected the text written by student 3 to represent the NS texts. This is a relatively longer text of 238 words with all three generic structure elements and 4 errors. Figures 2 and 4 show the annotated and unannotated versions of this text, respectively. Similarly, the text of student 2 from the NNS group was chosen to represent its group. Figures 3 and 5 show this text, with its 99 words, "procedure" and "recapitulation" elements only, and 12 errors.

Before undertaking investigations of single texts, I provided a transition from the study of group data. A look at "thematic structure" exemplifies the scope for qualitative analysis using a systemic functional perspective and

---

(1)	First, take the white block place along the long side of the red block in such a way that the joining short side of the white and red block.
(2)	Second, take the unused black block place against the joining width side of the white and red block.
(3)	Third, place the unused white block long side against the black block.
(4)	Then take the remaining black block to place the long side against the red block.
(5)	Finally, take the remaining yellow block to placed in the empty space to form a four side rectangle shape which the short side is facing you.

Figure 5: Unmarked set of instructions written by student 2 of the NNS group. The numbers in parentheses have been added to number sentences.

shows how an investigation of the group corpus data can set this up. The question of how a sentence begins is more simply answered in a set of instructions than many other text types. "Topical theme" is the first reference in a clause to meaning as content: it will be the first "subject", "circumstantial adjunct", or "complement" in the clause in terms of mood structure. From the perspective of "transitivity (ideation/content) structure", a "subject" is a "participant" (subject or complement in the mood structure) or a "circumstantial adjunct". In imperative clauses, I analysed the "topical theme" as the "predicator" (the "process" in the "transitivity structure"). This is because of the strong association of first position with "thematic" value in the clause; this structure has the effect of giving the verb the status of a theme, so "theme" is conflated with "predicator" instead of "subject", "adjunct", or "complement".

Looking at the data shown in Table 4 below, the NNS students noted how the type of "topical theme" seemed to be dependent on the generic structure element in which the clause was found. When I told them this feature is identified as the first reference to content, they recalled the kind of clause they had typically written for the "procedure" element, and how they had begun it with an imperative in order to direct the placement of a block. They contrasted this with what they had written in the orientation and recapitulation elements. From this they could deduce that the "topical theme" is a focus on a "participant" in a "proposition", or "statement", and a focus on "process" in a "proposal", or "command". A look at Table 3 confirmed that they had written almost all of their imperatives, that is, "proposals", in the "procedure element" of their texts. This is an example of wording that is related and responsive to the realization of discourse features, the conflation of use and usage. Examples such as these helped students to begin to grasp the relation between context, discourse, and text, that the situation called for a command, which logically was placed in the "procedure" element of the generic structure of the text. Moreover, they took note of the similarities between their texts and those of the NS students in this regard.

This provided an opportunity to make a further comparison between NS and NNS texts and led into an analysis of the individual texts my students had chosen to represent each group. The purpose was to illustrate what was meant by a "topical theme" serving as the "message focus" of a clause, and to relate wording, discourse, and situation. One way to bring out the differences between the NS and NNS texts is to present the students with the "topical themes" of the texts and show them the method of development of each text. In

Table 4: Types of "topical themes" in different elements of the generic structure

	(orientation, procedure, recapitulation) NS	NNS
topical themes	293 (22, 208, 63)	255 (21, 192, 42)
– subjects	146 (18, 73, 55)	112 (21, 62, 29)
– predicators	139 (4, 133, 2)	125 (0, 123, 2)
– circumstantial adjuncts	8 (0, 2, 6)	18 (0, 7, 11)

the manner of Halliday (1994:66) and Fries (1983), I took the "topical themes" of each clause and placed them in sequence under the general topical area to which they refer (see Figures 6 and 7 below). Across the top of each figure I put the areas of reference: textual reference to the reader and writer of the texts, such as 'you' or 'I', to the sequence of the block placement, to the procedure of placing the blocks, references to the blocks themselves, which are "participants" in the "transitivity" structure, and references to the design as a whole, also "participants". The sentences were numbered for ease of reference.

These visual layouts clearly showed the students how the NS text is more diverse, with three exophoric references to the reader and a concluding reference to the design as a whole, "the rectangle". All but one of the "topical themes" of the NNS text refer to the sequence and procedure. Lack of reference to reader and design in the NNS text accounts in part for the brevity as does the smaller number of procedural clauses.

My NNS students had by now become able to identify "clauses" and their "themes", and the difference between "propositions" and "proposals". They could differentiate between "process"," participants", and "circumstance". By looking at these diagrams of "topical themes" they could follow how the "message focus" changes from "reference" to the context in sentence 1 of the NS student's text to "procedure" and back to a concluding "recapitulation" in sentences 12 and 13. They contrasted this with the limited meaning communicated by the NNS students text. The "circumstantial themes of sequence" in this text are useful, but a simple count of clauses and a check of their "message focus" made it apparent to the students that shortcomings such as the minimal generic structure and lack of development of the text limit its effectiveness. Problems with clause formation and lexicogrammar below clause rank also became apparent from such an analysis and a closer look at errors.

The investigation of the small learner corpus had led students from initial

Reader/Writer	Sequence	Procedure	Blocks	Design
1. you				
	2. first			
		2a. join		
		3. put		
			4. the width	
		5. take		
		5a. join		
			5b. which (its longer side)	
		6. take		
		7. join		
8. you				
		9. take		
		10. place		
		11. take		
		11a. join		
12. you				
				13. the rectangle

Figure 6: Method of development of topical themes in the set of instructions written by student 3 of the NS group.

Reader/Writer	Sequence	Procedure	Blocks	Design
	1. first			
		1a. place		
				1b. the joining side
	2. second			
		2b. place		
	3. third			
		4. take		
		5. take		

Figure 7: Method of development of "topical themes" in the set of instructions written by student 2 of the NNS group.

quantitative investigation of texts written by groups of students to the more qualitative study of representative texts written by individual students in response to the demands of a particular writing situation. This was a task based activity calling for the writing of sets of instructions for other students to follow in assembling a block design. With discussion of the shortcomings of the representative text written by an NNS student came awareness of how a lack of proficiency can be understood in terms of situation, discourse, and wording. The notion of error was expanded beyond the wording of clauses to include the discursive function of text and responses to the needs of readers in the situational context.

The students had not forgotten the task based nature of their original writing of the sets of instructions. Their introduction to the relation between situation, discourse, and wording culminated in the evaluation of their own texts.[3] As part of the conclusion of the TBLL activity, I gave the representative text written by the NS student to a group of 25 NS students, and the representative text written by the NNS student to a different class of 25 NS students, along with sets of colored wooden blocks. They were asked to follow their set of instructions and individually make a design with their blocks. The success with which they built the design was considered a measure of the effectiveness of the texts. The broadest evaluation of the outcome of this task, but a relevant one of great interest to the students who had written the texts, was a count of the number of correct designs. In the first group of 25 students, 21 students were able to construct the design correctly in response to the NS student's text. However, only 6 out of 25 students in the other group were able to make the design by following the NNS students' instructions.

This evaluation motivated my students to further investigate their small learner corpus, the two representative texts, and their own set of instructions. Students enjoyed looking for empirical language data because it offers an explicit, concrete understanding of the relation between wording, discourse , and writing situation. Moreover, their experience with the range of features was transferable to other writing situations and text types. This final stage of activity relied on the *OCP* text-analysis program to produce lists and concordances from the small learner corpus to investigate specific features chosen as "key word" in different textual contexts. These included errors in context, lexicogrammatical features of multi-clause sentences in different elements of the generic structure, and comparisons of the variety of lexical choice in NS and NNS groups. In addition to being annotated for systemic functional features of language, this small learner corpus remains a tool that may be used to study the lexical patterns of these learner texts.

Conclusion

This paper has provided a theoretical and practical introduction to the use of a systemic functional small learner corpus by instructors in the classroom. Examples of classroom investigations of a corpus of student-written sets of instructions annotated using a systemic functional perspective of language suggest the pedagogical flexibility of this tool. By selective use of a text-analysis program with a small learner corpus, instructors can gain a better appreciation of their students' response to the demands of the use of language in context. This in turn will lead them to provide more appropriately for their students' language learning needs while promoting their language awareness of the relation between situation, discourse and wording. Finally, this functional perspective suggests a fresh understanding of language proficiency. A student's level of language proficiency can be measured in terms of the extent to which he or she can correctly deploy a range of features of wording and discourse appropriate for a particular situation and text type.

Notes

1.   The Polytechnic of Wales Corpus (POW), a corpus of some 100,000 words transcribed from a spoken corpus developed for a children's language development project, was manually parsed using a Hallidayan systemic functional grammar developed by Fawcett (1981) in order to develop a formalised systemic-functional grammar for automatic parsing (Souter 1990).

2.   This activity was part of a larger investigation of a task-based communicative coding cycle involving two phases of activity: (1) the presentation of different modes of a videotaped set of instructions on the construction of a design using colored wooden blocks, construction of the design, and subsequent writing of sets of instructions, and (2) use of the written instructions by other students to construct the design. The main corpus numbered some 34,000 words and was written by 200 students (Ragan 1987).

3.   A more detailed description of the systemic functional perspective of this classroom methodology for ELT and ESL writing can be found in Ragan 1989.

Bibliography

Biber, D., Conrad, S. and Reppen, R. 1996. "Corpus-based investigations of language use". *Annual Review of Applied Linguistics* 16: 115–136.

Biber, D. 1993. "Representativeness in corpus design". *Literary and Linguistic Computing* 8(4): 243–57.

Fries, P. 1983. "On the status of theme in English: Arguments from discourse". In J. S. Petöfi and E. Sozer (eds), *Micro and Macro Connexity of Texts*, 116–52. Hamburg: Helmut Buske Verlag.

Granger, S. 1992. "International corpus of learner English". In J. Aarts and P. de Haan and N. Oostdijk (eds), *English Language Corpora: Design, analysis and exploitation*, 57–71. Amsterdam: Rodopi.

Granger, S. 1994. "The learner corpus: A revolution in applied linguistics". *English Today* 39, 10(3): 25–29.

Greenbaum, S. 1993. "The tagset for the International Corpus of English". In C. Souter and E. Atwell (eds), *Corpus-based Computational Linguistics*, 11–24. Amsterdam: Rodopi.

Halliday, M. A. K., McIntosh, A. and Strevens, P. 1964. *The Linguistic Sciences and Language Teaching*. London: Longman.

Halliday, M. A. K. and Hasan, R. 1985. *Cohesion in English*. London: Longman.

Halliday, M. A. K. 1994. *An Introduction to Functional Grammar*. London: Arnold.

Halliday, M. A. K. 1978. *Language as a Social Semiotic: The social interpretation of language and meaning*. London: Arnold.

Hockey, S. 1993. *MICRO-OCP*. Oxford: Oxford Computing Service.

Hockey, S. and Marriott, I. 1982. *Oxford Concordance Program*. Oxford: Oxford Computing Service.

Holborow, M. 1991. "Linking language and situation: A course for advanced learners". *ELT Journal* 45(1): 24–32.

Kennedy, C. 1995. "Wish you were here: 'Little' texts and language awareness". *Language Awareness* 4 (3): 161–172.

Kittredge, R. and Lehrburger, J. (eds). 1982. *Sublanguage*. Berlin: Walter deGruyter.

Linguistic Data Consortium. 1996. "Air traffic control corpus". Available World Wide Web: <http://www.ldc.upennedu–me_files/atc.readme.html>.

McEnery, T. and Wilson, A. 1996. *Corpus Linguistics*. Edinburgh: EUP.

Milton, J. C. and Tong, K. S. T. (eds), 1991. *Text Analysis in Computer-Assisted Language Learning*. Hong Kong: Hong Kong College of Science and Technology.

Owen, C. 1996. "Do concordances require to be consulted?" *ELT Journal* 50(3): 219–224.

Pere-Woodley, M-P. 1990. "Contrastive discourses: Contrastive analysis and a discourse approach to writing". *Language Teaching* 23: 143–151.

Pienemann, M. 1992. "COALA: A computational system for interlanguage analysis". *Second Language Research* 8(1): 59–92.

Quirk, R., Greenbaum, S., Leech, G. and Svartvik, J. 1985. *A Comprehensive Grammar of the English Language*. London: Longman.

Ragan, P. H. 1999. "Aviation English: Idiosyncrasy, predictability and problem". Presentation at The First International Congress on English Grammar. CIEFL, Hyderabad, India. 12–20 July.

Ragan, P. H. 1989. "Applying functional grammar to the teaching of ESL".*WORD* 40(1–2): 117–127.

Ragan, P. H. 1987. Meaning in the Communication of a Set of Instructions. Ph.D. Thesis, National University of Singapore.

Souter, C. 1990. "Systemic-functional grammars and corpora". In J. Aarts and W. Meijs (eds), *Theory and Practice in Corpus Linguistics,* 179–211. Amsterdam: Rodopi..

Warren, L. 1992. "Learning from the learners' corpus". *Modern English Teacher* 1: 9–11.

CHAPTER 9

Specialised Corpus, Local and Functional Grammars

Geoff Barnbrook
Department of English, University of Birmingham

John Sinclair
The Tuscan Word Centre

"In any identifying clause, the two halves refer to the same thing; but the clause is not a tautology, so there must be some difference between them."
M. A. K. Halliday, *Introduction to Functional Grammar,* 1994, page 124

Abstract

This paper describes the use of a small corpus of definition sentences in the investigation of the structure of a restricted language — the language of definitions. The corpus, extracted from the *Collins Cobuild Student's Dictionary*, was used to construct a taxonomy of definition sentence structure types, and this taxonomy in turn was used as the basis for the development of a grammar of the functional components of the definition language and of the corresponding parser. It describes the basic nature of the defining sentences used in the Cobuild dictionaries, and examines their status as a restricted language. It also outlines the process of development of the taxonomy, the grammar and the parser, and the operation of the current version of the software, developed by the authors over the last ten years. This research links with a broader investigation of defining language (Pearson 1998), and with the development of local grammars (Gross 1993, Hunston and Sinclair 1999).

Introduction

Halliday's remark quoted above is intended to apply to sentences such as *Sarah is wise* and *Tom is the leader*. It is easily adapted to be true of all definition sentences:

Every definition sentence consists of two parts; the two parts refer to the same thing, but the sentence is not a tautology, so there must be some difference between them.

The difference is that one part is more *explicit* than the other. The task of a grammarian of definitions is to divide the definition sentence into two parts, identify what is being defined and how it is being defined, and produce a description of the gain in explicitness that the definition provides.

The corpus used in this study consists of all the definition sentences printed in the *Collins Cobuild Students' Dictionary* (*CCSD*). There are 31,407 word senses defined in that book, and the sentences containing the definitions have been extracted from the surrounding text. The size of this corpus is 434,220 running words.

This corpus forms the basis for the investigation and description of the restricted language of definition, and for the development of a grammar and parser for that restricted language. It provides an adequate sample of almost all of the sentence structures used within it. The availability of more example definition sentences would not necessarily increase the accuracy of the grammar or parser.

The grammar and parser have been developed for a wide variety of applications in lexicography and natural language processing. In this paper we consider some issues in grammatical theory and description that arise from the specialised nature of the corpus.

Background and acknowledgements

This work has been in progress for some years. It was first proposed in Sinclair (1987) and elaborated a little in Sinclair (1990), and a feasibility study was done as part of the Chamberlain Project supported at the University of Birmingham by IBM. Then it was developed into a working application in a European Commission funded project which extracted lexicon data from a

Cobuild dictionary (Project ET-10/51, see Barnbrook and Sinclair 1995). A full presentation of the theory, methodology and strategy of the parser is to be found in Barnbrook (1995).

The copyright in *CCSD* is held by Messrs Harper Collins, who permit members of the University of Birmingham to make use of Cobuild texts for research purposes. The authors are grateful to all those who have supported this work.

Small corpora

The overall trend in corpus linguistics is towards bigger and bigger corpora, providing ever-increasing power to resolve the fine details of linguistic behavior. Cobuild's *Bank of English*, currently containing around 340 million words of running text, is at the top end as regards size, but from some points of view this is an extremely small selection of a language spoken and written all over the world every day.

There is no virtue in the smallness of a small corpus, but some corpora cannot get bigger and some do not need to for a particular study or application. The present corpus has both these features; it is finite and exhaustive as regards *CCSD* definition sentences, and as mentioned above, it provides an adequate sample of all the regular sentence types.

The definition corpus is not intended to be representative of the near-infinite variation of general language, but it can claim to contain examples of the principal kinds of definition sentences that will be found in the language at large. This claim arises from two features of the construction of *CCSD* definitions; the underlying study of people's defining behavior and the instructions given to Cobuild lexicographers.

In the period 1970–1980 there was a lot of work done in the study of spoken discourse, and in particular of language interaction in classrooms (see for example Sinclair and Brazil 1982). From the transcriptions of many lessons, the characteristic forms of defining behavior can be retrieved, and various types of definition sentence were found. The team compiling Cobuild dictionaries were given guidance in how to phrase definitions (Hanks 1987) but no specific rules were laid down. The corpus then is "open text" in that it is not restricted artificially, and specialised only in the communicative objectives of the definitions. Compilers were urged to be consistent as far as possible, so that similar types of sense were treated with a similar phraseology.

There are several other Cobuild dictionaries published, and others with whole-sentence definitions from Harper Collins and other publishers. By adding these in, the size of the corpus could be much extended, no doubt with some additions to the types of definition sentences. Also, Pearson (1998) shows that in addition to the separate and clearly motivated acts of definition, there are other structures found in text which have a similar function. So the present small corpus may be seen as exhibiting the core types of definition, and the grammar and parser will be adapted to cover a wider range of defining language in due course.

The grammar

Before considering the general nature of grammars, it is important to understand the basis on which this grammar of Cobuild definition sentences has been constructed. It is intended to describe the operation of the definition sentences purely as definitions, rather than as manifestations of the English language in general. The functional components of the sentences and their relationships to each other are framed entirely within the context of the act of definition and do not necessarily provide any information about their behavior as general manifestations of English.

The nature of grammar

A grammar in the broadest sense is an account of the way utterances in a language are organised to create meaning. In a specialised variety of a language the organisation is not expected to have all the features of the language as a whole, and so an adequate grammar for it may be considerably smaller and simpler than a grammar that is expected to account for a complete language.

The language of whole-sentence dictionary definitions — as shown, in modern times, by the Cobuild dictionaries — is a specialised variety of current English. Compared with general English, it makes use of only a small part of the structures available, particularly in the higher units of language patterning. While most of the words and phrases in it are used in their normal senses and patterns, the range of sentence types, the functions of the sentences and the higher organisation of the discourse are markedly specialised.

The point of specialisation is not obvious nor even relevant to a general grammar, especially a generative grammar. An adequate generative grammar of English will generate all the sentences that are instantiated in this variety, along with many others that could function as definition sentences. It will also of course generate many more sentences, being much too powerful for this limited task. Given this starting point the likely strategy for someone writing a grammar of the restricted language would be to reduce the rules of the general grammar to prohibit non-definition sentences being produced. The discussions about sublanguages (e.g. Lehrberger 1986:19–23) reflect similar positions.

The approach of the general grammarian to specialised forms of a language, then, is primarily reductionist. In contrast, the approach adopted in this project, arising from a detailed study of the restricted language of definitions, is to devise a unique grammar that stays very close to the functions of the restricted language, and relies very little on received categories.

We believe that the grammar is largely successful, providing an accurate description of the way the definitions are organised to create meaning. Since the definition sentences are in ordinary English, the specialised grammar might also help to improve general grammars. All the definition sentences in our everyday usage now have an alternative grammar. Either they can be treated like any other sentence, or they can be described by this grammar, which assumes that they are intended as definitions.

Experiment will tell us whether the definition grammar is always superior to the general grammar, or whether there are some conditions where it is better to ignore the potential of some sentences as definitions. The likelihood is that such a specialised grammar will outperform a general grammar, and that raises some interesting questions for the future of grammars. The general grammar would be seen as a structurally oriented grammar, capable of performing labelled bracketing on the sentences but not able to work out their functions. In conventionally asking general grammars to cover both structure and function with one set of categories we may be overloading them.

We are so accustomed to the apparatus of a conventional grammar that it is difficult at first to avoid assumptions that are not stated in the text. As an example, within the definition grammar Main and Subordinate clauses are not necessary categories except in the detailed analysis of discriminators, which is the place where the specialised grammar comes closest to a conventional one. Elsewhere they are replaced by more specialised and useful categories, such as Projection and Left-part. It is possible to use a surface label like Left-part because position is much less variable in the definition sentences, and this leads to major simplifications in the grammar.

Unique features of specialised varieties

A specialised variety of a language is not always just a restricted selection from the full set of possible sentences of the language. Its rules do not necessarily form a proper subset of the rules for the language as a whole, contained precisely within the general rules of the grammar of the language. As well as lacking some of the features of the general language, the variety may have some of its own rules, which are not found in the general rule set.

Where this is the case, the general grammar cannot be expected to generate the sentences of the specialised variety. If there is only one rule for the specialised variety that is not contained within the general rule set, then the general grammar can be declared inadequate in advance.

In the case of the definition sentences, there is a structural requirement that is of central importance to the analysis, and which is unique to this variety. The word or phrase that the sentence purports to define, the *definiendum* (or head-word in modern usage), is printed in bold face type. Such a typographical choice is available in the general language to emphasise a word or phrase, but it has no pre-set structural value.

Clearly the efficiency of analysis of the definition sentences is improved by this typological requirement. No doubt much if not all of the information it provides is redundant, and can be retrieved from other features of the sentences; later, in the section *Matching* below, it will be shown that it is not always an accurate identification; but it certainly obviates the need for devising initial heuristics that will retrieve the information. In comparing the performance of a general and a specialised grammar, it should be noted that the specialised grammar is given an unfair advantage at the start, by having one of the most important structural items identified typographically.

Local grammars for restricted language

The idea of differential grammars for different sentence functions is interestingly similar to a strategy proposed by Gross (e.g. 1993) at another level of language description. He devises "local grammars" to deal with organised text that normal grammars do not handle, such as dates and addresses in correspondence. Local grammars might also (Gross, personal communication) handle unique structures like the "ne…pas" negative in French.

Since the development of the definition grammar, this principle has been applied to other areas of language. Hunston and Sinclair (1999) have explored the structural basis of evaluative sentences, and Allen (1998) has used a similar approach for sentences dealing with causality.

Hunston and Sinclair (1999) stress the importance of the application of local grammars to meet the demands of users of natural language processing applications, and the improvement in efficiency which can come from their use. This efficiency gain is directly related to the fact that the rules of local grammars are "inherently simpler, weaker, more limited than the other kinds of rules".

It must be noted here that local grammars carry an extra burden over general grammars, in that they have to identify in the flow of open text the textual units that are relevant to them, and that they are capable of analysing. In the present study the definition sentences were automatically retrieved from an electronic structured text file, but in open text, where local grammars operate, they must be capable of deciding which sentence or other textual units are to be analysed by them.

The nature of definitions

Pearson (1998, Chapters 3, 4 and 5) provides a thorough survey of the nature of definitions in both dictionaries and general text. In her survey of the strategies used in dictionary definitions she questions the conflict established by other writers in this field between precision and accuracy on the one hand, and simplicity of language and greater ease of understanding on the other. The Cobuild definition style is aimed firmly at simplicity. Whether this reduces the value of the definitions as a source of linguistic information can only be judged on the merits of the data that can be extracted by the parser.

The grammar of Cobuild definitions

This is a sentence grammar in a very restricted meaning of the term. In each paragraph of a Cobuild dictionary there is one, and only one, sentence that carries the *definiendum*. No attempt is made to describe second or subsequent sentences in a definition statement. A dictionary paragraph can contain a variety of non-defining statements, phonetic transcriptions, style notes, enumeration of forms, examples of usage etc. The corpus described in this paper is the set of definition statements extracted from the dictionary. No connections are postulated between one sentence and another. Each sentence is a text in itself; cross-sentence cohesion is rare, for example a definition statement may refer back to a previous one as in "You can also say..."

The function of a sentence of this variety is to make explicit the meaning of the word or phrase chosen as *definiendum*, and the grammar developed to account for definition sentence structure is aimed entirely at this function. As pointed out above, the *definiendum* is already identified typographically.

Elements of structure

The structure of the various definition types is dealt with in detail in the section *Definition types and their parsing strategies* below. The following discussion outlines the general types of functional components found within the sentences and their relationship to the process of definition performed by the sentences.

A word must be said here about the way "meaning" is understood in lexicography, and similarity and difference in meaning. Lexicography is a practical skill, and is not an arena for purists. It can of course be argued, as it often is in "pure" linguistics, that there is no such thing as synonymy, and no way of precisely aligning language with life and the world. But lexicographers just have to do the best job that they can, subject to all sorts of constraints — in the case of *CCSD*, for example, the target users were expected to have English only at an intermediate level, and to be able to afford a dictionary of only 600 pages.

So when claims are made below that two segments of text "have the same meaning", this is to be understood at a practical level; similarly if a phrase is held to discriminate the meaning of one word as against another, this is not intended as having full scientific or philosophical authority.

First-level

A sentence is divided into two parts, called the *left-part* and the *right-part*. The left part contains the word or phrase that has been chosen as headword — that which is to be defined, and the right-part contains an explicit statement of its meaning. Very occasionally the bold face word (or words) appears towards the end of a sentence, and in such cases the sentences are considered to be reversed. If this variant was at all common it would invalidate the "left-part, right-part" terminology, but of the 31,407 sentences in the corpus only 472 are reversed.

There are two principal relations between the left part and right part. One is that of equivalence. Essentially the two parts of the sentence are held to mean the same thing. In a definition sentence such as:

A **guest house** is a small hotel. (p. 248)[1]

it is claimed that the phrases *guest house* and *small hotel* are equivalent.

From equivalence arise the two powerful notions of *paraphrase* and *substitutability*. A paraphrase of a segment of text is another segment of text which stands in an equivalence relation to it, so *small hotel* is held to be a paraphrase of *guest house*, and vice-versa. Substitutability is a relationship between two segments of text such that one can replace the other in a particular context without causing a change of meaning; so in the context *I stayed in a ...,* there might be general agreement that *guest house* and *small hotel* were in a two-way relationship of substitutability.

Part of the realisation of equivalence is in the syntactic feature of matching. Elements in the left-part prospect matching elements to be present in the right-part, so that in the above example the indefinite article *a* is matched. The structure of the right-part depends partly on the matching or non-matching of these prospections (see the section *Matching* below).

The other relation between the left part and the right part of a sentence is of explicitness; the right part is held to be more explicit than the left part. Although *guest house* and *small hotel* each have two words, it can be argued that *small hotel* is the more explicit of the two because the words each carry their normal meanings. *Hotel* carries the meaning of a building in which people can have accommodation and food if they pay for it, and *small* indicates the relative size. In contrast, the normal meanings of *guest* and *house* do not combine to mean a small hotel.

Explicitness can also lead to a shorter right part of the definition sentence. English often uses an idiomatic phrase which is composed of common words, but which has a meaning that is not deducible from the individual meanings of its component words. This can be confusing especially to learners of English. One well-known area is that of phrasal verbs; for example, within the phrasal senses of *give*, *CCSD* contains the entry:

If a structure **gives way**, it collapses. (p. 235)

Both *give* and *way* are common words, but their conjoined meanings do not create the meaning of the phrase. The lexicographer has assumed that *collapses* will be a word available to the user, and since it is unambiguous no further explanation is required. (This is a case of synonymy, which is further dealt with in *The right-part* below)

The left-part

The left-part contains the headword. Before the headword there may be elements of cotext, and after the headword, more cotext. This cotext can be analysed into various grammatical elements which fulfil different functions in different definition types, and these elements are labelled accordingly in the parser output described in the section *Parsing strategies* below. For the time being, we shall call cotext occurring before the headword *cotext 1*, and that occurring after the headword is called *cotext 2*. The structure of the left-part, then, may be:

[cotext 1] headword [cotext 2]

(where square brackets indicate options).

As an example, consider the left part of sense 2 of *herd*:

If you **herd** people or animals… (p. 261)

The function of the cotexts is to express preferences associated with the occurrence of the headword in the sense being defined, so that the above example implies that this meaning of *herd* only applies when the object of the verb is *people* or *animals*. Each cotext also sets up the possibility of one or more matches which prospect suitable elements in the right-part, so we may expect the pronoun *you* to recur in the second part, and possibly *them* referring to the *people* or *animals*:

If you **herd** people or animals you make them move together to form a group. (p. 261)

The relationship between the left and right parts of the definition is specified by an element called a *hinge*. The function of the hinge is to indicate the relationship between the left-part and the right-part. In some definition types, as with the initial *if* in the example of *herd* above, the hinge appears at the beginning of the left part. Hinges also express inferences (or, rather, meanings that are conventionally assumed to be inferences). In conventional grammar this initial hinge would turn the rest of the left-part into a subordinate clause structure, but since the two parts of the definition are equivalent, there is no motivation to subordinate one to the other, and indeed to analyse the above definition sentence as Subordinate Clause, Main Clause would be misleading; hence initial *if* is not a Subordinator in the definition language grammar

The left-part of some definition statements contains a further elaboration called a projection. A projection is realised by the occurrence of a reporting structure at the beginning of the definition:

If you say that you **are starving**,....(p. 550)

In conventional grammar this would turn the rest of the left-part after *say* into a reported structure, but again this is not a formal requirement of the definition language grammar.

The right-part

The function of the right part is to make explicit the meaning of the headword by means of one of various techniques. The most common technique is that of analysis of the "genus — species" kind. Hence the right-part very often consists of a superordinate and at least one discriminator, in the classic style of definitions. These are realisations of explicitness, since the superordinate refers to a set of actions, events etc. which includes the headword, and the discriminator ascribes some feature to the superordinate which distinguishes the headword referents from other members of the set. The two terms are reciprocal, since a superordinate requires a discriminator to express its relation to the headword, and a discriminator discriminates among hyponyms. The usual pattern is:

superordinate discriminator

In some cases the sequence is reversed, with the discriminator preceding the superordinate, and some definitions may use discriminators before and after the superordinate. As examples:

An **albatross** is a very large white sea bird. (p. 14)

A **marquee** is a large tent which is used at an outdoor event. (p. 343)

There are two other patterns in the right-part, not nearly as common as the one just described. Occasionally the pattern of superordinate and discriminator in the right-part is not clear, and the right-part consists simply of an explanatory clause or phrase, called here an *explanation*.

Your **parents** are your father and mother. (p. 404)

On a few occasions the right-part consists of just one word, with or without matches; this is called a *synonym*.

A **cascade** is a waterfall. (p. 73)

A synonym has the feature of substitutability but it only offers a gain in explicitness if the right-part is more accessible to a user than the left-part — it is hoped that many typical users of *CCSD* might know what a *waterfall* was although they had never met the word *cascade*. This type of accessibility was an effect that Cobuild lexicographers strove to achieve, guided by the comparative frequency of the words in question.

Also in the right-part there will be the matching elements to those prospected in the left-part; these are detailed in the next section.

Matching
Some words and phrases in the right-part of a definition sentence are recalled in the left-part by the normal conventions of *cohesion* in English. Examples of matching items include definite and indefinite articles, usually matching each other, and pronouns, either matching other pronouns or substituting for more specific cotext in the left part. Matches are assigned according to the local syntax; so for example *a place*, *a machine* will be matched by *it*, and someone, *a person* and plural nouns will be matched by *they*, *them*.

In grammars of open text such matching would be called *anaphora*. Anaphora works backwards — the cohesive pattern is set up by the occurrence of the second element, and the previous text is searched for the *antecedent*. However, in the local grammar of definition it is *prospective*, in that words and phrases are identified in the left-part as potential matches, and the right-part is searched for the items which would confirm the match.

Structurally, the matching allows the main components of the definition to be identified. Matching elements in the left-part form the cotext, which, as has been pointed out above, expresses preferences associated with the occurrence of the headword in the sense being defined. Matched elements in the right-part simply confirm the prospections. One of the main rules of well-formedness in this grammar is that all the cotexts must be matched in the right-part. Hence those words in the left-part that do not have a match must be part of the *definiendum*, whether or not they are in bold face, and those words in the right-part that do not have a match must be part of the paraphrase of the meaning.

This feature finally gives structural status to the headword. At the beginning of the analysis, the headword is superficially identified by the bold face type that is used in the dictionary. This is convenient, if not necessarily always consistent with structural categorisation. In the majority of cases, the head-word is confirmed by analysis as the word or phrase in bold type, but there are a few where the *definiendum* is in fact rather more than what the lexicographers have picked out as headword. Usually this analysis causes the headword to be extended by adding in an adjacent word, a preposition or a very common verb. Because the left-part and the right-part have to be precisely aligned with each other in the grammar, these extensions will show up initially as non-matches, and must then be incorporated in the headword, with consequent changes to the right-part.

It may not be coincidental that in translations of the definitions, being done in quite separate projects, the same phenomena are reported — that the *definiendum* has to be extended in a number of cases in order to achieve a sensible translation. In general the growing recognition of the importance of phrases in current English is undermining some of the very basic assumptions of lexicography and lexicon-building — that meaning inheres largely in the word.

The parser, local grammars and functional grammars

This study originally built a parser that satisfactorily processes almost all of the whole-sentence definitions given in *CCSD*; that is, it uses a computer program to provide an interpretation that is true to their function. Since the definition sentences are written in normal English (except for the systematic use of bold face), then the parser will also interpret any such sentences occurring in the language at large. Further, the parser will satisfactorily process many thousands of sentences of similar construction that do not happen to be used in *CCSD*. It can thus be seen as a local grammar with a strong functional orientation.

Let us assume that a battery of local grammars can be envisaged, each of which analyses a set of sentences in functional terms, and which taken together describe convincingly the vast majority of the sentences in ordinary text. Such a battery could claim to be more of a functional grammar than the general functional grammars of, for example, Dik (1978) or Halliday (1985, 1994), while retaining the features of simplicity and generative weakness.

One reason why a local grammar may be able to produce a more satisfactory analysis than a general one is that it has advance information of the communicative function of the sentence, and so it does not have to work this out in analysis. Putting this another way, a battery of local grammars could not be used on open text without some pre-processing to decide on the likely function. So at present our definition parser can only be applied to sentences which are pre-selected as genuine defining sentences; it is not equipped with the means of deciding which sentences are suitable for being parsed by it. For example if we pass the following bogus definition through the parser:

A dog is a damned nuisance,

it will produce the following output:[2]

article (cotext1)	A		
headword		dog	
hinge		is	
matching article	a		
discriminator		damned	
superordinate		nuisance.	

The above analysis is a misinterpretation of the sentence. No doubt some sentences will be acceptable in more than one sublanguage, and thus parseable by several of the specialised parsers, either inappropriately, as above, or, in the case of a multifunctional sentence, quite satisfactorily. So the provision of a battery of specialised parsers would need to have routeing software as well to direct sentences into the correct parser or parsers.

General outline of the development of the definition parser

The parser was developed on the basis that the definitions in the Cobuild dictionary range represent a subset of English which is sufficiently restricted in both lexis and syntax to allow automatic analysis. A taxonomy of definition patterns was constructed from the corpus of sentences and parsing strategies were devised to deal with each suitable pattern. The taxonomy is discussed in detail below.

The definition language used in *CCSD* is less complex than that used in the larger Cobuild dictionaries, and so provided the best starting-point for exploration and development of an automatic method for extracting semantic and syntactic information from the definitions. The final version of the software takes definition texts and associated information, extracted automatically from the machine readable text of *CCSD* as described in the next section, and produces an analysis capable of direct human use or of input to other software, e.g. lexicons for machine use.

Outline of processing

The parsing falls into three stages. From a superficial examination of the corpus it is clear that there are several distinct types of definition structure and phraseology, so the initial strategy of the parser is to identify the definition types and formulate criteria for assigning any particular definition to one of the types. Then a basic analysis is carried out, which divides the definition sentence into its major functional components. Finally there is an output stage which performs any further necessary analysis, and outputs the analysis in the required output format.

Extraction of data from the dictionary text

The machine readable version of the *Student's Dictionary* contains much more information than is needed for the analysis. As an example, the full entry for *abide*, including the field codes which provide typesetting information, is:

[EB]	
[LB]	
[HW]	abide
[PR]	/%eb*a*!id/,
[IF]	abides, abiding, abided.
[LE]	
[MB]	
[MM]	1
[FB]	
[GR]	PHRASE
[DT]	If you [HH]can't abide [DC]something, you dislike it very much.
[XB]	
[XX]	He likes you but he can't abide Dennis.[XE]
[FE]	
[ME]	
[MB]	

[MM]	2
[GR]	VB
[DT]	If something [HH]abides, [DC]it continues to happen or exist for a long time.
[ME]	
[CB]	
[VB]	
[VW]	abide by.
[GR]	PHR VB
[MB]	
[DT]	If you [HH]abide by [DC]a law, agreement, or decision, you do what it says.
[XB]	
[XX]	Both parties must agree to abide by the court's decision.
[XE]	
[ME]	
[VE]	
[CE]	
[EE]	

The information needed for the analysis is the definition text (marked [DT] above) and the grammar note (marked [GR]). To make cross-reference easier, the sense number [MM] and the inflected forms [IF] were also extracted, and a sequence number representing the position in the dictionary of the selected sense was calculated.

A set of simple extraction and editing programmes was written to collect this information and to convert the various dictionary field delimiters (such as [HH], [DC] etc.) to a uniform field separator ("I"). This provided in simple form the information needed for parsing. For example,the entries for *abide* in the file used for input to the parsing software were:

if you I can't abide I something, you dislike it very much. I 1 I phrase I 25 I abide abides abiding abided

if something I abides, I it continues to happen or exist for a long time.I 2 I vb I 26 I abide abides abiding abided

if you I abide by Ia law, agreement, or decision, you do what it says. I 0 I phr vb I 27 I abide abides abiding abided

The only pieces of information contained in these entries which are not present in the original dictionary are the definition number (25, 26, 27), calculated by the extraction programme to facilitate reference to individual definition texts, and the zero sense number assigned to *abide by*. This phrase has no sense number in the original dictionary entry, and so has been allocated the number "0" for uniformity of processing.

The forms of the headword found at the end of each entry are taken from the text used at the start of each entry in the dictionary relating to the same headword, and do not necessarily all apply to the specific sense of the word under consideration.

Definition type identification

The definition texts, extracted as described above, are put through an analysis programme which uses pattern-matching to identify the definition structure type to which each definition belongs and to annotate it for allocation to the appropriate parsing software. In most cases this is done using only the pattern of the definition text, although in some cases the current version of the software also uses the grammar code provided in the dictionary text as an aid to discrimination between similar structural types. This is simply a short cut for processing convenience.

Basic functional analysis

The software which performs the initial analysis works on two levels. Firstly, the analysis into functional components produces a subdivided version of the original definition text, with each specific item within the data record allocated to a component. The second level of analysis identifies the elements in the right parts of the definitions which match elements in the left parts, discussed above. Some matching elements realise separate components in the definition grammar, while others are embedded within other components, such as superordinates or discriminators. The first stage of analysis identifies these elements and sub-elements, and where necessary tags them.

As an example, the definition:

When the police **breathalyze** a driver, they ask the driver to breathe into a special bag to see if he or she has drunk too much alcohol. (p. 61)

would be analysed by the first stage of the parsing software into the following data items:

1   When
2   the police
3   breathalyze
4   a driver,
5
6   they
7   ask @M2_the driver_M@ to breathe into a special bag to see if
     @M2_he or she_M@ has drunk too much alcohol.

The matching pronoun *they*, which matches the cotext 1 element *the police* is allocated to its own data item, item 6, because it occupies a separate, well-defined position in the linear sequence of the definition. In contrast the elements *the driver* and *he or she* within data item 7 which match *a driver* in item 4, have tags placed before and after them. The opening tag is "@M2_", which contains four symbols. "@" signals the opening boundary of the tagged item, "M" classifies it as a matching item, "2" points to its antecedent as Cotext2, which in this example is found in item 4, and "_" fills in the space so that the tag is part of the same token as the following word *the*. The closing tag is "_M@". These tags allow the matching items to be treated correctly at the final display stage even though they are embedded within the explanation element E which makes up data item 7. For this definition data item 5 is blank. In some definitions, such as sense 2 of abdicate, further text is found in the first part of the definition:

If you **abdicate** responsibility for something, you refuse to accept the responsibility for it any longer.

In this case the text "for something" would be allocated to data item 5.

Detailed analysis and output formatting
In the second stage the analysed definition record produced by the first stage is arranged in the required output format. The separation of these two processes originated in the practical needs of software development, but it does have significant advantages. These are especially evident where a definition has complex components or embedded elements. To make it possible to deal with these and other problems adequately, some of the final stages of analysis are carried out in the second stage. In the example given above, this second stage of analysis would produce the final parsed output:

hinge	when
subject (cotext1)	the police
headword	breathalyze
object (cotext2)	a driver,
matching subject	they
explanation	ask
matching object	the driver
explanation	to breathe into a special bag to see if
matching object	he or she
explanation	has drunk too much alcohol.

In this final output, the tagged items from the first stage have now been interpreted as embedded matches for the original object of the verb headword, *a driver*.

Definition types and their parsing strategies

The taxonomy constructed for the definition types provides a specification both of the grammatical patterns which sentences follow, and thus the defining strategies available to lexicographers, and of the parsing strategies to be used in their analysis. Both of these are described in detail below.

The definition type taxonomy

The taxonomy contains seventeen structural types, arranged into four groups, and these account for all but six of the original 31,407 definitions. The six unclassified definitions are examined later in this section. For each of the sentence types the frequency within the dictionary is shown, followed by a typical example.[3]

Group A.

A1	10,494	An **issue** of a magazine or newspaper is a particular edition of it. (p. 301, sense 3)
A2	689	The earth's **crust** is its outer layer. (p. 127, sense 3)
A3	358	**Forgot** is the past tense of **forget**. (p. 218)
A4	2,212	A **secluded** place is quiet, private, and undisturbed. (p. 504)
A5	2,202	Something that is **hidden** is not easily noticed. (p. 263, sense 1)

| A6 | 1,441 | To **commit** money or resources to something means to use them for a particular purpose. (p. 101, sense 2) |
| A7 | 172 | New people who are introduced into an organization and whose fresh ideas are likely to improve it are referred to as **new blood**, **fresh blood**, or **young blood**. (p. 52, phrases) |

The seven definition types making up group A (covering 17,568 definition sentences, 55.94% of the 31,407 definitions in the dictionary as a whole), share a general pattern in which each definition forms a statement of identity between the item being defined, the *definiendum*, and its defining text or *definiens*. While this is true, in a sense, for all definitions, in group A the relationship is more straightforward.

The identity may be direct, as in the example from type A2, in which "the earth's crust" is capable of being replaced in use by "the earth's outer layer", or through a projection, as in the type A7 example. Here the "new people who are introduced into an organization" are not literally equated with "new blood" etc., but "are referred to" in that way. Similarly, the type A6 example explicitly equates the meaning of "to commit money or resources to something" with "to use them for a particular purpose".

The most common single part of speech to be defined using the strategy found in this group is the noun, defined in all the type A1 definitions (59.73% of group A). Type A4 (12.59%) uses a very similar sentence structure to define the adjective, but the focus of the definition is shifted. In the example given, the noun *place* is used as an illustration of the typical context of this meaning of *secluded*. The identity expressed in this case is between the two possible ways of describing this noun: *secluded* and *quiet, private, and undisturbed*. Type A5 uses a more complex version of the same structure to deal with predicative rather than attributive adjectives.

Type A3 is a slightly special case within group A, in that it represents a form of grammatical cross-reference, used particularly for linking irregular forms of words to their base forms.

Group B.

| B1 | 7,528 | When a country **liberalizes** its laws or its attitudes, it makes them less strict and allows more freedom. (p. 322) |

B2	1,813	If someone is **run-down**, they are tired or ill; (p. 491, sense 1)
B3	1,714	If you do something **in class**, you do it during a lesson in school. (p. 89, Phrases)
B4	14	You ask what has **got into** someone when they are behaving in an unexpected way; (p. 233, sense 3)

The group B definitions (11,069 or 35.24%) use a structure that conventional grammar would call "conditional" to define their headwords, most commonly verbs. The conditional structure can be introduced by *if* or *when*, with associated implications for the inevitability or otherwise of the linguistic item being defined. Type B1 is the typical structure, associated with verbs, while types B2 and B3 use the same sort of shift in focus described under group A above to define mainly adjectives and adverbial constructions respectively. Type B4 uses a form where the "conditional" is final in the sentence, to deal with a range of phrases.

Group C.

C1	1,524	You can also say you **admire** something when you look with pleasure at it. (p. 8, sense 2)
C2	561	If you say to someone that something is **their own affair**, you mean that you do not want to know about or become involved in their activities. (p. 10, sense 4)
C3	224	You can refer to a change back to a former state as a **return** to that state. (p. 480, sense 10)
C4	76	When someone creates something that has never existed before, you can refer to this event as the **invention** of the thing. (p. 298, sense 3)
C5	362	**Equatorial** is used to describe places and conditions near or at the equator. (p. 182)

Group C (2,747 definitions, 8.75%) consists of various kinds of projections, which describe the linguistic purposes and situations associated with the headwords. This is reflected in the lack of a typical part of speech defined by sentences within this group, and the rather elaborate and tentative constructions used to introduce the definitions. The optional use of *can* or similar words in several of the types within this group distances the lexicographer slightly from the usage being described.

Group D.

D1   17   In **humid** places, the weather is hot and damp. (p. 272)

This is a small group, consisting entirely of 17 type D1 sentences, all of which use a preliminary phrase beginning with *in* to introduce their head-words. In the context of the normal structure of the definition sentences, this introductory phrase has more in common with usage notes, which are not covered by this description. At an early stage in the investigation it was realised that the underlying structure of some definition sentences was being masked by extraneous information added to the beginning of the sentence. As an example, consider the definition of sense 3 of *queen* (p. 454):

In chess, the **queen** is the most powerful piece, which can be moved in any direction.

The introductory phrase *in chess* masks the underlying type A1 structure of this definition, and initially caused problems for the recognition. To avoid this, an extra stage was added to the preprocessing routines used to extract the data from the original dictionary files. The usage note element, *in chess* in this example, was removed from the beginning of the sentence and placed in its own separate field at the end of the new data record. But in type D1 definitions the headwords are actually part of these introductory notes, and so are identified and dealt with separately.

Unclassified definitions

The taxonomy outlined above accounts for 31,401 of the 31,407 definition sentences in *CCSD*. The remaining six are unclassified. They are:

a) **Around** can be an adverb or preposition, and is often used instead of **round** as the second part of a phrasal verb. (p. 26, sense 1)
b) **Eminently means** very, or to a great degree; (p. 175)
c) Roads, race courses, and swimming pools are sometimes divided into **lanes**. (p. 313, sense 2)
d) In a railway station or airport, you can pay to leave your luggage in a **left-luggage office**; (p. 319)
e) You can also give your impression of something you have just read or heard about by talking about the way it **sounds**. (p. 537, sense 6)
f) You can acknowledge someone's thanks by saying **"You're welcome"**. (p. 641)

For a variety of reasons, each of these exceptions to the taxonomy contributes to a confirmation of its validity. Definition a) is effectively a compound of two definition types, type A1 and type C5; b) is a simple misprint — the headword boundary is wrong; c) and d) both give information about their headwords which does not constitute a definition, and e) and f) are reversed versions of type B4. Of the six, therefore, only e) and f) could justify the creation of a new type within the taxonomy, and it was felt that two definitions hardly made a structural type.

Parsing strategies

Each of the definition sentence types identified in the taxonomy has its own individual parsing software (although type A2 is so similar to type A1 that it shares the same initial functional analysis routines). In each case the parsing software uses pattern-matching combined with the structural organisation of the sentences themselves, particularly the bold-face identification of the headword and the sequence of sentence elements. The pattern-matching combines predetermined wordlists with text-dependent routines which generate potential matching strings.

Examples of the parsed output are given below for each of the sentence types. The output for each example begins with the headword, followed by the sense number where appropriate, and the grammar code. A full explanation of the symbols used is given in the Appendix of this chapter.

This form of the parsed output assigns structural symbols to segments of text sequentially; higher order units like cotexts, left and right parts are not shown, although they can easily be identified.

Group A

Type A1.	current account
	COUNT N
A	A
H*d	current account
H*i	is
A~m	a
D*r~1	bank
S	account
D*r~2	which you can take money out of at any time using your cheque book

O*r	or
D*r~2	cheque card;
N*2	a British use.

Type A2. plumage
UNCOUNT N

M*r	A bird's
H*d	plumage
H*i	is
D*r~1	all
M*r~m	its
S	feathers.

Type A3 Does

H*d	Does
H*i	is
A	the
E	third person singular
L	of
E	the present tense
L	of
X	do.

Type A4. abrasive (1)
ADJ

A	An
H*d	abrasive
N*o	person
H*i	is
E	unkind and rude.

Type A5. fraught (2)
ADJ

N*o	Someone
B	who
H*i	is
H*d	fraught
H*i~m	is
D*r~1	very

S	worried
O*r	or
S	anxious.

Type A6.   anaesthetize
VB with OBJ

T*o	To
H*d	anaesthetize
O*b	someone
H*i	means
T*o~m	to
S	make
O*b~m	them
S	unconscious
D*r~2	by giving
O*b~m	them
D*r~2	an anaesthetic.

Type A7.   bush. (2)
SING N

A	The
D*r~1	wild
S	parts of some hot countries
H*i	are referred to as
A~m	the
H*d	bush.

Group B.

Type B1.   confirm (2)
REPORT VB

H*i	If
S*b	you
H*d	confirm
O*b	something,
S*b~m	you
E	say that
O*b~m	it
E	is true.

Type B2.   content (6)
PRED ADJ

H*i	If
S*b	you
H*i*2	are
H*d	content
A*d	with something,
S*b~m	you
H*i*2~m	are
E	satisfied
A*d~m	with it.
N*2	If you are *content* to do something, you do it willingly.

Type B3.   reaction (3)
COUNT N with "against"

H*i	If
S*b	there
H*e	is
A	a
H*d	reaction
A*d	against something,
A*d~m	it
E	becomes unpopular.

Type B4.   careless (2)
ADJ

S*b	You
V*p	do
O*b	something
A*d	in a
H*d	careless
A*d	way
H*i	when
S*b~m	you
E	are relaxed or confident.

Group C.

Type C1.	enviable	
	ADJ	
	P*r*s	You
	P*r*v	describe
	P*r*c	something such as a quality
	P*r*l	as
	H*d	enviable
	E	when someone else has
	P*r*c~m	it
	E	and
	P*r*s~m	you
	E	wish that
	P*r*s~m	you
	E	had
	P*r*c~m	it
	P*r*s~m	yourself.
Type C2.	amateurish	
	ADJ	
	H*i	If
	P*r*s	you
	P*r*v	describe
	P*r*c	something as
	H*d	amateurish,
	P*r*s~m	you
	P*r*v~m	mean
	P*r*c~m	it
	E	is not skillfully made or done.
Type C3.	return (10)	
	SING N with PREP 'to'	
	P*r*s	You
	P*r*v	can refer to
	A	a
	S	change
	D*r~2	back to a former state

P*r*2	as
A~m	a
H*d	return
D*r*2~m	to that state.

Type C4.   barrage
COUNT N with SUPP

H*i	If
S*b	you
V*p	get
O*b	a lot of questions or complaints about something,
S*b~m	you
P*r*1	can say that
S*b~m	you
V*p~m	are getting
A~m	a
H*d	barrage
O*b~m	of them.

Type C5.   Mini-
PREFIX

H*d	Mini-
H*i*1	is added
A*d*1	to nouns
H*i*2	to form
E	other nouns that refer to a smaller version of something.
N*2	For example, a mini-computer is a computer which is smaller than a normal computer.

Group D.

Type D1.   pressurized
ADJ

I*n	In
A	a
H*d	pressurized
N*o	container or area,
S*b	the pressure inside

H*i	is
E	different from
S*b~m	the pressure
E	outside.

Applications

The development of the taxonomy and parser described in this paper was originally undertaken to make the information contained in the definitions available
for applications in natural language processing (NLP). The creation of the corpus of definition sentences was the first stage of that project. But the corpus
and its parser have a valuable role to play in many other applications, some of
which are mentioned below. The contribution of the work to the use of the dictionary as a database for these systems or for other purposes is described in the
sections which follow. The direct use of the parsed output in lexicon-building
is currently being explored in the English section of the European
Commission-funded SIMPLE project, adding semantic information to the lexica produced in the PAROLE project.

In addition to these general NLP applications, there are also many ways in
which the definition language model and the software derived from it can be
applied directly in improving the construction and use of dictionaries prepared
on similar bases. The most important potential applications of the software in
this area are described in the sections below.

The dictionary as database

A set of parsed definitions can be used as a database for direct consultation by
users, and facilities for accessing dictionary entries on the basis of different
pieces of information are already well established. Dictionaries released on
CD-ROM, such as the *Oxford English Dictionary*, are pre-indexed on several
different pieces of information to allow searching to be carried out on most of
the fields within an entry. This can provide a powerful language investigation
tool when combined with an interrogation language or macro system. In the
case of the *Oxford English Dictionary*, it is possible to construct fairly sophisticated searches which can extract, for example, all the headwords with a particular language included in their etymology whose first quotation date in the

dictionary lies within a specified range.

Facilities like these are extremely valuable, but they still limit the user's access to the items of data specifically identified by the mark-up system when the dictionary was compiled. The main benefit arising from a dictionary whose definitions can be automatically analysed is the potential for the use of the whole text as an element of database structure without prior explicit indexing.

As an example, it would be useful if the dictionary database could be accessed by cross-references between words which share linguistic characteristics, including those not normally considered for indexing as individual pieces of information. For example, if you were considering the definition of sense 2 of "girlfriend" in *CCSD*:

A woman's **girlfriend** is a female friend. (p. 234)

you might feel a need to know what senses of other headwords had the same restrictive cotext,"a woman's". Once the definitions have been parsed, software can easily be produced to select these senses. Carrying out this exercise on the parsed type A1 definitions produced the following list of headwords and sense numbers:

admirers 1
bonnet 2
bosom 1
breasts 1
bust 5
cleavage 1
dowry
girlfriend 2
husband
maiden name
negligee
ovaries
period 3
suit 2
suitor
uterus
vagina
womb

At such a simple level, of course, it would be possible to use standard string search utilities to produce similar results, although these lack the structural information to identify "cotext1", and produce a less refined result, including all definitions containing the same sequence of characters regardless of their position or function within the sentence.

In the original electronic text of the dictionary the definitions are not internally analysed, and one of the main benefits arising from the availability of parsed definitions lies in the extent to which searches such as the one above can be carried out on the basis of analytic information which was not explicitly considered when the dictionary was set up.

The ability to access the information implicitly encoded in the definition sentences, in addition to that explicitly marked within the electronic text, greatly improves the usefulness of the dictionary as a source of lexical, semantic and syntactic information for the construction of lexica, or in the development of automatic disambiguation systems.

Dictionary construction

The detailed analysis performed on the definition texts during the development of the parser allowed the principles of dictionary construction to be investigated thoroughly, and identified certain anomalies in the production of the *CCSD*. As a result, it became obvious that the tools developed for the analysis of dictionary definitions could also be used both for quality control over the production of individual dictionaries, and to improve the general approach to dictionary construction.

Quality control

An important procedure in dictionary compilation is the validation of the text. A battery of checks is devised to ensure that all the headwords are defined, that all examples contain the headword, that all cross-references have referents, and many other details; much of this is now capable of being done automatically or semi-automatically. The availability of parsed text brings a new precision to the task of validation.

Six definitions detailed earlier proved impossible to allocate to types within the definition taxonomy. These and similar anomalies identified during the investigation proved helpful in highlighting problems and errors in the production of the dictionary. As examples, the recognition software which forms the first part of the parsing routines could be used as an automatic basis for detecting some types of compilation errors, while the ability to identify the functional components of the definitions makes it possible to check relationships between them, and their internal consistency, simply and efficiently.

General dictionary construction strategies

The overview of definition strategies provided by the taxonomy, and the detailed critique of individual definition sentences provided by the parser, together form the basis of a thorough review of the approach adopted to dictionary construction. This has already been used in a project to translate the *CCSD* into other languages. The definition types revealed by the taxonomy were used to identify potential translation problems before the detailed work began, and to select methods of overcoming them.

Full sentence definitions are much more explicit than the normal abbreviated style of lexicographers — which is why they are considered appropriate for learners of the language. They can of course also relate systematically to a set of abbreviated definitions, and provide a sophisticated quality control for "ordinary" dictionaries. Indeed, the draft text of the first Cobuild dictionary was automatically generated from a database using a set of conversion rules. Nowadays the large effort required to build and manage the database would not be justified, and the alternative of building and storing parseable text is much more attractive and economical.

New kinds of reference books can also be designed on the basis of parseable text. For example, the ability of the parser to pick out superordinates makes it possible to produce, automatically, the draft of a semantic tree structure:

Beer…is a…drink

A **drink** is…a…liquid

A **liquid** is a substance

A **substance** is a solid, powder, or liquid

The last definition is called *ostensive*, because it lists the substances; no superordinate is available at this level of generality.

Similar connections can be made in the cotexts (here underlined):

Beer is…<u>alcoholic</u>

An alcoholic <u>drink</u> contains alcohol

A drink is also an <u>alcoholic</u> drink

Alcohol is drink <u>such as beer, wine and whisky</u>…

Drink is alcohol…<u>beer, wine or whisky</u>

Alcohol is also a…liquid <u>which is found in drinks such as beer, wine and whisky</u>…

It is clear from the above that a set of definition texts and a parser can be used to establish a wide variety of semantic relationships among words and phrases. This kind of information has not been available automatically before.

Local Grammars

The definition parser can be adapted to accept open text. For this it would have to be able to recognise potential definition sentences, and reject those that had a similar form but were not definitions. It would not have the benefit of a pre-selected headword, though — as is pointed out above — this is not always fully reliable and has to be checked against the matching. It would also lack the word-class information provided by the dictionary.

The adaptation would clearly not be straightforward, but there is no reason to believe that it would not perform satisfactorily. It could also be further developed to deal with quasi-definitions of the kind described in Pearson (1998). A software tool that identified and described a full range of defining behavior would be a powerful asset, for example in future lexicography, in terminology and in translation.

General grammars deal with definition sentences according to their conventional structure; for example, the most frequent type, type A1 above, would be classified in systemic-functional grammar (SFG) (Halliday 1994:119) as realising a relational process of being, intensive and identifying. Many of the other types could be fitted into Halliday's classification, but with some queries arising. For example, (a) many non-definition sentences are classified in the same way as the definitions; (b) a classification may superficially fit a definition sentence (e.g. type A4 seems to fit the intensive, attributive category of the relational process of being, but definitions are not attributive, and the essential symmetry of the definition statement is lost; (c) there is no apparent place for ostensive definitions; (d) SFG is not automated.

There is clearly a lot of overlap, and indications of similar reasoning and classification. Definition is surely a relational process, relating a word and its definition. It is a process of being, rather than a material or mental process. Halliday analyses identifying clauses into two components, token and value, related by a verb that could well be a hinge. The correspondence here is close, but many of the definition types do not fit here; type B4, for example, would be analysed in a completely different part of a SFG.

This is another classic example of form versus function. The existence of the set of definition statements is objective evidence that all the sentence types function as definitions in the real world, but the general grammars will treat those with several clauses in them in a different way from single-clause sentences, and assign them different functions.

Let us briefly compare the kinds of analysis offered by the general grammar and the local grammar. First, there is the role of cohesion, which is called matching here to emphasise that it has a different status in the grammar of definitions from what it is normally assigned in a general grammar. For Halliday cohesion is non-structural (1994:309) which means that it is a feature of discourse rather than grammar; the analysis presented here does not make such a distinction. In the language of definition the matching rules are as strict and predictable as any concord rule in a grammar.

Here is an example, set out diagrammatically to show the matching.

If you / wrest \ something away from someone
   you /   take \ it   from them
      / by pulling \ it
      /   violently \

The matches provide a coherent background against which the definition holds; that is to say it will normally be found to be a correct definition when the circumstances of the use of the word correspond to the features expressed in the matches. Here the matches are:

you as subject of the headword verb indicates that the action is within the accepted social norms (*someone* instead of *you* would indicate a distancing of the action from this state of acceptance, a stance of neutrality.) Matched by *you*–cohesion type: repetition.

something as object of the headword verb indicates its transitivity; there is no guidance needed as to what sort of things can be wrested. Matched by *it*, *it*–cohesion type: reference.

from someone as an adjunct indicating that another person is involved, who has possession of whatever is wrested. Matched by *from them*–cohesion types: *from* = repetition, *them* = reference.

The word *if*, which is the hinge, is unmatched and indicates that the action defined is not obligatory. Wresting is not the same as for example breathing, which is unavoidable and so its definition begins "When people or animals *breathe…*"

The word *away* is not matched, and the parser at present simply reports that it has no status. It is not a discriminating word — the lexicographer might easily have repeated it with take, and then it would match. It does not seem distinctive enough to become part of the *definiendum*.

What is left is shown in the diagram above within slashes, and equates *wrest* with *take by pulling violently*.

The claim made by the local grammar of definition is that such an analysis shows an understanding of the text that is not reached by any general grammar, and probably could not be, because for example the way in which cohesion is handled in relation to definitions may not be applicable in other sentence types.

In the following final example on the next page, an attempt is made to show the difference between a local and a general grammar with respect to definitions that are made up of more than one clause.

One of the main differences between the two analyses is the discrepancy between the unit boundaries, suggesting that it would not be easy to reconcile them. The local grammar (LG) divides the sentence into two elements, and the general grammar (GG) into three. However, the first element of each has the same boundary. Within that, LG makes a three-part division, while GG makes a division into six parts. The concord matching of LG is not noted in GG, and the subordinations noted in GG are not found in LG. Clearly these are quite different ways of "understanding" the same event.

Note that GG is used as a default in LG, where there is no reason in the functional analysis to vary from the structural norms; so the Subject-Verb-Complement (SVC) structure of the projection mirrors the SVC of GG, and also the projection match SV; also the SVC of the explanation. So if precedence were given to local grammars where they applied, the two types of analysis dovetail.

left part	*hinge*		If		*subord conj*	*cond clause*
	projection	*p*r*s*	you		*sub*	
		*p*r*v*	describe		*verb*	
		*p*r*c*	someone		*comp*	
		*p*r*l*	as	*prep*		*prep phrase*
		A	a	*article*		
	headword		**paragon**	*noun*		

right part	*projection*	*p*r*s~m*	you		*subj*	*main clause*
		*p*r*v~m*	mean		*verb*	
			that		*subord conj*	
	explanation	*p*r*c~m*	their	*det*	*subj*	*reported clause*
		subj	behavior	*noun*		
		verb	is		*verb*	
		comp	perfect		*comp*	

Conclusion

The taxonomy, grammar and parser described in this paper, based on the small corpus of definitions extracted from the *CCSD*, provide a basis for describing the definition language used in the Cobuild dictionaries, for assessing its general properties and for identifying the functional components of individual definitions. Within lexicography these tools can be developed in order to analyse other dictionaries which use whole-sentence definitions, and they could be applied to a wide range of tasks in dictionary navigation and production.

    They have a wider potential role in lexicology and lexicon-building, in that they can in principle identify and describe semantic explicitness; definition sentences have an important property that the European Commission project "ET-10" demonstrated — they map relatively easily onto formulae, and vice versa. The parser is an intermediate stage, preparing the sentence for "translation" into a formula which can then be manipulated by machine. A generator can be built to operate in the reverse direction, as Cobuild showed some years ago (Clear 1987:59).

Finally, there is the relation between this highly specialised language and the general grammar of English. Sentences of the kind found in the corpus are also found in open text, where a general grammar would give them an almost totally different analysis. This raises two important questions that we hope will be followed up in new work:

(1) The grammar of definitions is above all a functional grammar; the fact that each sentence is a definition is given before the parser starts work. The parser reveals the way in which the definition does its job, how it "explicitises".

But general grammars, including those that call themselves "functional", do not as yet explain how a definition defines. There are signs of partial alignment in e.g. Halliday (1994), and one could envisage, for example, many type A1 definitions being linkable to intensive identifying relational clauses. The cost from one point of view would be the scattering of the definition sentences all over the grammar, as function gave way to form; and from the general grammar perspective it would be necessary to review the structural role of cohesion. The question is: Can these two views of (functional) grammar be reconciled?

(2) The grammar of definitions is a local grammar, in that it only performs properly on one type of sentence; correspondingly it is very modest in scope, very simple in structure and very "weak" in terms of the variety and type of rules. There is parallel work going on to develop other local grammars with similar functional goals and simple apparatus. Perhaps in a few years' time there will be a battery of local grammars and routeing procedures which among them can analyse satisfactorily the bulk of open text. General grammar fits in residually, when the special structures of the type have been identified by the parsers.

Would general grammars make better progress if the function of sentences, as demonstrated here, was (a) taken into account in the GG, and (b) not duplicated in the GG?

Notes

1. All quoted definitions are from *Collins Cobuild Student's Dictionary*, First Edition, 1990.
2. The descriptive terms are informal at this stage; the set of symbols in use is given in the Appendix of this paper.

References

Allen, C. M. 1998. A Local Grammar of Cause and Effect: A corpus-driven study. MA dissertation, University of Birmingham.

Barnbrook, G. 1995. The Language of Definition. PhD dissertation, University of Birmingham.

Barnbrook, G. and Sinclair, J. McH. 1994. "Parsing Cobuild entries". In J. McH.. Sinclair, M. Hoelter and C. Peters (eds), *The Languages of Definition*, 13–58 [Studies in Machine Translation and Natural Language Processing7]. Luxembourg: The European Commission.

Clear, J. 1987. "Computing". In J. McH. Sinclair (ed), *Looking Up*, Chapter 2. London: Harper Collins.

Collins Cobuild Student's Dictionary, First Edition 1990: London: Harper Collins.

Dik, S. C. 1978. *Functional Grammar* [North-Holland Linguistic Series 37]. Amsterdam: North-Holland.

Foley, J. A. (ed), 1996. *J. McH.. Sinclair on Lexis and Lexicography*. Singapore: Unipress.

Grishman, R. and Kittredge, R. 1986. *Analysing Language in Restricted Domains*. Hillsdale NJ: Lawrence Erlbaum Associates.

Gross, M. 1993. "Local grammars and their representation by finite automata". In M. P. Hoey (ed), *Data, Description, Discourse: Papers on the English language in honour of John McH. Sinclair*, 26–38. London: Harper Collins.

Halliday, M. A. K. 1985; 1994. *Introduction to Functional Grammar*, 1st and 2nd editions. London: Arnold.

Hoey, M. P. (ed), 1993. *Data, Description, Discourse: Papers on the English language in honour of John McH. Sinclair*. London: Harper Collins.

Hanks, P. W. 1987. "Definitions and explanations". In J. McH. Sinclair (ed), *Looking Up*, Chapter 6: 116–136. London: Harper Collins.

Hunston, S. and Sinclair, J. McH. 1999. "A local grammar of evaluation". In S. Hunston and G.Thompson (eds), *Evaluation in Text: Authorial stance and the construction of discourse*, Oxford: OUP.

Hunston, S. and Thompson, G. (eds), 1999. *Evaluation in Text: Authorial stance and the construction of discourse*. Oxford: OUP.

Lehrberger, J. 1986. "Sublanguage analysis". In R. Grishman and R. Kittredge (eds), *Analysing Language in Restricted Domains*. Hillsdale NJ: Lawrence Erlbaum Associates.

Pearson, J. 1998. *Terms in Context* [Studies in Corpus Linguistics 1]. Amsterdam: John Benjamins.

Sinclair, J. McH. 1987. "The dictionary of the future". (Collins Dictionary Lecture, given at the University of Strathclyde) In J. A. Foley (ed), *J. McH. Sinclair on Lexis and Lexicography*, 121–136. Singapore: Unipress.

Sinclair, J. McH. 1990. "The nature of lexical statement". In Yoshimura et al. (eds), *Linguistic Fiesta*, 183–197.Tokyo: Kurosio. Revised version "Words about words", Chapter 9, Sinclair 1991: 123–137.

Sinclair, J. McH. 1991. *Corpus, Concordance, Collocation*. Oxford: OUP.

Sinclair, J. McH. (ed), 1987. *Looking Up*. London: Harper Collins.

Sinclair, J. McH. and Brazil, D. C. 1982. *Teacher Talk*. London: Harper Collins

Sinclair, J. McH., Hoelter, M. and Peters, C. 1994. *The Languages of Definition* [Studies in Machine Translation and Natural Language Processing 7]. Luxembourg: The European Commission.

Yoshimura, K. et al. 1990. *Linguistic Fiesta*. Tokyo: Kurosio.

Appendix: Explanation of symbols

Symbol	Meaning
A	Article
A*d	Adjunct
B	Binder e.g. "that" in type A5 definitions
D*r*1	Preceding discriminator
D*r*2	Following discriminator
E	Explanation
H*d	Headword
H*e	Headword element
H*i	Hinge
I*n	Operator "in" introducing type D1 definitions
L	Linker in type A3 definitions
M*r	Modifier, preceding a noun
N*o	Noun or noun phrase cotext
O*b	Object of a verb
P*o	Possessive pronoun or possessive noun phrase

P*r	Projection structure
P*r*s	Projection subject
P*r*v	Projection verb or verb phrase
P*r*c	Projection complement
P*r*l	Projection link
Q*r	Qualifier, following a noun
S	Superordinate
S*b	Subject of a verb
T*o	Operator "to" in type A6 definitions
X	Cross-reference
V*p	Verb or verb phrase

Where similar components occur more than once they have numbers added (as *1 etc.), and matching elements have "~m"attached to the label for the original component.

SECTION V

CHAPTER 10

Collecting, aligning and analysing parallel corpora

Ann Lawson

Institut für Deutsche Sprache

Abstract

In parallel corpora, each text collected is a translation of another. A parallel corpus can comprise simply two texts, one in the original language of production, and one in translation. It can also, however, consist of several, indeed dozens, of different translations of the original text. Such corpora are able to furnish researchers with considerable information about language patterning, for instance on translational equivalents, collocational and phraseological units.

This article will describe the theoretical background and practical experiences of creating such a multilingual corpus. Within the Trans-European Language Resources Infrastructure (TELRI) Project, a parallel corpus consisting of versions of a central text has been collected, encoded and subsequently aligned. This collection is still growing and is available on the Internet. An overview is also given of the research opportunities made possible by a multilingual aligned corpus with practical examples of such research findings.

Introduction

In the early stages of corpus research, the corpora collected and analysed for the exploration of language use were largely monolingual. In recent years, with the growing mass of information on the Internet in the so-called global village, easier, cheaper travel and communications and increased computing

power and expertise, multilingual corpora are coming into their own as reposi-
tories of information which can feed the ever-growing demand for language
pedagogy, translation skills and semi-automated translation systems.
Improved communication and translation are the keys to meeting the challenge
of this millennium. An investigation of form and meaning as contained in texts
in different languages can make a vital contribution to this effort.

By definition, all translation involves change of the text and its context, and
involves both linguistic and extra-linguistic features. Every language teacher
and learner has experience of work which may consist of strictly accurate translations of a word or phrase but which results in a loss of style and vitality and
thus often fails to render the meaning accurately in context. Translation equivalents are corresponding units of meaning in the languages explored (see Barlow
1997; 13). The "lexical item" is proposed by John Sinclair as an alternative to
the assumption that the word is the primary unit of lexical meaning (Sinclair
1998:1). Lexical items balance "syntagmatic and paradigmatic patterns", and
such units of meaning can comprise single words, multi-word units, fixed
phrases, idioms, proverbs, technical terms, and jargon. The correspondence in
translation mirrors these units, which often differ in other languages. The equivalence could be word-to-word (German *Haus*/English *house*), word-to-phrase
(*Schadenfreude*/malicious pleasure in someone else's misfortune), phrase-to-
phrase, and so on. Usually, the translation of individual words or phrases has an
effect on the rest of the sentence or even paragraph.

Researchers from a diverse range of disciplines have turned to corpora as
unique stores of latent linguistic knowledge. Corpus linguistics provides a
methodology for accessing and extracting authentic data about language use in
context. This paper aims to show the role of parallel corpora in the sphere of
language learning and the development of human language technology.
Working with parallel corpora can help identify the systematic, i.e. rule-based,
the idiosyncratic, i.e. list-based, and the contextually determined, i.e. frequen-
cy-based relations between form and content of linguistic utterances. I shall
begin with an introduction to multilingual corpora, then present a brief survey
of resources and texts already available. Then follows a description of the
process of creating a parallel corpus.

Small Corpora

What constitutes a small corpus is of course highly dependent on the context, the content and the timing of the corpus in question. Technological developments over the last decades have led to the compilation of enormous bodies of textual resources. No large-scale lexicography in a well-documented language would be undertaken at the start of the third millennium with corpus resources of less than several hundred million words. However, a corpus of spoken language is highly unlikely to reach more than a fraction of that total, and yet may still be considered large enough and, more importantly, entirely adequate for the purpose in hand.

Despite, or perhaps because of, the availability of what are currently considered to be very large text collections and corpora, many users require subject-specific and goal-oriented corpora. It is no longer the case, if indeed it ever was, that small corpora are a poor or amateur substitute for "proper" corpora. Rather, in fact, it is precisely due to the growing ease with which large corpora can be accessed and analysed, either on site, on the WWW or via CD, that users increasingly find themselves wishing to have data more relevant to their particular subject-field, with the additional information they wish to analyse. In this way, many users are not turning away from the possibilities offered by massive text collections, but rather selecting or creating their own data which can then be compared with and contrasted to the larger monolingual text collections. To borrow from the jargon of foreign language teaching, such resources could be called corpora for specific or special purposes (see also Kennedy 1998). Many experts in the use of corpora in language teaching such as Douglas Biber (1990:269) and Christopher Tribble (1997:106) advocate the use of smaller, specific corpora in language teaching. Moreover, it is now possible for relatively inexperienced computer users to consider creating and using custom-made, improvised corpora in a way that, in the past, only computational experts could attempt.

The focus of this chapter is on corpora produced for specific purposes using normal office or home computing hardware and software which is free or cheap, widely available and requires little or no programming expertise. Such small corpora can, depending on resources and purpose, reach millions of words of running text and can be much larger than their name suggests.

Multilingual corpora

I shall take the opportunity to explain some terminology at this juncture. Many widely available corpora contain material in one language only. Sometimes this material may inadvertently contain translations from another language, for instance in newspaper reports from other countries, but on the whole, translated texts are avoided. The most cogent reason for the exclusion of translated texts in monolingual corpora of general language is that translated language is not naturally occurring, and always involves some distortion, which at its worst can be referred to as "translationese". Examining a monolingual corpus can obviously only provide information about that language. To compare two languages or a group of languages, a multilingual corpus must be consulted. There is a lesser, but steadily growing body of multilingual corpus material, of which the two main types are parallel and comparable corpora.

Comparable corpora contain original, naturally occurring language material produced in one or more languages. In order to be truly contrastive, like should be compared with like. That is to say, the composition of the corpora in each language collected should be similar in size, distribution, age, topic and so on. McEnery and Wilson describe these as "small collections of individual monolingual corpora" (McEnery and Wilson 1996:57) which are sampled from similar sources. They ideally contain, like monolingual corpora, no translated texts. To make the corpora truly comparable, it is usually best to decide on common features, proportions, similar function and register etc. One major European project, PAROLE (Preparatory Action for Linguistic Resources Organisation for Language Engineering), for instance collected comparable corpora of 20 million running words for 14 languages with restrictions and guidelines for the proportions of text to be taken from different media (book, newspaper, fiction), the date of the texts, the subject, genre, style and so on.[1] In practice, however, much of this information is hard to capture and define, as many texts do not fit into such neat categories. Information about the subject of a text can often only be captured by reading the text, and many texts, such as newspapers, contain sections on many different subjects. For these reasons, comparable corpora usually do not correspond exactly, but their usefulness is not diminished by this.

Comparable corpora may consist of, for instance, parliamentary proceedings from the same time-span in two or more languages, transcripts of radio programmes of similar style and level, and so on. An ad hoc comparison could be made between similar quantities of, say, quality daily national newspapers published in various language communities in the same time-span downloaded from published CD-ROMS. Strictly speaking, such a compilation cannot be called a corpus, since any analysis will be undertaken on the data from the separate CDs. Indeed, many so-called parallel corpora should more properly be termed "text collections", since content restrictions are usually hard to enforce on material which is rather specialist and hard to compile. However, with careful thought as to the text typology and analyses conducted, the results can be outstanding with minimal effort. Another ongoing corpus project is building a comparable corpus of at least 10 million words of English and Italian legal language.[2] Comparable corpora are useful because the language is naturally occurring, thus reflecting better the language use as well as the interests and preoccupations of the society creating the language. Translation is by definition "secondary text production" (Schäffner 1998:83) and is often made in an entirely different age and place from the original text. Comparable corpora are therefore more reliable sources of natural language lexical equivalents. Since comparable corpora can usually be created from individual monolingual corpora, they are also relatively easy to find and compile, and can thus be much larger. However, for a comparison of particular language phenomena and translation equivalents, comparable corpora reach their limits and a parallel corpus must be consulted.

Parallel corpora, sometimes called "translation corpora", or "bitexts" in the computing world (Melamed 1997:305), are similar to comparable corpora in that they consist of material in two or more languages.[2] However, in parallel corpora, the material collected consists of both original texts and their translations. That is, texts are chosen which were originally produced in one of the languages, and their translation into one or more languages is included. This is a familiar concept in bilingual editions of books, but having the material in machine-readable form has a series of advantages. This should not be confused with what the translatina community commonly refers to as "parallel text(s)", or "parallel documents/documentation". This is used to describe (often non-electronic) collections of language material used as an aid to idiomatic translation, which compare roughly to comparable texts as described here. See Williams (1996) and Schäffner (1998) for more details. Some corpus linguists, such as Kennedy (1998:54), have tended to use "parallel" to describe what I here call "comparable", in line with the majority in the field. As Michael Barlow points out:

Taking a language to consist of form-meaning links, what we have in parallel corpora are two sets of form-meaning linkings, one for each language. And since the two texts are translations, the meaning part can be assumed to be approximately the same in both texts. Thus we are able to see how two different languages encode equivalent meanings. The art of translation is undeniably complex and involves many different kinds of processes, but we can consider three main aspects of translation, namely, language particular encodings of (i) event structure, (ii) discourse structure, and (iii) lexis. Each of these areas can be profitably analysed using parallel corpora. (web quote from 1996a)

In order to defend them, Anna Mauranen sums up the traditional complaints against parallel corpora as follows:

1. translation distorts the target language (TL) because it reflects the source language (SL)
2. translated language is different from original language
3. translators are unreliable and make mistakes (Mauranen 1997:160)

Her argument that translated language is a normal part of any natural language, and can highlight the contrasts between languages, is persuasive. After all, for languages of lesser diffusion like Finnish, more than 50% of all printed texts may be translations from other languages.

A parallel corpus may comprise simply two texts, one in the original language of production, and one in the translated language. It can also, however, consist of several, indeed dozens, of different translations of the original text. Wolfgang Teubert, who has worked on several projects building and analysing comparable and parallel corpora, lists the different kinds of parallel corpora as follows:

–   a parallel corpus containing only texts originally written in language A and their translation into languages B (and C ...)
–   a parallel corpus containing an equal amount of texts originally written in language A and B and their respective translations
–   a parallel corpus containing only translations of texts into the language A, B and C, whereas the texts were originally written in language Z (Teubert 1996:245)

The second kind, often called reciprocal corpora, are arguably the most useful as they contain language translated in both directions, although achieving a balance between languages of variant diffusion can be difficult. A description of the production of this third kind (called "multitexts" by Melamed), centred round a hub language, is presented below. Such corpora have the advantage that interference between translations in closely related pairs of languages is reduced. One may also be interested in collecting and comparing several versions of a text in the same language to see where the translation differ and agree in order to highlight common problems and consistency of terminology. Parallel corpora in general, since they involve versions of the same text in more than one language and rely on good translations, are harder than comparable corpora to collect in large quantities.

Parallel corpora are most useful when they are aligned, that is, when the texts are matched up so that they can be more easily compared. Much research is carried out into ways of automating this process (see section on alignment below). In language teaching, parallel corpora have the advantage over comparable corpora that they provide the student with a bridge between the two languages being worked on, to ease comprehension problems and allow first-hand the investigation of variance in structure and style of different languages. It is highly recommended to have access to a comparable corpus of similar material alongside any parallel corpus. The results of queries can then be checked against naturally occurring, non-translated language in order to confirm the results from and judge the representativeness of the parallel material.

Benefits of a parallel corpus

Parallel corpora were originally developed, and are still intensively used, for developing and improving technology to assist multilingual communication. A brief overview of the main fields is given below. Corpora, often by-products from other projects rather than specially produced, have been used to great effect as a classroom resource since the 1980s. Parallel corpora, too, have a role to play in language pedagogy. I will describe some of the main ways, referring to material designed by language teachers.

Parallel corpora are most often developed and used as training corpora in order to improve, for instance, stochastic parsing techniques and machine translation platforms (see for instance Brown et al 1990:82 for a discussion of the use of the Hansard corpus). The search for adequate equivalents and ways of identifying them accurately is fundamental in translation research and the development of translation tools. Although the early hopes of machine translation have been largely thwarted by the idiosyncrasies of natural language, a computer-aided translation system taking these into account may yet be feasible. Since much of translation is routine and repeated, it makes sense to automate as much as possible (see also Sinclair 1996:172). Example-Based Machine Translation uses parallel corpora to achieve preliminary translations quickly, as described by Allen and Hogan (1998:747).

Cross-language information retrieval (CLIR) is the meeting-point of traditional information retrieval and machine translation. Its focus is on the capture of efficient and accurate information in various languages, rather than direct correspondences between languages. So-called "transfer dictionaries" are used, that is, existing dictionaries available in electronic form which provide equivalents which can then be searched for.

Parallel corpora also have a role to play in monolingual language studies in the realm of word sense disambiguation. Many words, especially those which occur frequently, have several senses which can be disambiguated by the human reader but pose problems for computers. Since, in the bilingual context, ambiguity is usually resolved (see Leacock, Towell and Voorhees 1993), parallel corpora, especially with grammatical annotation, would assist to an even greater extent.

In multilingual lexicography, parallel corpora are a rich source of translation equivalents and usages not contained in the classical bilingual dictionary (see also Sinclair et al 1996). Language learners are often frustrated when they attempt to use bilingual dictionaries to translate a text into a non-native language. The amount of information and the way it is presented are clearly inadequate. After all, it is not a single word in isolation, but a "unit of meaning", embedded in a specific context, that needs to be translated. Very often, the "equivalents" offered in the bilingual dictionary are either not suitable in the context required, or do not offer enough information in order to be able to choose the right one. Comprehension is usually more or less adequately satisfied since the learner translating into the mother tongue can use expert knowledge of that language, but production proves more difficult. As Wolfgang Teubert says, "a parallel corpus of a reasonable size contains more knowledge about translational equivalents than any bilingual desk dictionary" (1996:249). It is to be expected and hoped that the current generation of electronic bilingual dictionaries largely based on traditional print dictionaries will be superseded by resources allowing access on demand to material drawing on multilingual corpora.

Language Pedagogy

Language teachers have long been aware that empirical, real-life examples of language use are invaluable to their students, especially when the learning environment is a country where the language being learned is not widely spoken and exposure to the language is therefore low. Modern learner's dictionaries take corpus evidence into account in their choice, ordering, definitions and the examples now included in most dictionaries. Corpus material has been used increasingly in the design and preparation of language teaching material and in the classroom over recent years. Giving students increased direct classroom access is the next obvious step.

Corpus material allows authentic material to be used in the classroom by the student as analytic researcher into lexical, semantic and syntactic topics. Students find their preconceptions and intuitions challenged, and are encouraged to build and test their own hypotheses and discover for themselves the rules governing language, instead of relying on dictionaries and grammars for explanations which may be insufficient in the context or not easy to put into practice. As Tim Johns puts it (1991:2), "we simply provide the evidence needed to answer the learner's questions, and rely on the learner's intelligence to find answers." Data-driven learning encourages students' discovery as an integral part of the learning process. Students also experience increased exposure to natural language, which they can search for the items or structures which are of most relevant and interest to them at any given time. Parallel corpora have the additional advantage that a bridge can be built between the language of study and the language the students are already familiar with. As students have become increasingly familiar with computers, websites and basic programming, their competence and independence has increased. However, very little research on the uses of parallel corpora and concordances in the classroom and the results achieved has as yet been undertaken.

Students require at least initial guidance in working with computer-based material, and the teacher must plan and prepare materials thoroughly. Using corpus- or computer-based material does not necessarily lessen the work-load, and may indeed increase it, at least at the start, as presuppositions are broken down and new approaches must be found. More advanced students may work more independently on larger, longer-term projects, but usually corpus material must be integrated into language teaching resources. There are several excellent websites devoted to the preparation of such material.[3] The findings and results from monolingual corpus use, in which area the main focus has been on teaching English language have been adapted for use in the multilingual sphere.

In addition, Joseph Rézeau has made available some examples of his classroom exercises.[4] The "Virtual Language Centre" in Hong Kong offers a large range of useful information for language teachers and learners alike. The site also offers ways of creating crosswords, multiple-choice and cloze tests.[5] The Virtual CALL Library offers a large number of freeware and shareware programs and suggestions on using computer material in the classroom.[6]

Parallel corpora can be used as a resource for the teacher to extract information, design language teaching material and present the edited material to the student. There is a danger of overwhelming the student with data which is too plentiful and varied, too hard to analyse and order. This is likely to result in frustration and confusion. For that reason, most initial classroom use of parallel corpus data is pre-organised by the teacher in the form of material presented to the class on paper or on-line. A typical model for such classroom material prepared from parallel corpora could be as follows:

- presentation of lexical or syntactic problem to be tackled — typical learner questions or mistakes
- investigation of how the issue is described in reference works (grammar/dictionary)
- examination of corpus evidence — parallel sentences (chosen, edited and ordered, either side by side or interspersed)
- creation of a hypothesis — rule-building by the student or group of students
- testing of the hypothesis on further examples
- comparing with material from comparable corpora as a further test

In addition, subject-specific vocabulary lists can be built up in electronic form by the students, with their favourite examples in context for differing translations stored for future learning. Statistical tests also have a place in the classroom in the form of comparative frequency, collocational and grammatical analysis. Cognates or apparently "true friends" (Partington:54) can be examined to see if they are really used in exactly the same way in context. In addition, self-testing can be undertaken in the form of multiple choice or word translation drills.

Several projects have concentrated on the preparation of parallel corpus material for the classroom. The Lingua Parallel Concordancing Project, funded by the European Union to develop software to assist language teachers and learners and trainee translators, has made many results publicly available.[7] The project, which began in 1993, involves several European partners from Denmark, Greece, Italy, England and France but the results are designed to be adapted to other languages. The project is gathering and managing a multilingual parallel corpus which aims at developing translation aids and language learning tools in order to ease students' and teachers' work in second language learning. The *MultiConcord* program allows the user to select a source and target language for which there are available corpora, then enter a query in the chosen search language.[8] The search queries are simple, allowing words or phrases, wildcards, and context queries which search for a word in the vicinity of another. Since the alignment is carried out anew on each search, the process is relatively slow on large and complex queries. Even so, this program is one of the most useful for the classroom, not least because of the test creation facilities. The webpage describes some practical examples of use of the program in a classroom setting and allows a demonstration version to be downloaded.

Parallel corpora can also be made available to the student, either in the classroom if facilities are available, or in electronic form for study elsewhere, for independent research. Some initial assistance is clearly required in the handling and analysis of corpus evidence. More advanced students may find it fruitful to design and prepare their own specialised small parallel corpora (see below). Such advanced study could focus on genre- or subject-specific features, or examine syntactic or semantic patterning in general language.

Parallel corpora also have a secure place in the teaching of special language translation and multilingual terminology. Bilingual dictionaries are often wholly unsuitable for specialised fields, and terminologists and translators have long found themselves compiling glossaries to assist their work. In the multilingual sphere, understanding a term in one language is not enough, as the appropriate equivalent must be found in the second language. The best source of information translators can use are previous successful translations. No dictionary can provide so much information about language use in context. Corpora of successful translations provide contextual evidence because not single words but sentences with their component parts are included. Jennifer Pearson, who investigates methods of teaching future language experts, describes the production of glossaries of terminology for specialist work from electronic resources (Pearson 1996). Students are encouraged to learn the procedures in order to be able to use them independently in their professional careers, since terminology is highly subject-specific.

Resources

Once a teaching topic or research area in which consulting a parallel corpus could be of interest has been identified, certain questions should be addressed. Any use of parallel corpora will depend on the answers to these questions:

–   what particular benefit can be drawn from a parallel corpus?
–   what is the primary purpose for using a parallel corpus?
–   who will be using the resources? (single researcher, particular group of students, future classes, distance learning)
–   what level of familiarity do they have with corpora and electronic resources? (less experienced users are more likely to gain benefits from material derived from corpora, rather than direct corpus access)
–   what corpus and computational resources and expertise are at your disposal already? (machine-readable research papers which have been translated for publication, student translations, university website information and the like can all have their place)
–   what other resources are easily available?

This last question is arguably the most important. It is a vain hope to expect that a large general purpose kind of parallel corpus will be soon at hand for use by researchers, language engineers and language students alike. It is, however, not only unrealistic, impracticable and expensive, but not even desirable in the context of small corpora for specific purposes. It is generally more fruitful to concentrate on the task in hand in order to derive the maximum benefit from corpus work. A large amount of material has been collected and produced during research projects; the survey below offers some pointers but cannot hope to be comprehensive. As a general rule, more is always becoming available all the time so it is worth searching thoroughly on the Internet.

Tools

The most well-known and commonly used tools for parallel corpus analysis are *Wordsmith* and *ParaConc. Wordsmith* (see chapter 3) is a suite of tools created by Mike Scott of Liverpool University available via the World Wide Web from Oxford University Press.[9] It consists of a range of tools including *Wordlist*, which generates word lists in alphabetical and frequency order and provides various statistics, *Concord*, which creates concordances, finds collocates of the word and identifies common phrases, *Keywords*, which identifies key words in a given text and a *Dual Text Aligner*, which aligns sentences in two files, allowing you to carry out sentence by sentence comparison of texts, amongst other tools. It runs on PC/Windows and is inexpensive in the personal version or site licences. It is possible to test the system and to take advantage of a trial period. *ParaConc*, a parallel text concordance program, is available from Michael Barlow for Windows and Macintosh platforms.[10] It allows the user to search for a word or phrase, then display the results in two windows. It can be downloaded from the web, although permission is needed for use on a site. A manual is available, as are some sample texts, while more can be loaded into the program. *ParaConc* offers the very useful option of acquiring a list of "hot words" which are suggested as possibly suitable translations by the software.

The searches can be based, as in monolingual concordancers, on a morpheme, word or phrase in Language A. The program then finds and displays all the occurrences of that search term, typically in KWIC (Key Word in Context) format, and shows a second window with the corresponding sentences in Language B. As Barlow describes (1997:18), parallel concordancing easily confirms the absence of one-to-one correspondence between languages, and can highlight the contextual and subject-defined reasons for particular lexical and grammatical choices. Search results can be sorted alphabetically according to the word before or after the search item, and so on. It is to be hoped that future development of such and similar tools will offer the chance for more sophisticated queries, such as for grammatical, statistical and collocational information, and more analysis tools for the results achieved.

The PEDANT project run by Daniel Ridings has also produced results with applicability in the classroom.[11] Indeed, one of the focuses of the project has been to support translator and language teaching. To date, material in 17 languages has been collected, classified by medium and genre. The solution adopted by PEDANT involves creating a text that contains nothing other than the alignment information based on the Text Encoding Initiative, or TEI, (see section on Encoding below) with hyperlinks back into the base corpus. The website offers searching facilities based on a number of language pairs, presenting the results on screen in real-time. All texts are first aligned at sentence level, using a program based upon the Church and Gale algorithm (see section on Alignment below), which has been shown to be over 95% reliable.

The Multext Project is developing a series of tools for accessing and manipulating corpora, including corpora encoded in SGML, and for accomplishing a series of corpus annotation tasks, including token and sentence boundary recognition, morphosyntactic tagging, parallel text alignment, and prosody mark-up. Annotation results may also be generated in SGML format.[12] (See section on Encoding below.)

Text Collections

There is a considerable and ever-expanding number of organisations publicly offering text collections, the most useful of which are listed in Appendix One. In addition, websites themselves are excellent sources of material in specific fields. An increasing number of publications and projects now produce CD-ROMs which can be used, as described by Tribble (1997). However, much of this material is monolingual or comparable, and there are not many options available when it comes to parallel texts. Much early work in the multilingual sphere was undertaken on the so-called "Canadian Hansard", the Proceedings of the Canadian Parliamentary Debates in French and English.[13] This resource was made available in electronic form to the research community, and the example of the Canadian government is now followed by the United Nations and the European Community, which produces a huge amount of translated material each year because it is committed to provide its legislation in all the official languages of the Community. This is due to increase in coming years with the extension of the European Union to countries of the former Soviet bloc. In addition, the European Union sponsors many multilingual projects in on-going work programmes and makes available the resources produced. Many such projects have focussed in recent years on the design, standardisation and production of parallel corpora; a list of some of these projects follows in Appendix Two.

Corpus Creation

Design

If no suitable corpus is available, the alternative is to make one. It could be the case that one has material at one's disposal already which could relatively easily be formed into a parallel corpus with additional input. Corpus design is, as always, vital. As John Sinclair says, "the results are only as good as the corpus" (Sinclair 1991:13). While material, resources and the time available usually delimit the scope of the corpus, the corpus planning should be undertaken carefully. Matters to be considered include size and balance. For general language corpora, it is widely held that a corpus should be as large as possible in order to provide information about low-frequency words. Size is less of an issue now that computational advances mean that even large corpora can be manipulated quickly. A current standard for monolingual corpora is 500 million words of running text, and this is set to increase. At the same time, attention had turned increasingly to monitor corpora, which are ever-changing collections of language resources passing through our systems rather than static collections (Sinclair 1994:11). The emphasis on size is of less relevance, however, for corpora for specific purposes, where quality is more important than quantity. Parallel corpora, due to their content and the compilation process, tend to be much smaller than monolingual corpora.

Balance is an issue much discussed and hard to decide on in general language corpora. It is not generally a problem for small parallel corpora as long as it is understood and accepted that any corpus is only able to provide information about that portion of language which it contains. If a corpus contains almost entirely newspaper texts, then clearly any results can only be related to journalistic style and topics, and not to general language. This, however, is not normally a concern for the producer of corpora for specific purposes, since often one text-type is of particular interest, the topic and purpose of the survey are known, and there is no intention to claim that the language collected reflects the whole body of naturally occurring language. Depending on the purpose of the corpus collection, it may be decided that balance is more important than size. It is currently inconceivable that a parallel corpus could reflect the whole spectrum of language use. Parallel corpora of spoken language are unlikely, for instance, to be created because of the problem of cost and effort in the original language, and the almost impossible nature of translation of idiomatic spoken material into the target language. When a relatively small amount of data is processed, this inevitably has an effect on the analysis conducted.

On the whole, it is best to choose texts already available in accepted translations, i.e. those produced by professional translators and published. This increases the chance of the translation being good, although it should also be borne in mind that some types of writing such as literature are often highly idiosyncratic. Often, parallel corpora to date have focussed on famous and widely-read literary texts, because they are easily available in several languages. This has the advantage that the texts are well translated and made available via publishers or specialist sites. However, the major drawback is the idiosyncratic use of language in creative writing. Research undertaken on literary texts cannot, clearly, be understood as representative of other text types. The World Wide Web is the major source of much multilingual material, often subject-specific, although the translations are often by amateurs and unreliable.

Collection

Once the corpus design has been decided and the texts have been identified, the collection "proper" can begin. Even at the start, the texts can be compared by simple searching, rather like having two books open side by side and glancing between the pages in the different languages. Gaining access to electronic versions is greatly facilitated by the websites and CD-ROMs described above. If all else fails, scanning and optical character recognition software is increasingly cheap and efficient nowadays. See Barnbrook (1996:30–32) for a discussion of the issues surrounding scanning and other practical considerations about corpus creation. Keyboarding is only an option for small amounts of text, as it is very time-consuming.

Copyright

Intellectual Property Rights and copyright are thorny issues which should not be discussed only after the event, but rather should form an integral part of corpus design and creation. The copyright status of any material used in a corpus must be investigated prior to its use. Even though the primary aim of a corpus may be localised and seem of little interest to others, it is a good idea to bear in mind that the data may be made more widely available at a later date. The publishing house is generally the first port of call, although often copyright rests with the author. If student texts are being used in corpus collection, a copyright declaration should be submitted with the electronic data. The fact that material is available on the web does not mean that it can be used by anyone for any purpose. In a parallel corpus, permission for the use of the original text does not suffice; the copyright on the translation should also be cleared. Many copyright holders are aware of language corpora and most are prepared to agree to academic use. However, their agreement should not be assumed in advance, nor should the amount of time to reach such an agreement be underestimated.

If the texts are to be quoted extensively, used in language teaching or training materials, this should also be specified explicitly in the request. Copyright holders may wish to stipulate that only extracts of a certain length may be used. If the corpus may have commercial value at a later date, copyright holders should be made aware of this, and they may choose to impose a fee or claim royalties. On the whole, it is better to avoid such arrangements as they are time-consuming and costly. If many texts come from one publisher, blanket agreement may be given. Anonymisation may have to be undertaken in some specific corpora where confidential or personal material is used, such as company reports or private letters.

Encoding

It is important to be able to retain as much bibliographic and structural information about the text as possible, such as typographical conventions, headings, paragraphs, location of diagrams or links, etc. In general, as much information as possible should be retained and recorded about the corpus design and creation, the text origin and author details and of course any encoding scheme and codes used. Most corpora contain such information implicitly, but often in an idiosyncratic format which is not transparent to a new user and not easily convertible. While it is to the human reader reading a print version what is a chapter-heading or list, the computer will only recognise such structural features if they are explicitly marked. Making such information machine-readable is the purpose of encoding (or mark-up). There is much discussion about encoded versus "raw" text, and it may well be the case that for the purpose in hand, plain text is adequate and more easily manipulated. However, given a good, user-friendly and well-documented scheme, sophisticated processing and retrieving of information from corpora can be facilitated by encoding. If the "raw" text is needed or desired for any reason, such encoding can be subsequently stripped from the text.

The chief advantage of such schemes is that data preservation and transfer is promoted: proprietary, "in-house" formats may be easier in the short-term but incomprehensible and not easily converted later. Using such schemes also means that many problematic decisions and considerations have been taken into account already, and do not have to be approached again. As additional computing space and effort is decreasingly an issue, the main disadvantages are the initial awkwardness of such schemes and the fact that the standards sometimes do not seem very standard. Much work has been and is still being undertaken to establish international standards. The Text Encoding Initiative (TEI) devises and maintains conventions for text encoding.[14] It is a project run by several associations interested in humanities computing. The TEI has adapted for corpus creation and text encoding an established encoding scheme, Standard Generalised Markup Language (SGML), which is similar in form and design to the language used for creating webpages. SGML is an ISO standard widely used and recognised by programs such as SARA, the retrieval application supplied with the British National Corpus. An introduction to SGML is available on the Internet.[16] The *WordPerfect* and "emacs" data-editors offer built-in facilities for working with SGML. An Extensible Markup Language (XML) version of the TEI material is under development.[17] In general, the information needed for the encoding is extant in the text and "search and replace" functions, or simple scripts, can insert the codes automatically.

In TEI encoding, each text consists of a "header" with information about the text (creation, collection, all bibliographical details, codes), followed by the text as such, interspersed with annotation in the form of tags (marked with <start> and </end>) and entity references (which can be recognised because they begin with "&" and end with ";"). A document type description (dtd) is the formal representation which tells the user or computer how the text is structured. The TEI has made standard dtds for various text-types, which already take into account their special features. The dtd can be extended or updated as required following the guidelines set out. The level of encoding can be chosen according to the task, and can thus be more or less detailed. The legality of the encoding, that is, whether the text fits the rules set out in the header, is checked by parsing. This examines the internal consistency and coherence to the dtd. If a document "parses", it conforms to the rules in the dtd.

Encoding is certainly unwieldy for the human user, since it is designed to be read and analysed by computer. For subsequent work on the text corpora, software makes it is possible to hide the mark-up, so that it is not visible on the screen to the human user (as is the case on webpages). Many projects around the world now make use of the TEI guidelines, including the British National Corpus, most European Union-funded projects and the TELRI parallel corpus, described below.[18] Other initiatives, such as the Expert Advisory Group on Language Engineering Standards (EAGLES), explore and adapt the standards in the European context for European Union-funded projects.[19] For more information on the TEI, see Ide 1999. A slimmed-down version of the scheme, called TEI-Lite, has also been developed.[20] Appendix 3 contains a sample of text from the Plato corpus encoded according to TEI with a key to the codes. Some basic encoding assists the process of automatic alignment greatly. Depending on the level used, encoding means that searches may be made more specific, for example searches could be made only within the first paragraphs of sections, or only in the sports section of newspapers.

Annotation

Annotation, rather than retaining information from the print version, as encoding seeks to do, adds to a text linguistic, interpretative (Leech 1993; 275) information such as grammatical tags or parsing information, prosodic or semantic information. This means that this information can be further processed by the computer. Leech (1993) discusses several rules for annotation of corpora, chiefly that the annotated corpus should be flexible and manipulable, the annotation used well-explained and not considered infallible. There are, of course, many layers of annotation and many schemes giving more or less fine-grained linguistic information. As McEnery (1996:23) points out, most annotation schemes are a compromise between practicalities and maximum potential utility (see also Králiková's article in Teubert et al, 1997:102–110). The TEI has prepared guidelines and encoding schemes to enrich texts within the framework. Annotation schemes fall outside the scope of this paper, and will not be further discussed.[21] If a parallel corpus has been tagged, it is possible to search for grammatical features in one language and compare how they are rendered in the other.

Alignment

Accurate alignment is vital in order to be able to extract information out of the parallel corpus. The first thing most people want to do with a parallel corpus is search for words or phrases in one language, perhaps well-known problem words, and find the corresponding equivalents in the translated text. A search query can be typed in in one language and all occurrences (lemmatised or according to part of speech, if that is available) found in that language. The program then looks up all the corresponding sentences, located by paragraph and sentence number, in the second language. This procedure works well because, on the whole, sentences in Language A are translated in the same order into Language B. Furthermore, long sentences in Language A tend to be translated into long sentences in Language B, and shorter sentences tend to be translated into shorter sentences. However, it is not sufficient to line up texts sentence by sentence, as translations do not correspond exactly and the alignment could go askew in a long section of text. Therefore, more accurate ways of aligning texts are required.

A huge amount of research in recent years has concentrated on ways of automating the alignment process. This will be sketched out here. There are two main ways of aligning. Internal linguistic criteria such as lexical equivalence can be used, or alternatively information about the structure of the text (sentence and paragraph breaks previously encoded, for instance). The first option has the advantage that the mark-up stage is avoided, but the second is currently more straightforward and reliable. In fact, the most elegant and fruitful solution for the future looks to be a combination of these two, using both content-based internal and external factors.

Three main ways of aligning parallel texts using statistical measures have been proposed, such as Hidden Markov Models (Brown, Lai and Mercer 1991), using reliable words as "anchors" (Kay and Röscheisen 1993) and sentence length in words or, even more reliably, characters (Gale and Church 1991). The most widely used methods have been based on the Gale and Church algorithm of length-based aligning, with a reliability of around 95%. First the method aligns paired paragraphs, then moves on to sentences within those paragraphs, making various assumptions about the probability of translation, such as that most sentences are translated by at most two sentences.

Correspondences between some kinds of words, such as names, some proper nouns and terminology (which tends to be translated straightforwardly) can also be searched for by the computer, thus achieving partial alignment. Ruta Marcinkeviciene has examined *hapax legomena*, that is, words occurring only once in a text, as possible anchors for alignment.[22] Language occurs as text, not as single words, and the significance of multi-word units (units of meaning) has been increasingly acknowledged in recent years. Mutual information, a statistical measure of the degree of relatedness of two elements, can be used to help align parallel texts by identifying associations between pairs of words with similar distribution. Statistically significant word pairs can be identified in the two texts, and the occasions aligned where they are repeated.

"Mechanical" aligning, that is, alignment processes relying on encoding and text structure, requires some pre- or post-processing, as described above. This is because even in closely related languages, sentence boundaries often do not correspond. What is given as one sentence in one language may well be rendered in two in translation, or vice versa. Since good translations, which are in general the only ones worth exploring, are creative, words or phrases are sometimes expanded, contracted, word order altered to sound idiomatic, items even omitted or added. It is relatively easy to make "anchors" in texts, say at paragraph or sentence level, which may assist the alignment algorithm and prevent it from going too far off course. Alignment usually takes place at sentence level within paragraphs. In the Lingua project, an accuracy rate of 90% in the alignment process is anticipated, therefore some editing is necessary to correct the remaining 10%. It is possible to work with the texts without such checking, of course, but searches may be rather unsatisfactory because one side will not match up with the other. The parallel concordancing packages described earlier offer various ways to ease the process of adding texts. Other aligners are freely available, such as the "Vanilla" aligner and "MARK ALISTeR".[23] Once the alignment is satisfactory, the texts can be examined using the tools and the results either extracted into teaching material or further analysed.

A case study: East meets West

TELRI (Trans-European Language Resources Infrastructure) is an on-going project funded by the European Commission in order to encourage transfer of knowledge between Western, Central and Eastern European research sites in multilingual language engineering and more specifically, corpus research.[24] Its main focus has therefore been on the languages of Central and Eastern Europe, along with the major languages of Western Europe, thus including Romance, Slavic and Finno-Ugric languages. The Working Group "Joint Research" was set up within the project with the objectives of building links between TELRI partners and of using these links to encourage research projects between partners. The main concrete result to emerge from this Working Group was the Plato parallel corpus. This work proved not only to be an excellent way for partners to gain expertise and experience in parallel corpus collection and manipulation, which was new to most, but also produced a useful resource which is still being extended, improved and used by a large number of researchers in the field.

Plato's "Republic" was chosen as the main text for developing a parallel corpus. A single text was chosen for reasons of practicability. A well-known classical text was chosen on the grounds that translations into most, if not all, of the TELRI project languages would be likely to exist. It was hoped that all the texts produced and examined in the parallel corpus would be "target texts", since only the Greek is the "source". In fact, it became apparent during the course of work that certain of the translations were effected via another translation, often the English.

Each project member initially sought out suitable translations of the text in their own language. Translations could be found in all the project languages, with the exception of Estonian and Albanian. In several languages, more than one translation was available, and these were included as an interesting comparison. Versions of the texts already in electronic form were sought, whenever possible. These were variously downloaded from the Internet, bought on CD-ROM or acquired direct from the publishers. If no electronic version was available, partners scanned the texts and proof-read them. In exceptional cases, when the quality of the type was too poor to be recognised by the scanner, the text was input by hand. Copyright holders were approached for permission to use their texts in academic research work. Although the original text is not covered by copyright restrictions, the translations are. When texts were not or no longer in copyright, usually because of their age, no permission was sought but the publisher and/or source of the text was always acknowledged.

The data was then encoded. While a plain-text version of the "Republic" was retained in each version, it was also encoded according to the TEI convention. To assist the later alignment process, all folio markings from the early version were encoded, together with all the book and section headings. One translation, the Latvian, it was found, was only in that language as an abridged edition, but that text was marked up to correspond, with gaps, to the others. Several workshops were organised where partners could get together to learn more about the processes and work on the texts. All available information on folio-markings and sub-chapter headings was retained to ease the alignment process, but it was found that consistency between the versions was not high.

Nevertheless, the alignment was largely successful and the Working Group used the texts to test corpus alignment software and make subsequent improvements. The encoded and aligned Plato texts, as well as their plain-text versions, have been put onto the TELRI CD-ROM "East meets West" (Erjavec et al. 1998) along with software tools and information about the project, including research work undertaken using the texts. Since producing the CD-ROM, several more languages have been added to the original collection of 18, and the aligned versions have been made available on the Internet[25]. Many research projects have used the resource, many of which are collected and published in Teubert et al 1997. The CD-ROM was distributed with corpus and lexicon resources produced within the Multext-East Project, including an aligned parallel corpus of George Orwell's 1984.

The parallel corpus described here is small and specialised. It was the result of a research project and the process of creating it threw up many questions and issues. Development is continuing; in particular, ways of improving the alignment of the texts are being explored, and a new version of the corpus will be made available shortly. Although several academic papers have already focussed on findings from the Plato corpus (Lewandowska-Tomaszczyk, e.g. Oakes & Wynne 2000), it is perhaps most useful as an example of how small parallel corpora including a large number of languages can be compiled.

In order to be usable, it is not necessary for parallel corpora to contain huge amounts of text. Indeed, too much text is often disruptive in the teaching arena to the student with a limited amount of time in class, and a specific subject of study. Students who have access to the methodology and tools described in this paper will find themselves able to compile corpora which are tailor-made to their interests. Much of the material can be freely found on the Internet. For example, learners of English who plan to work in the financial sphere may find a small parallel corpus of bank brochures and information highly informative, while a corpus of company reports may be of more interest to the business student. The opportunities for exploration of text-based language are virtually limitless. Once the parallel corpus has been compiled, the student can undertake many different research projects. He or she could, for instance, explore the relative frequencies across languages of word-pairs for which dictionaries claim translational equivalence. Collocational and prosodic patterns may indicate that usage is rather more complicated than suggested by the translation equivalents favoured by dictionaries. For a description of the investigation of grammatical and/or lexico-semantic features, please see Mohsen Ghadessy and Yanjie Gao's paper in this volume.

Conclusion

It has been shown that parallel corpora can provide vital information about correspondences between form and meaning in the multilingual context, information which can be used to improve translation technology and be put to good use in the classroom. They can be exploited to gain insights into the structure and function of specific languages and the relationships between language pairs, and furthermore to ease access to the wealth of information latent in comparable corpora. This paper cannot hope to have covered all the options and possibilities offered, but has aimed to indicate the range of tools and resources already available to the language teacher and researcher, and to show that such work is feasible and worthwhile even with limited time and computational power. While the emphasis in monolingual corpora will remain on general-language, large, balanced corpora, parallel corpora provide the ideal opportunity for creation and use of small corpus resources, aided by existing software and resources.

Notes

1. for more details see http://guagua.echo.lu/langeng/projects/parole/ann978.html

2. Bologna corpus http://www.cilta.unibo.it/progetti.htm

3. http://web.bham.ac.uk/johnstf/paracon.htm and
    http://www.uhb.fr:80/~rezeau_j/mltcn03.htm

4. http://www.uhb.fr:80/~rezeau_j/mltcn03.htm

5. http://vlc.polyu.edu.hk/Authoring/authorin.htm

6. http://www.sussex.ac.uk/langc/CALL.html

7. http://web.bham.ac.uk/johnstf/paracon.htm

8. http://web.bham.ac.uk/johnstf/timconc.htm

9. http://www1.oup.co.uk/elt/catalogu/multimed/4589846/4589846.html

10. http://www.ruf.rice.edu/~barlow/parac.html

11. www.gusd.holding.gu.se/~ridings/pedant.html

12. http://www.lpl.univ-aix.fr/projects/multext/

13. http://www-rali.iro.umontreal.ca/TransSearch/TS-simple-uen.cgi

14. http://www.uic.edu/orgs/tei/index.html

16. http://www-tei.uic.edu/orgs/tei/sgml/teip3sg/index.html

17. http://www.tei.c.org and http://www.loria.fr/~bonhomme/xml.html

18. see the applications page on http://www.uic.edu/orgs/tei/app

19. http://www.ilc.pi.cnr.it/EAGLES/home.html

20. http://www.uic.edu/orgs/tei/lite

21. To view a sample of tagged text, see http://svenska.gu.se/~ridings/parabank/node18.html

22. http://donelaitis.vdu.lt/publikacijos/hapax.htm

23. http://www.loria.fr/projets/XCorpus/ See also Paskaleva and Mihov 1997

24. http://www.telri.de

25. All of the Plato texts and aligments are available in TRACTOR, the TELRI Research Archive of Compatational Tools & Resources at www.tractor.de.

References

Allen, J. and Hogan, C. 1998. "Expanding lexical coverage of parallel corpora for the EBTM approach". In A. Rubio, N. Gallardo, R. Castro and A. Tejada (eds), *Proceedings of the First International Conference on Language Resources and Evaluation,* 747–754. Granada.

Baker, M. 1992. *In Other Words: A coursebook on translation.* London: Routledge.

Barlow, M. 1995. *A Guide to ParaConc.* Houston: Athelstan.

Barlow, M. 1996. "ParaConc: A Parallel concordancer for parallel texts". *Computers and Texts* 10:14–16.

Barlow, M. 1996a. "Analysing parallel texts with ParaConc". ALLC/ACH '96. University of Bergen, Norway. URL: http://www.ruf.rice.edu/~barlow/norway.html

Barlow, M. 1996b. "Parallel texts in language teaching". In S. Botley, J. Glass, T. McEnery and A.Wilson, (eds), *Proceedings of Teaching and Language Corpora*

1996 [Technical Paper 9], 45–56. University Centre for Computer Corpus Research on Language, Lancaster.

Barlow, M. 1998. "Investigating form and meaning using parallel corpora". In W. Teubert, E. Tognini-Bonelli and N. Volz (eds), *Translation Equivalence: Proceedings of the third European seminar*. The Tuscan Word Centre: The TELRI Association e.V.

Barnbrook, G. 1996. *Language and Computers* [Edinburgh Textbooks in Empirical Linguistics]. Edinburgh: EUP.

Biber, D. 1990. "Methodological issues regarding corpus-based analyses of linguistic variation". *Literary and Linguistic Computing* 5: 257–269.

Botley, S., Glass, J., McEnery, T. and Wilson, A. (eds), 1996. *Proceedings of Teaching and Language Corpora 1996* [Technical Paper 9]. University Centre for Computer Corpus Research on Language, Lancaster.

Brown, P., Cocke, J., Della Pietra, D., Della Pietra, V. J., Jelinek, F., Lafferty, J. D., Mercer, R. L. and Roossin, P. S. 1990. "A statistical approach to machine translation". *Computational Linguistics* 16 (2): 79–85.

Brown, P., Lai, J. C. and Mercer, R. L. 1991. "Aligning sentences in parallel corpora". In *Proceedings, 29th Annual Meeting of the Association for Computational Linguistics,* 169–176.

Chen, S. 1993. "Aligning sentences in bilingual corpora using lexical information". In *Proceedings of the 31st Annual Meeting of the Association for Computational Linguistics,* 9–16.

Davis, M., Dunning, T. and Ogden, B. 1995. "Text Alignment in the Real World: Improving alignments of noisy translations using common lexical features, string matching strategies and N-Gram comparisons". In *Proceedings of the Seventh Conference of the European Chapter of the Association of Computational Linguistics,* 67–74. Dublin, Ireland.

Dunning, T., Cowie, J. and Waka, T. 1991. *Analysis of Parallel Japanese and English Corpora.* CLR Tech Report. (MCCS-91–233).

Erjavec, T., Lawson, A. and Romary, L. (eds), 1998. *East meets West — A Compendium of Multilingual Resources.* CD-ROM.

Fung, P., and Church, K. "K-vec: A new approach for aligning parallel texts". *COLING 94:* 15th International Conference on Computational Linguistics, Kyoto: Aug 94, 1096–1102.

Grefenstette, G. (ed), 1998. *Cross-language Information Retrieval.* Dordrecht: Kluwer.

Ide, N. and Greenstein, D. (eds), 1999. *Computers and the Humanities.* 33 (1–2), Special Double Issue, Tenth Anniversary of the Text Encoding Initiative.

Johns, T. 1991. "Should you be persuaded: Two examples of data driven learning". In T. Johns, and P. King (eds), *Classroom concordancing. ELR Journal* 4:1–16. University of Birmingham.

Kay, M. and Röscheisen, M. 1993 "Text-translation alignment". *Computational Linguistics* 19 (1): 121–142.

Kennedy, G. 1998. *An Introduction to Corpus Linguistics Studies in Language and Linguistics*. London: Longman.

Klavans, J. L. and Tzoukermann, E. 1990a. "Linking bilingual corpora and machine readable dictionaries with the BICORD system I". In *Proceedings of the Sixth Conference of the University of Waterloo Centre for the New Oxford English Dictionary and Text Research: Electronic text research*. Waterloo, Canada. University of Waterloo.

Klavans, J. L. and Tzoukermann, E. 1990b. "Combining lexical information from bilingual corpora and machine-readable dictionaries". In *Proceedings of the 13th International Conference on Computational Linguistics: COLING*. Helsinki, Finland.

Klavans, J. L. and Tzoukermann, E. 1996. "Dictionaries and corpora: Combining corpus and machine-readable dictionary data for building bilingual lexicons". *Journal of Machine Translation*. Dordrecht: Kluwer.

Leacock, C., Towell, G. and Voorhees, E. 1993. "Corpus-based statistical sense resolution". *Proceedings of the Human Language Technology Workshop Princeton*. 260–265.

Leech, G. (1993). "Corpus annotation schemes". *Literary and Linguistic Computing* 8 (4): 275–81.

Lewandowska-Tomaszczyk, B. and Melia P. J. 1997. *PALC '97 Practical Applications of Language Corpora*. Lodz.

Lewandovska-Tomaszczyk, B., Oakes and Wynne M. 2000, "Automatic alignment of Polish and English texts". In PALC '99: Practical Applications in Language Corpora. Hamburg: Peter Lang.

Mauranen, A. 1998. "Form and sense relations as seen through parallel corpora. *TELRI Proceedings of the Third European Seminar "Translation Equivalence"*. Scheßlitz: IDS/TWC.

McEnery, T. and Wilson, A. 1996. *Corpus Linguistics* [Edinburgh Textbooks in Empirical Linguistics]. Edinburgh: Edinburgh University Press.

Melamed, I. D. (1997). "A portable algorithm for mapping bitext correspondence". *ACL 97*. 305–312.

Partington, A. 1998. *Patterns and Meanings* [Studies in Corpus Linguistics 2]. Amsterdam: John Benjamins.

Paskaleva, E. and Mihov, S. 1998. "Language acquisition from aligned corpora". In *Proceedings of the International Conference "Language Teaching and Language Technology"*, Groningen, April 1997, 43–53. Swets and Zeitingler, The Netherlands.

Pearson, J. 1996. "Teaching terminology using electronic resources". In S. Botley, J.

Glass, T. McEnery and A. Wilson (eds), *Proceedings of Teaching and Language Corpora 1996* [Technical Paper 9], 203–216. Lancaster: University Centre for Computer Corpus Research on Language.

Peters, C., Picchi, E. and Biagini, L. 1996. "Parallel and comparable bilingual corpora in language teaching and learning". In S. Botley, J. Glass, T. McEnery and A. Wilson (eds), *Proceedings of Teaching and Language Corpora 1996* [Technical Paper 9], 68–82. Lancaster: University Centre for Computer Corpus Research on Language.

Peters, C. and Picchi, E. "Bilingual reference corpora for translators and translation studies". www.ilc.pi.cnr.it/pisystem/artcomparab.htm

Picchi, E. and Peters, C. 1998. "Cross-language information retrieval: A system for comparable corpus querying". In G.Grefenstette (ed), *Cross-language Information Retrieval,* 81–92. Dordrecht: Kluwer.

Schäffner, C. 1998. "Parallel texts in translation". In L. Bowker, M. Cronin, D. Kenny and J. Pearson (eds), *Unity in Diversity? Current trends in translation studies.* Manchester: St. Jerome.

Sinclair, J. McH. 1991. *Corpus Concordance Collocation: Describing English language.* Oxford: OUP.

Sinclair, J. McH. 1994. Corpus Typology: Draft — work in progress. http:// www.ilc.pi.cnr.it/ EAGLES/typology/typology.html

Sinclair, J. McH., Payne. J. and Hérnandez, C. P. 1996. "Corpus to corpus: A study of translation equivalence". *Special Issue of International Journal of Lexicography* 9 (3): 28–264.

Sinclair, J. McH. 1996. "The search for units of meaning". *TEXTUS* 9:75–106.

Sinclair, J. McH.1998. "The lexical item". In E. Weigand (ed), *Contrastive Lexical Semantics* [Current Issues in Linguistic Theory 171], 1–24. Amsterdam: John Benjamins

Stevens, V. 1995. "Concordancing with language learners: Why? When? What?" *CAELL Journal* 6 (2): 2–10.

Teubert, W. 1996. "Comparable or parallel corpora". In J. McH. Sinclair, J. Payne and C. P. Hérnandez (eds), *Special Issue of International Journal of Lexicography* 9 (3): 238–264.

Teubert, W., Tognini-Bonelli, E. and Volz, N. 1998. *Translation Equivalence: Proceedings of the third European seminar,* IDS/TWC.

Tribble, C. 1997. "Improvising corpora for ELT: Quick and dirty ways of developing corpora for language teaching". In B. Lewandowska Tomaszczyk, and P. J. Melia (eds), *PALC '97 Practical Applications in Language Corpora.* Lewandowska-Tomaszczyk, 106–117. Lodz.

Weigand, E. (ed), 1998. *Contrastive Lexical Semantics* [Current Issues in Linguistic Theory 171]. Amsterdam: John Benjamins.

Williams, I. A. 1996. "A translator's reference needs: Dictionaries or parallel texts?" *Target* 8 (2): 275–299.

Wilson, A. and McEnery, T. 1994. *Corpora in Language Education and Research: A Selection of Papers from Talc94*, Unit for Computer Research on the English Language Technical Papers 4 (Special Issue), Lancaster University.

Zanettin, F. 1994, "Parallel words: Designing a bilingual database for translation activities". In A. Wilson and T. McEnery, *Corpora in Language Education and Research: A selection of papers from Talc94*, 99–111. Unit for Computer Research on the English Language Technical Papers 4 (Special Issue), Lancaster University.

Appendix 1: Some Sites with Text Resources (mono- and multilingual)

- TRACTOR — The TELRI Research Archive of Computational Tools and Resources — distributes corpus tools and resources — http://www.tractor.de
- OTA — Oxford Text Archive — http://sable.ox.ac.uk/
- ELRA — European Language Resources Association — http://www.icp.grenet.fr/ELRA/
- Gutenberg Project — on-line electronic publications, chiefly books — http://www.promo.net/pg/epub.html
- ICAME — The International Computer Archive of Modern English — www.hd.uib.no
- LDC — Linguistic Data Consortium — www.ldc.upenn.edu
- CETH — Centre for Electronic Texts in the Humanities — http://www.ceth.rutgers.edu/
- Elsnet — http://www.cogsci.ed.ac.uk/elsnet
- COBUILD — access to the Bank of English — http://titania.cobuild.collins.co.uk/
- BNC — British National Corpus ñ http://info.ox.ac.uk/bnc/
- World Language Resources — http://worldlanguage.com/info
- European Corpus Initiative — have produced a CD-ROM including some non-aligned parallel texts — http://www.elsnet.org/resources/eciCorpus.html
- Canadian Hansard French/English texts searchable on the Web — http://www-rali.iro.umontreal.ca/TransSearch/TS-simple-uen.cgi

Appendix 2: Some Recent Projects on Parallel Corpora

- Multext — Tools and sample multilingual corpora — http://www.lpl.univ-aix.fr/projects/multext/
- Multext-East — Parallel and comparable corpora in Eastern European languages

(available via TELRI on "East meets West" CD-ROM) — http://www.lpl.univ-aix.fr/projects/multext-east/
- Crater — English, French, Spanish tagged aligned corpora (available via ELRA)
- TELRI — the "East meets West" CD-ROM — http://www.telri.de
- MLCC — Multilingual Corpora for Co-operation — translated data in nine languages from the EU — http://www.icp.grenet.fr/ELRA/cata/ text_det.html
- BAF — small English/French hand-aligned corpus — http://www-rali.iro.umon-treal.ca
- Knut Hofland's English/Norwegian texts: http://www.hit.uib.no/enpc/
- Scania Corpus Project — emphasis on Scandanavian languages — http://stp.ling.uu.se/~corpora/scania/
- PEDANT project — parallel corpora in European languages — http://svenska.gu.se/~ridings/parabank/parabank.html
- INTERSECT (International Sample of English Contrastive Texts) Project — parallel bilingual corpus of French and English written texts — http://www.bus.bton.ac.uk/Staff/RSalkie/RSalkie.html
- LINGUA — multilingual corpora in language pedagogy — http://web.bham.ac.uk/johnstf/paracon.htm
- TRIPTIC: Trilingual Parallel Text Information Corpus in English, French and Dutch (2 million words each). Paragraphs are aligned. For further information, contact Hans Paulussen hpa@elv.fundp.ac.be.
- Translation Corpus of English and German — http://www.tu-chemnitz.de/phil/english/real/transcorpus/index.htm
- Thai On-Line Library TOLL of parallel Thai/English texts — http://seasrc.th.net/toll/index.htm

Appendix 3: Sample of text encoded according to the TEI guidelines

```
<!DOCTYPE TEI.2 PUBLIC "-//TEI//DTD TEI Lite 1.0//EN">
<tei.2 teiform="TEI.2">
<teiheader type="text" status="new" teiform="teiHeader">
<filedesc teiform="fileDesc">
<titlestmt teiform="titleStmt">
<title teiform="title">Plato's Republic — New Translation</title>
</titlestmt>
<publicationstmt teiform="publicationStmt">
<p teiform="p">Made within Telri</p>
</publicationstmt>
<sourcedesc default="NO" teiform="sourceDesc">
```

<p teiform="p">Harvard University Press</p>
</sourcedesc>
</filedesc>
</teiheader>
<text teiform="text">
<body teiform="body">
<div type="book" n="1">
<div type="section">
<head>I</head><p>
<milestone unit ="folio" n=327a><seg> Socrates: I went down yesterday to the
    Peiraeus with Glaucon, the son of Ariston, to pay my devotions to the Goddess,
    and also because I wished to see how they would conduct the festival since this
    was its inauguration.</seg>
<seg> I thought the procession of the citizens very fine, but it was no better than the
    show, made by the marching of the Thracian contingent.</seg>
<seg>
<milestone unit ="folio" n=327b> After we had said our prayers and seen the spectacle
    we were starting for town when Polemarchus, the son of
Cephalus, caught sight of us from a distance as we were hastening homeward and
    ordered his boy run and bid us to wait for him, and the boy caught hold of my
    himation from behind and said, "Polemarchus wants you to wait."</seg>
<seg> And I turned around and asked where his master was.</seg>
<seg> "There he is," he said, "behind you, coming this way.</seg>
<seg> Wait for him."</seg>
<seg> "So we will," said
Glaucon,
<milestone unit ="folio" n=327c> and shortly after Polemarchus came up and
    Adeimantus, the brother of Glaucon , and Niceratus , the son of Nicias , and a few
    others apparently from the procession
.</seg>
<seg> Whereupon Polemarchus said, " Socrates , you appear to have turned your faces
    townward and to be going to leave us."</seg>
<seg> "Not a bad guess," said I.</seg>
<seg> "But you see how many we are?" he said.</seg>
<seg> "Surely."</seg>
<seg> "You must either then prove yourselves the better men or stay here."</seg>

CHAPTER 11

Corpus, comparison, culture
Doing the same things differently in different cultures

Geoff Thompson

University of Liverpool

Abstract

This paper focuses on the comparative analysis in the classroom of
small corpora of equivalent genres in different languages. The case is
argued for including explicit attention to language forms even within
communicative language teaching approaches, and for using cross-linguistic comparison as an awareness-raising resource. However, attention should be shifted away from isolated structures and towards
exploring the "discourse value" of lexical, structural and other choices
in context. One way of implementing this shift in perspective is by comparative genre analysis. Using comparable corpora of familiar genres as
the basis for language awareness activities can help learners explore the
ways in which language is deployed in the FL to achieve particular
communicative goals. In addition, it can often lead naturally to discussion of aspects of the other culture as reflected in the language. The
paper explores these issues through the examples of Chinese and
English tourist brochures, and Swiss and English job advertisements.

Introduction

Although communicative language teaching emerged largely as a reaction
against the narrow emphasis on grammatical structure in approaches that were

dominant at the time, there has in more recent years been a general move towards accepting that, in conjunction with extensive practice in meaningful communication, it is important to include explicit focus on language forms. One factor in this movement has been the growth of corpus linguistics and the realization that this provides not only fundamental insights into language in use but also effective techniques for exploring language that can be applied with learners. Initially the impetus came from concordances produced with the help of computers. Tim Johns, for example, developed the idea of "data-driven learning", where students work on language data in the form of concordance lines (Johns, 1994). The Collins COBUILD project drew on the Bank of English corpus held at the University of Birmingham to produce not only descriptive grammars, but also a series of "concordance samplers" for use in class, covering areas such as prepositions and reporting verbs. However — as the present volume demonstrates — the potential of corpora as resources for language teaching and learning goes well beyond concordances: there are many other ways in which they can be used to stimulate guided, purposeful exploration of a range of language features. In fact, although many writers, including the majority of the contributors to this volume, take it for granted that corpora and computers are natural partners or even inextricably linked, there is no reason why corpus work in the classroom needs to rely on computers at all. I shall be arguing that using a computer in the kind of exploration of small corpora that I outline would be difficult and in some respects positively unhelpful.

What I want to discuss in this paper is the use of comparable corpora in two languages — the foreign language and the mother tongue — as the basis for sensitising learners to the ways in which language choices work in specific genres (the term "genre" is used here to refer to any type of text that people generally recognize as having distinctive characteristics which set that type apart from others: business letters, science textbooks, news reports, political speeches, and recipes are all examples of different genres).[1] The approach proposed here involves the learners looking at complete texts rather than concordance lines, so that they develop a sense of the genre as a whole; and it also involves them comparing examples of the same genre in their own language, as a way of sharpening their sense of what precisely it is about the language in the foreign language genre which makes it distinctive. This emphasis on genre is based on the simple insight that native speakers can normally recognise very easily what kind of text (i.e. what genre) a stretch of language comes from, even if the extract consists only of a sentence or two.[2] This means that all language must vary — in ways that may be subtler or more obvious — according to the context in which it is used; and that learners need to become aware of, and eventually able to manipulate, this variation if they are to reach any level of proficiency beyond the most minimally utilitarian. At the same time, the variation is within the overall language system — with very few exceptions, it is not a question of features being found only in one genre, but of the relative frequency of different features in a genre, and the ways in which they are combined. Thus attention to the language of one genre contributes to strengthening learners' grasp of the system as a whole.

Explicit focus on language

One of the recurrent controversies within language teaching has been whether or not explicit attention to generalisable facts about the foreign language has a useful function in helping learners to master that language. For much of the time, the controversy has been seen almost exclusively in terms of grammar rules. In audio-lingual methods, for example, learners are drilled in producing structurally correct sentences by imitating models, but do not receive any explanation of the grammatical rules which those models are designed to exemplify. It is assumed that the learners develop a native-speaker-like, unconscious sense of what the rules are by being exposed to numerous examples of each rule in operation, and that teaching them the rules as rules does not contribute helpfully to this process. In the grammar-translation method and many versions of structural approaches, on the other hand, learners are explicitly told at an early stage in the teaching cycle what the rules are and then asked to use them to construct correct sentences. Here, it is assumed that explicit knowledge of the rules serves as a kind of "sentence-generator", allowing learners to construct sentences which they have not come across amongst the particular examples that they have met in class (see e.g. Richards and Rodgers, 1986, for a full discussion of the differences).

With the emergence of communicative approaches to language teaching in the early 1970s, the debate continued but in a slightly different form. Initially, explicit focus on grammar was strongly discouraged, partly at least in reaction to the fixation of prevailing methodologies on structure at the expense of meaning. It was argued that learners acquire language by engaging in meaningful communication, and that distracting their attention from meaning by asking them to look at structure simply slows down, or actively hinders, the process of acquisition. Some EFL theorists, most notably Stephen Krashen (1988), claim that explicit knowledge of grammar is qualitatively different from the unconscious knowledge which a native speaker draws on in using the language and which the learner needs to acquire, and that it is not possible to convert the first kind of knowledge into the second. Others, such as N. S. Prabhu (1987), base their rejection of grammar in the classroom on the belief that the knowledge needed to be proficient in a language is so complex that it simply cannot be taught but must be picked up through concentrated meaningful use.

However, it has increasingly been recognized that there is no inherent reason why communicative approaches should not include attention to all aspects of the language used to effect communication, including the grammatical structures (Thompson, 1996), and that this can contribute usefully to the process of learning. Keith Johnson (1996) recasts the debate in terms of what he calls DEC (declarative knowledge — i.e. explicit knowledge about language) and PRO (procedural knowledge — i.e. ability to use language), and he argues forcefully that learners need to be helped to develop both — the only real question for him is over the order in which the two are focused on in the classroom: DECPRO (a "grammar-first" approach) or PRODEC (a "communicate/practise-first" approach). In a series of books and papers, Rod Ellis (e.g. 1992, 1998) has proposed a methodology in which the learners are guided first towards understanding and responding meaningfully to language, and subsequently towards noticing and describing the grammatical structures whose meaning they have understood without necessarily "recognising" them as structures (proponents of task-based approaches, such as Willis, 1996, and Skehan, 1994, have put forward proposals for dealing with grammar which are similar in most essential respects). In this approach, it is not assumed that getting the learners to focus on a grammatical rule will lead to them learning that rule immediately; instead the purpose is to make them aware of it so that they keep noticing it in the language that they come across in the future and thus gradually assimilate it over time. In Johnson's terms, the approach can therefore be described as PRODECPRO. For example, a sequence of this kind could be based on an astrology column from the previous day's newspaper, predicting readers' futures according to their star signs:

PRO: Decide how many of the predictions were accurate for you.

DEC: Look at how the predictions are expressed, focusing on the ways modal verbs are used to express different degrees of certainty ("may", "will", etc.) and obligation ("should", "must", etc.); formulate rules for the use of modals in predicting.

PRO: With prompting from the teacher, keep noticing similar ways of making predictions in other texts and other contexts (e.g. weather forecasts); and gradually build up a sense of when predictions are expressed in certain ways, and develop the ability to express them in those ways yourself when appropriate.

A further crucial feature of the approach is that it is the learners, not the teacher, who formulate the grammatical rule, using the evidence of the examples in the language that they have been responding to in terms of its meaning. The process of working out the rule for themselves helps the learners to invest more in understanding it and therefore encourages more effective learning.

Despite the shift of perspective and terminology, one aspect of the debate which has tended to remain constant is the restricted view of what constitutes grammar: it is seen primarily in terms of morphology (the study of word parts such as the -s and -ing endings on verbs in English) and syntax (the study of structures). However, in parallel with the developments in ideas for handling grammar within a communicative approach outlined above, but to some extent separate from them, there have been developments in views of what grammar is — or, more broadly, what proficient users of a language know about, and can do in, that language. Influenced especially by the ideas of the linguist Michael Halliday (e.g. 1994), learning grammar is seen less in terms of mastering decontextualisable structures such as "the past tense", and more in terms of getting to grips with the systems of resources available in the foreign language for expressing meanings in particular types of contexts. These resources include the formal structures; but the structures need to be presented primarily in terms of their function and the kinds of contexts in which their use is natural for native speakers (for a survey of the increasingly extensive literature on the teaching of spoken discourse from this kind of perspective, see S. Thompson, in press). Much of the impetus for the adoption of this wider view of grammar in language teaching has come from the proponents of Language Awareness (see e.g. James and Garrett, 1991), who take it as a basic assumption that an essential part of what learners need to understand and, eventually, use and exploit is what may be called the "discourse value" of lexical and structural choices. For example, both tag questions (e.g. "it hurts here, doesn't it?") and queclaratives (declarative sentences used as questions — e.g. "it hurts here?") can be used in speech to ask for confirmation; but they have different discourse values and are not discoursally interchangeable — each is appropriate in different contexts, and the choice of one or the other is dependent on factors such the speaker's status in relation to the hearer (see G. Thompson, 1999).

Although the two developments outlined above, in methods for teaching grammar and in views of what grammar is, have on the whole proceeded separately, they are fully compatible — indeed, a corpus-based approach can bring them together very naturally. It is a simple matter to extend the methodology proposed by Ellis to cover the explicit investigation by learners of discourse value: in my experience, learners take rather more readily to examining language choices in terms of the contextual and social factors than in terms simply of syntactic rules. In the field of English for Academic Purposes, for example, many of the applications of genre analysis (see Swales, 1990) rely on training learners as discourse analysts: having read and responded to an academic article, students may be asked to decide when and why present, present perfect and past verb forms are used in the introduction section. The approach to working with corpora outlined below is based on this pattern of focus on meaning followed by discourse analysis: there is explicit attention to facts about the language established by the learners themselves on the basis of the data (as is typical of all corpus-based classroom activities), but the facts explored go beyond narrowly lexical or structural aspects to look at the ways in which specific linguistic choices are related to wider discourse and socio-cultural factors. The assumptions are that an understanding of how the foreign language functions in its environment — an ecological approach, as it were — will help learners cope better with the task of coming to terms with the language; and that this understanding can most effectively be developed by conscious, guided scrutiny of the language at work (see Tribble, this volume, for a similar view).

Cross-linguistic comparison

For a number of decades now, the term "grammar-translation" has been used as an easy synonym for bad language teaching. Curiously, however, we seem to be returning to a new version of grammar-translation methods within a communicative framework.[3] Just as explicit "grammar" has re-emerged — though metamorphosed into the wider concepts of language awareness and discourse analysis — from the limbo to which it had been assigned, so it can be argued that "translation" has started a come-back, in the guise of cross-linguistic comparison (see e.g. Soars and Soars, 1986 etc.). It is argued that comparison of the foreign language with the mother tongue, if carefully handled, can be a highly effective way of highlighting what can be thought of as the different "internal logic" of the foreign language. For example, gaining a reasonably secure grasp of what the present perfect is for can be facilitated by an explicit comparison with the way in which the mother tongue divides up the semantic space covered in English by the present, present perfect and past verb forms, and with the contexts in which each of the equivalent forms is used.[4] The objection might be raised that the learners are quite probably not aware of how their mother tongue works and that the comparison will therefore be at best difficult and at worst an unhelpful distraction. A counter-argument to this is that helping them to explore their own language is a way of developing their sensitivity to language generally, which may be an important support in learning a foreign language. It certainly seems odd that teachers generally expect learners to cope simultaneously with both an unfamiliar language and an unfamiliar way of looking at language; encouraging them to try out the linguistic categories on their mother tongue, where they can draw on their existing rich knowledge of the language, is likely to help them to develop a better sense of what the categories mean, which will in turn help them to arrive at a better sense of how the categories function in the other language.

As with grammar teaching, cross-linguistic comparison — at least as exemplified in textbooks — has tended to focus on structure; and, again as with grammar, it is clear that a broader view of the aspects of the two languages that can be compared is likely to be beneficial. There are in fact ways in which this broader view is already accommodated in the ordinary practices of many language teachers. Explanations of vocabulary often rely on cross-linguistic comparison, and this frequently involves issues of appropriacy to different contexts, and even socio-cultural norms. For example, I remember being surprised the first time one of my students in China told me that there was going to be a "demonstration" in Beijing on May 1st: for me, demonstrations are always directed against something or someone, and it took a few moments to clarify that we were actually talking about the politically innocuous May Day Parade. Another area where wider issues are typically brought in is when social customs are compared: for example, what British people do at the start of meals instead of saying something like "good appetite"; or on what occasions people exchange formalised greetings (birthdays, namedays, etc.), and what the typical greetings are. From these kinds of comparisons, it is potentially only a small step to a more systematic approach to cross-discourse comparison, focusing on a range of different ways in which the two languages each operate in their own environments to carry out equivalent functions. The examples of comparable corpora discussed below are designed to illustrate this kind of approach in action (see Lawson, this volume, for a discussion of comparable corpora from a different perspective).

Cross-linguistic corpora

If we accept the desirability of the approach outlined above — explicit investigation by the learners of lexical and grammatical choices from a discourse perspective, supported by comparisons with the mother tongue — we then need to think of practical ways of implementing it in the classroom. One way is through the use of cross-linguistic corpora of particular genres.

It is worth noting that the way corpora are used in the approach proposed here is to some extent the reverse of how they are used in corpus linguistics. Linguists generally start with as few preconceptions as possible about what they will find in a corpus. What they are looking for are the patterns of repetition (e.g. of words appearing together in collocations, or of structures used with marked frequency — or infrequency — in particular genres) which reflect the patterns that build up in native speakers' minds as they are exposed to, and use, the language over years and which form the basis of their sense of what sounds "natural". An important function of corpora in the language classroom, on the other hand, is to provide the learners with concentrated exposure to particular patterns of repetition, which will usually be at least partially identified in advance by the teacher, in order to accelerate the development of their sense of what sounds natural in the foreign language.

One advantage of including texts in the mother tongue — apart from the general advantages of cross-linguistic comparison already mentioned above — is that it helps to alleviate the problem that the learners may not have declarative knowledge of how their mother tongue operates. In my experience, asking learners to explain something about their language using their intuition alone frequently leads either to baffled silence or to confusion and disagreement. Giving them data to look at provides a concrete basis which helps them to discover and formulate facts about the language. This contributes to a non-vicious circle: identifying features in texts in a familiar language gives them relatively easy practice in the fairly specialised skill of working with corpora; and this supports their efforts to explore corpora in the foreign language by giving them a better sense of what to look for and how to look for it.

The teaching sequence starts with the learners responding to a single text in terms of meaning. This involves, amongst other things, establishing the context and genre of the text: who has produced it, what audience it is intended for, what its purpose is, and so on. In the second step, the learners are guided towards focusing explicitly on certain features of the language of the text which are distinctive for the genre in some way. The final step is when the corpus is brought in to allow them to explore the use of those features more widely: the text as a single example of its genre is, as it were, projected outwards onto the genre as a whole. This helps the learners to see the generic background against which the individual text "makes sense" — the pool of potential meanings on which it draws for its language choices; and it encourages a sense of the genre as a relatively identifiable type of language use within the overall language system. It also gives a good deal of the exposure which native speakers get gradually over a longer period, together with the explicit noticing that Ellis argues leads to effective learning. At the same time the mother tongue corpus is brought in so that the learners can identify more precisely what it is about the language choices that is distinctive, and can notice where the choices that seem intuitively natural to them as speakers of their own language can be transferred to the other language and where other choices need to be made in order to sound natural in the other language.

Example 1: Travel brochures

The rest of this paper will exemplify how this general approach can be put into practice. The first example that I wish to look at is drawn from a study by Angela Yan (1998). She carried out a small-scale comparison of travel brochures in English and Chinese, focusing especially on the ways that the writers interact with their readers. She was interested in features such as the use of imperatives addressed to the reader, and the forms used to refer to the reader (*you, people, tourists,* etc.).

One of the aspects that she notes relates to the use of the imperative. In the English brochure, this is remarkably frequent: no less than 22% of the clauses in her data are imperative. The following are typical examples:

(1)   The highlands of Scotland has something for everyone. <u>Take</u> a closer look and <u>be</u> rewarded by the majesty of its scenery and wildlife …

(2)   <u>Visit</u> Culloden Battlefield, scene of the last great land battle in Britain, and <u>walk</u> the milelong ramparts of Fort George. <u>Tour</u> Cawdor Castle, home of the Thanes of Cawdor immortalized in Shakespeare's Macbeth …

It is clear that, although these are imperative in form, they are not primarily to be interpreted as commands in the usual sense. The prototypical imperative — e.g. "be quiet!" — can be paraphrased as "you must be quiet". On the other hand, the first example above is closely related to conditional promises ("If you take a closer look, you will be rewarded …"), while it seems more appropriate to paraphrase the second example not as "you must tour Cawdor Castle" but as "you can tour Cawdor Castle". Their primary purpose can be seen as projecting the reader into the scenery, constructing a description that unfolds as if the reader were travelling through it. This orientation towards the reader as potential actor is reinforced by both explicit and implicit reference to the reader: explicitly by use of *you* as Subject, and implicitly by reference to activities for which the most plausible potential "doer" is the reader:

(3)   Wonder at the works of nature as <u>you</u> visualize a cathedral inside the vast embrace of Snoo Cave.

(4)   The <u>climb</u> through the startling hairpin bends of the Bealach Na Ba (Pass of the Cattle) leads to picturesque Applecross.

In all, 13% of the Subjects in Yan's data are of these types: when the imperative clauses which have *you* as understood Subject are added, 35% of the clauses are therefore reader-oriented in one way or another.

In her Chinese data, on the other hand, the orientation is rather more strongly towards the locations being described, projecting less a tour by the reader than a panoramic, bird's-eye view.[5] The reader is referred to, but typically indirectly in the third person, or implicitly in verb forms without an expressed Subject — such cases account for 20% of the clauses.[6]

(5) | <u>yóu rén</u> | wú | bù | lè | ér | wàng | fǎn
| <u>visitors</u> | no | not | happy | so | forget | back

"Visitors are so happy that they are reluctant to leave."

(6) | lìng | <u>rén</u> | zàn tàn | | de | shān hú | jǐng sè
| make | <u>people</u> | gasp admiringly | | PART | coral | scenery

"The coral scenery makes people gasp in admiration"

PART = *particle which signals a relationship of modification between a preceding group/clause and a following nominal group*

(7) | <u>jū</u> | mù | <u>sì wàng</u> | | de | shì | qīng cuì
| <u>raise</u> | eye | <u>look around</u> | | PART | be | verdant
| de | shān luán | | | | |
| PART | mountain | | | | |

"Looking around, there are verdant mountains."

In some ways, these appear similar to example (4), which also refers only implicitly to the reader. However, in context the effect is different: the instances in the English brochure resonate with the other more overt reader-oriented choices and contribute to the overall sense of "you" "acting"; those in the Chinese brochure, in contrast, have few overt interactive choices to resonate with and their potential reader-orientation remains dormant (on the concept of resonance in text, see Thompson, 1998). On the rare occasions (3% of clauses) when the reader is referred to as *you*, the form *ní* is used: in the context this is equivalent to the generic use of *you* (= *one*) in English and is less overtly interactive than, for example, the respectful form *nín*, which is used for direct address to an individual.

Most strikingly, Yan found only one imperative form, and even this is mitigated in that it is the softener 'try' which is imperative rather than the main process *imagine*:

(8) | shì | xǐng
| try | imagine

"Try to imagine"

She argues (1998: 118) that if imperatives were used they would sound inappropriate, in that they would tend to retain their association with commands and appear unfriendly. This suggests that Chinese learners might avoid using imperatives in similar contexts in English where they would be appropriate, and that the apparent resemblance between imperatives in English and Chinese might hide important differences in their discourse value. More generally, there appears to be a fairly marked difference in the level and type of interactivity in the travel brochures. In English marketing genres (advertisements, brochures, etc.), interaction is one of the primary techniques of involvement, through which the advertiser tries to persuade the reader (Thompson and Thetela, 1995). A key resource for the writer in making the text interactive are reader-oriented Mood choices such as imperatives (which are common in brochures, but less so in advertisements) and interrogatives (which do not occur in the brochure data, but are frequent in advertisements). This appears not to be the case in Chinese, at least for brochures; instead, there is a tendency to rely more on describing the salient features of the place to which the brochure relates.

From the perspective of the classroom, one great advantage of brochures (apart from the fact that they are sent out free on demand, so that it is fairly easy to build up a collection) is that each in itself forms a mini-corpus, since it includes many different short texts of the same type. Each text referring to a different location in the country or region described in the brochure is designed to be free-standing and can be read alone; and each is a separate example of the same genre as the others. Michael Hoey (1986) has coined the term "discourse colony" for this kind of collection of related but separate texts gathered into a single book / brochure / etc. (other examples of colonies are dictionaries, encyclopedias and telephone directories). By their very nature, discourse colonies in general are excellent candidates for mini-corpora for use in the classroom.

Example 2: Job ads

The other example that I wish to discuss also relies on texts from discourse colonies: in this case, job advertisements. Sibylle Alder (1998) compiled an annotated computer-based corpus of 400 job ads in English and 400 in German from the relevant sections of newspapers in the UK and Switzerland. She analysed them from various perspectives, concentrating — as Angela Yan did — on the extent to which the writers engage in overt interaction with the readers, and the ways in which they do this. Alder examined particularly the balance between requirement and persuasion and the related dimension of distance and personalisation: that is, whether the wording of the ads suggests that the companies see their role in the interaction as magisterially bestowing jobs "downwards" on those applicants who manage to demonstrate their worthiness, or as attracting ideal candidates to work for them by offering benefits and a relationship of equality. The critical discourse analyst Norman Fairclough (1996) argues that we are going through a process of "technologisation of discourse" — changes in language which reflect new ways of visualising and organising workplaces in our culture. Using this idea, Alder presents the options in job ads as reflecting the general pressures on companies nowadays to act and project themselves not simply as employers deciding who goes where in a hierarchy but as human resource developers providing environments in which the best qualities of their employees can be nurtured.

One way of attracting applicants is, of course, by stating the benefits associated with the job. There are examples of this in both sets of ads; but there is a clear tendency for more of the English ads to do this (67% as against 45% of the Swiss ads):

(9)   Excellent terms and conditions includes: fully paid holiday entitlements, accident insurance, company pension scheme, free uniform.

(10)   Wir bieten Ihnen eine umfassende Einführung sowie Unterstützung bei fachlicher Weiterbildung
        "We offer you a comprehensive induction as well as support for professional development."

One of the benefits that the English ads frequently mention is the salary:

(11)   Salary pro rata full-time pay scale (£7275-£11,166).

Exact salaries are mentioned in none of the Swiss ads, and even the following vague kind of information is given only rarely:

(12)   … bieten wir Ihnen einen zeitgemässen Lohn, Spesenvergütung und im Hintergrund ein gut eingespieltes Team.
        "… we offer you an up-to-date salary, expenses and in the background a well adjusted team."

At the same time, the English ads tend to be equally open about projecting their authority in making demands on candidates. As a simple indicator of this, the modal markers of obligation *require(d), must* and *should* occur 230, 96 and 57 times respectively. For example:

(13)   The posts <u>require</u> self motivated persons of graduate calibre with good organizational skills.

(14)   Above all you <u>must</u> have natural people skills.

(15)   Applicants for the role of QA Controller <u>should</u> have a good understanding of the principles of Quality Assurance …

The most frequent single modal marker is *will* (over 500 occurrences). This has many meanings, but one common location for its use is in the section of the ad setting out what is required of the applicant, where it has a strong element of obligation:

(16)   The successful candidate <u>will</u> be able to:
        undertake a wide range of servicing and repair work …

Overall, therefore, the English ads seem to separate out persuasion and requirement and deal with them overtly in different parts of the text; and even the persuasion is done without a strong tendency to establish personalised contact with the applicant.

In the Swiss ads, in contrast, the two are more subtly merged. These ads tend to be much less overt in expressing their requirements and more likely to choose wordings which project choice on the applicant's part. The markers of obligation *verlangen (require), müssen (must)* and *sollte/n (should)* occur no more than 23, 6 and 24 times respectively.

(17)   Aus diesem Grunde <u>sollten</u> Sie Kentnisse und Erfahrung … mitbringen
        "For this reason you <u>should</u> bring knowledge and experience …"

A different kind of marker of obligation, the noun *Aufgabe (duties)* and its derivatives such as *Aufgabengebiet (range of duties)*, is used frequently (170 times in all); but these typically occur as headings, with relatively little repetition of expressions of obligation within the descriptions of the duties. The single most frequent modal verb is *können (can*–55 occurrences). This is mainly used to express potential benefits for the applicant:

(18)   hier <u>können</u> Sie sich in einem Bereich weiterentwickeln, der die besten Zukunftsaussichten bietet.
        "here you <u>can</u> develop yourself in a field which offers the best prospects for the future."

Related to this is frequent use of markers of possibility such as *möglich (possible)* and *eventuell (possibly)*–57 occurrences in all — which allow for negotiation rather than imposing a particular set of conditions on the applicant:

(19)   Sie verfügen über Erfahrung, <u>eventuell</u> eine spezielle Ausbildung.
"You have experience, <u>possibly</u> specialised training."

Whereas *will* is frequently used in the English ads in prescribing the characteristics required of the applicant, the Swiss ads use the equivalent *werden* very rarely (13 times in equivalent senses) and instead show a marked tendency to use the Present Simple tense, as in example (19). This can be seen as describing the ideal candidate (it still, of course, indicates what the company requires):

(20)   Sie <u>sind</u> aufgeschlossen, selbständig, <u>haben</u> Freude am Kundenkontakt.
"You <u>are</u> outgoing, independent, <u>take</u> pleasure in contact with customers."

This option is often taken even when the duties of the post itself are being described:

(21)   Sie <u>sind</u> verantwortlich für das gesamte Lager sowie das Bestellwesen im Servicecenter und <u>koordinieren</u> alle damit verbundenen Aufgaben.
"You <u>are</u> responsible for the whole stock room as well as all orders at the service centre and <u>coordinate</u> all duties related to that."

In comparison with the relatively authoritative *will*–especially as it resonates with the other overt obligation-oriented choices in the English texts — the choice of the Present Simple seems to leave it to the candidates themselves to judge how far they match the description. It contributes to a tone of negotiation, of willingness to allow the candidate space to decide whether or not to apply. In these contexts the present tense in German has a similar discourse value to *will* in English; and the difference in the forms used relates to the broader issue of the relationship being established between the company and the potential candidate in the two cultures: whether the bias is towards prescription or equality.

The greater tendency of Swiss ads to project interaction and negotiation is reflected in other choices as well. For example, questions, which are inherently interactive, occur in only 12% of the English ads as opposed to 31% of the

Swiss ads. The Swiss questions typically come near the end and project an interest in the potential applicant's reaction:

(22)   <u>Interessiert?</u> Dann senden Sie ihre vollständigen Bewerbungs-unterlagung.
       "Interested? Then send your full set of application documents."

(23)   Fühlen Sie sich angesprochen?
       "Do you think this sounds like you?"

There is also a difference in the use of direct address to the applicant. As a number of the examples above have shown, this occurs frequently in the Swiss ads (*Sie–you*): 82% of the ads include at least one case of direct address, compared with only 42% of English ads. The majority of the English ads either avoid referring to the applicant, or use third-person forms such as *persons* or *applicants* (see examples (13) and (15) above). In addition, 87% of Swiss ads have self-reference (*wir–we*), whereas only 43% of English ads do. Here is a typical example from the Swiss corpus which also shows the company projecting itself as having feelings (a humanising touch which is found in only about 5% of the English ads):

(24)   <u>Wir möchten Sie gerne</u> kennenlernen, wenn <u>Sie</u> als sympatische und engagierte Frau …
       "<u>We would like</u> to meet <u>you</u> if <u>you</u>, as a friendly and committed woman, …"

Alder's analysis of the two sets of ads as summarised here covers both the presence or absence of content (benefits, salary, etc.) and the frequency and distribution of specific lexicogrammatical choices (modality, interrogatives, reference to the two interactants, etc.). This would allow a flexible approach if the analysis were drawn on in the classroom, focusing on these different aspects as appropriate. As with the Chinese data, the corpus does not throw up "new" uses or meanings that are outside the standard explanations/translations of, say, the modal verbs (although the *will*–Present Simple equivalence is unlikely to be mentioned in most textbooks). For example, the modal verbs *must* and *müssen* in the ads are in one sense very close in meaning. However, in terms of their discourse value in this context, they are clearly very different: *must* in the English ads is a much more "normal" choice than *müssen* in the Swiss ads. Part of the normalness comes from the whole approach to requirement vs. persuasion in the ads. The analysis therefore suggests that investigation and comparison of a single feature, though useful, may be less rewarding than looking at a range of related features — a point which also emerged through the discussion of resonance between choices in Yan's brochures.

Implications for the classroom

There are a number of ways in which the kinds of analyses carried out by Yan and Alder lend themselves well to classroom activities. The linguistic analysis is relatively straightforward, since the categories are deliberately simple to identify and talk about. Yan's analysis was done by hand, since she was mainly interested in grammatical structures and classes of verbs (action vs. mental processes) rather than particular lexical items, and she found no existing software which could do the initial analysis for her automatically. Alder was looking, amongst other things, at the use of modality; and she was therefore able to draw up a list of modal verbs, etc. and to search for them in her corpus using a concordance programme (Mike Scott's *WordSmith Tools*–see Chapter 3) for part of the analysis. This would not be essential in a classroom application, but it adds an extra dimension if computers are easily available.

It is relatively straightforward to apply the approach sketched out in the earlier part of this paper to these corpora. The initial stimulus in exploiting, say, the brochures with learners could be one text in English, read with a focus on the meaning. As part of the subsequent conscious examination of the language, the issue of interactivity could be raised; and different groups could be given a brochure each and asked to work through them rapidly to identify the choices which contribute to the interactivity and to gain some idea of the relative frequency of the various choices. The primary focus could be on a specific feature (e.g. imperatives in brochure data, modal verbs in the ads), particularly if this would make the lesson fit in with what has been dealt with in other lessons. However, it would seem sensible to encourage the learners to consider a wider range of related features, since the discourse value of one feature cannot really be judged in isolation. At the same time, to highlight the differences, they could be given a brochure in Chinese, or whatever their mother tongue is, and asked to analyse it as far as possible in the same way. The discussion of the groups' findings could follow through into various broader socio-cultural issues: the interpersonal implications of the use or non-use of imperatives found in the brochures; the different techniques used by brochure writers to involve the readers; the types of attractions and activities that appeal to tourists in the two cultures; and so on.[7] The same basic sequence could be applied equally to the job ads, with equally rich issues to explore relating to the social set-up reflected there (the common British preconception that the Swiss tend to be stiff and formal is certainly undermined by the overall finding that the Swiss ads are more interactive and "friendly" than the English ones).

It could be argued that such a sequence of activities demands more time and energy (not least from the teacher), than the potential benefits warrant. From a purely practical point of view, some time could be saved by dividing the corpus analysis amongst different groups and pooling their findings in the round-up discussion. This would anyway be sensible on other grounds, since it encourages the groups to listen and react to what the other groups say, and gives the round-up stage greater weight in the activity: as Jane Willis (1996) points out, the public presentation of the results of a task carried out in groups or pairs has a central function in helping learners move towards greater accuracy as well as fluency. However, there are also broader methodological justifications for devoting the necessary time to this kind of activity. The analysis of the corpus data is essentially a purposeful task involving the use of language, and therefore fits in well with current views on the efficacy of task-based learning; but it has the added advantage that it is a task which involves language not only as the means of communication to get the task done, but also as the subject-matter under investigation. In analysing examples of a genre in this way, the learners are being involved in constant, language-oriented attention to text, and they will be exposed to and may well notice many aspects of the language used that are not the main focus. Perhaps more importantly, the analysis gets the learners used to looking at text in this way, exploring a range of contextualised, culturally conditioned aspects involved in the linguistic choices — including grammatical structures. By doing this they gradually build up a sense of the importance of repeated choices across a number of examples of a genre in creating "naturalness". The specific findings that the learners come up with may seem relatively restricted in some cases, but the findings are only part of the learning outcome.

Looking at the issues from the perspective of corpus-based study, other questions arise. Alder's corpus was designed to be large enough to be representative (she justifies her decision not to go beyond 400 ads in each sub-corpus by the fact that she found no significant differences in the findings when she compared analyses for 200 and 400 ads). On the other hand, Yan's corpus of one brochure in each language is clearly small (even allowing for the fairly large number of separate texts within each brochure), and would be a weak basis for claims about the genre as a whole. However, in the classroom we are not aiming at a full, accurate, watertight description: the exploration is more important than the findings. A large corpus becomes unwieldy, and soon reaches the point where it is essential to use a computer, which may not always be easily available. Even with Alder's corpus, it would seem sensible to select a manageable number of ads for hands-on exploration in class. The full corpus could be made available on computer for back-up, to allow the learners to follow through specific points that they notice and see how far they apply to the larger corpus. In this case, the projection from individual instance to general use would be a two-stage process: first, with a broader focus, from the text to the hands-on corpus of complete texts, and then, with a more detailed focus, to the computer-based corpus which provides extracts — concordance lines — from texts. There is no great risk that a small corpus will lead to conclusions which are actually wrong: this would seem likely to arise only if, say, the brochure chosen happened to have been deliberately written to break or bend the generic conventions in some way. It is more likely that the data might suggest certain choices as more or less frequent than they would be if a larger corpus were used; but the benefits outlined above outweigh this possible disadvantage.

In some ways, a concordance programme which could do the mechanical trawling for specific features in a larger corpus might actually be a hindrance. For one thing, the searching is an important part of the process for the learner, since it involves purposeful scanning of a fairly large amount of text. In addition, concordance lines can make it difficult to get a sense of the overall context and of the ways in which the various features work together in individual texts. If a concordancer is available, it will often be most useful (as in Alder's study) as a way of locating where specific features can be found so that they can then be examined in the context of the whole text where they occur. There are certainly things which a computer analysis of a large corpus can show which are likely to be missed by a human scan — particularly collocational patterns of words typically occurring near each other in text; but the current equation of corpus *linguistics* with computer-based approaches does not need to apply in the classroom since we are acting as educationalists rather than as linguists. The crucial role of the corpus is to wean learners away from an understandable but ultimately unhelpful reliance on oversimple "rules" packaged by the teacher and towards an awareness that the development of proficiency depends to a great extent on focused, purposeful exposure to and use of language in specified contexts. In the language classroom, corpus is not a term of measurement but a state of mind.[8]

Conclusion

One of the problems that has faced language teachers in recent years is how to talk about language with learners in a stimulating, accessible way. In the 1960s and 1970s a consensus built up that the kind of talking about grammar that was possible within a structural approach was off-putting to the majority of learners: it seemed boring, over-technical, abstract and far removed from commonsense ways of talking about language. The first reaction was to avoid language as a topic altogether, and to introduce all kinds of fascinating other subjects from the "real world", from astrological predictions to zoo layouts. This was theoretically justified, in that teachers realised that it was vital to involve learners in meaningful communication and that this could be achieved more easily with topics which the learners found inherently interesting; but it was also to some extent a cop-out. It is certainly true that language is a system of communication, and so it makes sense to spend much of the time in class using it to communicate; but it seems a strange classroom in which the only topic that is banned is the subject being studied — especially if one of the reasons for banning it is that it is not interesting enough. From the outside, this has often — understandably — looked like a loss of nerve on the part of language teachers.

The approach set out in the present paper is intended to bring together three resources which can help overcome the problem. The first of these is, very broadly, discourse analysis (or genre analysis, or register analysis): what I have called an ecological approach to language, exploring it in relation to the environments in which it is used and the ways in which it adapts itself to each of the environments. This encourages talk about language which draws a good deal on commonsense notions of what language is doing. Metalanguage — labels for the grammatical and textual features identified, such as "modal verb" and "direct address" — is still necessary, but the rationale for having many of the technical terms is more transparent since the features that are being labelled are clearly related to the communicative purpose and context of the language.

The second resource is corpus analysis: projecting the individual text onto a wider range of similar texts which represent the background against which language choices in the text make sense. This encourages talk about the genre as a whole, and about the frequency and combinations of particular choices; and it gives a sense of the central importance of variation in language use. It also encourages talk about the socio-cultural implications of how the genre is performed: seeing repeated patterns of choice across a genre provides a far more memorable image than a single example can ever do of how the speakers of the other language go about conducting their lives through language.

The third resource is cross-linguistic comparison: looking at examples of the same genre in the mother tongue. This encourages talk which draws on the learners' existing but largely unconscious knowledge of how language works in their own social context, and thus grounds the discussion even more firmly in the kind of commonsense notions about language that native speakers have. As noted earlier, the data provided by the mother-tongue corpus is essential to help the learners bring to the surface their unconscious knowledge; and the insights that they gain about their own language can be stimulating in themselves and thus increase their willingness to investigate language in general.

Put the three resources together, and you have corpus-based cross-linguistic genre comparison: not, of course, the answer to all our problems by any means, but, I would argue, a useful tool in the fight to keep our nerve as teachers of language and to make language itself a viable object of study in the classroom.

Notes

1. I would like to express my thanks to Angela Yan and Sibylle Alder for permission to draw on their dissertation studies for the examples in this paper, and for the discussions which helped me develop the ideas put forward here.
   I also think it is worth pointing out explicitly that the view of language and text taken in this paper is an application of concepts from Systemic Functional Grammar: meaning as choice, the centrality of variation, the text as an instance of the language system as a whole, etc. I have opted to talk about "genre" since this term is likely to be familiar; but in an SFG approach the examples discussed in the body of the paper are more properly referred to as "register analysis". For a full introduction to the concept of register, see Ghadessy (1993).

2. Interestingly, when I have tried this out with native speakers, the only extracts they have any difficulty in identifying are those lifted from specially written texts from EFL textbooks. The problem is that these are "genre-free": contextless, purposeless, neutered. One can only wonder

about the effect of feeding our learners an unrelieved diet of such texts even at elementary levels.

3.   In some ways, the ghost of grammar-translation has rarely disappeared completely. In many textbooks using structural approaches during the 1960s and 1970s, for example, all the texts and exercises were transparently designed to illustrate and practise specific structures, even though these were often not explicitly stated anywhere in the form of grammar rules. At the same time, the near-mechanical exercises which occupied most of the practice time allowed a focus on getting the forms right without having to worry about the meaning (since that was always specified by the textbook). This had, of course, been the prime advantage of translation: the meaning of what was to be said was given by the sentence to be translated, and the learner simply had to concentrate on expressing that meaning correctly in the other language. In other words, structural approaches can be seen as embodying the spirit of grammar-translation without its external manifestations — grammar-translation without the grammar and without the translation.

4.   The crucial difference between this kind of comparison and contrastive analysis (James, 1980), which appears to be very similar, is that, on the whole, the latter was carried out surreptitiously by teachers and textbook writers: the results were administered to the learners in the materials, but the learners were not involved in the process of discovery. Cross-linguistic comparison is something that the learners themselves do, with the teacher as guide. This is thus part of the more general movement — as with grammar — towards discovery learning and greater transparency in teaching.

5.   The choice between tour and bird's-eye view is comparable with the two options that Linde and Labov (1975) found when they asked people to describe their apartments. It would be interesting to explore the parallels with different types of narratorial orientation in novels and short stories (see e.g. Simpson, 1993): the English option is related to having the narration from the restricted viewpoint of a character in the novel, whereas the Chinese option is closer to having an omniscient narrator. However, this is beyond the scope of the present study.

6.   There are practical difficulties with identifying "clauses" and "Subjects" in Chinese which there is no space to cover here. Many of the issues are discussed in Fang *et al.* 1995 (this is also the source of the description of the particle *de* used in the examples).

7.   It is worth noting that in principle the examples discussed in this paper are reversible: that is, they could equally well be used with English learners of Chinese, etc. Looked at from this side, one thing that would be highlighted in the brochures is the *absence* of a feature (imperatives) in the foreign language. This reinforces the value of doing a cross-linguistic comparison, since it is more difficult to notice things that aren't there unless you are actively looking for them.

8.   The same is in fact true for the linguist. However, size matters more in linguistics, partly at least because corpus-based work has had to justify its existence against a dominant approach based on linguists' intuitions, and it is large corpora which have provided the most striking evidence that many insights are not accessible to intuition.

References

Alder, S. 1998. Requiring the Ideal Candidate: Genre and interaction in English and Swiss job ads. Unpublished MA dissertation, University of Liverpool.

Ellis, R. 1992. *Second Language Acquisition and Language Pedagogy.* Clevedon: Multilingual Matters.

Ellis, R. 1998. *Second Language Acquisition Research and Language Teaching.* Oxford: OUP.

Fairclough, N. 1996. "Technologisation of discourse". In C. R. Caldas-Coulthard and M. Coulthard (eds), *Texts and Practices,* 71–83. London: Routledge.

Fang, Y., McDonald, E. and Cheng, M. S. 1995. "Theme in Chinese". In R. Hasan and P. Fries (eds), *On Subject and Theme: A discourse functional perspective,* 235–73. Amsterdam: John Benjamins.

Ghadessy, M. (ed), 1993. *Register Analysis: Theory and practice.* London: Pinter.

Halliday, M. A. K. 1994. *An Introduction to Functional Grammar.* (2nd edition). London: Arnold.

Hoey, M. 1986. "The discourse colony: A preliminary study of a neglected discourse type". In M. Coulthard (ed), *Talking about Text: Studies presented to David Brazil on his retirement* [Discourse Analysis Monograph 13], 1–26. Birmingham: Birmingham University.

James, C. 1980. *Contrastive Analysis.* London: Longman.

James, C. and Garrett, P. (eds), 1991. *Language Awareness in the Classroom.* London: Longman.

Johns, T. 1994. "From printout to handout: Grammar and vocabulary teaching in the context of data-driven learning". In T. Odlin (ed), *Perspectives on Pedagogical Grammar,* 293–313. Cambridge: CUP.

Johnson, K. 1996. *Language Teaching and Skill Learning.* Oxford: Blackwell.

Krashen, S. 1988. *The Input Hypothesis: Issues and implications.* London: Longman.

Linde, C. and Labov, W. 1975. "Spatial networks as a site for the study of language and thought". *Language* 51(4): 924–39.

Prabhu, N. S. 1987. *Second Language Pedagogy.* Oxford: OUP.

Richards, J. C. and Rodgers, T. S. 1986. *Approaches and Methods in Language Teaching.* Cambridge: CUP.

Scott, M. 1996. *WordSmith Tools.* Oxford: OUP.

Simpson, P. 1993. *Language, Ideology and Point of View.* London: Routledge.

Skehan, P. 1994. "Second Language Acquisition strategies, interlanguage development and task-based learning". In Bygate, Tonkyn and Williams (eds), *Grammar and the Language Teacher,* 175–99. Englewood Cliffs NJ: Prentice Hall.

Soars, J. and Soars, L. 1986. *Headway.* Oxford: OUP.

Swales, J. 1990. *Genre Analysis: English in academic and research settings.*

Cambridge: CUP.

Thompson, G. 1996. "Some misconceptions about communicative language teaching". *ELT Journal* 50(1): 9–15.

Thompson, G. 1998. "Resonance in text". In A. Sánchez-Macarro and R. Carter (eds), *Linguistic Choice across Genres: Variation in spoken and written English,* 29–46. Amsterdam: John Benjamins.

Thompson, G. 1999. "Acting the part: Lexico-grammatical choices and contextual factors". In M. Ghadessy (ed), *Text and Context in Functional Linguistics,* 103–26. Amsterdam: John Benjamins.

Thompson, G. and Thetela, P. 1995. "The sound of one hand clapping: The management of interaction in written discourse". *Text* 15(1): 103–27.

Thompson, S. In press. "Understanding spoken interaction: Recent developments in the analysis of spoken discourse and their applications for language teaching". *Australian Review of Applied Linguistics.*

Willis, J. 1996. "A flexible framework for task-based learning". In J. Willis and D. Willis (eds), *Challenge and Change in Language Teaching.* 52–62. London: Heinemann.

Yan, A. 1998. Interactions between the Writer and Reader in Travel Brochures. MA dissertation, University of Liverpool.

CHAPTER 12

Small corpora and translation[*]
Comparing thematic organization in two languages

Mohsen Ghadessy
Zhongshan University, Guangzhou, P.R.C.

Yanjie Gao
Xian Jiaotong University

Abstract

Recent studies of a text in one language and its translation in another (parallel texts) have revealed many syntactic, semantic, and discourse similarities and differences that can be focused upon in preparing bilingual dictionaries, materials for machine translation and teaching translation methods to university students. To our knowledge, no one has yet analyzed the thematic organization of parallel texts quantitatively. The present study looked at the thematic development of one text-type in English (the source language) and the corresponding translations in the other language, i.e. Chinese (the target language). Halliday's (1994) categories for Theme classification in English with some modification were used for this investigation. The findings based on a statistical analysis indicate that despite a significant difference in the number of clauses and hence thematic features for the parallel texts, there is a significant degree of correlation (translation equivalence) between the Themes in English texts and their Chinese translations in terms of selected thematic patterns. Some implications of the findings for teaching translation and establishing registers/text-types across languages will also be discussed.

Introduction

In the course of learning a foreign language all of us go through many hours of translating, consciously or subconsciously, from the first language into the second one and vice versa. In the majority of cases we are not taught how to do this but we do it as a shortcut to understand the messages in the other language or "reformulate" our L1 messages in L2 ones. In the history of the teaching of foreign languages, teachers have used translation extensively for their purposes, the total procedures and techniques being referred to as *The Translation Method*. Although in the last few decades this method has lost some of the importance attached to it in earlier times, as an academic subject translation has retained its popularity all over the world. Translation departments have been established in many universities in the East and West and, in some countries like China, translation is an obligatory subject for most university students.

Today translation is big business for producers of "equivalent" materials in two languages as the need for machine translation is increasing. For some languages there already exist commercially prepared packages for bilingual dictionaries and guidebooks of phrases and sentences common in what has been referred to by Halliday as "closed registers", i.e. language with a limited set of vocabulary and syntactic structures, for example The International Language of the Air, the bidding system in bridge, the language of menus, etc. (Halliday and Hasan 1985: 39–40). Machine translation is " an option only for a relatively small segment of text-types". However, there is a growing need for translating "general language texts" (Teubert et al. 1998).

Research on translation has focused on different linguistic features of the languages concerned, i.e. the source and the target language. In a seminar in Europe (Third European Seminar, "Translation Equivalence", Italy, Oct.1997), the following topics, among a number of others, were discussed in some "parallel texts" — "performative verbs, agreement and disagreement, multilingual language resources, parts of speech comparison, syntactic tagging, lexical alignment, etc.".

To our knowledge, there is no study to date of the thematic development (Fries 1983) in parallel texts which the present research tries to carry out. If we agree with the claim that "…operationally, most translation is done at the level of the smaller units (word and clause)…" (Newmark 1995: 67), then similar to the study of other linguistic features in parallel texts, an analysis of the clause Theme selections and consequent thematic development in the source as well as the target language would provide valuable aids to all translation practitioners.

Review of literature

The expression "word-for-word translation" is used in most cases to criticize the way a passage from L1 has been translated into L2. This is a method popular with novice translators. Experienced and professional translators, however, use other methods, i.e. "semantic translation, free translation, communicative translation, etc." (Newmark 1995), to provide parallel texts that are accepted by the target language community. A comparison of the L1 text and its parallel translation in L2 would provide findings that can be used as aids by translation practitioners.

Research on parallel texts has focused on different levels of language description and analysis (Arziculov 1998, Barlow 1998, Blanta 1998, Feng 1998, Xiao and Oller 1994). Not necessarily related to translation, thematic organization in a number of different languages and a variety of registers/genres in the same language has been studied by applied linguists. In relation to English and Chinese, the following are of interest (Fries 1983, Fang, Edward, and Cheng 1995, Ghadessy 1995a). Fang et al. study thematic organization at both clause and discourse levels within the framework of systemic functional theory (Halliday 1994). After discussing the notions of *subject* and *topic* in Chinese, they give four characteristics of Chinese clause structure, which, are quite similar to the structure of the clause in English, i.e.

(a) The clause is commonly defined in "message" terms; in other words "the clause ... has some form of organization giving it the status of a communicative event" (Halliday 1985:38);

(b) structurally, the clause divides into two parts : the first part, the beginning of the message; the second part, the continuation of the message;

(c) the different parts of the clause tend to have different information status : the first part known, definite; the second part new, indefinite; and

(d) the first part of the clause is significant in the creation of discourse.
    (Fang et al. 1995:240)

Fang et al. do not specify the Chinese data for their thematic analysis. The examples may be made up or belong to actual samples of written and/or spoken Chinese. This is not made clear.

Fries (1983: 119) refers to the "method of development" of a text. This deals with the lexico-semantic content of Themes. "Thematic content correlates with the method of development of a text (and the nature of the text)".

Ghadessy (1997: 141) concludes that by doing thematic analysis of texts in English "we can provide a more valid profile of English registers based not only on the ingredients of the products, i.e. words and phrases, but also the processes of meaning that underlie them".

Ventola (1995: 85), working on English and German, considers thematic organization as one of the "tools" for shaping discourse in parallel texts, in her qualitative analysis of some parallel texts maintains that " ...both the writers as well as the translators must be trained to be sensitive to these tools in order to use them effectively."

As to the value of a functional grammar for the analysis of parallel texts, we would like to quote Newmark (1995: 9). "In a narrow sense, translation theory is concerned with the translation method appropriately used for a certain type of text, and it is therefore dependent on *a functional theory of language.*" (emphasis added) We believe that a comparative study of the elements placed in the first part of the clauses in an English text and the corresponding translations in Chinese would reveal a number of interesting points, i.e. similarities and differences, that can be considered for commercial as well as pedagogical and practical purposes in the field of translation.

Method

1. Sample: The text-type used in the present study comes from a text book used for teaching translation to university students in China (Liu 1989). All the texts belong to the category of political commentary which deals with an evaluation/assessment of national/international events, present, past, or future. Using a framework provided by Ferguson (1983) for the discourse of spoken sports commentary, we can say that such commentaries provide both a description of events "play-by-play" and an evaluation of them, "colour commentary". The proportion of the two "phases" of the discourse is not equal. However, in the present texts, there is more of the colour commentary than the narration of the events. In all of the commentaries, the writers assume that the readers know what the events are, i.e. knowledge of the background information is shared.

2. Design: The first step in our analysis was to identify the boundaries of clauses in both languages. Embedded clauses were not analyzed for the thematic organization. All together for the nine texts, there were 426, average of 47 per text, clauses in the English texts and 548, average of 61 per text, in the Chinese texts. Halliday's 1994 definition and methodology for thematic analysis was used with some modifications based on Fries (1992) and Ghadessy (1995b).

"The Theme is the element which serves as the point of departure of the message; it is that with which the clause is concerned. The remainder of the message, the part in which the Theme is developed, is called ...Rheme" (Halliday 1994: 37).

All clause Themes in both English and Chinese texts were analyzed in relation to two sets of features, 11 grammatical features, and 10 lexico-semantic ones. Appendix 1 provides an example of each of these features in the English clause together with an example from Chinese. All the examples come from the analyzed texts. Examples for some thematic features did not occur either in the English or the Chinese texts. This may be due to the characteristics of the text-type or register under consideration. These features may very well occur in other registers of both languages. The Themes for all examples in English and Chinese have been underlined.

Procedure
Thematic organization in English and Chinese clauses
English examples (given first) are followed by Chinese examples. Numbers preceding examples refer to the text and clause numbers. If an English clause is rendered into more than one Chinese clause, then additional numbers are added at the end of numbers for Chinese examples. In the majority of cases, the Theme of the clause includes everything right up to the first finite verb of the clause, i.e. it is the subject of the clause. There are, however, differences if we have a Marked Theme, i.e. the Theme is not the subject of the clause. All the possibilities are shown in the examples in Appendix 1. In most examples, the Chinese version is the translation of the English equivalent. In the rest, where equivalent examples are not possible, two separate examples are given to show the Theme types in the two languages.

Theme properties
The Theme essentially comprises everything placed initially in a clause right up to the first finite verb. It may have three elements, i.e. (1) ideational (topical), (2) interpersonal, and/or (3) textual. The ideational element is obligatory. It relates the topic/ideas of the present clause to the previous/following clause(s). The interpersonal element is optional and provides an expression of the speaker/writer's opinion on the proposition made. The textual element is

also optional and overtly connects adjacent clauses. The following provides two examples of the form and the content of Themes analyzed (see Appendix 1 for all Theme types). For a detailed discussion of the grammatical properties see Halliday (1994 chapter three). Fries (1992) and Ghadessy (1995b) provide more details for the lexico-semantic properties.

Grammatical properties
simple Theme: (includes only the ideational or topical Theme without the interpersonal and/or textual elements)

   1.3   <u>China's central government</u> ...
   1.3   <u>dangshi de zhongyang zhengfu</u> ...
             <u>then particle central government</u>

Lexico-semantic properties
abstract Theme:

   1.10   <u>China's real strength</u> ...
   1.10.1 <u>ta jinyou de yidian lilian</u> ...
             <u>it only par little strength</u> ...

Results

Tables 1 below gives all the statistics for text 1 in English and Chinese (see Appendix 2 for all the results). For each text in English and Chinese the raw score for each feature and the percentage out of the total number of clause Themes are provided. For example, text 1 in English has 32 clauses and hence 32 Themes. 21 of these 32 Themes are Simple, i.e. do not have either textual or interpersonal Themes in them. Thus 67% of all the Themes in text 1 in English are of the Simple type.

On the other hand, for the Chinese translation of text 1, we have 45 clauses and hence 45 Themes. 30 of Theme Themes are Simple, i.e. they also constitute 67% of all the Themes in the Chinese translation1. If the Themes in both English and Chinese texts do not have the features in question, this is shown by (-) placed in each box.

Table 1: List of grammatical features (items 1–11) and lexico-semantic features (items 12–21) of the Themes in text 1, English and Chinese. In each box, first the raw number and then the % (out of total clause Themes) are given for the feature in question. Item 22 gives the total number of analyzed clause Themes for each text. The legend below this table gives the features considered.

Texts/Features	English	Chinese
1	21/67%	30/67%
2	11/34%	15/33%
3	11/34%	14/31%
4	-	1/2%
5	20/63%	34/76%
6	12/38%	11/24%
7	4/13%	3/7%
8	-	7/16%
9	-	1/2%
10	-	-
11	4/13%	5/11%
12	-	-
13	4/13%	5/11%
14	9/28%	11/24%
15	6/19%	17/38%
16	1/3%	2/4%
17	8/25%	8/18%
18	-	-
19	1/3%	1/2%
20	-	-
21	3/9%	1/2%
22	32	45

Legend:
1. Simple Theme, 2. Multiple Theme, 3. Textual Theme, 4. Interpersonal Theme,
5. Unmarked ideational Theme, 6. Marked ideational Theme, 7. Clause as Theme,
8. Ellipted Theme, 9. Predicated Theme, 10. Thematic equative, 11. Grammatical
metaphor, 12. Speaker/hearer as Theme, 13. Major text participant (animate) as
Theme, 14. Object/portion of scene as Theme, 15. Abstract Theme, 16. Process/event
as Theme, 17. Time as Theme, 18. Location as Theme, 19. Manner/means as Theme,
20. Cause/purpose as Theme, 21. Condition as Theme, 22. Total clause Themes

Discussion of findings

Statistical analysis

Comparing averages
The above table shows that there are similarities and differences between the English and the Chinese Themes. As Halliday (1993: 127) points out, "In both Chinese and English the noun is a clearly defined grammatical category; in both languages its core meaning is that of an object — an object possessing certain properties and capable of participating in certain processes." The Themes in the English clauses, which in the majority of cases are nominal groups (noun phrases), are translated into corresponding nominal groups in Chinese and placed initially in the Chinese clauses. The differences, on the other hand, relate mainly to the number of clauses in the two languages and the effect that this has on the rest of the Theme features and thematic development. In order to see where the differences are and also measure the significance of the differences, the procedure of *paired samples statistics, the T-Test*, was applied to all the 22 features of Themes in both languages. Table 2 below shows the results.

Number of clauses
There are significant differences, indicated by **, in English and Chinese texts in relation to a number of features. The main reason for the differences relates to the number of clauses in the nine English texts, a range of 32 to 75, as compared to the nine translations in Chinese, a range of 45 to 79. The average clause number in Chinese is 60.88 per text, in English it is 47.33. The crucial question to be asked is: What happens to the English Clause when it is translated into Chinese? A general answer is that in many cases the English clause is rendered into more than one clause in Chinese, each with its own Theme.

Simple Themes
Related to the significant increase in the number of Themes in Chinese is the significant increase in the number of Simple Themes, average of 25.33 in English but 35.66 in Chinese per text. However, the difference between English and Chinese in relation to Multiple Themes is NOT significant, average of 19.77 in English and 21.88 in Chinese per text. In other words, almost all of the additional Themes in the Chinese samples are of the Simple type. These Themes can be nominal groups (noun phrases), processes (infinitives

Table 2: Results of T-Tests for all feature frequencies in English and Chinese texts

Number	Features	T-Statistics	Significance
1	Simple Theme	-3.653	.006**
2	Multiple Theme	-1.040	.329
3	Textual Theme	-.243	.814
4	Interpersonal Theme	-2.874	.021**
5	Unmarked Theme	-2.680	.028**
6	Marked Theme	-3.216	.012**
7	Clause as Theme	-2.101	.069
8	Ellipted Theme	-9.000	.000**
9	Predicated Theme		
10	Thematic Equative		
11	Grammatical Metaphor	-.300	.772
12	Speaker/Hearer as Theme	-2.294	.051
13	Major Text Participant-animate	.833.	429
14	Object/Scene as Theme	-.963	.364
15	Abstract Theme	-.735	.483
16	Process/Event as Theme	-2.128	.066
17	Time as Theme	-2.562	.034**
18	Location as Theme	.426	.681
19	Manner as Theme	.000	1.000
20	Cause as Theme		
21	Condition as Theme	-1.200	.264
22	Number of Clauses	-6.616	.000**

** Significant (p<.05)

and — ing forms with or withour objects), or circumstances (adverbs) without the accompanying Textual and/or the Interpersonal Themes.

Interpersonal Themes

Although there is no significant difference between the two samples in relation to Multiple Themes, there is a significant difference in relation to Interpersonal Themes, which average 1.77 in English and 3.55 in Chinese per text. The low percentages in both samples indicates that, in this register, the expression of the opinions, views, and modality is rarely included in the clause Themes; it is to be found in the clause Rhemes.

Unmarked and Marked Themes

Another important effect of the increase in the number of Themes in Chinese is that the frequencies of both the Unmarked (Theme is subject) and Marked Themes (Theme is not subject) are significantly different from the English texts, averaging 35.77 in English and 44.00 in Chinese for Unmarked and 11.55 in English and 16.88 in Chinese for Marked per text. Thus unlike the Simple and Multiple Themes, the increase in the number of Themes belongs to both Unmarked and Marked categories.

Ellipted Themes

Another significant difference between the two samples is related to the number of Ellipted Themes (Theme is omitted), with a frequency of 1.22 in English and 7.22 in Chinese per text. The ellipsis is of course related to the Unmarked Themes, i.e. the subject of the clause in Chinese is omitted. This process affects the thematic progression as all the Ellipted Themes create an identity chain (same Theme) related to the first subject. Maintaining the same Theme for a number of consecutive clauses is a method of text development different from the same corresponding Themes in the English texts.

Time as Theme

The last significant difference between the two samples is related to the frequency of Time as Theme examples. Chinese clauses have more of this type of Theme, with a frequency of 5.66 in English and 7.77 in Chinese per text. This process creates more Marked Themes in Chinese, which as we saw above, is significantly different in the two samples. Also the frequency of Time as Theme in Chinese creates thematic progression, i.e. a similarity chain, based on the actual dates of events and happenings in the past. Maintaining the same Theme type (referring to time) for a number of consecutive clauses in Chinese is also a method of development different from the corresponding Themes in the English texts.

Correlations:

Despite the significant differences in the means for thematic features in the above table, we can show that there is a significant degree of relationship (correlation) between the Theme patterns in the two samples. By Theme pattern we mean the combination of features, grammatical and lexical, that can be assigned to each Theme. For example, the most frequent Theme pattern in English has the

Table 3: Frequency of Theme patterns in the two samples and their correlation

Theme Patterns	English	Chinese	Correlation
			.884**
1, 5, 15	64	77	
2, 3, 5, 15	52	33	
1, 5, 13	41	55	
2, 3, 5, 13	39	36	
1, 5, 14	28	34	
1, 6, 17	27	43	
2, 3, 5, 14	22	13	
1, 6, 7, 21	17	21	
1, 5, 16	11	15	
2, 3, 6, 17	11	12	
1, 5, 11, 15	10	14	
1, 6, 19	11	10	
2, 3, 5, 16	9	10	
1, 5, 8, 14	0	11	
2, 3, 5, 8, 13	4	11	
1, 5, 8, 13	1	15	

features 1, 5, 15. This means that the Theme is Simple, Unmarked and Abstract, e.g. *China's real strength* .... The same pattern is also the most frequent in Chinese, e.g. *America's idea* .... The following table gives the most frequent patterns in the English samples with their corresponding patterns in Chinese texts. The numbers in the left column refer to the Theme features discussed above. Only frequencies of 10 and above are given for both samples. The English correspondences in some cases have lower frequencies. We believe that the correlation can show the degree of "translation equivalence" between the parallel texts.

Correlation between the two sets of data is .88 which is significant at the .05 level. This indicates that the clauses in the two sets of texts are very similar, in terms of Theme patterns selected, i.e. have "translation equivalence". The above results show that it is also possible to establish similarities and differences for registers across languages by considering a discourse feature, i.e. thematic development in parallel texts.

The second set of statistics given below belong to correlations between Theme features across samples. Paired samples correlations across texts for all the features were as follows.

Table 4: Correlations for features across samples

No	Feature	Correlation	Significance
1	Simple Theme	.874	.002**
2	Multiple Theme	.788	.012**
3	Textual Theme	.779	.013**
4	Interpersonal Theme	.814	.008**
5	Unmarked Idea. Theme	.577	.104
6	Marked Idea. Theme	.673	.047**
7	Clause as Theme	.878	.002**
8	Ellipted Theme	.400	.286
9	Predicated Theme		
10	Thematic Equative		
11	Grammatical Metaphor	.124	.751
12	Speaker/Hearer as Theme	.971	.000**
13	Major Participant-animate	.544	.130
14	Object/Scene as Theme	.873	.002**
15	Abstract Theme	.858	.003**
16	Process/Event as Theme	.764	.017**
17	Time as Theme	.851	.004**
18	Location as Theme	.866	.003**
19	Manner as Theme	.384	.308
20	Cause as Theme		
21	Condition as Theme	.693	.039**
22	Number of Clauses	.914	.001**

** Significant ($p<.05$)

The strong positive and significant correlations between the thematic features across texts also indicate that in both samples full use is made of the range of thematic options available in both English and Chinese i.e. there is "translation equivalence".

Nominalization in both samples

In discussing the similarities and differences between English and Chinese for the register of science, Halliday (1993) maintains that "In both languages the grammar "packages" what has gone before by nominalizing the Process [verb] (attribute or event), and making the Medium [subject or object] of that Process a "possessive" modifier. This enables it to function as the Theme of the next clause." What Halliday attributes to the register of science in the two languages is less evident in the English political commentaries and their Chinese translations. The Themes in Chinese are not as packed with information as the ones in English, i.e. there are fewer nominalizations. Indeed, in many places, especially due to the process of ellipsis (omission), the same Theme is repeated.

Halliday (1993) also states that "It is often said that Chinese does not go in for nominalizations the way that English does; it prefers verbs." This can be given as an explanation for the additional number of clauses and hence simple Themes in the present study. Another explanation could be that more clauses and simple Themes in Chinese texts indicate a common trend in all translations. The proof for this is by way of reversing the directionality of translation in this case, i.e. from Chinese into English. Halliday's own research, though helpful, is not based on translations but a comparison of the scientific register in the two languages. We emphasize that our claim about the additional number of clauses and simple Themes apply only to the results of the present study and not to all other Chinese registers.

Pedagogical implications

As a register, the nine political commentaries in English have associated with them certain linguistic features not found in other English registers. This register makes use of the two "phases" of discourse, i.e. a report of the events, past, present, or future, and a commentary on these events. In the first phase, the events are presented grammatically by material processes (activity verbs) with participants (subjects and objects) and circumstances (adverbs). In the second phase, the commentary uses relational processes (linking verbs) with mainly carriers (subjects) and attributes (adjectives). There are, of course, other processes like verbal (saying) and mental (thinking) ones but the majority of processes are of the first two kinds.

In teaching translation strategies from English into Chinese, any of the similarities and differences established in the present study for thematic organization can be exemplified, discussed and practiced. This can constitute an important part of the syllabus for the whole course. The following paragraphs briefly discuss some of the possibilities.

Number of clauses

In the following examples all Themes are <u>underlined.</u> The numbers preceding each example correspond to the number of text (given first) and the number of clause Theme (given next). If the English Clause is rendered into more than one clause in Chinese, then this is shown by the third number.

English
1.8   <u>With a curious arrogance, made even stranger by its weakness,</u> China at first continued to refuse to accept the West on equal terms and negotiate with them as such.

Chinese
8.1   <u>zhongguo</u> aoman zishi
      <u>China</u> proud arrogant
8.2   <u>geng youyu ta de ruanruo wu neng</u> er ling ren gandao qiguai.
      <u>more because it par weakness incapability</u> thus make people feel strange.
8.3   <u>ta</u> zuichu yizhi bu cheng ren yu xifang guojia de pingdeng diwei
      <u>It</u> first never not acknowledge with Western nations par equal status
8.4   <u>(ta)</u> bing jujue yi pingdeng diwei yu xifang guojia jinxing tanpan.
      (it) and refuse with equal status with western nations make negotiations.

In the above example, while the English clause starts with a manner adverbial, the Chinese translation reinterprets the whole clause as two sets of two paratactic (independent) clauses each. There is thematic progression in three of the clauses, i.e. *China, It, it* (ellipted), with an abstract noun, i.e. *weakness*, given as the Theme of the second clause. In other words, only *China* and *weakness* are thematised; the rest of the information in the English Theme has become part of the Chinese Rhemes.

English
2.16   <u>Such investments</u> have been generally welcomed by various American communities which stand to benefit from the infusion of outside capital that would create jobs.

Chinese
2.16.1   <u>yiban shuolai, zhexie touzi</u> shi shoudao meiguo shehui ge
      <u>Generally speaking, these investments</u> be received America society various
      jieceng de ren de huanying de.
      communities par people par welcome par.
2.16.2   <u>yinwei tamen</u> zhuzhang liyong waibu liuru de zijin tigong jiuye

Because they advocate use outside flow in par capital create employment
jihui.
chances.

In the above example, the English clause with a Simple Unmarked Theme (Theme is subject) has been reinterpreted as two clauses with Multiple Themes. The same Theme has been repeated, once with an Interpersonal Theme, *Generally speaking*, and once with a Textual Theme, *Because*.

English
4.27   To have five bowls of rice in a society where the majority have a decent, balanced meal is a tragedy.

Chinese
4.27.1   zai yige shehui li, ruguo daduoshu ren chi de shi yingyanfenfu de
           In a society par, if majority people eat par be nutritious par
           meiwei jiayao
           delicious food
4.27.2   name you wu wan fan chi yie shi yige beiju.
           then have five bowl rice eat still is a tragedy.

In the above example, the Theme of the English clause, a process/event (an infinitive followed by an object) has been reinterpreted in the Themes of two clauses in Chinese which are related by a cause and effect relationship. The first Theme in Chinese is a Location Theme, *In a society*, and the second a Multiple Theme (has textual element *then*) with a process/event as the ideational element, *having five bowls of rice to eat*. We should also note that the post-modifying element for *society* in the English Theme, *where the majority have a decent balanced meal*, is now a conditional clause in the Rheme of the first Chinese clause, i.e. *if the majority of people have a decent balanced diet..*

Much less noticeable is the reverse process, i.e. the combination of two English clauses in the Chinese translation. The following are two sets of examples.

English
1.4   So out of tune with the world of nation states was China
1.5   that it did not even posses a ministry of foreign affairs until as late as 1858.

Chinese
1.4/ 1.5   ta yu shijie shang qita guojia geme hen shen,
            It with world on other nations misunderstanding very deep,
            jing chi zhi 1856 nian cai jianli yige zhuguang waijiao shiwu de jigou.
            even late till 1858 year par establish a managing foreign affairs par ministry.

In the above examples the Marked English Theme (Theme is not subject) in 1.4 and the Multiple Theme (Theme has textual element *that*) in 1.5 have been replaced by the unmarked Theme (Theme is subject) *It* in the Chinese translation.

English
3.4   <u>however, it</u> is still true to say
3.5   <u>that international law</u> is *primarily* concerned with states.

Chinese
3.4/ 3.5 <u>raner, shuo "guoji fa zhuyao shi guanyu guojia jian</u>
          <u>however, "saying international law mainly is about states among</u>
          <u>de fa"</u> reng shi zhengquede.
          <u>par law</u> " still is correct.

In the above examples the two Multiple Themes in the English clauses have been replaced by one Multiple Theme in the Chinese translation.

Teaching points
It is assumed that the students are able to produce "good" grammatical clauses (sentences) in both English and Chinese.
a.   Select 2 short parallel texts of another register.
b.   Teach students how to underline the Themes.
c.   Ask students to compare and contrast the Themes.
d.   Give students a short English text.
e.   Ask them to translate it into Chinese.
f.   Ask them to compare the two texts for thematic organization.
g.   Give students a short text in Chinese and reverse the process.

Pre- and post-modification : nominalization

Halliday (1993: 128) states that,

> It is often said that Chinese does not go for nominalizations the way that English does; it prefers verbs. *It may very well be that in other registers this process of nominalization has not gone so far as in English*; but as far as the discourse of science is concerned there is no noticeable difference. (*italics added*)

Based on the findings of the present research, we can say that the translations of the political commentaries in Chinese compared to the English texts have a more "verbal" style. This is a logical consequence of having more clauses in Chinese translations, i.e. every finite clause must have a finite verb. The increase in the number of clauses and hence the number of finite verbs can also be related to another important observation by Halliday (1993: 129) that "In Chinese ... there is no post-modification; all modifiers precede the Head noun". This can be seen in the following examples where the post-modification in the English nominal groups has been rendered into either pre-modification of the Head noun in the Themes or a separate additional clause in the Chinese examples.

English (given first) and Chinese (given next)

1.7   when a ministry of tribute and capitulations (Theme)
1.7   yige jieshou gongpin he touxiangtiaoyue de jigou
        a receiving tribute and capitulations par ministry (placed in Rheme)

1.21   The complete colonization of China (Theme)
1.21   zhongguo de quanpan zhimindihua
        China par total colonization (Theme)

3.8   The initial reaction of law students and laymen alike (Theme)
3.8   falu xi de xuesheng he waihangren chuci tingshuo guoji fa law department par
        students and laymen first heard of international law , zuichu de fanying
        tongchang shi feichang huaiyide.
        initial par reaction usually is highly skeptical. (placed in Theme and Rheme)

Teaching points
a.   Select 2 parallel texts of another register.
b.   Show the students how to underline all the Themes.
c.   Select all the topical Themes (Theme is the subject).
d.   Establish the head-noun in the nominal group (noun phrase).
e.   Mark all the pre-and post modifications.
f.   Ask students to compare and contrast the Themes for pre-and post-modification in English and pre-modification in Chinese.
g.   Give students texts in English or Chinese only and ask them to translate.
h.   Ask students to compare and contrast their Themes for pre- and post-modification.

Method of development

One set of significant differences in Table 2 relate to the number of Ellipted (omitted) Themes and Time as Theme categories in Chinese. In both cases the differences are significant. There are more examples of both categories in Chinese texts. The grammatical processes involved create identity chains with Ellipted Themes and similarity chains with Time as Theme options. Both these result in methods of development different in Chinese than in the English texts. Discussion and exemplification of how clauses are related in terms of the topical/ideational elements in the Themes can raise students' awareness of some of the cohesive thematic patterns achieved in both English and Chinese. Introducing the concepts of "identity and similarity chains" (Hasan 1985) can be useful at this point.

Teaching points
a. Select two parallel texts.
b. Mark all the Themes in the two texts
c. Show students by drawing lines how the topical element in the Theme of the first clause in each text is/is not related to the Theme of the following clauses.
d. Discuss the concepts of *identity* and *similarity chains* (Hasan 1985).
e. Discuss if the Theme is repeated or if it is related to the Rheme of the previous clause.
f. Give single texts to students for translation.
g. Compare and contrast the Themes for possible lexical chains established.

Finally, the present findings also has significance for the study of registers across languages. Biber (1995) and Biber and Finegan (1986) have carried out pioneering research on the similarities and differences in text-types within one language and across languages by their Multi/Feature Multi/Dimensional Approach. Their focus has been on individual morphemes/words from a variety of spoken and written registers. Their approach has been criticised for not considering patterns of language above word level (Ghadessy 1997a, 1997b). Thematic organization can be used as an additional criterion for establishing cross-linguistic registers.

Conclusion

An analysis of the thematic organization of parallel texts does not provide us with all the answers necessary for achieving a "perfect" translation which, according to Newmark (1995: 6), does not exist. "There is no such thing as a perfect, ideal, or "correct" translation." It does, however, guide us towards a better understanding of one significant discourse aspect of texts that plays an important role in our decisions about translation equivalence. Assuming that we have some "valued texts" in English with good and reliable translations in Chinese, the results of the present study show that despite significant differences in clause numbers and some Theme types, the two sets of data are similar in terms of selected thematic features and Theme patterns.

Note

* Some of the materials presented in this paper were first published in *TEXT* 20(4)2000, Walter de Gruyter, Germany. The authors are grateful for the publisher's permission to reprint the materials here.

References

Arziculov, H. 1998. "Turkic language automaton: Existing software and Turkic language resources". In W. Teubert,. E. Tognini-Bonelli and N. Volz, (eds), *TELRI TransEuropean Language Resources Infrastructure: Proceedings of the third European seminar "Translation Equivalence"*, 9–12. The Tuscan Word Centre: The TELRI Associationùe.V.

Barlow, M. 1998. "Investigating form and meaning using parallel corpora". In W. Teubert,. E. Tognini-Bonelli and N. Volz, (eds), *TELRI TransEuropean Language Resources Infrastructure: Proceedings of the third European seminar "Translation Equivalence"*, 13–28. The Tuscan Word Centre: The TELRI Associationùe.V.

Biber, D. 1995. *Dimensions of Register Variation: A cross-linguistic comparison.* Cambridge: CUP.

Biber, D. and Finegan, E. 1986. "An initial typology of English text-types". In J. Aarts and W. Meijs (eds), *Corpus Linguistics II: New studies in the analysis and exploitation of computer corpora.* Amsterdam: Rodopi.

Blanta, R.1998. "Performative verbs in Plato's Republic". In W. Teubert,. E. Tognini-Bonelli and N. Volz, (eds), *TELRI TransEuropean Language Resources Infrastructure: Proceedings of the third European seminar "Translation Equivalence"*, 29–36. The Tuscan Word Centre: The TELRI Associationùe.V.

Fang, Yan, McDonald, E. and Cheng, M. 1995. "On theme in Chinese: From clause to discourse". In . R. Hasan and P. H. Fries (eds), *On Subject and Theme: A discourse functional perspective,*235–273. Amsterdam: John Benjamins.

Feng, Zhiwei. 1998. "A study of translation equivalence in the Chinese-English text of Plato's Republic". In W. Teubert,. E. Tognini-Bonelli and N. Volz, (eds), *TELRI TransEuropean Language Resources Infrastructure: Proceedings of the third European seminar "Translation Equivalence"*, 9–12.The Tuscan Word Centre: The TELRI Associationùe.V.

Ferguson, C. A. 1983. "Sports announcer talk: Syntactic aspects of register variation". *Language in Society* 12:153–72.

Fries, P. H. 1983. "On the status of theme in English: Arguments from discourse". In S. Janos and E. Sozer (eds), *Micro and Macro Connexity of Texts* [Papers in Textlinguistics 45]. Hamburg: Buske.

Fries, P. H. 1992. "Theme, methods of development, and texts". Unpublished manuscript.

Ghadessy, M. (ed), 1995a. *Thematic Development in English Texts.* London: Pinter.

Ghadessy, M. 1995b. "Thematic development and its relationship to registers and genres". In M. Ghadessy (ed), *Thematic Development in English Texts.* London: Pinter.

Ghadessy, M. 1997a. "Thematic organisation as a criterion in establishing English text-types". *Studios Ingleses de la Universidad Complutense* 5:129–145. Madrid: Universidad Complutense.

Ghadessy, M. 1997b. "Review of D. Biber's 1995 Book: *Dimensions of Register Variation: A cross-linguistic comparison". Language Awareness.* 6(1):58–62.

Halliday, M. A. K. 1985. *An Introduction to Functional Grammar.* London: Arnold

Halliday, M. A. K. 1993. "An analysis of scientific texts in English and Chinese". In M. A. K. Halliday and J. R. Martin (eds), *Writing Science,* 124–132. Pittsburgh: The University of Pittsburgh Press.

Halliday, M. A. K. 1994. *An Introduction to Functional Grammar.* (second edition). London: Arnold.

Halliday, M. A. K. 1998. "Things and relations: Regrammaticising experience as technical knowledge". In J. R. Marin and R. Veel (eds), *Reading Science: Critical and functional perspectives on discourse of science.* London: Routledge.

Halliday, M. A. K. and Hasan, R. 1985. *Language, Context, and Text: Aspects of language in a social-semiotic perspective.* Geelong: Deakin University Press.

Liu, Miqing 1989. *A Workbook for English-Chinese Translation Skill Training.* Beijing: Tourist Education Press.

Newmark, P. 1995. *A Textbook of Translation.* (second edition). Englewood Cliffs NJ: Prentice Hall.

Teubert,. W., Tognini-Bonelli, E. and Volz, N. (eds), 1998. *TELRI TransEuropean Language Resources Infrastructure: Proceedings of the third European seminar*

"Translation Equivalence", 29–36. The Tuscan Word Centre: The TELRI Associationùe.V.

Ventola, Eija 1995. Thematic Development and translation. In M. Ghadessy (ed), *Thematic Development in English Texts*. London: Pinter.

Xiao, Suyi and Oller, J. W. 1994. "Can relatively perfect translation between English and Chinese be achieved?" *Language Testing* 11(3): 267–285. London: Arnold.

Appendix 1

Examples of Themes in English and Chinese showing the grammatical (1–11) and lexico-semantic (12–21) properties considered in this study.

Grammatical properties:

1. *simple Theme : (includes only the ideational or topical Theme without the interpersonal and/or textual elements)*
    1.3   China's central government ...
    1.3   dangshi de zhongyang zhengfu ...
           then par central government

2. *multiple Theme : (includes a textual element and/or an interpersonal element followed by an ideational Theme)*
    3.55   and so they think that the reported breaches of international law ...
    3.55.2 er shijishang (ellipted Theme)...
            but actually (it) ...

3. *textual Theme: (the presence of a textual element, i.e. the first word in the following examples)*
    1.17   But this ...
    1.14   lingwai, dangshi cuixianyu tunbin zhongguo de guojia ...
            Besides, then wanting to swallow China par nations ...

4. *interpersonal Theme: (the presence of an interpersonal element, i.e. the first word in the following examples)*
    9.28   Fortunately the storm ...
    9.28   xingyun de shi zhetian de fengbao ...
            Fortunate par be the day par storm ...

5. *unmarked ideational Theme : (Theme is the subject of clause)*
    1.3   China's central government ...
    1.3   dangshi de zhongyang zhengfu ...
           then par central government ...

6. *marked ideational Theme : (Theme is not the subject, i.e. an adverbial or a process)*

    1.8   <u>With a curious arrogance</u> ...
    1.19.1   <u>genju zhexie youxiao qi wei 99 nian de zuqi</u> ...
            <u>According to these validity period for 99 years par leases stipulations</u> ...

7. *clause as Theme : (the whole clause in a clause complex is taken as Theme)*
    1.9   <u>When ultimately it began to negotiate</u> ,...
    1.9   <u>dang zhongguo zuihou kaishi tong xifang jinxing tanpan shi</u> ...
            <u>When China finally began with west make negotiations par</u> ,...

8. *ellipted Theme : (Theme is omitted but can be recovered by looking at previous clause)*
    6.6   <u>and (we)</u> ...
    7.25.2   <u>(Watt)</u> zhizaochula kegong chushou de zhengqi ji
            <u>(Watt)</u> built for selling par steam engines.

9. *predicated Theme : (the ideational Theme comes after the introductory "it")*
    3.44   ... <u>it</u> is only <u>the violations of the law</u> ...
    1.16.1   shi ta de 1899 nian menhu kaifang zhengce ...
            be it par <u>1899 year door open policy</u> ...

10. *thematic equative : (ideational Theme is "equated" with something else, i.e. X=Y)*
            no examples in English texts
            no examples in Chinese texts

11. *grammatical metaphor : (usually nominalisation of a process)*
    2.1   <u>The excessive importation of these items</u> ...
    2.1.2   <u>meiguo de guoliang chukou</u> ...
            <u>America par excessive exportation</u> ...

Lexico-semantic properties:

12. *speaker/hearer as Theme : (referring to "I, we, you, etc.")*
    5.25   <u>You</u> ...
    5.25.1   <u>ni</u> ...
            <u>You</u> ...

13. *major text participant (animate) as Theme : (referring to "he, she, they, etc.")*
    1.24   <u>Sun Yat Sen</u> ...
    1.25   <u>Yuan Shih K'ai</u> ...
            <u>Yuan Shih Kai</u> ...

14. *object/portion of scene as Theme : (inanimate)*
    7.17   and <u>the early factories</u> ...
    7.17   <u>yinci, zaoqi de gongchang</u> ...
            <u>Therefore, early par factories</u> ...

15. *abstract Theme :*
    1.10   <u>China's real strength</u> ...
    1.10.1 <u>ta jinyou de yidian lilian</u> ...
    <u>it only par little strength</u> ...

16. *process/event as Theme : (infinitive, — ing verb forms, event words, i.e. "war, accident, etc".)*
    4.25   <u>To have one bowl of rice in a society where all other people have half a bowl</u>
    4.34   <u>najiu jihu biran hui zenjia</u> ...
    <u>then almost surely will increase</u> ...

17. *time as Theme :*
    1.32   <u>but between 1920 and 1926</u> ...
    1.32   <u>dan zi 1920 nian zhi 1926 nian</u> ...
    <u>but since 1920 year to 1926 year</u>...

18. *location as Theme :*
    3.35   <u>In some other countries</u> ...
    3.35   <u>zai ling yixie guojia li</u> ...
    <u>In other some countries par</u>...

19. *manner as Theme :*
    4.35   <u>And finally, in defining poverty</u> ...
    4.43   <u>raner, yi laodong funiu shuliang shang de jiju zeng zhang</u> ...
    <u>Yet, by means of the tremendous growth in the number of working wives</u> ...

20. *cause as Theme :*
    no examples in English texts
    2.12   <u>youyu riben gongsi kaishi xiang meiguo touzi</u> ...
    <u>Because Japanese company begin to America invest,</u> ...

21. *condition as Theme :*
    3.14   <u>If cabinet ministers and diplomats shared the popular</u> ...
    3.14   <u>ruguo neige buzhang he waijiaojia ...... de yingxiang</u> ...
    <u>If cabinet ministers and diplomats ...... par influence</u> ...

Appendix 2

Table 5: List of grammatical features (items 1–11) and lexico-semantic features (items 12–21) of the Themes in nine English texts analyzed.. In each box, first the raw number and then the % (out of total clause Themes) are given for the feature in question. Item 22 gives the total number of analyzed clause Themes for each text. The legend below this table gives the features considered.

Texts / Features	1	2	3	4	5	6	7	8	9
1	21/67%	25/61%	34/45%	34/57%	25/64%	23/66%	29/69%	28/58%	29/54%
2	11/34%	16/39%	41/55%	26/43%	14/36%	12/34%	13/31%	20/42%	25/46%
3	11/34%	15/37%	38/51%	22/37%	13/33%	11/31%	13/31%	20/42%	23/43%
4	-	1/2%	7/9%	4/7%	1/3%	1/3%	-	-	2/7%
5	20/63%	32/78%	59/79%	46/77%	33/85%	30/86%	29/69%	39/81%	34/63%
6	12/38%	9/22%	16/21%	14/23%	6/15%	5/14%	13/31%	9/19%	20/37%
7	4/13%	6/15%	9/12%	3/5%	2/5%	3/9%	3/7%	4/8%	-
8	-	1/2%	-	1/2%	-	5/14%	-	1/2%	3/6%
9	-	-	1/1%	-	-	-	-	-	-
10	-	-	-	-	-	-	-	-	-
11	4/13%	4/10%	1/1%	1/2%	3/8%	2/6%	2/5%	2/4%	5/9%
12	-	-	-	-	7/18%	2/6%	-	-	-
13	4/13%	14/34%	10/13%	19/32%	12/31%	2/6%	6/14%	5/10%	13/24%
14	9/28%	9/22%	2/3%	3/5%	1/3%	-	14/33%	2/4%	11/20%
15	6/19%	8/20%	37/49%	25/42%	13/33%	25/71%	5/12%	25/52%	2/4%
16	1/3%	1/2%	11/15%	2/3%	-	-	2/5%	8/17%	8/15%
17	8/25%	5/12%	4/5%	3/5%	-	3/9%	11/26%	3/6%	14/26%
18	-	-	4/5%	-	2/5%	-	-	-	2/4%
19	1/3%	3/7%	2/3%	5/8%	2/5%	-	2/5%	2/4%	2/4%
20	-	-	-	-	-	-	-	-	-
21	3/9%	2/5%	5/7%	3/5%	2/5%	3/9%	2/5%	3/6%	2/4%
22	32	41	75	60	39	35	42	48	54

Legend:
1. Simple Theme, 2. Multiple Theme, 3. Textual Theme, 4. Interpersonal Theme, 5. Unmarked ideational Theme, 6. Marked ideational Theme, 7. Clause as Theme, Ellipted Theme, 9. Predicated Theme, 10. Thematic equative, 11. Grammatical metaphor, 12. Speaker/hearer as Theme, 13. Major text participant (animate) as Theme, 14. Object/portion of scene as Theme, 15. Abstract Theme, 16. Process/event as Theme, Time as Theme, 18. Location as Theme, 19. Manner/means as Theme, 20. Cause/purpose as Theme, 21. Condition as Theme, 22. Total clause Themes

Table 6: List of grammatical features (items 1–11) and lexico-semantic features (items 12–21) for the Themes in nine Chinese texts analyzed. In each box, first the raw number and then the % (out of total clause Themes) are given for the feature in question. Item 22 gives the total number of analyzed clause Themes for each text. The legend below this table gives the features considered.

Texts / Features	1	2	3	4	5	6	7	8	9
1	30/67%	31/52%	38/48%	45/68%	40/68%	35/69%	51/81%	31/54%	50/74%
2	15/33%	29/48%	41/52%	21/32%	19/32%	16/31%	12/19%	26/46%	18/26%
3	14/31%	26/43%	34/43%	17/26%	15/25%	12/24%	12/19%	24/42%	16/24%
4	1/2%	3/5%	11/14%	3/5%	4/7%	5/10%	-	3/5%	2/3%
5	34/76%	43/72%	52/66%	49/74%	52/88%	34/67%	51/81%	40/70%	41/60%
6	11/24%	17/28%	27/34%	17/26%	7/12%	17/33%	12/19%	17/30%	27/40%
7	3/7%	8/13%	10/13%	5/8%	3/5%	3/6%	3/5%	4/7%	3/4%
8	7/16%	9/15%	7/9%	3/5%	8/14%	9/18%	7/11%	6/11%	9/13%
9	1/2%	-	-	-	-	-	1/2%	-	-
10	-	-	-	-	-	-	-	-	-
11	5/11%	5/8%	1/1%	5/8%	3/5%	1/2%	4/6%	1/2%	1/1%
12	-	1/2%	1/1%	-	8/8%	4/8%	-	-	-
13	5/11%	24/40%	14/18%	18/27%	23/39%	5/10%	14/22%	5/9%	12/18%
14	11/24%	3/5%	2/3%	1/2%	)2/3%	-	20/32%	5/9%	19/28%
15	17/38%	15/25%	24/30%	26/39%	18/30%	22/43%	9/14%	26/46%	4/6%
16	2/4%	1/2%	15/19%	4/6%	1/2%	7/14%	8/13%	8/14%	6/9%
17	8/18%	5/8%	9/11%	6/9%	-	9/18%	10/16%	6/11%	17/25%
18	-	1/2%	2/3%	-	2/3%	-	-	-	2/3%
19	1/2%	3/5%	3/4%	2/3%	3/5%	1/2%	1/2%	2/4%	3/4%
20	-	4/7%	-	-	-	-	-	2/4%	2/3%
21	1/2%	3/5%	9/11%	9/14%	2/3%)	3/6%	1/2%	3/5%	3/4%
22	45	60	79	66	59	51	63	57	68

SECTION VI

CHAPTER 13

The Exploitation of Small Learner Corpora
in EAP Materials Design

Lynne Flowerdew

Hong Kong University of Science and Technology

Abstract

This article first reviews the research-based studies which have been undertaken into learner corpora and the few applications of learner corpora to materials design. The second part of the article describes how the findings from learner corpora in the areas of collocational patterning, pragmatic appropriacy and discourse features can be used in conjunction with expert corpora to prepare EAP materials. I also suggest that the area under investigation has implications for teaching methodology. Although the article supports the use of corpora and concordancing in EAP language teaching some caveats in implementing this approach are also given.

Introduction

Over the last decade, the field of corpus linguistics has widened in two senses, i.e. it now encompasses more and bigger large corpora and also more small corpora. Much larger-scale, mega-corpora are now in existence (see Kennedy 1998). For example, the original *Cobuild Corpus* has been expanded into a 300 million word monitor corpus, named the *Bank of English*. New text is continually being added to the database, which has been used to inform an updated series of dictionaries and grammars (see Sinclair 1995; Willis and Wright

1995). There also now exists the 100 million word *British National Corpus, BNC* (Aston and Burnard 1998). However, in another sense, the field has widened to include the recognition of much smaller, specialised genre-based corpora, which was first initiated by Biber in 1988. As Aston (1997) points out such corpora are usually in the 20,000–200,000 word range and are more specialised than the larger ones in terms of topic and/or genre. The majority of these corpora are in the field of science and technology and consist of written rather than spoken academic discourse (e.g. Johns' (1994) 100,000 word *Plant Biology Corpus*). Many of the small corpora which have been compiled for various academic purposes are described in Stevens (1995) and Flowerdew (1996).

However, all the applications of corpora to EAP materials development which are surveyed in Stevens (1995) and Flowerdew (1996) rely on native speaker or expert corpora. The concordance-derived materials are either based on what practitioners view as constituting salient features of academic writing, what the practitioners themselves perceive as areas of weakness in learners' writing, or areas which their students themselves identify as weaknesses (Stevens 1991; Pickard 1994; Thurstun and Candlin 1998). The reason why learner corpora have not played much of a role to date in materials design is probably due to the fact that they there do not exist in the public domain any ready-made learner corpora, such as the *MicroConcord Collection of Academic Texts* (Scott 1996), for individual teacher's use. Teachers therefore have to compile their own corpora by either scanning their students' work or asking their students to save their work on disk from which a learner corpus could be created (see Barnbrook 1996 for further details on corpus compilation). In spite of the difficulty of accessing learner corpora, I would still like to suggest that for materials to address students' needs and deficiencies fully, insights gleaned from learner corpora need to be employed to complement those from expert corpora for syllabus and materials design.

The aims of this paper are twofold. First, I will review the studies which have been carried out into learner corpora and then survey the few applications of learner corpora to pedagogy which have been undertaken on a small-scale. In the second part of the paper, I will illustrate with some examples from my own work, how the findings of small learner corpora, i.e. subcomponents of the *Hong Kong University of Science and Technology (HKUST) Learner Corpus*, have been used in conjunction with expert corpora to prepare EAP materials.

Exploration of learner corpora: a review

To date, several studies have been carried out on subsections of two large-scale learner corpora, the *International Corpus of Learner English (ICLE)* and the *HKUST Learner Corpus*. In order to identify which grammatical structures, lexis or discourse items are underused or overused by students in academic writing, findings from a learner or non-native speaker (NNS) corpus are either usually compared with a parallel corpus of native speaker writing (NS), or sometimes with a larger reference corpus of expert writing.

A suite of contrastive studies using the French component of the *ICLE* corpus and the *Louvain Corpus of Native English Essays (LOCNESS)* as the control parallel corpus has been undertaken by Sylviane Granger (1998a), founder and coordinator of the *ICLE* project, in collaboration with other researchers. The French component of the *ICLE Corpus* consists of c. 280,000 words of argumentative essays by advanced EFL university students whereas the parallel NS corpus consists of about 230,000 words of similar writing by British and American university students. In one contrastive study, Granger and Rayson (1998) examined significant patterns of over- and underuse of various word categories (articles, determiners, pronouns, prepositions, adverbs, adjectives, nouns and verbs) in the learner corpus and noted a very significant overuse of the first and second personal pronouns, but an underuse of prepositions, a category often associated with nominalisations in informative academic writing (cf. Biber et al. 1998). However, Granger and Rayson also point out that within the general category of prepositions there exist considerable differences between individual prepositions. For example, informal prepositions such as *in spite of* and *till* are overused whereas their more formal counterparts *despite* and *until* are underused. They thus conclude that their learner data displayed many of the stylistic features of spoken English, and practically none of the features typical of academic writing. Similar studies on connector usage are reported in Granger and Tyson (1996) and on formulaic sentence builders, e.g. *It is said/thought that ...* in Granger (1998b). Altenberg (1997) describes some exploratory studies in the areas of vocabulary, noun phrase complexity, and personal involvement and detachment that have been carried out on the Swedish component of *ICLE*.

Research into the German subcomponent of the *ICLE Corpus* has been carried out by Lorenz (1998). Lorenz investigated overstatement in German advanced learners' writing by comparing the German component of the *ICLE*

Corpus, consisting of about 100,000 words with the *LOCNESS Corpus*. The findings reveal that German learners used far more intensifiers than the native speakers and that their typical attributive position was in thematic position whereas when the native speakers intensified adjectives inside noun phrases, they were almost exclusively placed in rhematic position. Hyland and Milton (1997) have also investigated the issue of "directness" in students' writing. They analysed the expressions of doubt and certainty in NS and NNS writing by comparing a 500,000 word subcomponent of the *HKUST Learner Corpus*, consisting of Hong Kong "Use of English" examination scripts with scripts receiving the highest grades transcribed from the Cambridge Examinations Syndicate "General Studies" Examination held in the UK. Their findings reveal that Hong Kong students do not moderate their claims sufficiently as their writing displays firmer assertions, a more authoritative tone and stronger commitments to statements when compared with NS writing.

Although a significant amount of research has been undertaken in recent years on learner corpora, not many of the findings have been applied directly to pedagogy and tend to remain at the level of implications. I would suggest that the findings from comparative studies of learner and expert corpora could be applied to materials design as has been the case in the compilation of dictionaries for non-native speakers. For example, many of the entries in the *Longman Dictionary of Common Errors* (2nd ed.) (Turton and Heaton 1996) are based on a comparison of usage in the *BNC* and the *Longmans' Learner Corpus*, a 10 million word learner corpus made up of samples of formal and informal written English from learners of English of over eight different levels of proficiency from over 160 different language backgrounds. The following section reviews the few applications of learner corpora to pedagogy.

Exploitation of learner corpora: a review

Some of the first work to be carried out on a small learner corpus was by Tribble (1990, 1991) on the use of "speech" verbs in a 54,861 word *Student Corpus* mostly taken from English language examination scripts extracted from the *Longman Corpus of Learner English*. Tribble notes the overuse and inappropriate use of *said* in his *Student Corpus* compared with its use in the *English Historical Review Corpus*. Tribble suggests that such examples of concordance data from a learner corpus could be exploited in the classroom by having learners work on re-wording the concordance lines shown in Table 1 below and encouraging them to use a broader range of vocabulary.

Table 1: Concordanced lines for said (from Tribble 1991)

PROF-AL	s to local places of interest as it is **said** the advs. brochure,
PROF-AL	say lack of freedom. But in my opion I **say** nuclear is the greatest
PROF-AL	even though they starve. At last, I'll **say** about the difference
PROF-AL	ht. You are definitely wright when you **say** the sea to be just
PROF-AL	riends house, I heard an opinion which **says** our Japanese are not

Another corpus-based study with some suggestions for pedagogical applications can be found in Granger and Tribble (1998) who compared the French sub-section of the ICLE corpus comprising 227,964 words with the larger reference corpus of the core British National Corpus (BNC) of c. one million words. They used the *Keywords* tool in the *WordSmith* programme (Scott 1996) which can compute words of unusually high and low frequency in a small corpus through comparison with their relative frequency in a larger reference corpus (see Scott 1997, and this volume). Granger and Tribble's (1998) findings reveal that learners were too reliant on superordinate adjectives such as *important* in their academic writing, which they used to the exclusion of words with a higher degree of specificity. They suggest the following concordance-based exercise, shown in Figure 1 below, to help learners increase their awareness of words that they tend to overuse:

In much student writing 'important' is a word that is used very frequently. The concordance samples below have been edited to remove all instances of 'important'. The attached concordance information will help you to complete the tasks below — as well an appropriate reference work such as the *Longman Language Activator* or the *COBUILD Collocations* CD ROM.

Task 1   Extend your vocabulary by deciding which of the words in the list below would make the best replacement for 'important' in following contexts given here — in some instances it would be better to continue to use 'important'.

Task 2   Using the corpus data you have been studying and other reference works, make a list of the nouns which collocate strongly with each of the adjectives given in the list.

Alternative word list: critical / crucial / major / serious / significant / vital

1.	nd imagine. This is the first and most	....	advantage of science and tech
2.	nimal and human lives. One of the most	....	consequence of pollution is the
3.	shown that they could work hard, take	....	decisions, and become involved
4.	ties seem to ignore completely another	....	factor people are slaves to:
5.	efficiency seem to be some of the all	....	factors in our hypersophistica
6.	television set. This has of course a(n)	....	impact on our mind: we are, ev
7.	e cause of women." This raises an	....	issue: according to me people
8.	g the environment. Air-pollution is a(n)	....	kind of pollution. Without be
9.	e in a world where television plays a(n)	....	part and it is highly probable
10.	ir reintegration in society. This is a(n)	....	point because in a sane and c
11.	itely answer this question. A third	....	problem is the polution due to
12.	the choice of the programmes, the most	....	question seems to be: Does te
13.	s in so critical a situation. The most	....	reason is pollution. Gas from
14.	concerned, it is the object of a very	....	requirement in the world of ad
15.	he influence of the media also plays a(n)	....	role. According to the amoun

Figure 1. Concordance-based exercise (from Granger and Tribble 1998).

Other applications of learner corpora to pedagogy are reported in Milton (1999). Based on his error analysis of the 10 million word *HKUST Learner Corpus*, Milton has devised a wordlist driven concordancing program, *WordPilot*, made interactively available to learners from their wordprocessor, which calls up databases of expressions that learners are either unaware of or avoid (see Figure 2 below).

Milton's application of learner corpus findings to pedagogy in the form of CALL-based activities is probably the most comprehensive to date. However, it demands a high level of computer knowledge and expertise to implement, which is not accessible to the average language teaching specialist. Moreover, learner corpora are not, for the time being at least, readily accessible to language teachers as they are not available for purchase. Even if they were available, their use would be limited to a specific teaching context so it is probably more expedient for language teachers to compile their own small-scale learner corpora to suit there own particular teaching situation. I would therefore like to offer some suggestions on how the findings from small learner corpora, i.e. subsections of a large-scale corpus, could be exploited without too much difficulty in a tertiary EAP setting. At the same time, I would like to put forward some caveats for using corpora in language teaching and suggest that certain types of errors should be dealt with in particular kinds of ways. Below, I con-

AutoConc-pap.txt_		
Search:	though it may	
WordList1		
However, in some	it could be said that	It may well be
However, it could be argued that	It has been claimed	It would seem that
It can be argued	It has been found	Perhaps one of the
It can be said	It is possible to believe in	Perhaps: the most obvious
It could also be	It may also be	Tis is not to say that
it could be argued that	It may be argued	This may have been
It could be said	It may be that	though it may
Untitled		
No. Preceder	Target Succeeder	Position
1 ...or communicative experience,	though it may enhance it by providing practic	8%
pap.txt		
Declarative and procedural knowledge of how to write can sure be useful for effec communication if there is also attention to what is written. The system described he substitute for communicative experience, though it may enhance it by providing pra use of specific written language features through timely access to authentic and app texts, and by making available writing tools that can assist with the composing proce		
For Help, press F1		

Figure 2: Example of a list-driven concordancer (from Milton 1999).

sider the role of small-scale learner corpora for both identifying and raising students' awareness, using concordancing techniques, of the following three areas (i) collocational patterning (ii) pragmatic appropriacy, and (iii) discourse features.

Exploiting the HKUST Learner Corpus: the role of concordancing

Collocational patterning

Several corpus-based applications to EAP writing have focused on vocabulary as an area meriting attention. For example, in response to her students' comments on "inadequate vocabulary" as a factor affecting their essay writing stan-

---

Vocabulary of Research Reports 1

Task 1
Replace the nonsense words with words commonly used in the writing of research reports.
Use as many contextual clues (both before and after the nonsense word) as you can. Each
block provides 10 examples of the use of the same word. The 17 missing words are:

analysis	questionnaires	categories	questions	data	research
designed	respondents	factors	responses	figures	significant
found	statistics	information	survey	questionnaire	

is of the questionnaires that each of our **jalkoplurga** participated in a separate trial. Ou
the general population of Hong Kong. Male **jalkoplurga** accounted for 57%. The relatively yo
nteresting to note that only three of our **jalkoplurga** were between 21 (the minimum age for
ucated and middle class. Thus, 75% of our **jalkoplurga** listed their occupation as business
an anticipated difference in the types of **jalkoplurga.** The initial section contained detai
The latter section, which was open to all **jalkoplurga,** was designed to elicit more general
lish and/or English to Cantonese. Only 12 **jalkoplurga** stated that they were unable to unde
cusation against the defendant. Of the 58 **jalkoplurga,** 55 answered in the affirmative, wit
d after the Chinese takeover in 1997? All **jalkoplurga** were asked this question and 84% of
que for protecting the confidentiality of **jalkoplurga** and, further, it avoided trespassing

iginally, these were the main aims of the **quargalip.** A third aim eventually developed: to a
jury service. Originally, our principal **quargalip** aim was to assess the extent to which j
ng to do so. As is normal in this type of **quargalip,** all questionnaires would have been kep
id. Working within these limitations, our **quargalip** appears to indicate that the judge does
onstitutes a correct verdict. The present **quargalip** attempts to examine the jury in Hong Ko
support for the jury is based upon. Our **quargalip** confirms that, in general, both those w
of evidence and judicial direction. These **quargalip** instruments were designed where possibl
aced in attempting to carry out empirical **quargalip** into the jury in Hong Kong, and our ada
ge extent, the difficulty of carrying out **quargalip** into the jury is because such endeavour
rt Act (UK) 1981 which impedes scientific **quargalip** into the jury represents a setback for

---

(Extracts from *Juries: A Hong Kong Perspective*, by Peter Duff, Mark Findlay, Carla Howarth and
Chan Tsang-fai, Hong Kong University Press, 1992.)

Figure 3: Example of a concordance-based exercise (from Pickard 1994).

dard, Pickard (1994) devised a set of concordance-based vocabulary exercises
to familiarise them with the language of research reports (see Figure 3 above):

With access to the *HKUST Learner Corpus* I decided to conduct a similar
type of study looking at students' use of this vocabulary in a subsection of the
corpus on report writing. I examined key vocabulary items such as *findings,
research, survey, questionnaire, respondents* and so forth, in the first drafts of
90 analytical project reports (about 200,000 words) written by second and

third year undergraduates on a Technical Communication Skills course at the Hong Kong University of Science and Technology. My examination of the KWIC (key-word-in-context) revealed that students knew all the key vocabulary but were not familiar with the lexico-grammatical environment in which the word usually occurs. Many collocational mismatches such as the following examples were found (see Flowerdew, 2000 for other examples):

- We have performed a survey.
- A questionnaire has been conveyed to the public.

Such errors have been researched extensively by Howarth (1998) who analysed the extent to which NNS deviate from NS phraseological norms which he established on the basis of collocational patterning in the social sciences text from the *Lancaster-Oslo-Bergen (LOB) Corpus* and a collection of university texts. Howarth drew up a collocational framework of three major categories: free combinations, restricted collocations and idioms. He found that it was the category of restricted collocation, i.e. (i) substitution is allowed of both the noun and verb (e.g. *introduce/table/bring forward a bill/an amendment*) (ii) the choice of noun is restricted, but some substitution of the verb is allowed (e.g. *pay/take heed*) (iii) there is complete restriction on the choice of verb, but some substitution of the noun (e.g. *give the appearance/impression*), which was the most salient category in NS writing. Not surprisingly, he found that it was also this category which was the most problematic for learners who made errors such as the ones given above involving lexical substitution.

In order to raise students' awareness of these collocational mismatches I suggest that first students could be given a list of nouns and verbs and asked to match them. After this hypothesis-testing exercise, students could verify their answers by using concordancing software to check the collocations in a corpus of similar reports. They could also note down the prototypical syntactic structures in which these collocations occur; for example, whether the combination *carry out a survey* prefers the active or passive form. I would also like to argue that for these types of errors, having the students either use the concordancing software (provided that they are not swamped with too many examples) or examine printouts of concordances is an ideal means of alerting them to these collocations as they occur at the sentence level and can easily be gleaned from the truncated concordanced lines.

However, one drawback of exercises involving concordancing is that students sometimes tend to get bored if they are presented with too many exercises of this nature. Such exercises could be interspersed with pen-and-paper exercises or follow-up discussion work to offset the rather repetitive nature of these activities.

Pragmatic appropriacy

In the same corpus mentioned in the previous section, I also examined pragmatic appropriacy, which concerns the writer's attitude to the message and is typically realised through modal verbs (e.g. *should, may*), modal adjuncts (e.g. *probably, obviously*) and boosters and downtoners. Another aspect of pragmatic appropriacy concerns whether the writer's attitude to the message is formulated appropriately in keeping with "context of situation" and "context of culture". For example, in the sections of the student reports detailing the survey data students had collected, the downtoner *only* was frequently used in a way which I considered to be inappropriate, as in the example below.

Only 40% of respondents reported that they had used the
Self-Access Centre.

I was surprised by how frequently students used *only* with, what I considered to be, fairly significant percentage figures, as in the above example. When I queried this use, students replied that they considered 40% as a low percentage of 100%, working on the assumption that all students would use the Self-Access Centre. On the other hand, I had compared 40% against my expected norm of 10%, a higher percentage of use than that predicted, which would therefore make *only*, from my point of view, inappropriate in this context.

Other examples which may be indicative of pragmatic inappropriacy occurred in the recommendation sections of the reports. Phrases such as *Therefore, we highly (strongly) recommend that …*were frequently used to introduce a set of recommendations. Such phrases were socio-culturally inappropriate as the students were addressing their reports to authorities, such as the Director of the Computer Centre, in which case a more hedged and deferential expression such as *We would like the Director of the Computer Centre to consider the following recommendations* would be used instead. When I questioned students about their use of this unhedged and too direct phrase, their response was that they thought such strongly-worded phrases made their set of recommendations sound persuasive and some even thought that using a more mitigating expression would indicate that the evidence contained in the body of the report was also weak as well.

These two cases demonstrate how important both the "context of situation" and the "context of culture" are in determining pragmatic appropriacy. Sometimes it is difficult to tell from an examination of the corpus text alone if the pragmatic force of an expression is appropriate or not without having knowledge of the wider context and culture, such as the reader/writer relationship and the social practices of the discourse community in which the text is created. As Aston (1995:260) points out, concordance data portrays "the decontextualisation of individual instances from their original communicative setting". Because the corpus is divorced from the context of situation in which it was created, Widdowson (1998:712) argues that it can only be viewed as the textual product of a discourse as "it cannot tell about the discourse processes whereby pragmatic meaning is appropriately achieved".

These observations have important implications for pedagogical applications of corpus data. Widdowson (1998) argues that teachers have to "authenticate" the language as discourse in their own terms and relate it to their own familiar cultural contexts and concerns:

> ... language teachers should indeed be concerned with pragmatic meaning, but this can only be achieved if they localise the language, create textual conditions that make the language a reality for particular communities of learners so that they can authenticate it... (Widdowson 1998:715)

Therefore, in certain circumstances, there is an inherent danger in transferring directly corpus-based findings to pedagogy — what is pragmatically appropriate in the corpus might be inappropriate in the students' own "context of situation", and "context of culture" and thus not directly transferable. For this reason, concordancing techniques should be used judiciously. In certain situations students can best be alerted to their pragmatic deficiences, not through employing concordancing techniques, which may provide misleading information, but rather, in a far more indirect way, through discussion-type activities which are grounded in a well-defined contextual framework with which students are familiar to enable them to assess the pragmatic appropriacy of such devices.

Discourse Features

In a recent article (Flowerdew 1988c), I pointed out that a decade ago most corpus-based research focused on the lexico-grammatical patterning of a text at sentence level, but now much more research is being undertaken on discourse features. Thompson's article in this volume also advocates shifting attention from isolated structures toward exploring the "discourse value" of lexical and structural items in context.

In a study of cause and effect markers, I examined the use of connectors and nouns with a discourse organising function in an expert and student corpus of about 40,000 words each (Flowerdew 1998b). The expert corpus was the *Greenpeace Report on Global Warming*, a subcorpus of the *MicroConcord Collection of Academic Texts*, and the parallel student corpus was a set of 80 essays on the topic of pollution, extracted from the *HKUST Corpus*. I classified the students' and experts' semantic use of connectors marking causality according to a framework of reason-result, means-result and grounds-conclusion. One striking difference between the student and expert writing was the overuse of connectors as markers of local coherence. For example, there were 32 occurrences of *therefore* in the student corpus, but only 13 in the expert corpus. Moreover, in the expert corpus *therefore* occurred in sentence initial position in only one line whereas in the student corpus it was always sentence initial except in one instance. In contrast, in the student corpus there was a virtual absence of connectors used globally, such as *so, thus* and *then* to signal the grounds-conclusion relationship resulting in essays which lacked concluding inferential statements. These connectors were present in the expert writing where they very often signalled a concluding summary to a paragraph wrapping up a previous stretch of text, which was very much evaluative in nature. In Figure 4 below from the expert corpus, most of the occurrences of *then* are used in this way (e.g. *This, then, is the heart of the matter*).

This use of *then* contrasts with its use in the student corpus where it was always used at a local level to signal the reason-result relationship, as shown in Figure 5 below. These two contrasting uses of *then* correspond to Halliday and Hassan's (1976) distinction between "internal" and "external" conjunction, where the former term denotes that the conjunction is located in the interaction itself, and the latter that the conjunction is "located in the phenomena that constitute the content of what is being said" (1976:321).

Interestingly, the discourse-organising nouns such as *reason, result,* and

1	much coal; if the last tree is felled,	**then** we can say goodbye to the world as w
2	me or even greater priority. <p> This,	**then,** is the heart of the matter. For org
3	rica and the Philippines. <p> How far,	**then,** can we engage in a realistic progno
4	st certain to make matters worse. How,	**then,** could forests be sustainably manage
5	02 emissions). <p> For sundry reasons,	**then,** increased use of natural fertilizer
6	pectively. For purposes of this paper,	**then,** the "current" deforestation rate, m
7	tation appears likely. <p> All in all,	**then,** deforestation presents a decidely

Figure 4: Concorance lines for *then* extracted from the expert corpus.

1	d education system for the citizens.	**Then** It can raise the living standard and
2	to be exposed to different cultures.	**Then** general education level will be incre
3	s labours will be required on farming.	**Then** it is more difficult to find jobs in
4	increase the load of the government.	**Then** it will lower the competition ability
5	ny nations in China are unemployed.	**Then** the labours supply and the relative w
6	nd rights are insecure and limited.	**Then** the businessmen would fear this inve
7	xist in such a large domestic market.	**Then** income generated by the large firms
8	secondary schools should be provided.	**Then** every child Southern China can have
9	ter sense of belonging of the labour.	**Then** the workers can be willing to contri
10	opportunity is a vast avail. The GDP	**then** climbs up companying with the increas
11	of the transporation is quite high,	**then** the investors may not put their inve
12	enterprises invest in China. It	**then** helps the development of industr
13	ea to the surrounding suburbs and	**then** the situation of too many people

Figure 5: Concordance lines for *then* extracted from the learner corpus.

cause had different grammatical patternings in the two corpora. In the expert corpus, such nouns were very often used in rheme position, e.g. ... *factors already described are already powerful causes of deforestation*, or were of the pattern there *is/are*, e.g. *There are many reasons why developing countries have espoused....* It was found that students invariably used all these nouns in sentence-initial position with premodification as in the following examples of concordanced lines:

in a good example. The major	**reasons**	for Guangzhou become an industrial
especially for industry. The	**reason**	is that the industrial infrastructure
by cheap products. One minor	**reason**	is of geographical sense. Unlike in

To alert students to these kinds of discourse features, I would advocate more exploitation of the viewfinder option in the concordancing software (a facility which allows the learner to see a screenful of cotext for an individual KWIC concordance line). For example, students can use the viewfinder to examine the previous stretch of text to determine what the precise summative function of a connector signalling global coherence is. In this case, it is not always appropriate for the students to examine, either on screen or on a printout, the truncated KWIC lines in which these connectors occur as such phrases can only be fully explained with recourse to the preceding paragraph(s) of text. Students could also be asked to compare the use of these connectors in the two corpora as a means of raising their awareness of overuse at a local level and underuse at a global level of coherence (see Flowerdew 1998a for other examples of concordance-based exercises).

However, a few words of caution are in order here. I noticed that there were some instances of resistance to data-driven learning by students, a problem which of course can also occur with teachers. I also found that the reactions of science and engineering students and business students to hands-on concordancing were quite different. Whereas the science and engineering students had no difficulty in manipulating the concordancing software and were able to ignore punctuation details (e.g. <p>, see the concordance lines in Figure 4) contained in the text, the business students found the insertion of punctuation details distracting and took far longer to familiarise themselves with the programme. Not surprisingly, the business students found the text uninteresting as it was unrelated to their subject area. I would therefore suggest that it would probably be more motivating for students if they could choose the corpus text they wanted to work with. Possibly, under the teacher's guidance, they could browse a few texts first using concordancing techniques to see if the texts are suitable in terms of topic and level of language before embarking on a suite of exercises.

I also found that some of the students had reservations about examining examples of learner writing, commenting that they would prefer to compare the concordanced output of expert writing with the examples of the item in their own work, rather than be exposed to other students' errors which they might not make.

Conclusion

In this chapter, I have attempted to show that the findings from small learner corpora, i.e. sub-components of the large-scale *HKUST Learner Corpus*, can provide useful insights into which collocational, pragmatic or discourse fea-

tures should be addressed in materials design. I have also given some suggestions as to how the findings from learner corpora can be used in conjunction
with expert corpora to prepare EAP materials and suggested that the type of
error under investigation has implications for the way it is dealt with. At the
same time I have discussed a few caveats for using corpora in language teaching, and in this respect, I would like to reiterate the words of Cook (1998:57)
referring to Carter's (1998) standpoint "In his view, materials should be influenced by, but not slaves to, corpus findings ... and that pedagogic materials
should be corpus based not corpus bound". I would like to suggest that the
same applies to teaching methods.

References

Altenberg, B. 1997. "Exploring the Swedish component of the International Corpus of
   Learner English". In B. Lewandowska-Tomaszczyk and P. J. Melia (eds), *PALC
   '97-Practical Applications in Language Corpora*, 119–132. Lodz: Lodz
   University Press.
Aston, G. 1995. "Corpora in language pedagogy: matching theory and practice". In G.
   Cook and B. Seidlhofer (eds), *Principle and Practice in Applied Linguistics:
   Studies in honour of H. G. Widdowson*, 257–270. Oxford: OUP.
Aston, G. 1997. "Small and large corpora in language learning". In B. Lewandowska-
   Tomaszczyk and P. J. Melia (eds), *PALC '97-Practical Applications in Language
   Corpora*, 51–62. Lodz: Lodz University Press.
Aston, G. and Burnard, L. 1998. *The BNC Handbook*. Edinburgh: EUP.
Barnbrook, G. 1996. *Language and Computers*. Edinburgh: EUP.
Biber, D. 1988. *Variation Across Speech and Writing*. Cambridge: CUP.
Biber, D., Conrad, S. and Reppen, R. 1998. *Corpus Linguistics: Investigating language
   structure and use*. Cambridge: CUP.
Carter, R. 1998. "Orders of reality: CANCODE, communication and culture". *ELT
   Journal*, 52 (1): 43–56.
Collins COBUILD English Dictionary. 1995. London: HarperCollins.
Cook, G. 1998. "The uses of reality: A reply to Ronald Carter". *ELT Journal*, 52 (1):
   57–63.
Cowie, A. (ed), 1998. *Phraseology*. Oxford: Clarendon Press.
Flowerdew, J. 1996. "Concordancing in language learning". In M. Pennington (ed),
   The Power of CALL, 97–113. Houston TX: Athelstan.
Flowerdew, L. 1998a. "Concordancing on an expert and learner corpus in ESP". *CÆLL
   Journal* 8 (3): 3–7.

Flowerdew, L. 1998b. "Integrating expert and interlanguage computer corpora findings on causality: Discoveries for teachers and students". *ESP Journal* 17 (4): 329–345.

Flowerdew, L. 1998c. "Corpus linguistic techniques applied to textlinguistics". *System* 26 (4): 541–552.

Flowerdew, L. 2000. "Investigating errors in a learner corpus". In L. Burnard and T. McEnery (eds), *Proceedings of the Teaching and Language Corpora Conference 98*, 145–154. Frankfurt: Peter Lang.

Granger, S. (ed), 1998a. *Learner English on Computer.* London: Longman.

Granger, S. 1998b. "Prefabricated patterns in advanced EFL writing: collocations and formulae". In A. Cowie (ed), *Phraseology*, 145–160. Oxford: Clarendon Press.

Granger, S. and Rayson, P. 1998. "Automatic profiling of learner texts". In S. Granger (ed), *Learner English on Computer*, 119–131. London: Longman.

Granger, S. and Tribble, C. 1998. "Learner corpus data in the foreign language class-room: Form focused instruction and data-driven learning". In S. Granger (ed), *Learner English on Computer*, 199–209. London: Longman.

Granger, S. and Tyson, S. 1996. "Connector usage in the English essay writing of native and non-native EFL speakers of English". *World Englishes* 15 (1): 17–27.

Halliday, M. A. K. and Hasan, R. 1976. *Cohesion in English*. London: Longman.

Howarth, P. 1998. "The phraseology of learners' academic writing". In A. Cowie (ed), *Phraseology*, 161–186. Oxford: Clarendon Press.

Hyland, K. and Milton, J. 1997. "Qualifications and certainty in L1 and L2 students' writing". *Journal of Second Language Writing* 6 (2): 183–205.

Johns, T. 1994. "From printout to handout: Grammar and vocabulary teaching in the context of data-driven learning". In T. Odlin (ed), *Perspectives on Pedagogical Grammar*, 293–313. Cambridge: CUP.

Kennedy, G. 1998. *An Introduction to Corpus Linguistics*. London: Longman.

Lewandowska-Tomaszczyk, B. and Melia P. J. (eds), 1997. *PALC '97-Practical Applications in Language Corpora*. Lodz: Lodz University Press.

Lorenz, G. 1998. "Overstatement in advanced learners' writing: Stylistic aspects of adjective intensification". In S. Granger (ed), *Learner English on Computer*, 53–66.Oxford: Clarendon Press.

Milton, J. 1999. "Lexical thickets and electronic gateways: Making texts accessible by novice writers". In C. Candlin and K. Hyland (eds), *Writing: Texts, processes and practices*, 221–243. London: Longman.

Pickard, V. 1994. "Producing a concordance-based self-access vocabulary package: Some problems and solutions". In L. Flowerdew and K. K. Tong (eds), *Entering Text*, 215–224. Language Centre, Hong Kong University of Science and Technology.

Scott, M. 1996. *WordSmith Tools*. Oxford: Oxford English Software, UK.

Scott, M. 1997. "PC analysis of key words — and key key words". *System* 25 (2): 233–245.

Stevens, V. 1991. "Classroom concordancing: Vocabulary materials derived from relevant, authentic text". *English for Specific Purposes* 10: 35–46.

Stevens, V. 1995. "Concordancing with language learners: Why? When? What?" *CÆLL Journal,* 6 (2): 2–10.

Thurstun, J. and Candlin, C. 1998. "Concordancing and the teaching of the vocabulary of academic English". *English for Specific Purposes* 17(3): 267–280.

Tribble, C. 1990. "Concordancing and an EAP writing programme". *CÆLL Journal* 1(2): 10–15.

Tribble, C. 1991. "Some uses of electronic text in English for academic purposes". In J. Milton and K. S. T. Tong (eds), *Text Analysis in Computer Assisted Language Learning*, 4–14. Hong Kong: Hong Kong University of Science and Technology and City University of Hong Kong.

Tribble, C. 1997. "Put a corpus in your classroom: Using a computer in vocabulary development". In T. Boswood (ed), *New Ways of Using Computers in Language Teaching*, 266–268. Alexandria, VA: TESOL.

Tribble, C. and Jones G. 1990. *Concordances in the Classroom.* London: Longman.

Turton, N. D. and Heaton, J. B. 1996. *Longman Dictionary of Common Errors.* London: Longman.

Widdowson, H. G. 1998. "Context, Community, and Authentic Language". *TESOL Quarterly,* 32 (4): 705–716.

Willis, D. and Wright, J. 1995. *Collins COBUILD Basic Grammar.* London: HarperCollins.

CHAPTER 14

Small corpora and teaching writing
Towards a corpus-informed pedagogy of writing

Christopher Tribble

London University, Reading University, Lancaster University

Abstract

Writers need at least four kinds of knowledge when they approach a writing task: knowledge of *content, writing process, context,* and *language system.* An appropriate corpus of exemplars of the genre in which learners are interested provides them with an important resource, as it offers essential information about the lexico-grammar, patterning and organisation which have made these texts allowable contributions to the genre. This chapter considers ways in which teachers and learners can apply corpus methodologies to a micro corpus of web-published "leaflets" as part of a strategy for developing a capacity to write such texts. It argues for a corpus-informed pedagogy of writing in which the comparative analysis of small *exemplar* corpora in relation to larger *reference* corpora becomes part of the repertoire of the teachers and students of writing.

Learning to write in a foreign language

Foreign language students, especially those who wish to become writers in professional or academic settings, need to develop a wide range of knowledge, skills and competencies: what Ann Johns, a leading researcher in academic writing, calls *literacies* (Johns, A.M. 1997). The kinds of knowledge writers need can be categorised under four main headings (Table 1):

Table 1: What writers need to know (Tribble 1997:43)

content knowledge	knowledge of the concepts involved in the subject area
writing process knowledge	knowledge of the most appropriate way of carrying out a specific writing task
context knowledge	knowledge of the social context in which the text will be read, and co-texts related to the writing task in hand
language system knowledge	knowledge of those aspects of the language system necessary for the completion of the task

In the case of adult learners, it is usually the students who have the main responsibility for the development of their own knowledge and understanding of the content of the subjects they are studying and the professions in which they work. It still remains, however, the teacher's responsibility to create opportunities in which learners can develop and extend the process, context and language system knowledge they need in order to write successful texts.

Over the last twenty or so years, language teachers have developed a number of different strategies designed to help learners extend these kinds of knowledge. In current EFL/ESL writing pedagogy two major strands of applied research can be identified. One is often referred to as the *process approach* (Raimes 1993, White & Arndt 1991, Grabe & Kaplan 1996), the other as the *genre* approach (Cope & Kalantzis 1993, Gee 1997). While acknowledging the importance of ensuring that students are able to develop confidence in their individual "voices" as writers, in this paper I shall be focussing on ways in which teachers can use small corpora to help learners find out more about the context and language system knowledge of the factually oriented texts which many of them will find themselves having to write in professional or academic settings. Some of the insights which a genre approach to writing instruction offers provide a useful starting point to such a project.

Genre

Although the term *genre* remains the subject of some debate (Gee 1997), it nevertheless offers a useful explanatory framework for accounting for variation between texts. In this paper, I propose to use as my main working account of genre a definition elaborated by Ruqiya Hasan who, along with M.A.K. Halliday, was one of the founding theorists of the Australian genre school:

1. A genre is known by the meanings associated with it. In fact the term 'genre' is a short form for the more elaborate phrase 'genre-specific semantic potential'.
2. Genre bears a logical relation to Communicative Context [CC], being its verbal expression. If CC is a class of situation type, then genre is language doing the job appropriate to that class of social happenings.
3. Genres can vary in delicacy in the same way as contexts can. But for some given texts to belong to one specific genre, their structure should be some possible realisation of a given Generic Structure Potential [GSP].
4. It follows that texts belonging to the same genre can vary in their structure; the one respect in which they cannot vary without consequence to their genre-allocation is the obligatory elements and dispositions of the GSP (Halliday & Hasan 1985:108).

Hasan's notion of genre is based on the idea that spoken or written interactions can only be understood by seeing them against their social setting (the Communicative Context or CC). In this view of language as social interaction, each CC has the potential for a determinate number of meanings, and each of these meanings has associated with it a determinate range of realisations — the Generic Structure Potential (GSP). Hasan gives examples of two spoken "texts" which both arose from shopping interactions (Halliday & Hasan 1985:60–61), and demonstrates that, because the language is doing the same job in each instance, the linguistic structures used by the speakers are also similar. (Halliday & Hasan 1985:66). In written communication a simple example would be a letter of appointment issued by an employer. The CC is readily identifiable and the range of possible texts arising from the CC (the GSP) predictable. Of course, there will always be examples which contradict generic norms as language is a human phenomenon. This, however, does not undermine the *pedagogic* potential of such a view of language.

I find this approach to genre useful as it allows for narrower or broader specifications of genres as a function of the relative specificity of the Communicative Context (CC). By characterising the CC in terms of *situation types*, each with its associated Genre Specific Potential (GSP), Hasan offers an explanation of the way in which some textual realisations of a genre are considered more appropriate than others, i.e. are more allowable contributions, and also of the way in which some genres are more narrowly specifiable than others. It also dissolves the potential contradiction between narrow accounts of genre offered by authors focusing on the role of genres in academic settings such as John Swales (1990), and accounts of "protogenres" offered by Australian genre theorists such as Jim Martin (Martin 1989:7).[1] Thus one CC may be highly specific and have a very narrowly restricted GSP e.g. Swales' example of the *Journal / Newsletter of the Hong Kong Study Circle of Stamp Collecting Enthusiasts* (Swales 1990:27); or it might be of a more general nature e.g. "good-news" and "bad-news" letters in administrative correspondence (Swales 1990:53) with a correspondingly broader, though still identifiable GSP; or a CC might be so general that while it bears no relation to a particular discourse community e.g. Martin's categories of RECOUNT vs. PROCEDURE / DESCRIPTION vs. REPORT (Martin 1989:3–8), experienced readers will still be able to identify allowable contributions. Thus whether it is specific or general, each CC has associated with it a GSP which can be realised verbally through a (specifiable) range of allowable texts.

Whatever the problems associated with the notion of genre, it has been widely adopted (Bhatia 1993, Cope & Kalantzis 1993, Halliday 1978, Martin 1985, Swales 1990, Tribble 1997) and has provided the basis for a socially situated view of writing which complements the work of the process writing school. A genre approach has become increasingly influential in recent years, (Bamforth 1993, Gee 1997, Johns 1997) and has provided a useful framework for the use of language corpora in practical classroom learning and teaching (Flowerdew 1993, Tribble & Jones 1997, Tribble 1997a). Ways of extending the integration of corpora and specifically *small* corpora into ELT writing instruction will form the basis of the next sections in this chapter.

Preparing to write into a new genre — an example

Corpus linguistics has, to a large extent, developed from an agenda that has been driven by lexicographers, descriptive linguists and the NLP research community (Aston 1995, Tribble 1997b). This has tended to encourage a "biggest is best" view of the corpus (e.g. Sinclair 1991) which, while it may be valid for these communities, does not necessarily meet the needs of teachers and learners in ELT. The large corpus, whether it is "balanced" as in the case of the British National Corpus (Burnard 1995), or an open-ended "monitor" corpus in the case of the Bank of English at Birmingham University (Sinclair 1991), provides either too much data across too large a spectrum, or too little focused data to be directly helpful to the majority of language teachers and learners. Although these big corpora have made, and will continue to make, invaluable contributions to ELT lexicography and language description, large corpora *per se* appear to have limited direct relevance as a resource for students and teachers with an interest in learning about specific genres. Although I do not reject big corpora, along with other authors in this collection, in this paper I am interested in proposing practical ways of using smaller — or micro – corpora in language teaching.

An analytic framework proposed by Bhatia (1993) offers a useful starting point for a demonstration of the value of a small corpus in writing instruction. The framework was developed as a way of assisting teachers or students who have an interest in a specific genre, and involves seven steps:

1. Placing the given genre-text in a situational context
2. Surveying existing literature
3. Refining the situational/contextual analysis
4. Selecting the corpus
5. Studying the institutional context
6. Levels of linguistic analysis:
   – analysis of lexico-grammatical features
   – analysing the text-pattern or textualisation
   – structural interpretation of the text-genre
7. Specialist information in genre analysis (Bhatia 1993:22–34).

This approach offers teachers and learners a systematic way of developing the context and language system knowledge we have noted as being necessary if a writer is to make an acceptable contribution to a genre. It also provides an excellent starting point for the analysis and eventual pedagogic exploitation of specialist micro corpora.

The genre
The genre I have chosen to work with is related to one of the text categories specified in the syllabus for the written component of the Cambridge Advanced English Certificate (CAE). These are:

announcements	articles (newspaper / magazine)
directions	formal and informal letters

instructions	leaflets
notices	personal notes and messages
reports	reviews

As would be expected, such tasks also form the basis for the syllabus of most published materials that are designed to help learners who are preparing for this section of the examination.

In Tribble (1999) I have argued that this kind of syllabus can lead to confusion as it encourages teachers and text book writers to treat what are in fact *text types* as if they were discrete *genres*. As an example, we find that in a chapter on *Brochures* in recently published CAE preparation materials (O'Dell 1996), instances of written texts, whose only common feature is that they are printed on pieces of folded paper, are treated as if they are all analogous instances of a single genre. This approach presents students and teachers with real problems. Thus in the first stage of the chapter students analyse three leaflets publicising the London Transport Museum, and are guided to certain conclusions about the linguistic choices writers make in order to achieve this particular promotional purpose. They are then asked to undertake tasks such as:

(1) Your local area is keen to encourage foreign tourists. You have been asked to write a brochure to send to other countries in order to promote the area. You have been requested to pay particular attention to at least three of the following — landscape; local food and drink; leisure facilities; places of historic interest; transport. Write the brochure.

(2) You feel particularly strongly about an issue that is causing considerable discussion in your area. You decide to publicise your views by producing a pamphlet in which you lay out clearly what the issue is, why you feel as you do and why those with opposing views are, in your opinion, mistaken. Write the pamphlet.
(O'Dell 1996:87)

This is confusing because students are being asked to write texts which arise from strongly contrasting communicative contexts — neither of which bears a relation with the communicative context which had been the focus of the original analysis. There are plenty of analogues for the museum publicity leaflets, and it would have been possible to develop a coherent account of such leaflets as a specific genre of writing and then go on to develop new texts within these generic constraints. Unfortunately, this has not been done in this instance.

Instead, learner have been asked to write into genres which are the result of very different communicative contexts — and to make the assumption that these texts will be analogues of the original promotional leaflets. Ironically, the reality of the contrast is hinted at by the use of the text type names: "brochure" and "pamphlet". It is not, however, acknowledged in the text, and the assumption is made that lessons learned from the analysis of one piece of folded paper can be transferred to the writing of other texts which could be printed with the same format.

In the following discussion I propose to offer an alternative pedagogic account of an instance of a text type that is related to "leaflet" and, I hope, demonstrate how a genre-specific micro corpus can make a major contribution to a student's capacity to write into the genre realised by such texts. I shall use the notion of genre as a way of accounting for my selection of texts, and Bhatia 1993 as a starting point for the analysis of a micro corpus of examples of a specific genre. I shall then show how this genre approach can be used as the basis for a *pedagogic* account of a set of related texts

The text type I shall consider is an electronically published variant of the marketing leaflet. Although such promotional literature continues to be distributed in print form, the World Wide Web (WWW) has also become an important means for marketing many products from natural cosmetics to educational programmes. An example of the former can be seen in Figure 1 below, part of a Web catalogue of natural cosmetic and health products. An example of the latter is given in Figure 2 below.

These kinds of document share many features with one another, and with comparable print and Web leaflets. Some of these shared features arise from the potential of their electronic medium of distribution (e.g. "Go to" and "Search" buttons; hyperlinks to other documents), others arise from the similarity of the communicative purposes of the texts. Thus, each of our examples contains the following distinct sections:

- title — who are we?
- user specification — whom do we aim to serve?
- product specification — what do we offer? what are its special features?
- contact information — how do you contact us?

Although some of these sections are realised differently (for example, the *Smooth* page provides links to pages which give further information about "*who* are we?", while the *MA* page gives immediate information on the staff

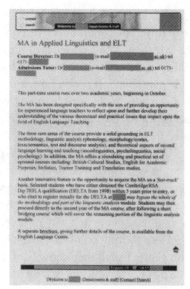

Figure. 1: Natural Cosmetics   **Figure 2:** MA Programme

who are involved in the programme) the overall structure is similar. The major difference between the two pages is that *Smooth* tells its readers how much the product costs, while the *MA* page is noticeably reticent with regard to the matter of fees!

In the rest of this paper I shall be using a micro corpus of Web leaflets promoting MA in Applied Linguistics / ELT (*MA-WEB_PAGE*). The texts used in the corpus were found by typing the keywords *Master, applied, ELT* and *linguistics* into the *Alta Vista* search engine, and following the links which were offered. I eventually collected examples from fourteen different universities, a total of 13,216 words. In order to prevent invidious comparisons (some of the texts strike me as being much less successful than others!) all text extracts will be given anonymously (01Uni.txt, etc.)

My justification for considering these texts as exemplars of the same genre is that each text has a precisely analogous communicative purpose: to give appropriate information to a clearly defined target readership so as to encourage them to enrol on the programme on offer. The communicative context of these "web leaflets" is (in Hasan's words) "a class of situation type" which we can call *academic product promotion* and the texts themselves are examples of "language doing the job appropriate to that class of social happenings". Swales supports such a reading when he says:

> Communicative purpose is both a privileged criterion and one that operates to keep the scope of a genre as here conceived narrowly focused on comparable rhetorical action. In addition to purpose, exemplars of a genre exhibit various patterns of similarity in terms of structure, style, content and intended audience. (Swales 1990:58)

I think it is clear that the fourteen examples I shall be working with are indeed "comparable rhetorical action". The extent to which they "exhibit various patterns of similarity in terms of structure, style, content and intended audience" remains to be seen.

Preparing the corpus[2]

Once the texts had been downloaded they were saved as HTML documents to a local hard disk. The HTML documents were then stripped down to plain text files for use as the main corpus resource. Although I am aware that, for example, McEnery T & A Wilson (1997) advocate the benefits of "multi-media" corpora (and the need for consistent "multi-media" encoding), in the present instance the HTML coding across the documents in the micro corpus was so inconsistent it would have involved more work to exploit the existing coding than it did to tag the text manually.[3]

The plain text files were tagged at two levels. The first provided a way of describing the overall organisation of each example in the corpus. This was achieved by developing a set of "move" tags which were then used to mark natural internal divisions in the text where a particular kind of purpose is being achieved.[4] In this system "<summary>" marks sections where the programme is outlined, and "<entry>" marks sections where entrance requirements and qualifications are stated. The categories used in this analysis were not taken from any pre-existing move structure such as Swales (1981), or Dudley-Evans (1994), but were derived from a reading of the texts, and the pre-existing section headings chosen by many of the writers. Figure 3 shows the section divisions that were identified. This is the complete set of move tags used in the corpus, the first tag marking the beginning of the move, the second closing the move, and, of course, not all texts contain all the tags.

```
<admin>,</admin>5
<assessment>,</assessment>
<department>,</department>
<duration>,</duration>
<entry>,</entry>6
<index>,</index>
<mode>,</mode>
<programme>,</programme>7
<qualification>,</qualification>
<resources>,</resources>
<staff>,</staff>
<summary>,</summary>
<title>,</title>
```

Figure 3: Tag-set

The second level of tagging marked the formal units "heading" "sentence" and "paragraph". The tags for these were:

- heading: /h — semantic units identified by a direct reading of the texts
- sentence /s — arbitrary units marked by the existence of sentence final punctuation (.?!) at the end of the immediately preceding text string (with the first sentence in the text marked by hand). The text had been pre-edited to remove strings such as Prof., Ms. etc., and so forth, and was post-edited to take into account anomalous formatting.
- paragraph /p — arbitrary units marked by the existence of a double hard-return code ({CHR(13)}{CHR(10)}) at the beginning of the string. A degree of post-editing was required to ensure that paragraphs had been reliably placed.

The resultant text looks as shown in Figure 4 below.

Having made this investment of time, it is now possible to get raw frequency data from the corpus, but also possible to make much more delicate analysis of the ways in which language is used at specific moments and locations in the texts.

/h <department> University of XXX — Applied English Language Studies
Unit </department>

/h <title> MA in Language Teaching and Learning </title>

/p /s <department> We offer Masters and PhD studies in Applied Linguistics. /s
Over the past ten years students have come to study here from many countries
including the UK, Switzerland, Brazil, Malaysia, Turkey, Korea, Japan,
Senegal, Angola, Mozambique, Spain, France, etc </department>

/h <summary> ABOUT THE COURSE
/p /s The course sets out to explore the three areas of language, language learning and language teaching methodology, with particular emphasis on the inter-
relationships between them.

Figure 4: Tagged text

Analysing the corpus

Bhatia's steps in genre analysis included:

1. Placing the given genre-text in a situational context;
2. Surveying existing literature;
3. Refining the situational/contextual analysis;
4. Selecting the corpus;
5. Studying the institutional context.

Given the scope of this paper, I do not propose to expand further on these five
steps (or on Step 7: "Specialist information in genre analysis"), although a
teacher approaching this kind of genre might wish, for example, to review
recent work in cultural studies (e.g. Myers 1999) as part of their preparation
for an analysis of the genre in question. In the following sections I shall, therefore, focus most of my attention on the three stages implied by Bhatia's Step 6:
"Levels of linguistic analysis":

– an analysis of lexico-grammatical features
– analysing the text-pattern or textualisation
– structural interpretation of the text-genre

Lexico-Grammatical Features

Wordlists

A frequency sorted wordlist offers an effective way of beginning to study a text or collection of texts (Tribble C & G Jones 1997, Stubbs M forthcoming), as it gives an immediate insight into words which appear with high frequency. What it does not do is to provide an insight into the extent to which these words may be statistically prominent in relation to other texts. This facility is provided by the *Wordsmith Tools Keywords* program, more of which anon. We will begin our analysis of the lexico-grammatical features of our micro corpus, however, with a frequency list, the top 20 words in the *MA-WEB_PAGE Micro Corpus*. As a basis for reference, we shall consider the top 20 words *BNC Written and Spoken "Sampler"* (approximately 1 million words in each set) (Figure 5 below):

One of the most obvious differences between the wordlist for *MA-WEB_PAGE* and the wordlists for the large corpora is the presence of a signifi-

MA	Freq.	%	BNCWR	Freq.	%	BNCSP	Freq.	%
THE	640	4.8	THE	67,075	6.21	THE	38,962	3.71
OF	552	4.14	OF	32,656	3.02	I	33,478	3.19
AND	429	3.22	AND	28,900	2.68	YOU	27,334	2.6
IN	355	2.66	TO	26,680	2.47	IT	26,983	2.57
TO	262	1.97	A	21,958	2.03	AND	26,013	2.48
LANGUAGE	239	1.79	IN	21,184	1.96	S	22,236	2.12
A	231	1.73	IS	9,954	0.92	THAT	22,210	2.11
FOR	151	1.13	FOR	9,590	0.89	TO	22,142	2.11
COURSE	128	0.96	THAT	8,537	0.79	A	20,450	1.95
ENGLISH	122	0.92	WAS	8,362	0.77	OF	15,916	1.52
STUDENTS	121	0.91	IT	7,915	0.73	IN	13,526	1.29
TEACHING	111	0.83	ON	7,338	0.68	N'T	13,291	1.27
IS	104	0.78	BE	7,200	0.67	WE	11,326	1.08
ON	99	0.74	WITH	7,137	0.66	DO	10,163	0.97
ARE	98	0.74	AS	6,547	0.61	ER	10,071	0.96
MA	98	0.74	I	6,315	0.58	IS	9,983	0.95
BE	96	0.72	BY	5,908	0.55	THEY	9,800	0.93
CREDITS	90	0.68	AT	5,651	0.52	YEAH	9,423	0.9
RESEARCH	86	0.65	ARE	5,012	0.46	ON	8,398	0.8
WITH	84	0.63	HE	4,995	0.46	WAS	8,093	0.77

Figure 5: The most frequent 20 words in the *MA-WEB_PAGE Micro Corpus* and the *BNC Written and Spoken "Sampler"*

cant number of content vocabulary items at the top end of the list. In the present instance it is 8/20 for the *MA-WEB_PAGE* list [language / course / English / students / teaching / MA / credits / research], as opposed to 0/20 in both the written and spoken lists. This difference is the result of the very narrow content domain of the *MA-WEB_PAGE* texts when compared with the range of topics which will be treated in a general corpus. It can be useful as it means that even with very simple software it is still possible for learners to find out about some of the more important content words in a set of closely associated texts.

Even more useful, however, is the information that raw frequency lists can give about where a genre is situated when compared with other examples of written and spoken production. Accounts of the contrast between written and spoken language in use (Biber 1998, Halliday 1989) stress the high frequency of certain word classes, and the low frequencies of others in texts arising from different production contexts, and account for these contrasts in terms of the fundamentally different communicative purposes of spoken and written production. Halliday argues that "in general, the more 'written' the language being used, the higher will be the proportion of lexical words to the total number of running words in the text." (Halliday 1989:64) and goes on to consider the relative "nouniness" of written production, where nouns are used in preference to verbs in order to realise different kinds of meaning or create different relationships. This leads to a typification of written production as *lexically dense* and spoken production as *syntactically intricate* (Halliday 1989:87).

In the present instance, we get an indication of this from the contrast between the highest frequency words in *MA-WEB_PAGE* and the other lists. Thus, *MA-WEB_PAGE* and *BNC Written* are strikingly similar in their top five words, unlike *BNC Spoken* where, although *the* is the most frequent word, it has a lower percentage value (3.71% compared with 4.8 / *MA-WEB_PAGE* & and 6.21 / *BNC Written*), and items 2 and 3 are *I* and *you*. The high percentages for *the* and *of* are also a clear indication of the higher percentage of determinate nouns in use in the instances of written production than in the spoken (indefinite articles are similar percentages across all three corpora (1.73 / 2.03 / 1.95). When lower frequency words are observed, the contrast becomes even clearer, with even *BNC Written* evidencing a relatively high frequency of first person pronouns (mainly accounted for by the journalistic and fiction texts in the corpus), and *BNC Spoken* offering examples of pause markers (*er*) and transcription indicators of casual speech (*yeah* / negative contractions).

A conclusion from this discussion (and one which it is possible, in fact, to make *before* reading the texts) is that the *MA-WEB_PAGE* micro corpus is not conversational in its tone (unlike, I would predict, some other kinds of promotional material addressing a different audience with less serious aspirations than potential MA candidates!). Rather, it is likely to be informationally oriented, and to present this information in extended noun phrases rather than with lots of verb phrases.

Not only can we gain insights into the kind of writing that is exemplified in the texts in our micro corpus, we can also identify patterns of use that are associated with high frequency items. While this may be of less interest in a large mixed corpus (where it is common practice to exclude high frequency words like *the* and *of* because they offer few insights), in a micro corpus it can be extremely useful to consider these words as a way of gaining an insight into the kinds of prefabricated unit which are used across the corpus.

Taking *of* in *MA-WEB_PAGE* as an example, and using *Collocates* and *Cluster* in *Wordsmith Tools*, it is possible to begin to identify classes of high frequency nouns in the texts, and the patterns in which they occur. A listing of the immediate left collocates (those words appearing immediately to the left of the node word) shows the nouns in *MA — WEB_PAGE* which are commonly post-modified with a prepositional phrase. *Cluster* reveals the kinds of phrases which occur in the environment of *of*. While these phrases will be (possibly overly) familiar to those of us who work in the field, for learners approaching the genre for the first time, they may be as bright and shiny as freshly minted pennies. A micro corpus combined with wordlisting and concordancing tools can provide instant pathways into texts which might otherwise remain opaque to the learner and (through *Cluster* analysis) offers access to the kind of phrase-bank which the expert writer is able to draw on unconsciously when composing within a particular genre. Figure 6, below, gives two lists: one of the collocates of *of* and the other of clusters involving *of*.

Keywords

Frequency sorted wordlists, combined with collocation and cluster information, can offer a great deal of information about the high frequency words in a text and the patterns in which they occur. They do not, however, provide direct information about which words are *unusually* frequent or infrequent in the text in question when it is compared with another text or collection of texts. Keyword analysis allows such comparisons to be made. Another part of the *Wordsmith Tools* suite, *Keywords* makes possible the study of those words

N	WORD	L1	N	cluster	Freq.
1	RANGE	25	1	part of the	16
2	UNIVERSITY	18	2	the teaching of	15
3	TEACHING	16	3	of language teaching	13
4	ONE	13	4	a wide range	12
5	ASPECTS	12	5	bank of english	12
6	BANK	12	6	of the course	12
7	AREAS	11	7	of the taught	12
8	PART	11	8	the university of	12
9	DEPARTMENT	10	9	wide range of	12
10	ANALYSIS	9	10	one of the	11
11	AREA	8	11	an area of	10
12	END	8	12	and invaluable collection	10
13	SCHOOL	7	13	components of the	10
14	TWO	7	14	of their own	10
15	VARIETY	7	15	on an area	10
16	APPLICATIONS	6	16	taught components of	10
17	GUIDANCE	6	17	the taught components	10
18	UNDERSTANDING	6	18	their own choosing	10
19	CHOICE	5	19	range of options	9
20	COLLECTION	5	20	school of education	9
			21	area of interest	8
			22	interest of their	8
			23	of interest of	8
			24	of language and	8
			25	of the programme	8
			26	the end of	8
			27	under the guidance	8

Figure 6: Collocates and clusters of *of*

which are statistically significantly more or less frequent in a small text when it is compared to a larger text or collection of texts.[8] Some of the keywords for *MA-WEB_PAGE* are given in Figure 7 below. Two different lists are given — the first was referenced against the *BNC Sampler Written* subset, the second against the *BNC Sampler Spoken* subset. The first pair of lists details *positive* keywords in *MA-WEB_PAGE*–i.e. those words that are statistically prominent in the genre as a result of their comparatively high frequency in the example texts. The second pair lists the *negative* keywords in *MA* i.e. those words that have strikingly *low* frequency in the micro corpus when it is compared with larger populations of texts.

N	Positive (ref BNCS)		N	Positive (ref BNCW)		N	Negative (ref BNCS)		N	Negative (ref BNCW)	
1	LANGUAGE	*	1	LANGUAGE	*	186	NOT	*	280	GOOD	x
2	MA	*	2	STUDENTS	*	187	SO	*	281	COME	x
3	TEACHING	*	3	ENGLISH	*	188	WHEN	*	282	ABOUT	x
4	CREDITS	*	4	TEACHING	*	189	WOULD	*	283	ALL	x
5	LINGUISTICS	*	5	CREDITS	*	190	BUT	*	284	ONE	x
6	ENGLISH	*	6	LINGUISTICS	*	191	THE	*	285	OUT	x
7	MODULES	*	7	MODULES	*	192	IT	*	286	NOT	*
8	DISSERTATION	*	8	MA	*	193	THAT	*	287	THEM	x
9	STUDENTS	*	9	MODULE	*	194	I	*	288	SEE	x
10	COURSE	*	10	DISSERTATION	*				289	HAVE	x
11	MODULE	*	11	RESEARCH	*				290	WOULD	*
12	RESEARCH	*	12	COURSE	*				291	UP	x
13	TAUGHT	*	13	OF	x				292	WHEN	*
14	PROGRAMME	*	14	TAUGHT	*				293	IF	x
15	APPLIED	x	15	APPLIED	x				294	LIKE	x
16	DISCOURSE	*	16	PROGRAMME	*				295	BUT	*
17	SEMESTER	x	17	DISCOURSE	*				296	THERE	x
18	METHODOLOGY	*	18	ANALYSIS	x				297	WHAT	x
19	ASSESSMENT	x	19	COURSES	*				298	SO	*
20	COURSES	*	20	METHODOLOGY	*				299	NO	x
									300	WELL	x
									301	THEY	x
									302	WE	x
									303	DO	x
									304	YOU	x
									305	THAT	*
									306	IT	*
									307	I	*

Figure 7: Keywords
Words marked "*" occur in both lists. Words marked "x" only occur in one list.

Two points are worth making in relation to these lists. The first concerns the value of using strongly contrasting reference corpora. This is shown by the fact that while the *BNC Written (BNCW)* referenced keyword list gives more or less the same set of keywords in the top 20 as the *BNC Spoken (BNCS)* list, there is one important difference. This is the presence of *of* in the BNCS list — underlining the nominally oriented style of *MA-WEB-PAGE* in contrast with the spoken corpus. The second concerns the use of negative keyword lists. The negative keyword list confirms the low levels of first person reference in *MA-WEB-*

WORD	R1	R2	R3	R4	R5
ARE	10	1	0	1	1
TAKE	8	0	1	2	1
MAY	7	0	0	0	0
PRODUCE	5	0	0	0	0
CAN	4	1	0	0	0
HAVE	4	7	0	1	0
WILL	4	0	0	1	3
CHOOSE	3	3	1	0	0
FOLLOW	3	2	0	0	0
IS	3	0	0	1	0
WORK	2	1	2	1	0
WRITE	1	5	0	1	0

Figure 8: Verb collocates of student
(R1, R2, etc. = Right context 1, Right context 2, etc.)

PAGE compared with general text populations, and also of conditional — *would* indicating that this kind of promotional literature is less likely to use polite or hedging modals.

This list gives us a clear picture of the things that students *do* (*take, produce, choose, follow, work, write*) and when they do these things (the present — or timeless future)

A point of comparison which makes clear the radical difference which can be shown between one micro corpus and another is offered below in Figure 9 and Figure 10. Here, the wordlist for a micro corpus (30,000 words) of romantic fiction texts taken from the *Lancaster Oslo Bergen corpus (LOB)* has been referenced against the *BNC Sampler Written* subset to derive a set of keywords. The most prominent keyword is *she*. The list of things *she* does is given below. Clearly students on MA courses can expect to have less fun and fewer conversations than heroines in romantic fiction!

Text-pattern or textualisation
So far we have considered some of the words that are used in the *MALEAFLET* micro corpus and have seen how concordancing tools can give learners rapid access to important features of the lexico-grammar of the genre under investigation. In the next paragraphs we will briefly look at how some of

SHE	S	HER	I	HE	YOU
LL	N'T	HAD	HIM	VE	WAS
NIGEL	JULIA	DIANA	GAY	GAVIN	PHILIP
HIS	PEPITA				

Figure 9: Romantic fiction keywords

HAD	WAS	SAID	WOULD	COULD	FELT
LOOKED	KNEW	'D	WENT	SAW	'S
ASKED	DIDN'T	THOUGHT	DID	IS	MADE
MIGHT	SAT	TURNED	WANTED	ADDED	FOUND
MUST	SPOKE	WATCHED	COULDN'T	HADN'T	HAS
LAUGHED	LOVED	REALISED	TOLD	TOOK	WHISPERED

Figure 10: Romantic fiction — she collocates

these features are used in a patterned way in the texts we are studying. In order to do this we shall exploit the work done earlier in tagging the texts in the micro corpus to show sentence and paragraph beginnings.

We have already noted that keyword analysis offers a powerful way of approaching the "aboutness" of a text. In addition, it has proved interesting to note how keywords have an important role in the development of the major text units of paragraph and sentence.

Using the /p and /s tags it was possible to count 408 "paragraphs" and 686 "sentences" in *MA-WEB_PAGE*[9]. Two concordances were then generated, one for the top 20 keywords in the corpus, and another for the top 100 (setting the /p tag as required left context, and then setting /s as required left context). The results of this search were surprising (see Figure 11 below). First of all, Keywords occupy an unpredictably high percentage of paragraph and sentence initial positions. Hoey has commented on the ways in which certain kinds of lexis have a text organising function, giving the example of the way in which a number like "60" tends to occur with exceptional frequency in theme position or text initial position in a corpus of newspaper articles (Hoey 1997:21–22). It would seem that keywords themselves are also strongly implicated in the organisation of the text, and as such, possibly have a central role to play in the cohesion of a text. Thus in *MA-WEB_PAGE*, the top 20 keywords are in the first three words of 34% of all paragraphs and 44% of all sentences. While this may not allow us to say that these words are in *theme* position in a theme / rheme structure in all instances, it is useful for this analysis to consider the first few words of a clause as having high informational significance, and interesting to note that the top 100 keywords occupy as many as 521 out of 686 (75%) of the potential theme positions in the *MA-WEB_PAGE* corpus.

Top 20 Keywords in paragraph theme position	140 instances / 408 paragraphs (34%)
Top 100 Keywords in paragraph theme position	240 instances / 408 paragraphs (58%)
Top 20 Keywords in sentence / paragraph theme position	302 instances / 686 sentences (44%)
Top 100 Keywords in sentence / paragraph theme position	521 instances / 686 sentences (75%)

Figure 11: Sentence / paragraph / keywords

It would seem that by studying keywords in an unfamiliar genre learners will be focusing on some of the most strategically important words in a text. As an example of the value that can be derived from studying keywords we will extend the analysis of *students* which we began earlier. We have already shown how the authors of *MA-LEAFLET* ascribe relatively subordinate roles to *students*. We will now consider two other words from the keyword list — this time taking items which represent another side of the power structure *MA* itself, and *course*.

It would seem that if students are given subordinate roles in the processes described in *MA-LEAFLET*, and their future teachers are difficult to trace at all, *MA* and "course" are much less backwards in coming forward.[11] Concordances on these two words can show learners how simple linguistic devices have been used to allow *MA* and *course* to occupy these theme / subject positions. In the examples given below, this becomes immediately clear (verbs are marked in bold). For the 12 instances of *The MA* in theme position, nine of the verb forms are agentless passives and three are copula *be* (Figure 12 below).

Course follows the same pattern (Figure 13 below). Eight out of 23 instances are agentless passives, two are passives with agent, one is copula *be* and in 13 instances *course* is given animate attributes by being allowed to *examine, include, introduce, look at, prepare, provide,* or *set out to explore.*

Apprentice writers with an interest in promoting their MA programme, would gain at least two important insights from this kind of study. First, they

1. /s The MA/Diploma **is intended** for graduates with a professional interest in language.
2. /s The MA **has been designed** specifically with the aim of providing an opportunity for exp
3. /s The MA in Translation Studies **is run** in conjunction with the Modern Languages departme
4. /s The MA in English Language Teaching **has been designed** for qualified, trained and exper
5. /s The MA in Special Applications of Linguistics **is intended** for new graduates and others
6. /s The MA in Applied Linguistics **is intended** for experienced teachers of English who wish
7. /s The MA in TEFL/TESL and the MA in Applied Linguistics **are** both **designed** for language t
8. /s The MA in TEFL/TESL **is intended** for teachers of English with at least two years' exper
9. /s The MA in ESP **is designed** for teachers who already specialise in that area or who wish
10. /s The MA in Special Applications of Linguistics **is** open to new graduates with an interes
11. /s The MA in Applied Linguistics **is** a full-time modular scheme with taught courses over
12. /s The MA in Teaching International Communication in English **is** part of the Institute's

Figure 12: "MA" as keyword

/s The course **includes** presentations by [a]
/s This course also **introduces** students t [a]
/s This course **introduces** students to a [a]
/s This course **introduces** students to cur [a]
/s This course **introduces** students to res [a]
/s The course **introduces** the major theor [a]
/s The course **is** the result of [a]
/s This course **looks** at issues and tech [a]
/s This course **prepares** students for their [a]
/s This course **prepares** students for their [a]
/s The course also **provides** a sound ba [a]
/s The course **sets out** to explore the th [a]
/s The course **will also examine** relation [a]
/s The course programme for each ten-week programme **is based on** [p]
/s The course **is designed** for teachers [p]
/s The course **is intended for** language t [p]
/s This course **is designed** for working t [p]
/s The course **is organised** [p]
/s This course **is organised** in three part [p]
/s The course **will be organised** thematic [p]
/s Other courses **may also be on offer**– [p]
/s This course **is mainly taught** by mem [p + agent]
/s The course is **taught** by means of lec [p + agent]

Figure 13: *Course* as keyword

would come to an understanding of the roles which writers have decided to ascribe to major participants in the MA process: students, teachers and the programmes themselves. Secondly they would have access to the lexis and phrase

structure which these writers and their departments have considered appropriate to the genre they were planning to write into. While neither of these should
be seen as placing an obligation on learners to write in the same way as the
writers of the texts in the corpus, any decision to write in a different way can
now be informed by an understanding of the state-of-the-art, and will represent
the writers' conscious decision to strike out on their own. It is in this sense that
it is possible to talk about a *corpus-informed* writing pedagogy.

Structural Interpretation
A final area of analysis proposed by Bhatia is the structural interpretation of
the genre. We have already seen (Figure 4) that it was possible to identify a
series of section headings in the corpus (tagged "/h"). An edited concordance
on "/h" across the full corpus reveals some common ground in the organisation
of the texts in *MA-WEB_PAGE*–and the range of variation across the micro
corpus.(See Appendix: Moves in *MA-WEB_PAGE* for a full listing of these).

Move	File	words
<title>	\14uni.txt	5
<summary>	\14uni.txt	86
<entry>	\14uni.txt	73
<programme>	\14uni.txt	582
<mode>	\14uni.txt	96
<assessment>	\14uni.txt	58
<admin>	\14uni.txt	38
	total	938

Figure 14: Sections

This sequence is common to all fourteen texts in the corpus, although there
is significant variation in the number of sections which are used. The smallest
set of moves is found in UNI08.TXT (Figure 15 below) while the largest is

<title>	\08uni.txt
<summary>	\08uni.txt
<programme>	\08uni.txt

Figure 15: UNI08

UNI02.TXT with 36 moves. This apparent anomaly arises because UNI02 offers information about five specific programmes, all of which come under the general heading of "MA in Applied Linguistics". The individual moves which constitute each subsection of the text in fact map closely on to the typical set given in Figure 14.

Below this level of informational organisation, the text also displays similarities. The major patterning of the discourse is General Particular, where an opening generalisation is qualified with statements at progressive levels of specificity.[12] This can be seen in the example below, where an opening generalisation (beginning with the keyword *MA*) comments on the profile of potential candidates for the degree programme. This is then specified by a series of specifying comments, with cohesion being maintained either by anaphoric pronominal reference (as in "UNI14.txt" below) or by elegant variation and pronominal reference to the initial information focus (as in "UNI09.txt" below):

The MA in English Language Teaching has been designed for qualified, trained and experienced teachers from a variety of professional backgrounds. They will normally be graduates although in rare cases other qualifications may be taken into account. They will be trained teachers since the MA is not an initial training course. They will have spent some years working in schools, curriculum development centres, Ministries of Education, advisory centres, training colleges or universities. (UNI14.txt)

Applicants should be graduates of British or overseas universities in subjects such as English and foreign languages who have at least one to two years' experience of English language teaching in secondary schools, language schools, further education colleges, teacher training institutions, polytechnics, universities, etc. Most students have taught abroad. We look for good honours graduates, though it is possible in a few cases to admit applicants who have other degrees, or degrees in other subjects or even, rarely, non-graduates. (UNI09.txt)

Some conclusions

This chapter has been premised on the assumption that part of the job of a teacher of writing is to help learners extend their knowledge of:

a) the context in which they must write and
b) the language system resources they need to draw on in order to compose allowable contributions in such a context.

I have tried to show that a micro corpus of *exemplars* of texts written with a common communicative purpose and for analogous communicative contexts can provide a useful basis for developing this kind of knowledge. By studying an exemplar corpus in relation to contrasting *reference* corpora it is possible to gain an understanding of the texts which are similar to and different from the texts that learners want to write. Having identified where a target genre is situated in relation to other texts, it is then possible to use frequency sorted wordlists and keyword lists as a way of building an understanding of how words are used in such contexts and the rhetorical effects which expert writers achieve through such linguistic practices.

I have also shown how it is possible to add tags to the raw text of a corpus to enable:

a) the analysis of how the language system is used in relation to text units such as "sentence" and "paragraph" and
b) the analysis of the organisational patterns across the texts in the corpus.

I hope that the discussion above has shown that micro corpora can offer learners a practical basis for extending the knowledge they need in order to develop as writers, and provide teachers and materials writers with a valuable means of coming to a clearer understanding of the genres they find themselves teaching. The approach to the analysis of a micro corpus I have outlined provides a starting point for all manner of classroom research activities and, when combined with the work which has taken place under the name of classroom concordancing and data-driven learning (Johns 1988, 1991, 1994, 1997, Murieson-Bowie 1993, 1996, Tribble 1989, 1991, 1997b, 1997c), indicates what a corpus informed pedagogy for writing might look like.

Notes

1. *"The rationale behind a genre establishes constraints on allowable contributions in terms of their content, positioning and form.* Established members of discourse communities employ genres to realise communicatively the goals of their communities. The shared purposes of a genre are thus recognised at some level of consciousness by the established members of the

parent discourse community; they may be only partially recognised by apprentice members; and they may be either recognised or not recognised by non-members" (Swales 1990:53).

2.   The analysis which follows can be carried out using what is now (1999) "entry-level" in PC terms a Windows 95/98 PC with Intel Pentium processor, over 32 MB RAM and a reasonably sized hard disk drive (e.g. over 2 GB). The software used has been *Microsoft Word 97*, *Excel 97* and *Wordsmith Tools 3.00* (Scott 1998).

3.   A more extensive analysis of para-linguistic features such as illustrations, logos, layout, typeface, colour schemes etc. has much to recommend itself, but has not been undertaken in this study.

4.   All of this was done in *MS Word 97*.

5.   equivalent to "contact" in the earlier analysis.

6.   equivalent to "user".

7.   equivalent to "product".

8.   See Scott (1997) for a discussion of the statistics which underlie keyword analysis.

9.   It must be remembered that many of these "paragraphs" are single line text elements such as listed items, which partially accounts for the rather low ratio of sentences to paragraphs. The other reason for this low ratio is that in this kind of leaflet text writers appear to use single sentence paragraphs as a means of emphasising each point they wish to make.

10. The "Theme" of the clause is that part preceding the first main verb. In this analysis I have assumed that any word in the first three words of an orthographic sentence occupies such a position.

11. While neither "teacher" (referring to staff member), "lecturer" nor "tutor" are prominent keywords in *MA-LEAFLET*, *MA* is number 2 and *course* number 10 in the keyword list referenced against *BNC Written*.

12. See Hoey (1983) for an account of discourse patterns in text.

References

Aston, G. 1996. "Corpora in language pedagogy: Matching theory and practice". In G. Cook and B. Seidlhofer (eds), *Principle and Practice in Applied Linguistics: Studies in honour of H.G. Widdowson*. Oxford: OUP.

Bamforth, R. 1993. "Process vs. genre: Anatomy of a false dichotomy". *Prospect: A Journal of Australian TESOL* 8(1):289–99.

Bhatia, V. K. 1993. *Analysing genre: Language use in professional settings*. Harlow: Longman.

Biber, D. 1988.*Variations Across Speech and Writing*. Cambridge: CUP.

Burnard, L. 1995. *The British National Corpus Users Reference Guide (SGML Version)*. Oxford: Oxford University Computing Services.

Clark, R. and Ivanic, R. 1997.*The Politics of Writing*. London: Routledge.

Cope, B. and Kalantzis, M. 1993.*The Powers of Literacy: A genre approach to teaching writing*. London: The Falmer Press.

Dudley-Evans, T. 1994. "Genre analysis: An approach to text analysis for ESP" In M. Coulthard (ed), *Advances in Written Discourse*, 219–228. London: Routledge.

Flowerdew, J. 1993. "An educational or process approach to the teaching of professional genres". *ELTJ* 47(4): 305–316.

Gee, S. 1997. "Teaching writing: A genre based approach". In G. Fulcher (ed), *Writing in the Language Classroom*. Hemel Hempstead: Prentice Hall ELT.

Grabe, W. and Kaplan, R. 1996. *Theory and Practice of Writing*. London: Longman.

Halliday, M. A. K. and Hasan, R. 1985. *Language Context and Text: Aspects of language in a social-semiotic perspective*. Oxford: OUP.

Halliday, M. A. K. 1989. *Spoken and Written Language*. Oxford: OUP.

Hoey, M. 1983. *On the Surface of Discourse*. London: George Allen and Unwin.

Hoey, M. 1997. "From concordance to text structure: New uses for computer corpora". In B. Lewandowska-Tomaszczyk and P. J. Melia (eds), *Proceedings of PALC 97*, 2–23. Lodz: Lodz University Press.

Johns, A. M. 1997.*Text, Role and Context: Developing academic literacies*. Cambridge: CUP.

Johns, T. 1988. "Whence and whither classroom concordancing?" In T. Bongaerts et al. (eds), *Computer Applications in Language Learning*. Dordrecht: Foris.

Johns, T. 1991. "Should you be persuaded: Two examples of data-driven learning materials". *English Language Research Journal* 4:1–16.

Johns, T. 1994. "From printout to handout: Grammar and vocabulary learning in the context of data-driven learning". In T. Odlin (ed), *Approaches to Pedagogic Grammar*, 293–313. Cambridge: CUP.

Johns, T. 1997. "Kibbitzing one-to-ones". In G. V. Langley, (ed), *BALEAP Professional Interest Meetings Report 1995–997*,. London: British Association of Lecturers in English for Academic Purposes.

Martin, J. R. 1989. *Factual Writing: Exploring and challenging social reality*. Oxford: OUP.

McEnery, T. and Wilson, A. 1997. "Multi-media corpora". In, B. Lewandowska-Tomaszczyk and P. J. Melia (eds), *Proceedings of PALC 97*, 24–33. Lodz: Lodz University Press.

Myers, G. 1999. *Ad Worlds: Brands, media, audiences*. London: Arnold.

Murison-Bowie, S. 1993. "Concordancing corner 1: What is concordancing and why should we do it?" *TELLandCALL* 4.

Murison-Bowie, S. 1996. "Linguistic corpora and language teaching". *Annual Review of Applied Linguistics* 16:182–199.

O'Dell, F. 1996.*CAE writing skills*. Cambridge: CUP.

Raimes, A. 1993. "Out of the woods: Emerging traditions in the teaching of writing".

In S. Silberstein (ed), *State of the Art TESOL Essays*, TESOL.

Scott, M. 1997. "PC analysis of key words — and key key words". *System* 25(1):1–13.

Scott, M. 1998. *Wordsmith Tools 3.00*. Oxford: OUP.

Sinclair, J. McH. 1991.*Corpus, Concordance, Collocation*. Oxford: OUP.

Stubbs, M. Forthcoming. "Computer-assisted text and corpus analysis: Lexical cohesion and communicative competence". In D. Tannen et al. (eds), *The Handbook of Discourse Analysis*. Oxford: Blackwell.

Swales, J. 1981. *Aspects of Article Introductions* [Aston ESP Research Reports 1]. Birmingham: University of Aston.

Swales, J. 1990. *Genre Analysis*. Cambridge: CUP.

Tribble, C. and Jones, G. 1997. *Concordances in the Classroom: A resource book for Teachers*. Houston: Athelstan.

Tribble, C. 1989, June. "The use of text structuring vocabulary in native and non-native speaker writing". *MUESLI News*.

Tribble, C. 1991. "Some uses of electronic text in English for academic purposes". In . C. Millom and K. Tong (eds), *Text Analysis in Computer Assisted Language Learning*. Hong Kong: Hong Kong University of Science and Technology and City Polytechnic of Hong Kong.

Tribble, C. 1997a. *Writing*. Oxford: OUP.

Tribble, C. 1997b. "Improvising corpora for ELT: Quick-and-dirty ways of developing corpora for language teaching". In B. Lewandowska-Tomaszczyk and P. J. Melia (eds), *PALC '97 Proceedings*, 106–118. Lodz: Lodz University Press.

Tribble, C. 1997c. "Corpora, concordances and ELT". In T. Boswood (ed), *New ways in using computers in ESL.*. TESOL.

Tribble, C. 1999. *Writing Difficult Texts*, unpublished PhD Thesis. Lancaster: Lancaster University.

White, R. and Arndt, V. 1991. *Process Writing*. Harlow: Longman.

Appendix: Moves in *MA-WEB_PAGE*

1.	\<title\>	\14uni.txt
2.	\<summary\>	\14uni.txt
3.	\<entry\>	\14uni.txt
4.	\<programme\>	\14uni.txt
5.	\<mode\>	\14uni.txt
6.	\<assessment\>	\14uni.txt
7.	\<admin\>	\14uni.txt

1.	\<index\>	\13uni.txt
2.	\<department\>	\13uni.txt
3.	\<title\>	\13uni.txt
4.	\<mode\>	\13uni.txt
5.	\<entry\>	\13uni.txt
6.	\<assessment\>	\13uni.txt
8.	\<admin\>	\13uni.txt
9.	\<programme\>	\13uni.txt
10.	\<title\>	\13uni.txt
11.	\<mode\>	\13uni.txt
12.	\<assessment\>	\13uni.txt
13.	\<entry\>	\13uni.txt
14.	\<admin\>	\13uni.txt

1.	\<title\>	\12uni.txt
2.	\<summary\>	\12uni.txt
3.	\<programme\>	\12uni.txt
4.	\<staff\>	\12uni.txt
5.	\<admin\>	\12uni.txt
6.	\<department\>	\11uni.txt
7.	\<title\>	\11uni.txt
8.	\<admin\>	\11uni.txt
9.	\<entry\>	\11uni.txt
10.	\<programme\>	\11uni.txt
11.	\<assessment\>	\11uni.txt

1.	\<department\>	\10uni.txt
2.	\<title\>	\10uni.txt
3.	\<department\>	\10uni.txt
4.	\<summary\>	\10uni.txt
5.	\<programme\>	\10uni.txt
6.	\<assessment\>	\10uni.txt

7.	\<programme\>	\10uni.txt
8.	\<staff\>	\10uni.txt
9.	\<entry\>	\10uni.txt
10.	\<department\>	\10uni.txt
11.	\<admin\>	\10uni.txt

1.	\<department\>	\09uni.txt
2.	\<title\>	\09uni.txt
3.	\<summary\>	\09uni.txt
4.	\<entry\>	\09uni.txt
5.	\<programme\>	\09uni.txt
6.	\<assessment\>	\09uni.txt

1.	\<title\>	\08uni.txt
2.	\<summary\>	\08uni.txt
3.	\<programme\>	\08uni.txt

1.	\<title\>	\07uni.txt
2.	\<admin\>	\07uni.txt
3.	\<summary\>	\07uni.txt
4.	\<entry\>	\07uni.txt
5.	\<admin\>	\07uni.txt

1.	\<title\>	\06uni.txt
2.	\<index\>	\06uni.txt
3.	\<programme\>	\06uni.txt
4.	\<mode\>	\06uni.txt
5.	\<assessment\>	\06uni.txt
6.	\<entry\>	\06uni.txt
7.	\<admin\>	\06uni.txt

1.	\<title\>	\05uni.txt
2.	\<department\>	\05uni.txt
3.	\<summary\>	\05uni.txt
4.	\<admin\>	\05uni.txt

1.	\<title\>	\04uni.txt
2.	\<department\>	\04uni.txt
3.	\<entry\>	\04uni.txt
4.	\<mode\>	\04uni.txt
5.	\<programme\>	\04uni.txt
6.	\<assessment\>	\04uni.txt
7	\<admin\>	\04uni.txt

1.	<department>	\03uni.txt
2.	<title>	\03uni.txt
3.	<summary>	\03uni.txt
4.	<programme>	\03uni.txt
5.	<department>	\03uni.txt
6.	<admin>	\03uni.txt

1.	<department>	\02uni.txt
2.	<index>	\02uni.txt
3.	<summary>	\02uni.txt
4.	<mode>	\02uni.txt
5.	<programme>	\02uni.txt
6.	<mode>	\02uni.txt
7.	<assessment>	\02uni.txt
8.	<resources>	\02uni.txt
9.	<entry>	\02uni.txt
10.	<admin>	\02uni.txt

11.	<title>	\02uni.txt
12.	<summary>	\02uni.txt
13.	<programme>	\02uni.txt
14.	<assessment>	\02uni.txt

15.	<title>	\02uni.txt
16.	<summary>	\02uni.txt
17.	<entry>	\02uni.txt
18.	<programme>	\02uni.txt
19.	<assessment>	\02uni.txt

20.	<title>	\02uni.txt
21.	<summary>	\02uni.txt
22.	<assessment>	\02uni.txt
23.	<programme>	\02uni.txt
24.	<assessment>	\02uni.txt

25.	<title>	\02uni.txt
26.	<summary>	\02uni.txt
27.	<entry>	\02uni.txt
28.	<programme>	\02uni.txt
29.	<assessment>	\02uni.txt

30.	<title>	\02uni.txt
31.	<summary>	\02uni.txt
32.	<assessment>	\02uni.txt

33.	<entry>	\02uni.txt
34.	<programme>	\02uni.txt
35.	<assessment>	\02uni.txt
36.	<programme>	\02uni.txt

118.	<title>	\01uni.txt
119.	<summary>	\01uni.txt
120.	<programme>	\01uni.txt
121.	<assessment>	\01uni.txt
122.	<admin>	\01uni.txt
123.	<staff>	\01uni.txt
124.	<admin>	\01uni.txt

Name index

Subject index

In the series STUDIES IN CORPUS LINGUISTICS (SCL) the following titles have been published thus far:

1. PEARSON, Jennifer: *Terms in Context*. 1998.
2. PARTINGTON, Alan: *Patterns and Meanings. Using corpora for English language research and teaching*. 1998.
3. BOTLEY, Simon and Anthony Mark McENERY (eds.): *Corpus-based and Computational Approaches to Discourse Anaphora*. 2000.
4. HUNSTON, Susan and Gill FRANCIS: *Pattern Grammar. A corpus-driven approach to the lexical grammar of English*. 2000.
5. GHADESSY, Mohsen, Alex HENRY and Robert L. ROSEBERRY (eds.): *Small Corpus Studies and ELT. Theory and practice*. 2001.
6. TOGNINI-BONELLI, Elena: *Corpus Linguistics at Work*. 2001.
7. ALTENBERG, Bengt and Sylviane GRANGER (eds.): *Lexis in Contrast. Corpus-based approaches*. n.y.p.